A CENTURY OF CARRIER AVIATION

The Evolution of Ships and Shipborne Aircraft

DAVID HOBBS

Seaforth
PUBLISHING

DEDICATION

Thousands of men and women have qualified to fly from aircraft carriers in the past hundred years in many different navies. This book, in its humble way, is dedicated to their vision and achievements.

Many of them died flying, and I remember especially Commander Tony Light RN, my Commanding Officer in 849HQ Squadron, and his observer, Lieutenant Commander J.P. Moody RN, who crashed and died yards in front of me in their Gannet in the MADDL circuit at RNAS Lossiemouth. My term-mates from BRNC Dartmouth, Lieutenant Commander Gordon Batt DSO RN and Lieutenant Commander Steve Van Someren RN, crashed into the sea at night and have no other grave. I am proud to have known them.

FRONTISPIECE:

A Royal Navy Phantom of 'C' Squadron, A & AEE Boscombe Down, carrying out deck landing trials on HMS *Eagle* in 1969. The ship had recently been modernised and was in far better material condition than her sister *Ark Royal* but was withdrawn from service early for political reasons and never embarked Phantoms operationally. (US NAVY)

Copyright © David Hobbs 2009

First published in Great Britain in 2009 by
Seaforth Publishing
An imprint of Pen & Sword Books Ltd
47 Church Street, Barnsley
S Yorkshire S70 2AS

www.seaforthpublishing.com
Email info@seaforthpublishing.com

British Library Cataloguing in Publication Data
A CIP data record for this book is available from the British Library

ISBN 978-1-84832-019-2

Typeset and designed by Roger Daniels
Printed and bound in Thailand

Contents

Acknowledgements

I am, as always, grateful to my wife Jandy for her help with research and administration, and to my son Andrew for his unfailing support for everything I do.

Much of the latter part of this work has been put together from my own experience of carrier flying in both fixed- and rotary-wing aircraft in roles as diverse as Airborne Early Warning and Commando Assault. Research into earlier generations of naval aviators has occupied a number of years, and has been carried out in the archives of the Naval Historical Branch, now at Portsmouth, and the Fleet Air Arm Museum at RNAS Yeovilton. I am grateful to the Head of Branch, Captain Christopher Page RN (Retired) and Librarian Jenny Wraight at the former for their constant support and interest in my writing. At the latter I am grateful to the Archivists Jan Keohane and Catherine Cooper, who have helped me to find a number of early references.

Most of the photographs are from the collection I inherited from my friend, the late J. David Brown, formerly the Head of the Naval Historical Branch. I have added to the collection with images I took myself over the years. These have been supplemented by others from the USA and Australia. I am grateful to Laura Waayers, Historical Services Manager of the US Naval Historical Foundation, for copying the photographs credited to the Naval Historical Center. Dr David Stevens, Director of Strategic and Historical Studies at the Sea Power Centre – Australia, sent me the images of Sopwith Camels and 1½ Strutters on HMA Ships *Australia* and *Sydney*, credited to the Sea Power Centre, for which I am extremely grateful. I am also indebted to Ken Ellis, Editor of *FlyPast* magazine, for the photographs that Key Publishing provided. My thanks also go to Steve Bush, editor of *Warship World* magazine, who gave valuable help in the selection of photographs. The books listed in the bibliography all come from my own library.

Conversations with naval aircrew from Australia, Canada, New Zealand and the USA, as well as those in the UK, have continued to widen my knowledge of the subject, and I am grateful to them all. They are too numerous to mention, but I will single out Gannet observers John Irving and Steve Hazell, who sat behind me on my first day catapult launch and subsequent deck landing. Peter Flutter and Peter Hulett flew with me through many of the more exciting launches and recoveries on nights that seemed particularly dark at the time, and on a practice bombing sortie when we hit and destroyed a splash target towed behind an RFA, an unusual triumph for an AEW crew. Their confidence meant a lot to me, even if I did not show it at the time, and I treasure the memories of a very happy era of deck operations.

Lastly, I am grateful to Rob Gardiner of Seaforth Publishing for the opportunity to publish this work.

Glossary

A & AEE	Aeroplane and Armament Experimental Establishment
ACA	Admiral Commanding Aircraft, Grand Fleet
ACNS	Assistant Chief of the Naval Staff
ACR	Aircraft Control Room
ACRO	Aircraft Control Room Officer
ADD	Airflow Direction Detector
ADDL	Airfield Dummy Deck Landing
ADR	Aircraft Direction Room
AEW	Airborne Early Warning
AFC	Air Force Cross
AIO	Action Information Organisation
AOC	Air Officer Commanding
AOR	Amphibious Operations Room
APU	Auxiliary power unit
ASI	Air speed indicator
ASW	Antisubmarine warfare
ATCO	Air Traffic Control Officer
Avgas	Aviation gasoline
BH	British hydraulic (catapult)
BLC	Boundary layer control
BPF	British Pacific Fleet
BRC	Base Recovery Course
BS	British steam (catapult)
BuAir	Bureau of Aircraft, USN
BuNav	Bureau of navigation, USN
BXS	British Experimental Steam (catapult)
CAI	Close-Approach Indicator
CALE	Catapult Aircraft Line-Up Equipment
CAM-Ship	Catapult Armed Merchant ship
CAP	Combat air patrol
CCA	Carrier Controlled Approach
CDS	Comprehensive Display System
CIC	Combat Information Centre
CNO	Chief of Naval Operations, USN
ComAirBatFlt	Commander Air Squadrons Battle Fleet, USN
CPO	Chief Petty Officer
CV	USN/NATO designation for an aircraft carrier
CVA	USN/NATO designation for an attack aircraft carrier
CVAN	USN/NATO designation for a nuclear-powered attack aircraft carrier
CVE	USN/NATO designation for an escort aircraft carrier
CVN	USN/NATO designation for a nuclear-powered aircraft carrier
CVS	USN/NATO designation for a support aircraft carrier
DAOT	Directorate of Air Operations and Training, RN
DAPS	Deck Approach Projector Sight
DCHQ	Damage Control Headquarters
DFC	Designated Flying Course
DGA (N)	Directorate General Aircraft (Naval), RN
DLCO	Deck Landing Control Officer
DLMS	Deck Landing Mirror Sight
DLPS	Deck Landing Projector Sight
DNAW	Directorate of Naval Air Warfare, RN
DNC	Directorate of Naval Construction, RN
DNOR	Directorate of Naval Operational Requirements, RN
DSC	Distinguished Service Cross
DSO	Distinguished Service Order
DTSD	Directorate of Tactics and Staff Duties, RN
EMCON	Emission Control (Policy)
EP	Estimated Position
'f'	Lieutenant Commander 'Flying'
FDO	Flight Deck Officer
'Flyco'	Flying Control Office
FOAC	Flag Officer Aircraft Carriers
GCA	Ground controlled approach
GF	Grand Fleet
GOP	General Operations Plot
HAPI	Harrier Approach Path Indicator
HCO	Hangar Control Officer
HCP	Hangar Control Position

HMAS	His/Her Majesty's Australian Ship	R-1	Rigid Airship Number 1
HMCS	His/Her Majesty's Canadian Ship	RAE	Royal Aircraft Establishment
HMS	His/Her Majesty's Ship	RAF	Royal Air Force
hp	Horsepower	RAN	Royal Australian Navy
IAS	Indicated air speed	RAS	Replenishment at Sea
IFF	Identification Friend or Foe	RATOG	Rocket-assisted take-off gear
IJN	Imperial Japanese Navy	RCN	Royal Canadian Navy
JBD	Jet blast deflector	RFA	Royal Fleet Auxiliary
JHDU	Joint Helicopter Development Unit	RHIB	Rigid Hulled Inflatable Boat
JTC	Joint Technical Committee	RN	Royal Navy
Knot	Speed measured in nautical miles per hour	RNAS	Royal Naval Air Service
		RNAS	Royal Naval Air Station
LAMPS	Light Airborne Multi-Purpose System	RNR	Royal Naval Reserve
		RNVR	Royal Naval Volunteer Reserve
lb	Pound/s in Imperial measurement	R/T	Radio telephone
LOP	Local Operations Plot	SAR	Search and Rescue
LSO	Landing Safety Officer	SHOL	Ship/Helicopter Operating Limit
MAC-Ship	Merchant Aircraft Carrier	SOC	Scheme of Complement
MADDL	Mirror-Assisted Dummy Deck Landing	SS	Steam Ship
		STOBAR	Short take-off but arrested recovery
MADGE	Microwave Aircraft Digital Guidance Equipment	STOVL	Short take-off and vertical landing
		TACAN	Tactical Aircraft Navigation System
MAP	Ministry of Aircraft Production	TAG	Telegraphist Air Gunner
MATCH	Medium Anti-Submarine Torpedo-Carrying Helicopter	TAG	Tailored Air Group
		TSR	Torpedo Spotter Reconnaissance
MCO	Mirror Control Officer	UK	United Kingdom
MDAP	Mutual Defense Assistance Program	U/S	Unserviceable
MRALS	Marine Corps Remote Area Landing System	USA	United States of America
		USN	United States Navy
NACA	National Advisory Committee for Aeronautics	USS	United States Ship
		VF	Heavier-than-air, fixed-wing fighter squadron designation, USN
NAD	Naval Air Division, RN		
NAS	Naval Air Squadron	VTOL	Vertical take-off and landing
NAS	Naval Air Station, USN	W/T	Wireless telegraphy
NASA	National Aeronautics and Space Administration		
NATO	North Atlantic Treaty Organisation		
NAVHARS	Navigation, Heading and Attitude Reference System		
ORO	Operations Room Officer		
PO	Petty Officer		
PPI	Plan Position Indicator		
'Pri-Fly'	Primary Flying Control Position, USN		
PSO	Projector Sight Officer		

Introduction

The capabilities that make naval aviation stand apart from flying ashore are the techniques and technologies that allow aircraft to take off from and land on moving vessels, and to navigate over the featureless ocean in between. That man would succeed in developing them was not always obvious, and the early pioneers literally risked their lives to make progress. In the century since Eugene Ely made his exciting first take-off from the USS *Birmingham*, much of the pioneering work has been carried out by the Royal Navy despite considerable opposition from politicians and the land-oriented RAF. I have written this book from a British perspective that reveals progress step-by-step as it occurred. The practical implementation of these developments has invariably been carried out by the US Navy, however, and I pay due credit to the USN, which has perfected the art of carrier operation with the magnificent *Nimitz*-class ships. The three major aviation technologies incorporated in their design; the steam catapult, angled deck and deck-landing projector sight, were invented in Britain because, with its smaller carriers and no immediate prospect of new ones in the early 1950s, the Royal Navy had to innovate if it was to keep its ships viable. With newer and bigger ships, the USN did not feel the same urgency.

While most of the book describes real ships and the techniques of the pilots who flew from them, I could not resist including a chapter on planned ships that were cancelled and the techniques they would have brought with them. While these projects were alive they exerted considerable influence on the way carrier technique developed, especially in the case of *Queen Elizabeth*, CVA01, the design of which still has relevance today. I have done little more than mention the Royal Navy's new *Queen Elizabeth* and *Prince of Wales*. A contract to build these two aircraft carriers, the largest warships ever ordered for the Royal Navy, was signed between the UK Ministry of Defence and BVT Surface Fleet, an amalgamation of BAE Systems and VT shipbuilding interests, on 3 July 2008. Due for completion after 2014, they will play an important part in the second century of carrier aviation.

In my naval career I achieved over 800 deck landings in both fixed- and rotary-wing aircraft, a quarter of them at night, and I was fascinated by reading accounts of the early pioneers when researching this book. Their achievements, which must at times have been terrifying, paved the way for today's operations, which have almost, but never quite, made deck landing a routine event. As we move into the second century of flying from aircraft carriers, unmanned naval aircraft are set to play a rapidly growing part, and I look forward to the time, two decades from now, when unmanned combat air vehicles will form a significant part of carrier air groups. The USN will lead progress, but I hope the Royal Navy will still be able to play a leading role.

David Hobbs MBE
Commander Royal Navy (Retired)
Twyford, Dorset
2008

A brief explanation of flight from a ship's deck

Aircraft of all types fly by generating a force known as 'lift', which is greater than their weight. In the case of airships the lift comes from filling suitable envelopes with a gas, such as hydrogen, which is lighter than air. As long as the total weight of the airship containing the envelopes is less than that of the volume of air it displaces, it will have lift sufficient to overcome its weight and will ascend. Aeroplanes generate lift by moving horizontal surfaces having aerofoil sections, known as wings, through the air. In conventional aircraft the wings are attached to the fuselage and the whole aircraft has to move to generate sufficient lift to exceed its weight. In helicopters the wings, known as rotor blades, are rotated above the fuselage to generate lift; the aircraft itself need not necessarily be moving and could be in a stationary hover. In the past fifty years jet lift, using rotating nozzles or banks of vertically-mounted lift engines, has offered some fixed-wing aircraft the means to take-off and land vertically.

Aerofoil sections have a minimum speed below which insufficient lift will be generated to allow the aircraft to fly, and a maximum speed which occurs when the thrust generated by the aircraft's engine can no longer overcome the drag induced by the wing's passage through the air. Aircraft are said to be in balanced flight when the forces acting on them are in equilibrium; that is when lift equals weight and thrust equals drag. The amount of lift generated by a given wing increases as the square of the aircraft's speed, a fact referred to as the 'V-squared Law'. In consequence, when the throttle is closed to reduce thrust, lift reduces rapidly and, if no corrective action is taken, a point will be reached where lift will be lost and the aircraft's nose will drop, causing it to descend rapidly under the influence of gravity until sufficient lift is regained. This is known as stalling, and the speed at which it occurs is the stalling speed. Military aircraft such as fighters have wings designed for high speed, giving them relatively high stalling speeds, and designers have always had to compromise between the need for a low landing speed, just above the stall, to land on an aircraft carrier, and high speed for combat.

Aircraft are fitted with systems that measure their speed relative to the immediate air mass that surrounds them. This is known as indicated air speed (IAS). The IAS takes no account of wind speed and so does not give 'speed over the ground' like that measured in a motor car. More complicated calculations of speed corrected for temperature and the reduced atmospheric pressure at altitude are beyond this simple explanation and are not relevant to landing on or launching from the deck of an aircraft carrier. Airspeed indicators in naval aircraft have always been calibrated in nautical miles per hour, or knots.

An aircraft flies relative to the air that surrounds it. Thus, when taking off from a runway on land, in still air, it will become airborne at an IAS governed by its weight and wing design. That speed and the distance taken over the ground to accelerate to it will be constant. Taking off into wind will not alter the IAS at which the aircraft becomes airborne, but will reduce the distance run over the ground required to reach it. For example, an aircraft that becomes airborne at 100 knots would only cover the distance over the ground needed to reach 85 knots when taking off into a 15-knot wind. At lift-off the airspeed indicator would read 100 knots. Conversely, an aircraft taking off downwind would cover a greater distance over the ground and would need to cover the distance needed to accelerate to 115 knots before lifting off at an indicated 100 knots.

When taking off from the deck of an aircraft carrier, the speed of the ship through the water contributes to the speed of the aircraft relative to the air that surrounds it. Invariably aircraft carriers turn into wind to operate their aircraft, and by increasing their own speed they reduce, still further, the deck run needed by an aircraft to achieve the IAS needed to get airborne at a given weight. Following the earlier example, if our aircraft launched from an aircraft carrier steaming into wind at 25 knots, it would still become airborne at 100 knots IAS but would already be moving at an indicated 40 knots before releasing its brakes to roll along the deck, 15 knots wind plus

25 knots ship speed. It would only require a deck run equivalent to the acceleration to 60 knots to get airborne.

When aircraft are launched by catapult, the design figure quoted for the equipment is an 'end speed', that is the speed which the shuttle, and the aircraft towed by it, can achieve relative to the deck. If the aircraft in our example was launched from a British BH III hydro-pneumatic catapult with a stated end speed of 66 knots, it would leave the deck with 106 knots IAS, that is 15 knots wind, 25 knots ship speed plus the end speed of the catapult. If the carrier in this example was capable of 30 knots, launching the aircraft by catapult would require only 4 knots of natural wind to achieve flying speed.

Aircraft in the landing pattern fly to their IAS, but the ship's speed has an effect on landing, just as it did on take-off. Take, for example, our earlier aircraft. As it has used fuel and possibly ammunition, its weight would be less than on take-off, reducing its stalling speed. It would fly the final approach of its landing circuit at 90 knots IAS, towards the carrier steaming at 25 knots into a 15-knot wind. Its speed relative to the deck, therefore, would be 50 knots and it is this energy that has to be absorbed by the arrester gear. Figures quoted for arrester gear always refer to the weight of the aircraft in landing configuration and speed relative to the deck. Aircraft that can land vertically or with very little forward momentum do not need arrester gear to halt them.

The Pegasus engine fitted in the Harrier AV-8 family of aircraft has allowed a significant variation on the operation of fixed-wing jets to and from the flight deck. These aircraft fly conventionally using lift generated by the wings during normal flight, but use engine thrust to augment or replace it in low-speed take-off and landing from the hover. By rotating the engine nozzles downwards through 90 degrees the full engine thrust can be used to lift the aircraft off the ground, provided engine thrust is greater than the aircraft's weight. This is known as vertical take-off and landing, or VTOL. The weight that can be lifted by the engine is less than the maximum permissible weight of the aircraft, however, so VTO has penalties in terms of the amounts of fuel and weapons that can be carried. These can be overcome by using a rolling or short take-off technique in which the nozzles are rotated down, typically through about 45 degrees, to augment wing lift as the aircraft leaves the deck. This technique is known as short take-off and vertical landing, or STOVL. The ski jump, described fully in Chapter 17, enhances the weight that be carried in STOVL take-offs still further. Recovery is by vertical landing from a hover over the flight deck after fuel and weapons have been used, reducing the aircraft weight below maximum engine thrust.

In normal flight Harriers use conventional elevators, ailerons and a rudder, but without airflow over them in the hover these surfaces are ineffective. For low speed control the aircraft are fitted with a duplicate system which comes into use when the engine nozzles are selected more than 10 degrees below horizontal. The conventional surfaces continue to move but, additionally, a series of 'puffer jets' fed by high-pressure air bled from the engine and fed to the jets by pipes provide forces that move the aircraft in pitch, roll and yaw. The pilot's control input to the puffer jets is made by moving the control column and rudder pedals in the normal manner to activate both systems. After launch the puffer jets are selected off when the engine nozzles are selected back to the horizontal. The changes of flight status from the hover into wing-borne flight and decelerating back into the hover are known as transitions.

CHAPTER 1 Beginnings

The first take-off from a ship. Eugene Ely trades height for speed as he leaves the forward edge of the uss *Birmingham*'s small deck in Hampton Roads, Virginia, on 14 November 1910. The ship in the background is the destroyer uss *Roe*, Destroyer Number 24, acting as plane-guard.

(US NAVY)

Although the Wright Brothers' first powered flights in December 1903 initially attracted scant attention, Wilbur Wright's first flights in Europe in August 1908 and Louis Blériot's cross-Channel flight in a powered aircraft the following year caused considerable popular excitement. The latter event led the press to claim that Britain was no longer protected by conventional sea power. The Channel had actually been crossed by air before, by a manned hydrogen-filled balloon in 1785, and the press had made similar claims then. These incidents gave continued validity to St Vincent's dictum that he did not say that an enemy could not come to England, only that 'he could not come by sea'. Despite the potential for aircraft to raid the British mainland, any practical invasion force would still have to travel by sea, and defeat the world's largest navy at the height of its power in order to do so.

The British Admiralty had nothing to gain by hastening the development of new technologies that would make the world's largest fleet obsolete. Outwardly it strove to maintain the impression that it was not interested in change, whereas, in truth, it sponsored extensive research into new weapons and, when necessary, used Britain's enormous industrial capacity to build new weapons faster than any other nation, thus maintaining a superior 'edge'. Watching and waiting was a sensible policy for the era before 1914, and the adoption of torpedoes, torpedo-boats and submarines just before man's first powered flight are relevant examples of the success of this approach.

In 1907 the Wright Brothers approached the Admiralty with an offer to sell their aeronautical patents outright but, like the US Government before it, the Admiralty was not prepared to spend taxpayers' money on an unproven idea and elected again to watch progress rather than hasten it. The offer was politely refused but did have the effect of focusing naval attention on the rapid development of aviation. To put the Wrights' offer into context, it should be noted that in early 1907 the Brothers' greatest achievement was a 24-mile flight in October 1905, which had lasted 38 minutes and was ended only because the aeroplane ran out of fuel. At that stage they knew they had developed a practical aeroplane, and ceased flying to concentrate on marketing their invention. By September 1908, when they were astounding both the USA and Europe with extended flights of over an hour's duration, there was considerable development of lighter-than-air craft in Germany and heavier-than-air craft in France, though the French were still well behind the Wrights. Early in 1907 Lady Jane Taylor, authorised by Charles Flint, the Wrights' European agent, to act as his agent for the sale of Wright aeroplanes to the British Government, had engaged in negotiations with Lord Tweedmouth, the First Lord of the Admiralty. The initial offer to the British Government was for fifty aeroplanes capable of a 30-mile flight, alighting at the point of departure within one hour after starting, each having a carrying capacity of two men and surplus fuel. These were to cost £2,000 each, the total sum of £100,000 being broken down into three payments; £25,000 on demonstration of efficiency and immediate delivery of the machine used for that demonstration, £60,000 in payments of £15,000 on each delivery of ten aircraft, and £15,000 on delivery of the remaining nine machines. Flint then increased the price to £4,000 per aircraft, saying: 'We ... deemed it desirable to increase the price to the British Government, feeling that an increased price for a machine of increased efficiency [as had been proposed by then] would cause them *to take us more seriously* ...'. However, despite Lady Jane's optimism the negotiations were concluded abruptly on 7 March 1907, when Lord Tweedmouth wrote to her: 'I have consulted my expert advisers with regard to your suggestions as to the employment of aeroplanes, and I regret to have to tell you, after the careful consideration of my Board, that the Admiralty, whilst thanking you for so kindly bringing the proposals to their notice, are of opinion that they would not be of any practical use to the Naval Service'.

In July 1908 Captain R.H. Bacon RN, the Director of Naval Ordnance, who was responsible for the development and procurement of new weapons systems, submitted proposals to the Board of Admiralty for the appointment of a Naval Air Assistant to the Board and the construction of a rigid airship. The proposals were accepted quickly, so quickly in fact

Eugene Ely lands on the uss *Pennsylvania*, Armored Cruiser Number 4, in San Francisco Bay on 18 January 1911. Note the flat approach and the nose-high attitude with the wheels only inches above the deck. The round-down and canvas screen forward of the deck are both prominent, as are the spectators crammed on to every vantage point including masts and yards.

(EUGENE B. ELY SCRAPBOOKS, COPYRIGHT THE US NAVY HISTORICAL CENTER)

that they may well have been expected before the formal submission was made.[1] This would be consistent with Bacon's close association with Admiral Fisher, the First Sea Lord, as his Naval adviser between 1904 and 1906; the first captain of the revolutionary HMS *Dreadnought* between 1906 and 1908 and then Director of Naval Ordnance. In the 1909/10 estimates £35,000 was allocated for the construction of HM Rigid Airship Number 1, R-1, by the shipbuilding firm of Vickers, Sons & Maxim at Barrow-in-Furness. By 1909 the airship was already a viable proposition,[2] capable of seeking out and observing enemy vessels on the open sea and reporting their position using wireless telegraph (W/T) transmitters. At the time of its order, R-1 was the largest flying machine yet designed, not much smaller in volume than a battleship. It was the first rigid airship ordered for any navy, and the only

previous military order had been for the German Army. Although R-1 broke up on being withdrawn from its shed at Barrow on 24 September 1911, the failed project was of direct interest to the operation of aircraft from ships at sea because the cruiser *Hermione*[3] was modified to act as an airship support vessel. It was used as an accommodation ship at Barrow, commanded by Captain Murray Sueter RN, the Inspecting Captain of Airships with his deputy, Commander Oliver Schwann RN as executive officer. The ship contained a plant for manufacturing hydrogen and a number of cylinders of the gas intended to 'top up' the airship's seventeen gas bags at sea, in addition to Avgas that could be pumped into the airship's fuel tanks. R-1 was designed with boat-shaped cars capable of floating on the sea surface, and the most successful aspect of her construction was

demonstrated when she rode out a gale attached to a mast set up for the purpose during tethering trials in Devonshire Basin in May 1911. It was the first airship designed to be 'moored' to a mast by a coupling in the nose, and operationally it was intended to moor the airship to a similar mast on *Hermione* while it was replenished at sea. The R-1 was designed to stay airborne for over 24 hours in her own right, and such a capability would have greatly extended the airship's radius of action, beside offering a command and control facility that would have linked the airship's relatively weak transmissions to the fleet command through *Hermione*'s more powerful W/T installation. The R-1 project included the training of the Royal Navy's first aircrew in 1910, their qualification being recognised by the introduction of flying pay by Order-in-Council in December 1910.

Some of the mechanics trained to maintain the new airship developed their skills by helping to fit out the airship during 1911.

Despite the focus on R-1, there was considerable interest in heavier-than-air craft across the navy. In April 1910 the Admiralty sent a group of officers to witness the state of aircraft development in France and to attend the first conference on what was known at the time as 'aerial navigation'. By then France led the world in the development of aviation, and the French Navy was one of the first military organisations to establish an investigatory commission to establish the Service's aeronautical needs.[4] Admiral Le Pord was charged with identifying them and deciding whether 'heavier-than-air' or 'lighter-than-air' aircraft were better suited to fleet use. In the summer of 1910 Le Pord's commission reported that aeroplanes were

The Royal Navy's first aircraft project, HM Rigid Airship Number 1, moored to a specially designed mast in Cavendish Dock, Barrow-in-Furness, on 22 May 1911 during trials. She was an innovative design which deserved more success than she achieved; a day later she successfully rode out a gale measured at up to 45 knots, attached to the mooring, but in September she was damaged on being extracted from her shed and written off. The cruiser HMS *Hermione* was modified with a mooring mast and hydrogen manufacturing equipment to support R-1 at sea.

(AUTHOR'S COLLECTION)

the better option and a ship capable of carrying them would be required. To reinforce the Commission's findings, in the autumn of 1910 Frenchman Henri Fabre became the first man to take off from and alight back on the water. His aircraft was a tail-first pusher monoplane of his own design, fitted with pontoon floats also designed by him. This was a key technical enabler, as it was thought that 'hydro-aeroplanes' would be ideal for naval use, able to operate from the sea surface in much the same way as army aeroplanes operated from fields ashore. Experience was to show that the concept was not that straightforward. The term 'hydro-aeroplane' was cumbersome and was soon replaced by the simpler word 'seaplane', coined by Winston Churchill in July 1913 when, as First Lord of the Admiralty, he took a keen interest in the development of naval aircraft.

The French Navy selected its first aircraft-carrying vessel in 1911. The torpedo-boat tender *Foudre* needed little alteration and was already fitted with extensive workshops and booms capable of lifting the aircraft from the deck on to the water and back again. It had been used for experiments with hydrogen balloons between 1898 and 1901. A canvas hangar, the first to be fitted to any warship, was rigged aft of the ship's three funnels, and there was ample space on deck to prepare aircraft for flight. Her first aircraft, a Voisin floatplane, was embarked on 27 May 1912 and took part in several naval manoeuvres before 1914. *Foudre* was the first warship in any navy to be altered permanently for the operation of aircraft, and the first to use them in exercises. The concept of operation was simple; she would proceed to an area of sheltered water and anchor. Seaplanes, having been prepared for flight on deck, were lowered on to the water with their engines running, since it would have been impractical and quite unsafe for a mechanic to try to swing the propeller while balancing on a float once the aircraft was in the water. Once clear of the boom, the pilot would taxi his aircraft clear of the ship, turn into wind and take off. After the flight the reverse procedure was followed, with the exception that the engine was stopped as soon as the aircraft was secured to the boom. In 1914 *Foudre* was fitted with a small flight deck over the forecastle to test the feasibility

of take-off by wheeled aircraft. Civilian aircraft designer and pilot René Caudron made the first French take-off from a warship at sea on 8 May 1914, in a Caudron G.III amphibian seaplane with wheels fitted to the floats. A second attempt by Lieutenant de Vaisseau Jean de Laborde, one of the French Navy's first pilots, resulted in a crash which, fortunately, he survived. By then both the Royal and United States navies had overtaken France both in terms of operating technique and numbers of aircraft.

The Imperial Japanese Navy (IJN) was keenly interested in aviation, and arranged for officers to examine *Foudre* in June 1912. While in France they ordered two Maurice Farman seaplanes which were shipped back to Japan. In the autumn the same team visited the USA, where they studied developments and ordered two Curtiss seaplanes. Subsequent trials favoured the Farman aircraft, and a licence was obtained for the type to be manufactured at the Yokosuka Naval Arsenal. In the autumn of 1913 the

IJN took a merchant ship, the *Wakamiya Maru*, from trade and rigged it with canvas hangars and booms to operate two Farmans during naval manoeuvres in October and November. Subsequently she was commissioned as a warship and the mercantile 'Maru' suffix was dropped. The vessel went on to play a significant part in the early development of Japanese naval aviation and operated as a static air base during the seizure of Tsingtao from the Germans in 1914. In 1920 she was fitted with a flight deck 66 feet long over

The steel hangar structure installed on the French *Foudre* in 1912 was the first to be built on any warship. The aircraft seen next to it is a Voisin, the French Navy's first floatplane, and it appears to be a tight fit, especially with regard to height. Note the canvas screen in the fully-open position, used to close the hangar and give some degree of protection once the aircraft was safely stowed inside.

(BORIS V. DRASHPIL COLLECTION
VIA STEPHEN MCLAUGHLIN)

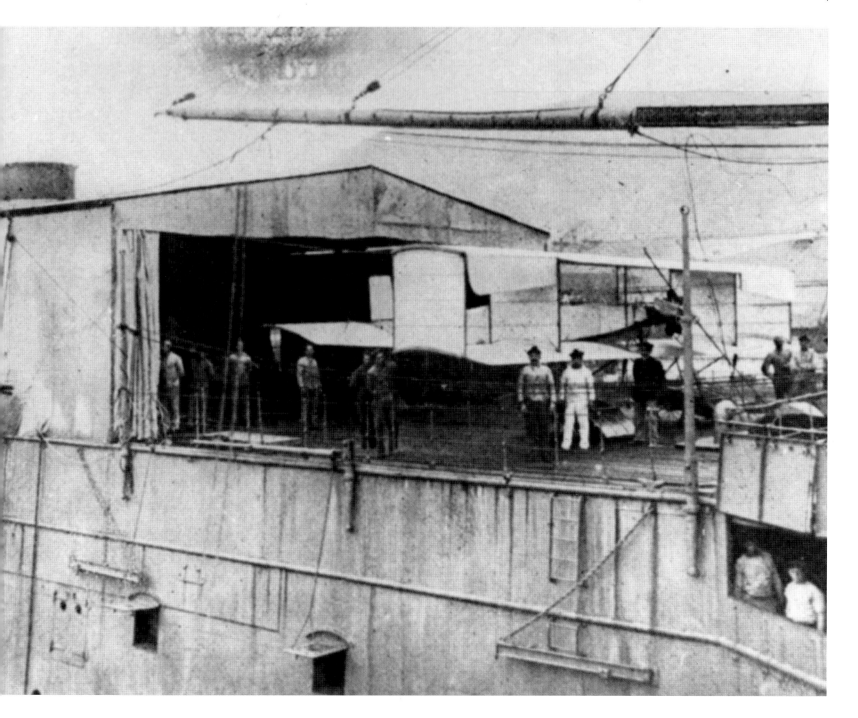

the forecastle, from which Lieutenant Torao Kuwabara made the first Japanese take-off from a ship under way in June of that year.

In the summer of 1910 Captain Washington I. Chambers USN persuaded the US Navy Department to bear the expense of rigging a warship for flying trials. Having gained approval, Chambers invited Wilbur Wright to fly one of his aircraft off the light cruiser *Birmingham*, but the pioneer turned down the opportunity to achieve another 'first'. Glenn Curtiss was approached instead, and accepted immediately, offering a 50hp Model D pusher biplane and a Curtiss company pilot named Eugene Ely, who Chambers had met at an air show at Halethorpe, Maryland.[5] A flying-off platform was erected on USS *Birmingham* in October 1910. Made of wood, it was 83 feet long and 22 feet wide, but was not intended to be a permanent structure. It sloped downward from the roof of the 6-inch gun mounting on the forecastle to the stem of the ship at an angle of 5 degrees. The aircraft was embarked on 10 November while the ship was alongside in Norfolk Navy Yard. Photographs show that, to give himself a measure of protection during the flight, Ely took the precaution of wrapping inflated bicycle inner-tubes around his shoulders to add buoyancy if he ended up in the water. He also wore a football helmet to ensure that a crash into the

water could be survivable. The cruiser had an escort of four torpedo-boat destroyers intended both to rescue the pilot, if necessary, and to form a line during the flight marking the route for the pilot to fly back to the shore, early recognition of the difficulty of navigating over open sea. The Curtiss biplane was just less than 30 feet long, giving an available deck run of 53 feet. *Birmingham* sailed from Norfolk on 14 November, and the original intention was for her to cruise in Chesapeake Bay at 10 knots, reducing the required aircraft take-off run relative to the deck. Rain squalls were encountered, however, and *Birmingham* anchored in Hampton Roads with her escorts to wait for the weather to clear. It seemed to clear after noon and they got under way, but heavy rain forced the ships to anchor again.

At about 15:00 the weather began to clear and the order was given to weigh anchor. Ely started his engine but the noise interfered with activity on the bridge and the ship was delayed getting under way. Impatient to be off, however, Ely gave his mechanic the signal to release the rope 'hold-back' that had prevented the aircraft from moving forward with the engine running, and took off into a 10 knot wind straight down the deck. The ship was technically under way with the anchor clear of the sea bed, but had no forward motion to assist the take-off. Ely

The Imperial Japanese Navy was quick to see the advantages of a mercantile hull for the operation of seaplanes. *Wakamiya* is seen here with a spread seaplane being prepared for flight on the upper deck forward and another, folded, in the forward hangar. Extended booms were fitted to the masts to swing aircraft over the side and recover them; the after one can be seen swung out to starboard ready to recover an aircraft that is not yet within the frame of the picture. Canvas awnings could be drawn across both hangars to protect the aircraft inside from the elements. (AUTHOR'S COLLECTION)

needed to accelerate by 20 knots to give him the necessary 30 knots flying speed, but he failed to do so and literally fell off the end of the deck. He pushed the stick forward and kept the nose down to trade height for speed, and the propeller disc just touched the surface of the water as he reached flying speed. The impact splintered the propeller tips and the resulting vibration as he climbed away forced Ely to land on the nearest point of land, Willoughby Spit, now part of Naval Air Station (NAS) Norfolk, less than three miles from the cruiser. Even though it had not gone as planned, the flight demonstrated the

feasibility of launching a wheeled aircraft from a flight deck built on a warship. It could also be said to indicate the desirability of having a naval pilot who understood what was going on in the ship around him and, later in the same month, Glenn Curtiss offered to train a naval officer to fly free of charge. The offer was accepted, but Captain Chambers had to fight hard for an appropriation of just $500 (a little over £100 at the time) to build a larger deck on another warship to demonstrate a landing.

The ship selected for the landing trial was the USS *Pennsylvania*, based on the Pacific west coast of the

Commander Samson (bearded and with outstretched arms) supervises the loading of aircraft number 2 on to the take-off platform on HMS *Africa* in Sheerness Dockyard. The aircraft was Short-Sommer biplane constructor's number S.38, originally allocated the RN serial number B2, then T2 and finally simply 2. Note the three floats lashed to the aircraft's undercarriage, fitted in November 1911.
(AUTHOR'S COLLECTION)

USA. During January 1911 a wooden deck 120 feet long by 32 feet wide was constructed over the cruiser's after turret and quarterdeck in Mare Island Navy Yard. It sloped gently downwards from the mainmast to the stern. To guard against the risk that an approach made too low might rip off the undercarriage on the 'lip' where the deck ended, a steeply sloping ramp was built up from the quarterdeck to join the after end of the flight deck. This feature was later named the 'round-down' by the Royal Navy and became a pronounced feature of most British-designed carriers, but was almost completely neglected by USN constructors despite its incidental benefit of smoothing the turbulence caused by the passage of the ship's hull through the air.

Lieutenant Ellyson USN, who became the Service's first pilot, is believed to have proposed the arrester wires used in the trial, adapting a system used to stop 'drag-racing' cars at automobile events. This comprised twenty-two lengths of rope laid across the deck at three-foot intervals, each length having a 50lb sandbag secured at each end. The ropes were held clear of the deck by two twelve-inch-high wooden battens which ran the full length of the deck, ten feet

apart. The aircraft used was the first Curtiss Model D-IV Military Machine, powered by a 50hp Curtiss engine and modified by the addition of a narrower extra wing bay on each side to increase wing area, and three hooks on the axle between the main wheels which were intended to engage with the arrester wires. Ely carried out the first deck landing in history on 18 January 1911. It was successful, but by the standards of later generations it should not have been. The original plan had been for *Pennsylvania* to be under way, but her captain felt there was insufficient room to manoeuvre in the crowded waters of San Francisco Bay and remained at anchor with a 10 knot wind blowing from astern. This had the effect of increasing Ely's speed relative to the deck to over 40 knots and giving him less time to correct errors of height and line-up in the last stages of his approach to the deck. After taking off from an airfield near San Francisco he flew a left-hand circuit around the ship, giving himself a long, low and straight final approach. At the last moment, he flared slightly to ensure a safe height over the round-down, causing the aircraft to 'float' over the deck in the ground effect caused by the increased incidence and excessive speed. Having

Number 2 on *Hibernia*'s take-off platform. Note the forward-facing boom on the fore-mast, installed to lift the aircraft into place, and the extent to which the flight-deck support structure prevents the forward turret from training. A temporary canvas screen has been rigged aft of the aircraft to protect the lower bridge from propeller blast.
(AUTHOR'S COLLECTION)

Commander Samson takes off from HMS *Hibernia* near Portland on 2 May 1912, becoming airborne well before reaching the bow. This was the first take-off from a ship under way and also the first by a naval pilot in a Service aircraft. After a short flight he landed at Lodmoor Marsh, near Weymouth in Dorset.

(AUTHOR'S COLLECTION)

floated over 40 feet of deck, he recovered the situation by pushing the stick forward, 'poling for the deck', which caused Ely's hooks to engage the eleventh and nine succeeding arrester ropes. The 1,500lb aircraft was quickly brought to a standstill, having collected a total of 1,000lb of sandbags, 50 feet short of the canvas screens rigged aft of the mainmast as a 'last-ditch' barrier to prevent the aircraft crashing into the superstructure. Ely stepped from the aircraft to a resounding cheer from the sailors who had watched the landing from every vantage point, and to be greeted by his wife, who exclaimed: "Oh boy, I knew you could do it!" While the deck was cleared of ropes and sandbags, Ely, his wife and Captain Chambers were entertained to lunch by Captain C.F. Pond USN, who commanded *Pennsylvania*. After lunch Ely took off over the cruiser's stern. The event went more smoothly than his previous take-off, assisted by the longer deck, a brisk breeze and his own experience.

A month later another important trial used *Pennsylvania* to demonstrate aircraft/capital ship compatability. To justify a purchase order for the US Navy's first aircraft, the secretary of the navy, George von Lengerke Meyer, insisted that it be demonstrated that an aeroplane could be launched and retrieved from a naval ship-of-the-line without impairing the vessel's combat efficiency. On 26 January 1911 Glenn Curtiss had become the second man to take off from and land back on water in an aircraft fitted with floats. To meet Meyer's demand, on 17 February in San Diego bay, using the Curtiss D-III Tractor Hydro, a biplane converted from pusher to tractor config-uration with the engine and propeller in front, he rose from the water, alighted again near *Pennsylvania* and taxied up to the ship's side. Once there he was hoisted inboard by one of the boat derricks and deposited on the upper deck amidships, where mechanics inspected the aircraft while Curtiss went for tea. These niceties completed, the engine was started and aircraft and pilot were hoisted back on to the water, from which Curtiss took off and made a short hop with a stalled landing. The aircraft was then taxied back to the Curtiss camp at Hammondsport without leaving the water. In fact the modified aircraft was not properly balanced for full flight, and its configuration was not used again, but the required demonstration had been made. The success of these three trials showed that, even at their present stage of development, aircraft could operate from ships, both from temporary platforms acting as flight decks and from the sea alongside them in calm weather. Captain Chambers had been able to demonstrate that aircraft might not yet be able to replace cruisers in the scouting role but, by taking eyes into the sky, they could make them more efficient. The point was noted, and the 1912 Naval Appropriations Act, passed in March 1911, included $25,000 for aviation. While this represented only a small fraction of the money allocated by the Royal Navy for the construction of its first airship two years earlier, it was a start which allowed the USN to order its first aircraft, an amphibian biplane known as the Triad and designated A-1, from Glenn Curtiss on 8 May.

By then the Royal Navy was beginning to make significant progress in developing an air capability. Training for airship crews had begun in 1910, and a year later, in March 1911, Francis Kennedy McClean, a wealthy member of the Royal Aero Club, lent two of his own Short Brothers' pusher biplanes to the Admiralty to enable naval officers to be taught to fly. The Club gave the Navy free use of its airfield at Eastchurch and club premises, themselves a near-gift from McClean. Flying tuition was provided free by George B. Cockburn, holder of UK Pilot Certificate Number 5, but the Admiralty did have to pay for the running costs and any repairs found to be necessary to the aircraft. A fee of £20 per pilot was paid to Horace Short for technical instruction at Short Brothers' factory. The course ended in September 1911, by which time the pilots had attended the French military aviation trials at Reims and visited several French firms, including the Gnome aero-engine works. Four had been selected out of two hundred Royal Navy and Royal Marines officers that applied for the course, but one went sick at a critical moment before it started and was replaced at short notice by one of the officers standing by the new airship at Barrow. Some of the officers who had not been selected learned to fly at their own expense, with the result that the navy had eight qualified aeroplane pilots by the end of 1911, in addition to a number of lighter-than-air pilots qualified to fly airships.

In order to put the experimental operation of aircraft from ships in the months ahead into context, it is worth taking a closer look at the flying training the first naval pilots received. Like most early aeroplanes, the early Short biplanes were so light that they could usually only be flown practically at dawn or dusk, when there was virtually no wind. Indeed, for the first week of training no flying was attempted when there was a wind of more than 4 knots. The aircraft had no system of dual control, and the pupil sat behind the instructor, watching what he did. When confidence was gained by both after a series of fast 'hops' across the airfield, the Training Manual advised the pupil to 'learn the movement of the lever by reaching over the instructor's shoulder and grasping it lightly, following the movements of the pilot'.[6] Conversation over the noise of the engine and the rushing wind was impossible, so the instructor would elbow the pupil's arm out of the way if he wanted him to release the control. After a series of straight flights twenty or thirty feet above the grass, shallow turns would be demonstrated with a radius of about four hundred yards, then the pupil would 'go solo', an experience then, as it is today, of mingled terror and delight. As with all aircraft fitted with the Gnome rotary engine, there was no throttle, so the engine was either flat-out or stopped. Speed on approaching to land was controlled by switching the engine on and off, always hoping that it would burst back into life when switched on. The aircraft were relatively straightforward to fly once the 'knack' had been learnt, easy to break with a heavy landing and easy to repair afterwards. Among the group of sailors generally referred to as 'air mechanics' trained at Eastchurch in 1912 were 13 sailmakers, responsible for the fabric, 6 carpenters responsible for the airframe structure and 4 blacksmiths responsible for the engines.

As well as the Eastchurch group, the officers standing by the airship at Barrow-in-Furness were responsible for a separate, but significant, line of development. The Assistant Inspecting Captain of Airships, Commander Oliver Schwann RN, had no time to take a flying course but raised £700 among his brother officers and their wives to buy a 35hp Avro Type D biplane. This was fitted with both wooden and metal[7] pontoon floats designed with the help of naval artificers working with him on the airship project. Schwann taught himself to control the machine and refined the float design through several improvements interspersed with duckings in Devonshire Basin at Barrow. On one occasion he is reputed to have shouted "save the damned aeroplane, I can look after myself" to the boat crew that rowed towards him after the aircraft had nose-dived during a high-speed run with what had proved to be inefficient floats.[8] After the loss of R-1 in September, the team at Barrow concentrated on the Avro and perfected new floats with which Schwann became the first British aviator to take off from water on 18 November 1911.[9] His lack of skill and the aircraft's marginal flying capabilities with the extra weight of the floats betrayed him, however, and the subsequent crash was not the first British controlled landing on water. That came a few weeks later when Lieutenant A.M. Longmore RN, an Australian who was one of the four Eastchurch pilots, took off from the airfield at Eastchurch and landed on the water of Sheerness Dockyard on 1 December 1911 in a Short S.27, Short constructor's number 38, allocated naval airframe number T2, as originally built with a 50hp Gnome engine. This aircraft was fitted with flexible air bags, two of which were lashed to the framework of the undercarriage and a third to the tailskid aft. Unlike Schwann's Avro, the Short's flexible floats did not allow the aircraft to take-off from water, and it had to be hoisted ashore before flying back to its airfield.

Another early pioneer was Lieutenant J.C. Porte RN, who was later famous for designing a series of flying boats for the Royal Naval Air Service (RNAS). In 1908 he was in command of a submarine at HMS *Dolphin*, the submarine base at Gosport in Hampshire. With a colleague, Lieutenant W.B. Pirie RN, he designed and constructed a biplane glider with highly staggered wings and a skid undercarriage. His intention, once it had proved itself in flight, was to fit a 35hp JAP engine to achieve powered take-off and flight. With the help of a number of sailors from the submarine base he had the aircraft hauled to the top of Portsdown Hill, north of Portsmouth, on a four-wheeled trolley on 17 August 1909. The launch comprised putting the unsecured aircraft on to the trolley and pushing it along a wooden trackway, constructed and laid down to create a smoother surface than the surrounding grass. When it reached flying speed the aircraft lifted off the trolley but never achieved controlled flight. *Flight* magazine of 25 September 1909 described the experiment as 'resulting in a smash which wrecked the aircraft', after which Porte abandoned the design and moved on. Its control arrangements were very like those of a submarine, in that two 'coxswains' sat side-by-side; one controlled the aircraft heading and the other attitude and altitude. Porte subsequently sought Admiralty funding for his experimental aircraft, but it was refused because the aircraft had not proved successful. It is interesting to consider what different course naval aviation might have taken had he flown successfully in 1909. By twenty-first-century standards of resource allocation, of course, the unstinted use of twenty or more sailors for some months was a significant investment by the Admiralty.

By June 1910 Porte was experimenting with a self-built copy of the diminutive Santos-Dumont Demoiselle single-seat monoplane in which he taught himself to fly. It was fitted with a 35hp Duthiel-Chalmers engine, and he made a number of modifications to the original design. These included fitting small wheels outboard of the main wheels on the end of 'stunsail booms' to make the machine more stable on the ground and prevent it from turning over sideways. He also gave it a 'bowsprit' to protect the propeller and prevent the aircraft from pitching on to its nose. He carried out a series of increasingly fast taxiing trials at the Hampshire Aeroplane Grounds at Fort Grange in Gosport, later to become RNAS Gosport. Unfortunately, during one of these he ran into what he described as a 'deep undulation' which caused him to be 'brought up suddenly'. The aircraft was wrecked. Porte was not one of the four officers selected for training at Eastchurch, but he went to France to qualify for his aviator's certificate, partly because the facilities were better there, and partly because the French officials were unaware of his medical limitations (he had tuberculosis, and was prematurely retired from the navy early in 1911). He did his training on a Deperdussin monoplane at Reims, and was awarded Aero Club de France Certificate Number 548 on 28 July 1911, flying a Deperdussin. Such were Porte's piloting skills that he became technical director and test pilot for the newly-formed British Deperdussin Company.

These experiments show a widespread belief among the Royal Navy's early aviation enthusiasts that aircraft in general, and seaplanes in particular, represented the way forward. The design of floats was a challenge, however. Those with flat bottoms could not break free of the surface tension/suction of the water, their undersides tending to 'stick' to the surface unless small ripples or waves enabled them to break free. The problem then was that, as speed increased towards the point where flight was possible, waves could impact and damage the floats or throw up spray into the wooden propeller and engine, damaging both. The struts holding the floats in place were not sprung, and, as speed increased, the waves imparted a juddering vibration which passed through the whole airframe and often led to structural damage. The artificers at Barrow experimented with metal hydroplanes, but these needed additional buoyancy at low speeds and could be smashed at higher speeds

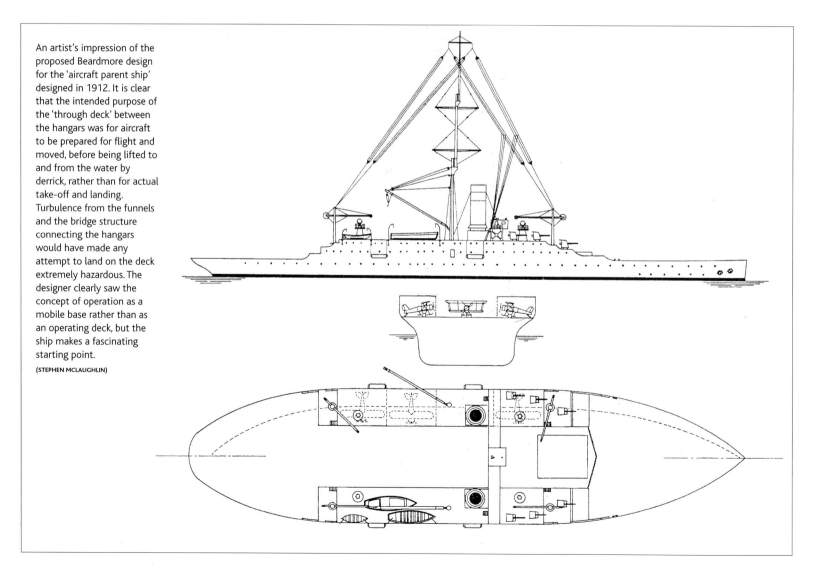

An artist's impression of the proposed Beardmore design for the 'aircraft parent ship' designed in 1912. It is clear that the intended purpose of the 'through deck' between the hangars was for aircraft to be prepared for flight and moved, before being lifted to and from the water by derrick, rather than for actual take-off and landing. Turbulence from the funnels and the bridge structure connecting the hangars would have made any attempt to land on the deck extremely hazardous. The designer clearly saw the concept of operation as a mobile base rather than as an operating deck, but the ship makes a fascinating starting point.

(STEPHEN MCLAUGHLIN)

if they touched weeds or driftwood in the water. The best solution, and the one that allowed Schwann his first, brief flight, was a 'vee-shaped' wooden float with a 'step' that allowed the float to 'unstick' from the surface as the aircraft lifted with increasing speed. Longmore's flotation bags were little more than buoyancy aids intended to save the aircraft if it came down in the water. Their successful use was, in effect, a proving trial to prepare the way for the first major achievement by Royal Navy pilots, a series of practical demonstrations that aircraft could operate from warships at sea under realistic conditions.

The most senior of the four Eastchurch-trained pilots was Commander Charles Rumney Samson RN, a dynamic officer who lost no time, once qualified, in seeking Admiralty approval to carry out take-off trials from a ship. Approval was given in December 1911, demonstrating that, contrary to popular opinion, senior officers were keen to see what aviation could achieve. Samson's total flying time would have

amounted to tens rather then hundreds of hours at the time, making both his enthusiasm and early achievements all the more remarkable. The vessel selected was the pre-Dreadnought battleship *Africa*, and two downward-sloping, parallel troughs were constructed from wood, forming a flight deck over the forward gun turret and the forecastle. Samson flew T2 from Eastchurch to Sheerness Dockyard where the ship was moored to a buoy, and had the aircraft hoisted aboard from a lighter. On 10 January 1912 he became the second man in history to fly from a ship's deck, using just over 100 feet of the available take-off run despite a slight tailwind. He flew back to Eastchurch and landed safely. The next logical step was to take off from a ship under way at sea, and this was achieved on 2 May 1912, again by Samson in T2, but by then the aircraft had been fitted with a more powerful 70hp Gnome engine. The troughs, this time without as much slope and nearly level, were built on to *Africa*'s sister-ship *Hibernia*, which steamed at 10½

HMS *Hermes* as she appeared when taking part in the Royal Navy's 1913 manoeuvres. Canvas hangars have been erected to protect the aircraft stowed on board forward and aft, and long handling booms have been installed on the forward and main masts to lift them on to and off the water alongside. The take-off platform forward is just visible, running from the canvas hangar to a position just forward of the bow.
(P.A. VICARY COLLECTION VIA STEPHEN MCLAUGHLIN)

Short 'Folder' number 81, constructor's number S.64, the first naval aircraft designed to fold in order to occupy less hangar space when embarked, at Eastchurch shortly after its construction. It passed its acceptance tests on 17 July 1913, embarked in HMS *Hermes* a day later and flew from her until badly damaged off Cromarty on 4 September 1913 when its rudder jammed at 1,000 feet and it dived into the sea.

(KEY PUBLISHING – GORDON SWANBOROUGH COLLECTION)

knots in Weymouth Bay for the trial. With a combination of natural wind over the bow and ship speed, the aircraft was airborne after a run of only 45 feet. A third launch took place in July from the older battleship *London*. In all three cases the aircraft took off with ease, well before the end of the deck, and was able to fly ashore to land. Had it been unable to do so it would have alighted on the water close to the nearest warship. Aircraft could, therefore, be taken to sea and could be launched and even recovered on to the water in calm conditions. The same flight deck had been used on all three ships, and was clearly capable of being erected and dismantled quickly, but

it restricted the tactical flexibility of the ship on which it was mounted in that if the forward guns were fired, the flight deck and any aeroplane on it would be destroyed by blast. A solution was to carry seaplanes on the upper deck amidships, near the ship's boats, where they could be lowered into the water to fly and recover, leaving the main armament's arcs of fire largely intact. Even then, though, there was still a problem, since battleships in the line and cruisers scouting ahead of them must not be handicapped by having to fall out of their stations in line or screen to operate seaplanes. Aircraft had obvious utility as airborne 'scouts', but with no real offensive capability

they could not yet be allowed to interfere with the primary functions of fighting ships.

The Royal Navy concluded that the best way to get seaplanes to sea was to embark them in a vessel specifically built or converted for the purpose of operating them. It was logical, therefore, to consider commissioning a ship whose only operational duty was the supply of aircraft, undistracted by tactical manoeuvring or gunnery considerations. Such a ship could also be fitted with workshop facilities for servicing the aircraft and, by centralising both the aircraft and the manpower needed to operate them, availability would be better than it would be if they were dispersed, with little support, on take-off ramps on several different ships, each with other priorities. In 1912 the shipbuilding firm of William Beardmore proposed a sketch design for an aircraft-carrying ship to the Admiralty. This featured a long flight deck with

workshops and hangarage either side of it connected, over the deck, by a bridge from which both ship and flying arrangements would have been controlled. With the wisdom of hindsight we can see that turbulence caused by the parallel structures and bridge would have made the flight deck inoperable. The proposed ship was not ordered by the Admiralty, which wanted more experience of aviation before taking such a step; the 'wait and see' doctrine. The design did, however, influence some of the subsequent attempts to design an aircraft carrier. In the autumn of 1912 the Admiralty decided to adapt the 5,600 ton protected cruiser *Hermes* into a seaplane carrier. The forecastle gun was removed and replaced by a sloping take-off deck similar to that used in *Africa*, *Hibernia* and *London*. Aft of the track, just forward of the bridge, a canvas hangar was constructed which was capable of protecting an aircraft from wind and

Winston Churchill, First Lord of the Admiralty, and Commander Samson in Short Type 74 number 76 in June 1914. The aircraft had been fitted with W/T equipment in April and was taking part in trials at the time. The propeller is not turning and the aircraft is floating with its nose into wind (note the sail on the small skiff). The rear cockpit, with its control wheel, is empty, and both occupants are in the front cockpit, where Churchill appears to be holding on to a taut rope attached to a sea anchor.

(SHORT BROTHERS VIA KEY PUBLISHING – GORDON SWANBOROUGH COLLECTION)

weather. A second hangar was rigged on the quarterdeck with a boom attached to the mainmast positioned to lift aircraft off the deck and on to the sea. A third aircraft could be carried on the deck but would be unprotected from the elements. Suitable workshops and store rooms were provided to support the embarked aircraft. She commissioned on 7 May 1913 as both an aircraft carrier and as the headquarters for the embryonic naval air service under the command of Captain G.W. Vivian RN. His terms of reference required him to administer all air

Commander Schwann's Avro Type D inside the airship shed at Barrow-in-Furness in 1911.

(KEY PUBLISHING – GORDON SWANBOROUGH COLLECTION)

personnel and the new coastal air stations in addition to the ship itself.

The US, French and Royal Navies all used aircraft in their 1913 fleet exercises with varying degrees of success. The USN shipped an 'Aviation Detachment' of Curtiss and Wright seaplanes to Guantanamo Bay in Cuba, from where they were used to publicise aviation rather than develop tactical doctrine. The French *Foudre* embarked Nieuport, Breguet and Farman seaplanes which flew patrols looking for 'hostile' shipping in the approaches to Toulon. Great difficulty was experienced in operating seaplanes in the open sea, and her commanding officer repeated the recommendation of Admiral Le Pord that a 'flat-topped' ship operating wheeled aircraft would be a

better concept, but he was ignored. The Royal Navy carried out its manoeuvres in the North Sea and in the Atlantic southwest of Ireland, and they proved to be the defining test of naval aviation before war broke out in 1914. The scenario matched the Blue against the Red Fleet, with 351 warships split between the two forces in almost exactly the ratio of the larger Royal Navy to the smaller Imperial German Navy. The only aircraft carrier, *Hermes*, was attached to the Red, or 'enemy', Fleet. She embarked two seaplanes, 80 hp Borel monoplane number 48, carried in the forecastle hangar, and 160 hp Short 'Folder' biplane number 81, carried in the quarterdeck hangar. The latter is of considerable historical significance as the first aeroplane designed for embarked operation. It was delivered on 16 July, only just in time for the exercises, after being developed by Horace Short in consultation with Commander Samson and Lieutenant Longmore. It could carry an observer, equipped with a Rouzet wireless transmitter, in addition to the pilot. As its name implied, however, the aircraft's principal feature was the wing-folding mechanism which allowed its wings to be folded into the minimum volume of stowage space in the hangar and spread quickly in readiness for flight. This was a great step forward from the earlier technique, which was to dismantle aircraft for stowage and reassemble them before flight, with the consequent need to re-rig them and adjust the control cables; a difficult and time-consuming task. Folding reduced the aircraft's width from over 56 feet to 12 feet, with no increase in the 40-foot length. The aircraft had a radius of action of about 65 miles from the parent ship, which was also the maximum effective range of the wireless transmitter. The transmitter alone weighed over 70lb, so, to save weight, a receiver was not carried. The noise and vibration in the aircraft's open cockpit would, in any case, have made it extremely difficult to use. The Red Fleet also had the new naval air station at Great Yarmouth, with three aircraft and four pilots, while Blue had air stations at Leven and Cromarty with similar numbers. The exercise instructions stated that aircraft were restricted to reconnaissance missions; they were considered immune from attack and could not, themselves, attack targets they sighted. *Hermes* had two specific roles, both of which generated considerable interest. Firstly she was to investigate whether it really was possible for aircraft to operate with the fleet under warlike operational conditions. Her secondary role was to replicate an airship in the reconnaissance role with a range of 800 miles, giving a radius of action of 400 miles. To fulfil this task she was allowed to proceed to any point within a 300-mile radius of Great Yarmouth and then launch an aircraft to complete the reconnaissance. To simulate an airship's endurance she had to return to Great Yarmouth within 48 hours of the time of her sailing. This aspect of her tasking gives evidence of the capability expected of R-1 had it been accepted for service.[10]

Hermes sailed from Sheerness for Great Yarmouth on 18 July 1913, and began to operate aircraft on 21 July, when Samson flew two sorties in the Folder, one in the forenoon and one in the evening. The Borel had to have some work done on it to make it serviceable, but both the aircraft and its hangar were completely wrecked by wind and waves when *Hermes* encountered very bad weather on 22 July. The Folder was slightly damaged in the after hangar but soon repaired by its mechanics.[11] Both fleets were at sea on that day, and 'war' was declared to have started at 16:00. On 24 July Red succeeded in landing troops near Immingham on a raid, and *Hermes* anchored nearby, north of Spurn Head, in the early hours of the morning, where, despite heavy swell, the Folder was hoisted out and took off. Dense fog forced it to turn back after only 30 minutes, but during the short flight several successful W/T messages were sent by the aircraft and received in 'mother' which re-broadcast them. Once the Folder was safely secured on board, *Hermes* closed Great Yarmouth and landed the wrecked Borel and took on Caudron G.III number 55 as a replacement.[12] The weather on 25 July was too bad for flying, with both fog and heavy seas, but by the afternoon of 26 July the waves had moderated enough to allow an attempt to be made to launch the Folder. Difficulty was experienced taking off, and during one particularly heavy bounce several struts that held the floats in place were broken. The aircraft was hoisted in and repaired overnight by the ship's air mechanics. The Caudron seaplane was stowed in a repaired forward hangar. It had a 100 hp engine and stepped floats, which represented a considerable advance over the pontoon-type floats on the Short-designed aircraft. Wheels were built into the floats to make the aircraft easier to handle on deck. On 28 July this aircraft, piloted by Lieutenant Bowhill, took off successfully from the forecastle ramp on *Hermes* while the ship steamed off Great Yarmouth, during a gap in the exercises while other warships took on coal. The Short Folder had been able to fly again from 27 July onwards, despite the driving rain and persistent swell. After coaling, the manoeuvres began again on 31 July, when a cruiser action was fought, followed by a major 'battle' between the Blue and Red battle-fleets which was judged by the umpires to have ended in a draw.

On 1 August *Hermes* launched the Folder for a general reconnaissance. It flew outbound to over 60 miles before turning back to return to 'mother'. Fourteen minutes later *Hermes* received a W/T message which was undecipherable and which ended abruptly. Officers in the ship deduced correctly that a malfunction had forced it to land on the water, so they calculated an 'estimated position' (EP) based on previous messages and the aircraft's planned track. It proved to be within 2 miles of the position where the aircraft had come down. As soon as the abruptly-ended message had been received, *Hermes* despatched the destroyer *Mermaid* to search for the aircraft and its crew of two, and followed as soon as steam was raised. On her way to the EP, *Mermaid* met the German steamer *Clara Mennig*, which had both the seaplane and its crew on board. They had landed near it and been hoisted on board by the crew, which had treated them well. When *Hermes* came up, the aircraft was lowered carefully back on to the water by the German steamer and hoisted back on to the carrier for repairs. The Folder's crew comprised Commander Samson as pilot and Lieutenant Raymond Fitzmaurice as observer. The latter subsequently gave an account of the flight which gives a good idea of the state that naval aviation had reached by mid-1913.[13]

> We started off from the *Hermes* at Yarmouth at 0900
> on a lovely day, making a good 75 knots, at about
> three to four thousand feet up; sometimes we had

to come down to within five hundred feet to get clear of the clouds and to get a good view. It is surprising how low clouds are; from below it looks as if the clouds are two or three thousand feet up, but on going up you often get into them at three or four hundred feet up. This is especially the case in the North Sea, and during the manoeuvres there were few days that you could see anything at a greater height than six hundred feet. We went about sixty-five miles out and, seeing nothing of the enemy, turned back. I had been sending signals by W/T all the time and had just reported a tramp steamer on the starboard bow, when the engine suddenly stopped. We unfortunately made a bad landing and completely smashed our undercarriage and part of the lower plane and tail; fortunately, however, the tramp came to our rescue and hoisted us on to her poop deck. She was a German timber boat, the *Clara Mennig*, bound from the White Sea to Tilbury; they were most kind and hospitable, but could not go out of their way to take us to Yarmouth. A few hours later, the *Hermes* hove in sight, having realised from our stoppage of signals that something was wrong; we hoisted out again from the *Clara Mennig* and hoisted into the *Hermes*, having had a very interesting day.

By the end of the 1913 fleet manoeuvres *Hermes*' Short Folder had flown six sorties and the Caudron at least one more. Flying operations continued into the autumn, and by October her aircraft had flown over thirty sorties, including another take-off by the Caudron from the flight deck off Cromarty. The period from May to October was the longest sustained evaluation of aircraft operations carried out by any navy, and had a considerable impact on the Royal Navy's perception of how aircraft should be deployed with the fleet.[14] There had been no new developments, and it could be argued that most sorties had repeated the experiments carried out in 1912, but the flying had been carried out as nearly as possible under operational conditions in less-than-ideal weather over a prolonged period. Fitting-out *Hermes* as an experimental aircraft carrier had been amply justified, and several important lessons had been learned. Among these, the most striking was the absolute need for W/T in naval aircraft intended for reconnaissance, both to report contacts and to ensure the safety of the crew if the aircraft came down many miles from 'mother'. Although an airborne observer could greatly increase the range at which an enemy fleet could be seen, that sighting was of little value if it could not be communicated quickly to the fleet command. In practical terms, one of the most important lessons was the need for long booms to keep the aircraft clear of the ship's side as it was lowered on to and lifted from the water. If the aircraft was too close to the hull while the ship rolled in a swell, there was a great risk that the airframe would bump into the side and suffer damage that would prevent it from flying. To be able to taxi clear once it was afloat, the aircraft had to be lowered with its nose forward so that the pilot could use rudder to turn away from the ship. This put the wings at particular risk during the lowering process, as even a gentle bump would impart stresses they were not designed to take. Another lesson brought home by experience was the need for shock-absorbers or springs on the struts between the floats and the fuselage, and for aircraft to be made generally more robust. It was now clear that aircraft intended for naval use needed to be specifically designed for the purpose, and not simply adapted from machines intended for operation ashore. The next step was to build a specialist aircraft carrier that would put the lessons learned into practice in the most efficient way.

HMS *Ark Royal* in Mudros Harbour in April 1915. The Anzacs in the boat in the foreground give an idea of scale.

After the successful conclusion of the flying experiments from *Hermes* during 1913, the Board of Admiralty decided to construct a specialist ship to carry and operate aircraft for operations with the fleet. A sum of £81,000 was made available in the 1914/15 estimates for the purpose. Using the experience gained to date, a design team comprising J.H. Narbeth, a constructor who was also an aviation enthusiast, his assistant C.J.W. Hopkins, Commodore Murray Sueter RN and Commander L'Estrange Malone RN discussed the ideal arrangements and considered options.[1] The Beardmore design was considered but thought to include too many features that had not yet been proven in practice, and a more extensive cruiser conversion was found, after calculation, not to justify the cost of conversion or the loss of such a ship from other duties. Narbeth listed the ideal properties that an aircraft carrier should possess, including aircraft stowage in hangars below the upper deck, unobstructed handling areas for the safe movement of aircraft on deck and a flying-off deck. There would also have to be cranes to handle aircraft, engine and airframe repair workshops, and ample space for spare parts to be stored. The stowage of high-octane aviation fuel (known later as Avgas), posed a particular problem because little was known about it other than the fact that the vapour was potentially more dangerous in the confined spaces within a ship's hull than live ammunition or its cordite propellant. As a mark of the faith the early aviators had in the future, he agreed that space should be included for offensive weapons to be carried by the aircraft. The ship needed good sea-keeping qualities and to be a steady platform capable of transferring aircraft to and from the water in moderate to rough seas. Above all, the aircraft carrier was to be a single-purpose ship, with no concessions to any role other than the operation of aircraft.[2] The work of this group produced a design that incorporated, in all essentials, most of the features required in every subsequent aircraft carrier.

No conventional warship hull could meet all these requirements without restriction. Only a mercantile hull could offer the volume needed if sacrifices in stability and efficiency were not to be prohibitive, but this meant that machinery capacity had to be

Seen from the air, HMS *Ark Royal*'s flat deck forward is cluttered with boats and washing lines with drying hammocks. It was never used, as intended, for launching aircraft. The steam cranes are flashed up and an awning has been rigged across part of the aircraft hatch to provide shade for the workshop and hangar. Note the empty space under the bridge where aircraft could be parked for engine runs.

(AUTHOR'S COLLECTION)

sacrificed or, rather, not increased above that found in a normal mercantile installation. To save construction time the Admiralty selected and bought a vessel laid down as a tramp steamer at the Blyth Shipbuilding Company which, by December 1913, was fully framed on the slipway with bottom plates and engine bearers in place. The latter were in the normal position amidships, and the revised design caused them to be removed and replaced right aft. This allowed the incorporation of a single hangar 150 feet long, 45 feet wide and 15 feet high, capable of holding ten aircraft on number 5 deck, the lowest continuous deck in the hull. A well-equipped airframe and engine workshop was sited over the hangar on number 2 deck. Access from the hangar to the handling area on deck and the 130-foot-long level flying-off deck forward was through hatches in the workshop deck and the upper deck, with two large steam cranes at the forward corners of the upper hatch, plumbing the opening. The cranes were used both to lift aircraft and components out of the hangar

and workshop and to hoist aircraft over the side on to the water. A simple five-ton derrick was also available for transfers between the hangar or workshop and the upper deck.

Accommodation for the ship's company was better than average, due in part to the mercantile origins of the vessel but mainly owing to the almost total absence of ship-mounted guns with their high demands for manpower and magazines. Air ordnance arrangements were in advance of those in any other navy, and included a bomb room, a torpedo warhead magazine and a separate torpedo body room. The first drop of a running torpedo, by Lieutenant Longmore in a Short Folder with extended, enlarged wings, took place on 28 July 1914, a few weeks before the ship was launched in September 1914. Avgas was carried in two-gallon cans stowed in bulk in a compartment forward of the workshop on number 2 deck. They were of commercial design and intended, originally, for the motor trade. Protection for and from the dangerous liquid was provided on all four

HMS *Ark Royal* moored at Kephalo in 1915, looking forward over the working deck from the bridge. Two Short seaplanes are being assembled; note the red-and-white roundels on the upper wing and the union flag on the fuselage of the nearer one; typical RNAS markings for the period.

(AUTHOR'S COLLECTION)

Fairy IIID N9499 is lowered into the water, with engine running, from the port steam crane. This aircraft was completed in September 1921 and served with 267 Squadron RAF in HMS *Ark Royal* between October 1922 and April 1923.

(AUTHOR'S COLLECTION)

sides and below by water jackets, and access was by means of a hatch in the flying-off deck. Aircraft were refuelled by pumping or pouring Avgas from the cans, chamois leather filters being used to filter out dirt particles and water. There was an area under the bridge which was open fore and aft in which an aircraft could be placed to run-up its engine under cover, and the flying-off area forward of the hatch was clear of all obstructions. This was intended to allow seaplanes with wheels, or mounted on a wheeled trolley, to take off, as the Caudron had done from *Hermes*. Water ballast tanks were built into the hull forward to trim her down by the bow to assist such take-offs with a downward-sloping deck, but there is no record of any ever having been carried out, since the deck was too short and the ship's speed too slow for it to be of practical use. To keep the deck clear, anchors and cables were worked from below the upper deck, on number 2 deck. A considerable amount of water ballast was carried high in the ship to reduce her excessive metacentric height and thus make rolling less severe to ease aircraft movement. A unique feature was a mizzen mast on which a sail could be hoisted to help keep her head-to-wind when she operated her seaplanes while at anchor.

Commissioned in February 1915 as HMS *Ark Royal*, this ship has a claim to be the first in the world to be designed and built specifically to carry and operate aircraft, another indication of just how much enthusiasm there was within the Admiralty to introduce aircraft to fleet operations. Overall, considering the minimal experience that had underpinned the design, she was a well-thought-out success. The main shortcoming was the choice of machinery and hull form. With a simple 'bluff' hull and a single coal-fired triple-expansion engine of 3,000hp she had a top speed of only 11 knots. This was considerably below the speed required for tactical manoeuvres with the fleet, and too slow for wheeled aircraft to take off from the deck. Another limitation was found to be the method chosen to move aircraft from the hangar to the deck. Seaplane operations from *Hermes* had shown that aircraft tended to swing when being lowered on to the water, with the resulting risk that they might bump the ship's side and be damaged. In *Ark Royal* they were lifted through relatively small hatches suspended from a crane, producing an even greater risk of impact in any but the calmest of sea conditions. In the event she sailed for the Dardanelles shortly after completion and spent most of the war as a mobile 'base' in the Mediterranean. During the Gallipoli Campaign her seaplanes were intended to spot for the guns of the warships bombarding the forts that guarded the narrows.

At the outbreak of war in 1914 the Royal Navy had the largest naval air component in the world, but it was virtually all based ashore. The Admiralty activated contingency plans and three small, fast ferries were requisitioned for use as seaplane carriers to work with fleets and squadrons. *Engadine, Riviera* and *Empress* were given simple conversions with the upper decks cleared aft and fitted with wooden platforms to take the weight of three seaplanes. Canvas screens and awnings gave side and overhead protection against the elements, and simple swinging derricks were fitted for handling the aircraft. In essence they were refined and slightly more capable improvements on *Hermes*, which was recommissioned for use as an aircraft transport. A fourth ferry, the *Ben-My-Chree*, and the retired Cunard liner *Campania* were taken up from trade late in 1914.

The aircraft available for operation from these ships included the big Short Folders, intended for reconnaissance and as weapon carriers, and the smaller Sopwith Tabloids, Schneiders and, later, Babies intended for use as fighters to counter enemy aerial activity. The difficulty of operating seaplanes was demonstrated in the winter of 1914/15. Attempted attacks on coastal targets were largely abortive owing to the poor performance of the aircraft on the water in the open sea. The Sopwiths were particularly hampered by their lack of power and the poor design of their floats and, since they tended to be used for the more ambitious offensive operations, the shortcoming limited the usefulness of the carriers. When the wheeled Sopwith Tabloid was adapted to become a seaplane and refined into the Schneider the 100hp Gnome engine was retained, even though three floats, their attachments and local strengthening added 200lb to the basic weight of the

aircraft. Weapons such as a Lewis Gun and ammunition plus small bombs or anti-airship Ranken darts added still further to the loaded weight. A fully armed and fuelled Schneider weighed about 1,300lb giving it a power-to-weight ratio of 13lb per horsepower. This ratio governs acceleration, which in turn governs take-off performance. Added weight without added power meant an increase in the distance needed to achieve flying speed and the time taken to reach it. To add to the problem, floats had a larger 'footprint' than wheels and thus a bigger area in contact with the surface, inducing more drag. This effect was lessened by using vee-shaped floats, like those pioneered by Schwann and his mechanics at Barrow, with which the 'footprint' decreased as the aircraft began to lift, and a step reduced the floats' waterline length still further as it came out of the water. The slab-sided, flat-bottomed floats fitted to Short, Sopwith and later Fairey aircraft in 1915 were not a good design and placed more, not less, of the lower surface in contact with the water as the aircraft lifted its nose to take off. The result, when the power available was only marginally sufficient to get airborne at all, was that waves were needed to break the contact between the float and the water. In calm conditions with neither wind nor wave to help, failures to get airborne were common. Choppy seas brought their own problems, however, since the spray thrown up by the floats hit the propeller, reducing engine revolutions and transmitted power, perhaps even causing physical damage. Rotary engines were generally enclosed in cowlings, named after their appearance as 'bull-nosed' or 'horse-collar' types. Both were cut away at the bottom to improve cylinder cooling in flight and to allow access for maintenance, but the opening could also allow significant quantities of 'solid' water to hit the engine and flood magnetos and ignition systems, causing the engine to stop. Shock absorbers were recommended in 1913 and were being fitted by 1915, but with the need to minimise weight growth neither they nor the fuselage attachment points were as substantial as was really necessary. The effect of bouncing from wave to wave at over 40 knots while taking off or landing was jarring on the aircrew, airframe and undercarriage; 'like being on the end of a stick pulled along park railings'.[3] Structural failures, like that encountered by *Hermes'* Folder, were common whether caused by a single rough-weather take-off or by a cumulative number of less spine-shattering experiences.

These early seaplane ships were the first generation of aircraft carrier to see operational service, and their usefulness can be illustrated by two sorties. The first involved Sopwith Type 807 number 808, a tractor-engine, folding biplane delivered from the manu-facturer in December 1914 and embarked in *Ark Royal* during the Gallipoli campaign. The ship's senior aviator was Flight Commander Hugh A. Williamson RNAS, who soon expressed the opinion that 'the heavy and cumbersome floats over-taxed the low-powered engines and we were constantly preoccupied with keeping our machines in the air'.[4] On 5 March 1915 *Ark Royal* was anchored near the new battleship *Queen Elizabeth* near Gaba Tepe on the western side of the Gallipoli Peninsula. Her aircraft were to spot for the battleship, which would fire over the peninsula

into the rear of the forts which faced the narrows. Since the ship would not be able to see its targets, air spotting was essential if the shoot was to be successful. So that Williamson could concentrate on transmitting the fall of shot, he elected to fly in the observer's seat of 808, and his pilot for the first sortie of the day was Flight Lieutenant W.H.S. Garnett RNAS. Williamson subsequently described the sortie: 'It was a perfect day, with just the right amount of wind for taking off from the water ... we soon reached 3,000 feet and were ready to cross the peninsula to the target. Then it happened, the propeller disintegrated and the aircraft went out of control and crashed into the sea.' Part of the shattered propeller had hit and damaged one of the starboard wings, causing the aircraft to depart from controlled flight and spiral into the water three miles west of *Ark Royal*. The pilot was slightly injured and Williamson more seriously hurt. Both were rescued by the destroyer HMS *Usk*. Williamson returned to the UK to convalesce, and while doing so he wrote a paper on what he considered to be the

A view down into the aircraft hangar from HMS *Ark Royal's* bridge. Work is in progress on a number of dismantled aircraft including 1577, a Sopwith Schneider issued to *Ark Royal* from the RNAS Depot at Imbros in September 1915. It was test-flown after erection in October, and was wrecked in May of the following year.

(AUTHOR'S COLLECTION)

ideal design for an aircraft carrier and even made a model, complete with a continuous flight deck and starboard-side island to illustrate his ideas. Unfortunately, it has not survived.

A typical flight from *Ark Royal* entailed preparing the aircraft on deck and starting the engine, the whole process taking about an hour from the time the aircraft was lifted through the hatch. Starting the engine required a mechanic to turn the propeller several times with the magnetos off – 'switches off' - to charge the cylinders with a fuel/air mixture. The magnetos would then be switched on – 'switches on' – and the propeller swung briskly to start the engine. If it failed to fire, the cylinders might flood with fuel and several minutes would elapse before a fresh attempt could be made. Engines stood more chance of starting if the aircraft was parked with its nose into wind. After start, the engine was run for several minutes to confirm oil pressure and to warm it up before the crew strapped into the cockpit and the aircraft was lowered on to the water, being kept clear of the ship's side by padded boat hooks. Once safely on the water, the pilot taxied clear of the ship into a clear patch of water and took off into wind. The distance required varied with surface wind and sea state, but took about 2,000 yards on average. As pointed out earlier, in a flat calm the seaplane might not get airborne at all and in rough conditions the floats might break up.

Once airborne, a fully-loaded Sopwith 807 took about three-and-a-half minutes to climb to 1,000 feet and climbed at about four minutes per thousand feet above that. When they were safely airborne the observer transmitted his call sign to the ship for which he was to spot but, with no receiver, he could not receive messages and relied on the pre-flight briefing, such as it was, for the conduct of the flight. Later in the Dardanelles Campaign the Turks succeeded in jamming the low-powered aircraft transmitters and, without a receiver, the observer had no means of knowing if his signals reached the ship with which he was working. Ideally, a replacement aircraft would relieve the spotter on task, but any problem in start-up or take-off would delay it, as was often the case. The spotter on task would operate until the pilot

calculated that he had reached his prudent limit of endurance (PLE) and then return to 'mother'. With the *Ark* at anchor for much of the campaign, navigation was not difficult and the ship would be over-flown before alighting on the water near it. Once safely down, the pilot would taxi to the ship, where the observer would hook the aircraft on to a wire lowered from the crane. Once the engine was stopped, the aircraft would be hoisted on to the deck and the crew would have the first chance to see how effective their sortie had been as visual signals from the battleship were deciphered. Similar sorties were flown by seaplanes from the Egypt and East Indies Seaplane Squadron until the end of the war in 1918.

The second illustrative seaplane sortie occurred during the Battle of Jutland on 31 May 1916. HMS *Engadine* formed part of the Battle Cruiser Fleet under Vice-Admiral Sir David Beatty, manoeuvring to try to gain information about the enemy battle fleet that was, for much of the time, invisible over the horizon. In his report on the battle,[5] Beatty stated:

> At 1445 I ordered *Engadine* to send up a seaplane and scout to the NNE. This order was carried out very quickly and by 1508 a seaplane with Flight Lieutenant F.J. Rutland RNAS as pilot and Assistant Paymaster G.S. Trewin RN as observer was well under way. His first reports … were received in *Engadine* at about 1530. Owing to clouds it was necessary to fly very low and in order to identify four enemy light cruisers the seaplane had to fly at 900 feet within 3,000 yards of them, the light cruisers opening fire on her with every gun that would bear. This in no way interfered with the clarity of their reports … which indicates that seaplanes in such circumstances are of distinct value.

When the signal from Admiral Beatty was received, all of *Engadine*'s Short Type 184 seaplanes were secured for sea, in her hangar with their wings folded. Before launching, the unwieldy doors of the hangar had to be opened, the aircraft manhandled on to the deck, its wings spread and engine run up before it could be hoisted on to the water.[6] Trewin's reports about the enemy cruiser's position, course and speed were deemed by the captain of *Engadine* to be 'admirably clear and succinct'[7] but unfortunately, although

HMS *Riviera* was requisitioned on 11 August 1914 and converted into a seaplane carrier by Chatham Dockyard, with canvas hangars fore and aft together with booms to lift aircraft on and off the water. She is seen here in her original civilian paint scheme shortly after completion of the work in September.

(AUTHOR'S COLLECTION)

Admiral Beatty congratulated the aircrew on their achievement, he never received their reports. *Engadine* attempted to pass the enemy contact reports to the Senior Officers of the Battle Cruiser Fleet and Fifth Battle Squadron by flashing light at 1530, 1532 and 1545, but none was acknowledged. The seaplane was forced to land on the sea because of a broken petrol pipe, which Rutland managed to repair using a piece of rubber tubing torn from his life-saving waistcoat.[8] He recovered to the ship and was hoisted in at 1600, after which, in deteriorating weather, no more sorties were flown despite the aircrew's enthusiasm to give it another go. For his efforts Rutland was promoted Flight Commander and awarded the DSO. His observer was awarded the DSC.

The work of the observers was significant. Unlike pilots, their role was not the subject of a formalised course of training until 1917. Before then, the second crew member in two-seat aircraft was usually a 'willing volunteer' from the carrier's wardroom, often the smallest and lightest who could cope. Midshipmen were frequently chosen for the task, and it was not unusual for officers from non-military branches, such as Assistant Paymaster Trewin, to volunteer, especially if they had hopes of becoming a pilot. In his book *Fights and Flights* (Ernest Benn, London, 1930), Samson gave a graphic picture of the observer's task:

> I leave to the imagination the job the observer used to have. He sat in a restricted space with a Lewis gun hitting him in the neck every time that he moved, nursing a camera on his knees with three or four 16lb bombs loose at his feet. Somewhere handy he had to have a pair of binoculars, writing pad, map and pencil. Added to this he had to attempt to understand what an excited and, in his view, imbecile pilot wanted him to do. Of course, he couldn't often hear what the pilot said amid the noise of the engine and general turmoil of flight.

After Jutland, Flight Commander Rutland described Trewin as 'one of the most courageous men I have ever met because he was obviously scared stiff whenever he was in the air and yet he always stuck to it and did his job well under any conditions'.[9] By January 1916 a start was made to recruit direct entry observers into the RNVR, but there were concerns that none would remain in the permanent force after demobilisation at the end of hostilities. Wing Captain F.H. Sykes RNAS suggested that such officers should be given flight rank and incorporated into an Intelligence Branch.[10] He also felt that they should receive flying pay since they 'encounter the same risks as the pilot' and had aviation skills 'though of a different kind to that of a pilot'.

The Grand Fleet's seaplane carrier, *Campania*, failed to sail with the fleet as intended and did not take part in the Battle of Jutland because of a signalling error. When she did sail, some hours adrift, she steamed flat out to catch up overnight, but was ordered back by the C-in-C on staff advice that she would be too far away from the battle fleet on 31 May.

The absence of her ten aircraft, three Short 184s, three Babies and four Schneiders, denied Admiral Jellicoe the use of a potentially significant reconnaissance force that might have contributed a 'picture' of the enemy fleet as it moved north before the daylight action. This unfortunate episode gives insight into Admiral Jellicoe's perception of aircraft operations at the time. The signalling error left his only aircraft carrier behind and his staff failed to realise the fact for several hours. Worse, the C-in-C and his staff were not aware that *Campania* had the speed to catch up and that, at roughly 21 knots, she was not likely to be intercepted and attacked by a U-boat. Most tellingly, however, they thought in terms of the carrier needing to be close to the fleet to be effective, whereas her Short 184s had the radius of action to locate enemy warships and transmit their position from a position 'over the horizon'. Clearly the GF Staff had not given enough thought to the actual, as opposed to theoretical, use of aircraft. Since Jellicoe had commanded the Red Fleet, which included *Hermes*, in 1913, this shortcoming is surprising.

The early seaplane carriers are best thought of as 'mobile hangars'. The limitation of having to stop to hoist aircraft on to and off the water in the open sea proved too great for them to be of real value in fleet actions, but they did serve a purpose with expeditionary forces in many relatively remote areas where fleet work was not required. A number of ships such as *Anne* and *Raven II* were taken up from trade and given conversions similar to *Engadine* and her half-sisters. Commissioned as HM Ships, they gave good service from sheltered anchorages off East Africa, the Aegean, the Red Sea, the Caspian Sea and the Eastern Mediterranean. The East Indies and Egypt Seaplane Squadron, led by Commander Samson from May 1916, gave particularly good service on the left flank of the British Imperial forces fighting the Turks in Palestine and Syria. While operating from sheltered anchorages solved the problem of ship movement and rough water, the high temperatures encountered in the Middle East introduced other problems. Samson wrote that the 'only chance of being able to fly with the Shorts was to try to get off very early in the morning or late in the afternoon, as the severe heat would inevitably not only boil all our cooling water away, but probably affect our lift'.[11] On 8 June 1916 he recorded that his Short 184 had needed a take-off run of two nautical miles, or 4,000 yards, to get airborne. Although the seaplane carriers brought their aircraft to remote conflicts they represented a 'dead end' in development terms, and an improved method of operation was needed if aircraft were to operate effectively.

HMS *Engadine* in 1915, after a more extensive conversion into a seaplane carrier carried out by the Cunard Steamship Company in Liverpool. She is seen here with a Short 184 on the working deck aft of the hangar, as she would have appeared at the Battle of Jutland on 31 May 1916. (AUTHOR'S COLLECTION)

CHAPTER 3

Take-off decks

A Fairey Campania is prepared for flight on HMS *Campania*'s take-off deck. The floats are resting on wheeled trolleys which would fall into the sea as the aircraft became airborne, and the tail of the aircraft has been pushed right aft between the split forward funnels to give the maximum deck run. As the name suggests, the Fairey Campania was designed specifically to operate from this ship.

His Majesty's Ships *Campania* and *Ben-my-Chree* commissioned within days of each other at Liverpool in April 1915. The latter was larger than the earlier ferry conversions and had a more substantial hangar aft, made of mild steel, measuring 82 feet long by 42 feet wide, and capable of holding four aircraft. Unlike the earlier conversions, *Ben-my-Chree* was fitted with a portable flying-off deck forward with a canvas shelter for a single Schneider seaplane. At 63 feet long and only 12 feet wide it was too small for a safe take-off in any but the strongest wind, but its installation showed recognition of the need for carriers to incorporate better ways of launching aircraft. On 11 May 1915, while operating as part of the Harwich Force, she attempted to launch a Schneider seaplane mounted on a jettisonable, wheeled trolley from her flying deck to intercept a Zeppelin shadower. The pilot warmed up the aircraft's Gnome engine after start, but in the process it backfired so violently that the aircraft fell off the trolley and was sufficiently badly damaged for the take-off to be abandoned. Admiral Jellicoe, the Commander-in-Chief Grand Fleet, began to doubt that seaplanes were of any practical value to the fleet after this incident. He feared that they could not be relied upon to get airborne to spot for his guns or to deny similar information from enemy aircraft 'unless it be by the use of aeroplanes (wheeled aircraft), rising from the deck of *Campania* .... able to land upon the water and be supported sufficiently long by air bags to allow of the rescue of the pilots'.[1]

A former Cunard liner, *Campania* was both larger and faster than previous carriers, if somewhat aged. She had been made available when a survey considered her too old for conversion into an armed merchant cruiser, and she had actually been sold for scrap when war broke out. Her conversion was basic, providing two hangars and a take-off deck 120 feet long by 30 feet wide which sloped downwards toward the bow over the forecastle. The shipyard did a good job refurbishing her coal-fired reciprocating machinery and she was capable of reaching 21 knots in short bursts. She was attached to the Grand Fleet and undertook trials after her completion in which, unfortunately, her performance operating seaplanes failed to match expectations. Her sheer size was a problem and caused considerable

difficulty in handling aircraft because of her greater beam and the height of the aircraft handling deck above the water. Derricks needed more 'reach' than those in *Hermes* or the converted ferries and, with the ship moving in sea or swell, aircraft at the end of a long rope on a long derrick arm always had a marked tendency to swing, particularly if there was any wind blowing. Even if the swing could be controlled with poles with soft pads on the end, there was still a risk that the aircraft would strike the ship's side or land in the water too heavily in adverse roll conditions. Unsatisfactory trials continued through June and July 1915 and added to the belief that seaplanes were not the way forward. On 6 July *Campania* launched a Sopwith Schneider from her flying-off deck. The event was described by Wing Captain Oliver Schwann RNAS, her commanding officer and the man who had experimented with seaplanes at Barrow five years earlier.[2]

Flight Lieutenant W.L. Welsh RNAS successfully flew a Schneider Cup seaplane from the flying deck of this ship on the evening of the 6th instant. The aircraft weighed 1,060lb, the pilot 160lb, fuel 30lb and the wheels 18lb giving a maximum all-up weight of 1,268lb. The ship was steaming at 17 knots directly into a 13-knot wind. The seaplane was placed on top of the forward hatch with the tail right up close against the fore bridge supports and was mounted on a wheeled trolley which could be released by the pilot after take-off. The wheels were 152 feet from the bows. The engine was run up to 1,050 revolutions and, with the tail float of the machine resting on the hatch, the seaplane was released at a given signal. As is usual with the 100hp Gnomes the engine spluttered a little as the seaplane moved ahead. It soon picked up and, on the whole, pulled well. The exact moment at which the tail lifted has not been definitely ascertained but it appears to have been after running about 30 feet. The elevator was kept hard down until the tail was up. It was then kept practically horizontal or slightly up for the whole run except just at the end when it was put considerably up. The steering of the machine was fairly good. No rails of any description were fitted to the flying deck. The seaplane started with a little port helm in order to counteract the

One of the last seaplane carriers to be converted by the Admiralty, HMS *Nairana* was capable of launching Sopwith Pups from the flight deck forward, and the gantry aft could lower Short 184s on to the water and recover them with the ship making way slowly.
(AUTHOR'S COLLECTION)

A Short Type 184 takes off from the water alongside HMS *Campania*. The ship is stationary and the port boom is still swung out from deploying the aircraft.
(AUTHOR'S COLLECTION)

HMS *Vindex*, showing the small take-off deck forward which covered the forecastle and an open storage space for two fighters. The two masts aft of the deck were each fitted with booms to move aircraft. She is at anchor and, since no jack-staff is fitted at the bow, the Union Jack is flown from the fore-mast.
(AUTHOR'S COLLECTION)

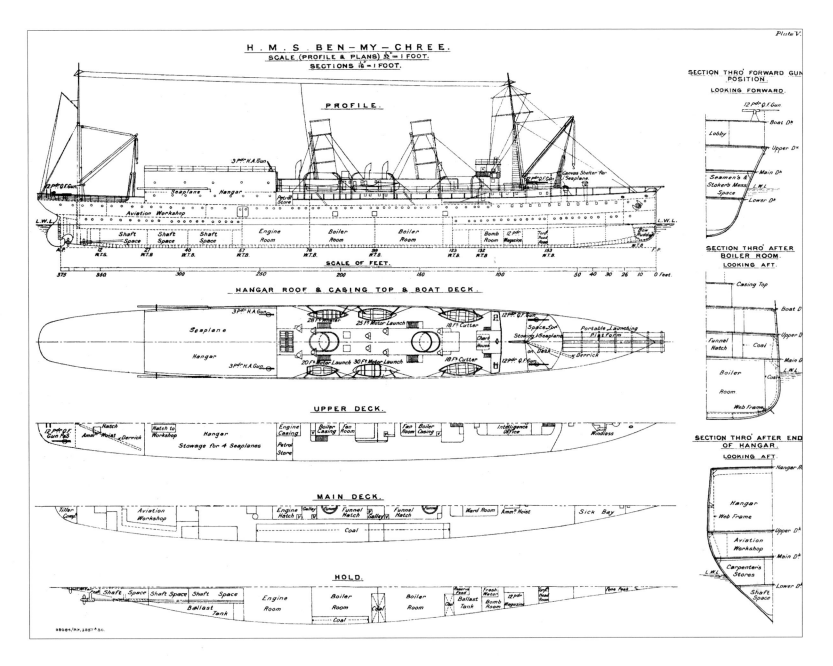

Plate V.

H.M.S. BEN-MY-CHREE.

SCALE (PROFILE & PLANS) 1/32" = 1 FOOT.
SECTIONS 1/16" = 1 FOOT.

PROFILE.

HANGAR ROOF & CASING TOP & BOAT DECK.

UPPER DECK.

MAIN DECK.

HOLD.

SECTION THRO' FORWARD GUN POSITION.
LOOKING FORWARD.

SECTION THRO' AFTER BOILER ROOM.
LOOKING AFT.

SECTION THRO' AFTER END OF HANGAR.
LOOKING AFT.

anticipated kick to the left on being released. The amount of helm given was rather too much and it went slightly over to one side as it reached the flying deck. It was then brought back to the centreline and crossed the bows exactly amidships. A proposal to keep the wheels of the seaplane running between rails or in grooved recesses is now finding favour among the pilots. The seaplane left the deck thirty-nine feet from the bows or about thirty-two feet from a point where the flying deck becomes so narrow that one of the wheels would have gone off the edge had it not been flying. The time from the moment of releasing the seaplane to the moment it left the deck was six seconds. The wheeled trolley was released by the pilot close to one of *Campania*'s motor boats and was recovered. A great deal of discussion is now going on as to what shall be done to enable the seaplane to fly off the deck more easily and with a full load, as it will be seen that this seaplane did not get off the deck any too easily.

In hindsight it was lucky for the pilot in *Ben-my-Chree* that his engine had backfired, as he would almost certainly have ditched over the bow at the end of his shorter take-off run. Captain Schwann's report goes on to speculate on the need for some form of external force to accelerate the aircraft during the first few feet

Plan and profile drawings of HMS *Ben-my-Chree* as she appeared after conversion to a seaplane carrier in 1915.

(AUTHOR'S COLLECTION)

of its take-off run. In view of Welsh's experience, no attempt was made to launch the heavier Short 184s from the deck, and by October disenchantment with *Campania* had grown to the extent that her outright disposal was considered. Wing Captain Schwann wrote[3] that considerable experience had been gained operating the ship and that improvements could be made that would improve her ability to operate aircraft. Among other comments, he noted that 'the officers and ship's company, including the air mechanics … were all new to the conditions on commencing work in May 1915. The observers, all RNR Midshipmen, had

Ditching was the inevitable end of a sortie from ships fitted with flying-off decks when they were too far from the coast for the aircraft to fly ashore. The pilot of a ditched WB.III clambers over the tailplane into a rescuing 32-foot cutter.

(AUTHOR'S COLLECTION)

An armed and fully equipped Beardmore WB.III takes off from HMS *Pegasus* in 1918.

(AUTHOR'S COLLECTION)

to be taught signalling, observation work from seaplanes, and in particular, the meaning of "initiative".' He also noted that 'flying from *Campania*'s deck is limited at present to very small light machines, suitable for the attack of airships but not for fleet scouting work', and that alterations to increase the size of the deck would improve matters. With his considerable experience of seaplane operations, he conceded that 'rising from the water must continue to be a difficulty for aircraft'. His views were supported both by Admiral Jellicoe and by the Air Department within the Admiralty and it was decided, therefore, to reconstruct *Campania* to operate aircraft more effectively and, as insurance against further failure, to carry observation balloons.

Ben-my-Chree was the first ship to embark Short Type 184 seaplanes, designed to carry a 14-inch Mark X torpedo between the floats in the strike role. With

the weight of the big aircraft itself and the weapon, 184s needed ideal conditions to take off from the water and could certainly not use the small flying-off deck, but the ability to operate them at all marked a significant advance in capability for embarked aircraft. In June 1915 *Ben-my-Chree* replaced *Ark Royal* off the Dardanelles, and it may well be that she and her new aircraft were deployed to the Eastern Mediterranean to seek out targets for the first operational aerial torpedoes. The first attack took place on 14 August 1915, flown by Flight Commander Charles H.K. Edmonds RNAS in seaplane number 842. *Ben-my-Chree* was anchored to the west of the Gallipoli Peninsula and Edmonds took off in calm conditions at 0455, crossing the Bulair Isthmus at 1,500 feet before locating the ship to be attacked west of Injeh Burnu. In his report to Squadron Commander C. L'Estrange Malone RNAS, who commanded the ship, Edmonds stated: 'I glided down and fired my torpedo at the steamer from a height of about 14 feet and

range of some 300 yards, with the sun astern of me. Looking back, I observed the track of the torpedo which struck the ship abreast the mainmast on the starboard side.'[4] In fact the target had been beached on 10 August, after being torpedoed and shelled by a British submarine, but on 19 August Edmonds set matters right by attacking and destroying a second supply ship which was under way.[5] On the same day Flight Lieutenant G.B. Dacre RNAS attacked and sank a steam tug close to the Asiatic shore. In his own report, L'Estrange Malone noted: 'One cannot help looking on this operation as being the forerunner of a line of development which will tend to revolutionise warfare'.[6]

Ben-my-Chree was sunk by Turkish shore batteries while anchored off Castelorizo Island on 9 January 1917; she was the only aviation vessel to be sunk during the First World War. Her Avgas was stored, like that of *Ark Royal*, in two-gallon tins which burned so furiously after she was hit that the ship's plating was

HMS *Ben-My-Chree* on fire and sinking off Castelorizo Island in 1917, after being hit by Turkish shore batteries. The explosion of petrol vapour in tins that were believed to be empty led to the steps subsequently taken by the Royal Navy to protect Avgas stowage in its carriers.

(AUTHOR'S COLLECTION)

HMS *Campania* after her second modification to operate aircraft in 1915-16. The original fore-funnel has been replaced by two mounted side-by-side, allowing the elongated take-off deck to be lengthened, running back between them at a slightly increased angle. Note the bridge structure fitted between the funnels, over the after part of the deck.
(AUTHOR'S COLLECTION)

By 1918 *Campania* was used mainly as a seaplane training ship. On 5 November 1918, while anchored in the Firth of Forth, she dragged her anchors in a gale and collided with both the battleship *Royal Oak* and the battle-cruiser *Glorious*. Fortunately her entire ship's company were taken off, but she is seen here sinking stern-first.
(AUTHOR'S COLLECTION)

buckled by the heat. The petrol vapour caused a number of the tins to explode, and the need to prevent similar damage influenced British views on Avgas storage for the next fifty years.

In September 1915 another ferry conversion joined the fleet. This was *Vindex*, which was smaller than *Ben-my-Chree* but larger than the *Engadine* group. A mild-steel hangar aft could house four Short 184s and a Sopwith Baby, and she had a take-off deck forward which was 64 feet long and 25 feet wide at the bows but only 9 feet wide over the well deck, from which two fully-assembled Sopwith Babies could be hoisted by derrick. It was appreciated that the deck was too small to launch the Babies, but they could be hoisted out for water take-offs and recoveries. This hardly made the best use of the deck, however, and in October the ship's officers obtained permission to evaluate Bristol Scout C biplane number 1255. The Scout was the only wheeled, single-seat fighter type in naval service at the time, and needed no wheeled trolley. The only modification required was a quick-release 'slip' to hold the aircraft back until the pilot was happy that the engine was delivering maximum power and the bridge staff were satisfied that the ship was steady into wind. Ely had used an improvised rope slip device five years earlier, but the *Vindex* trial used a wire hold-back capable of adjustment and frequent use, and which could be set in place quickly.

On 3 November 1915 *Vindex* steamed at 12 knots into a 15-knot wind, giving a relative wind of 27 knots from dead ahead, and Flight Lieutenant B.F. Fowler RNAS [7] flew the 80hp Scout off the deck in 46 feet. Fowler had started in the 'three-point attitude' with his tailskid on the deck, and it took 20 feet to accelerate to the flying attitude with the tailskid off the deck. The time from release to flight was 2.5 seconds, showing that the lighter Scout had a much greater rate of acceleration than the Baby launched from *Campania*. The wheels were covered with chalk, and left a track which showed clearly where the aircraft had flown off, 18 feet aft of the bow. In his report the captain noted that at 12 knots the flying deck was 'extending' forwards at a rate of 20 feet per second during the time taken to take off, giving an extra 'length' of 50 feet. Added to the physical deck

length, this meant that the pilot had an effective deck run of 96 feet available to him in the time it took his aircraft to travel from the point of release to becoming airborne. Subsequent trials showed that the minimum relative wind acceptable for a Scout launch using this technique was 22 knots. Directional control during the acceleration phase was marginal just as the aircraft passed the narrowest part of the deck, but experiments carried out ashore revealed a better technique which brought significant benefits. The tailskid was placed on to a small wooden trestle, lifting the rear of the aircraft up to the flying attitude while it was still attached to the hold-back. The take-off run was considerably reduced so that the minimum relative wind needed for a Scout launch came down to 19 knots, somewhat less than the maximum speed of the ship, making it possible to launch without natural wind if necessary. With this gear it was possible to launch two aircraft within 10 minutes of each other, most of time being taken to hoist the second aircraft out of the cramped hangar under the flight deck. Like all its contemporaries the Scout had no brakes, and the hold-back fulfilled the double function of keeping the aircraft stationary when the engine was running and allowing it to be slipped only when the pilot was happy that the engine was running smoothly, delivering full power.

The Scout take-off from *Vindex* demonstrated that launching a wheeled, high-performance aircraft from the deck of a ship was a practical proposition under operational conditions. It had been filmed, and was carefully analysed so that the technique could be fully understood and applied quickly to a wide range of ships. The one drawback, of course, was that there was no easy means of recovering the aircraft unless it was launched within range of land. If it was not, the pilot had to find a friendly warship, possibly miles away from the combat for which he had been launched, and ditch as close as he could alongside it. Assuming he survived his arrival in the water, the pilot had to swim long enough for a sea-boat to reach him, and survival equipment assumed importance. Most pilots wore inflatable life-preserving 'waistcoats' which could be purchased from Gieves' Naval Outfitters and others. Throughout the First World War British pilots did not

wear parachutes, as it was felt by authority that it might cause them to abandon their aircraft prematurely. They did not, therefore, have the option to bale out rather than ditch in rough weather. A technique was evolved in which the pilot flew low over a destroyer, to get the captain's attention, after which he ditched about 500 yards ahead of the ship. By the time the ship came up the sea boat would be swung out ready and could pick up the pilot after the minimum amount of time in the water. The waterlogged wreckage of the aircraft was seldom recovered.

On 12 April 1916 *Campania* rejoined the Grand Fleet with improved aircraft facilities, able to operate any shipborne aircraft in service. She had a larger flying deck, two large hangars within the original structure and extensive engine and airframe workshops. She also had a 'pit' aft, measuring 100 by 45 feet, from which a kite balloon could be operated. In addition to these major changes, there were a number of detail improvements. These included quick-release slip gear on the slings of the aircraft derricks which allowed seaplanes to be lowered on to the water while the ship was under way, making up to 10 knots. Under-way recoveries at up to 4 knots were also possible, but only for two-seater aircraft, as the pilot was fully occupied maintaining station accurately on the moving ship

while the observer attached the slip to the slings. The most important alteration was to the flying deck, which was lengthened by removing the navigating bridge and forward funnel. Two new athwartship funnels were installed 22 feet apart, with the deck passing between them, connected by bracing near the top and a navigating platform about 18 feet above the rear extension of the steeply sloping deck. The charthouse and wheelhouse were part of the supporting structure below the flying-off deck. The deck was 30 feet wide over the wheelhouse and flared to a maximum width over the forecastle. Although it followed the plan of the ship, coming to a point at the bow, a platform was added each side of the stem to extend the useful width right forward to 22 feet. The success of the new arrangements, created after little over a year of shipborne aircraft operations, was immediately apparent. *Campania* carried out a new series of flying trials with encouraging results, beginning with lowering and recovering 184s while under way and progressing through successful flying from the deck. On 29 May 1916, the day before the Grand Fleet sailed for the Battle of Jutland, she launched five Sopwith Babies from the deck before noon, demonstrating that an evolution which had been a major event before then had now become a matter of routine.

HMS *Pegasus* was the last and most sophisticated seaplane carrier to be completed during the First World War. She carried five Beardmore WB.III fighters in the forward hangar and four seaplanes aft.
(AUTHOR'S COLLECTION)

Take-off platforms, catapults and lighters

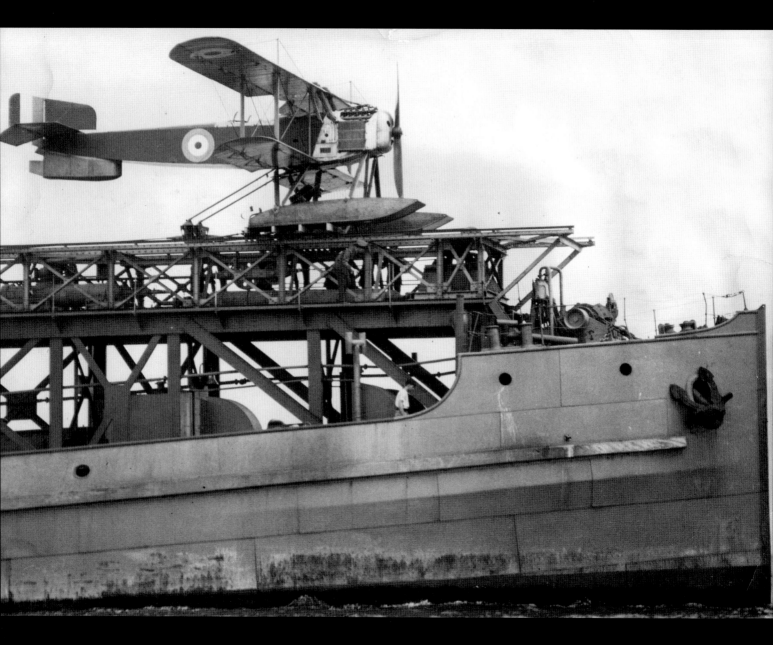

An un-numbered Fairey Campania
on HMS *Slinger*'s catapult.

It was recognised by 1917 that open-water seaplane operations were unsuccessful. Estimates vary, but one post-war study claimed that only 35 out of 66 seaplanes launched operationally in the North Sea succeeded in getting airborne [1]. These figures did not include the many occasions when launches were not even attempted because of unsuitable sea or wind conditions. Sopwith Baby seaplane fighters were faster than airships in level flight but could not climb as rapidly. Thus stopping the carrier to hoist out the interceptor robbed it of any chance of surprise, even if the aircraft managed to get airborne at all. In its attempts to get at airships that were scouting or transiting the North Sea to attack the UK, the Royal Navy embarked Sopwith seaplanes in a variety of vessels including the cruisers *Aurora* and *Arethusa*, the armed trawlers *Kingfisher* and *Cantatrice*, the requisitioned Humber ferries *Killingholme* and *Brocklesby* and even the submarine *E 22* experimentally. On 2 June 1915 *Arethusa* launched her Schneider against a scouting Zeppelin, and the pilot was overhauling his target when he broke off the action after misunderstanding a visual signal from the cruiser. This was the only sortie of its kind that stood a chance of an interception in over two years of seaplane embarkations in a defensive role.

In January 1917 Admiral Beatty, who had succeeded Jellicoe as Commander-in-Chief of the Grand Fleet on 29 November 1916, set up a Grand Fleet Aircraft Committee to report on and rationalise the Fleet's aviation requirements. At the same time, Commodore G.M. Paine RN was appointed Director of Air Services and, more significantly, Fifth Sea Lord, the first holder of an appointment which brought the navy's aviation representative on to the Board of Admiralty. The Committee rendered its report on 5 February 1917, the speed with which it did so giving further indication of the importance attached to the subject.[2] It recommended the deployment of wheeled fighter aircraft, specifically Sopwith Pups, aboard the largest possible number of capital ships together with *Campania* and *Manxman*, another seaplane-carrying conversion which was purchased by the Admiralty in March 1916 and commissioned for service with the Battle Cruiser Fleet in December 1916. The light

battle cruiser *Furious* was to be completed with a flying-off deck forward to act as a second large carrier.

In June 1917 the light cruiser *Yarmouth* was fitted with a flying-off deck 30 feet long mounted on the armoured conning tower forward of the bridge and cantilevered out over the forecastle six-inch-gun mounting. It did not affect the gun's arc of fire or

elevation and, thus, did not impair the cruiser's efficiency in a surface action. The deck was fixed and only offered a run of sixteen feet in front of the aircraft's wheels, but Squadron Commander Rutland RNAS, who had flown *Engadine*'s Short 184 at Jutland, took off with ease into a 25-knot relative wind on the first attempt. Following this successful demonstration, Beatty obtained Admiralty approval to fit an improved platform, including a frame and canvas hangar, to five light cruisers and the battle cruisers *Courageous* and *Glorious*. The *Yarmouth* platform had been the idea of Rear Admiral R.F. Phillimore, commanding the 1st Battle-Cruiser Squadron, and Wing Captain R.M. Groves RNAS, with support from Rosyth Naval Air Station. It represented the quickest way of getting high-performance fighters to sea without interfering over-much with the gunnery efficiency of the ships

Sopwith Pup N6453, the same aircraft that Squadron Commander Dunning had used for his first deck landing, on Y turret of HMS *Repulse* on 9 October 1917.

(AUTHOR'S COLLECTION)

involved, although the aircraft could not operate at night, in bad weather or low visibility, and it was still a 'one-shot' system. The major drawback with the fixed deck was that ships fitted with it had to turn out of line to launch their aircraft into wind. Since columns controlled by a senior officer using signal flags were still the most widely employed tactical formation, ships turning out of line could present a problem. If several did so at the same time, tactical cohesion could be lost.

On 21 August 1917 a Sopwith Pup flown from HMS *Yarmouth* by Flight Sub Lieutenant B.A. Smart RNAS achieved operational success, due in no small part to Smart's meticulous preparation and the skill with which he flew the sortie. The ship formed part of the 1st Light Cruiser Squadron and was at sea to support a minelaying operation off the German coast. The task force was due to pass through an area known to be patrolled by Zeppelins, and Smart and his two

mechanics got up before dawn to remove the canvas covers from Sopwith Pup N6430, test-run the engine and fire a few rounds from the Lewis gun to ensure that everything was ready.[3] Realising he would need the advantage of surprise to carry out an effective attack, Smart had his aircraft's red, white and blue national markings painted out with 'pusser's grey' paint and took the precaution of wearing two lifebelts and carrying a flask of brandy in his pocket to improve his chances after the inevitable ditching. He asked the ship's commanding officer, Captain H.E. Grace RN, for maximum speed when he launched, since he had such a short deck run in front of his wheels. The ship's executive officer lay under the aircraft, from where he could see the both the pilot's signals and the bridge in order that there should be no mistake working the quick release mechanism. Smart ran up his engine and raised an arm to signify to the captain that he was ready. The captain signalled

This photograph, although slightly damaged, gives a very good idea of just how small HMS *Yarmouth's* flight deck was. The cantilevered extension over the forward six-inch gun mounting is clearly visible with the Sopwith Pup lashed on top of it.

(AUTHOR'S COLLECTION).

the executive officer, who pulled the release cord and the aircraft flew off well before the end of the deck.

Smart took 15 minutes to climb to 10,000 feet, using cloud to avoid detection from L23, the German Zeppelin. Astutely he took compass bearings when he saw it so that he could continue to track it through cloud. Once he was close enough he carried out two diving, high-speed attacks with incendiary ammunition and saw L23 ignite and crash into the sea with no survivors. After the combat he flew a reciprocal compass heading to search for the British force, aware that the Danish coast was about 8 miles away to port. He sighted two destroyers and elected to ditch near them. Preparation for ditching involved undoing his straps and putting a plug in the tube that acted as an air valve for the rubber buoyancy bag in the after part of the fuselage.[4] He then switched off the engine and glided at just above stalling speed toward the sea surface, heading into wind. If a heavy sea had been running, a better alternative would have been to land across the swell, but this was not necessary. When he

estimated the aircraft to be about 15 feet above the water, Smart pulled hard back on the stick and stalled into the water with wings level. The heavy engine dragged the nose under, but Smart swam clear and held on to the tail, which was kept above the water by the buoyancy bag. He was rescued by a sea-boat from the destroyer HMS *Prince*. The airframe was not recovered, but the engine and Lewis gun were cut free and salvaged. Smart was awarded the DSO and promoted flight lieutenant for his achievement.

The obvious need to get aircraft to sea led to dynamic ideas, among them that of Lieutenant Commander C.H.B. Gowan RN, *Yarmouth*'s gunnery officer, in September 1917, for a platform 45 feet long capable of being fitted on to the main armament turrets of capital ships. This had the advantage that the turret could be trained into the relative wind, obviating the need for the ship to turn to launch its aircraft and making it possible for the ship to remain 'in line'. The first was fitted on to B turret of the battle-cruiser *Repulse*, and a successful trial launch was

Rigging a turret platform extension. Brackets and longerons have been fitted to the barrels of the super-firing turret, and the planks that will be laid on them to form the extension are piled ready for use on the platform on the turret roof.

(AUTHOR'S COLLECTION)

made from it on 1 October 1917 by Squadron Commander Rutland. In his Report of Proceedings on this important event, Captain J.S. Dumaresq CB MVO RN, an Australian serving in the Royal Navy, explained that the ship was 4 miles off Inchkeith at 10:00 on an initial course of 145 degrees at 24 knots. The true surface wind was observed to be 230 degrees at 17 knots. Two course adjustments totalling 45 degrees towards the true wind were made to strengthen the wind over the deck 'felt' on the turret platform. The turret was trained in local control using the left sighting hood, from where the trainer could see a wind vane fixed to the left gun muzzle in line with his eye. Final, small adjustments were made under the pilot's instructions, using a flag held in front of him as a sensor.[5] With the turret pointed into a relative wind of just over 30 knots, Rutland took off without difficulty in Sopwith Pup N6453, the same aircraft that Dunning had used two months earlier for his first landing on *Furious*. A tail guide trestle and hold-back device were essential to the successful launch. The former was basically similar to the device first used in *Vindex* and had the double effects of holding the aircraft's tail up into the flying attitude from the start of the take-off run and providing directional stability until sufficient airspeed was achieved for the aircraft's rudder to become effective. The tailskid was modified to incorporate a ball fitting attached near the lower end by a bracket and which ran along a groove in the top of the trestle. The hold-

Sopwith 1½ 'Ship' Strutter N5644 is lifted on to HMAS *Australia*'s Q turret from a lighter in the Firth of Forth in March 1918. Aircraft were brought out to ships of the Grand Fleet in this way from an 'air park' at Donibristle, near Rosyth.

(SEA POWER CENTRE – AUSTRALIA)

back was the standard device used on cruiser platforms and seaplane carrier decks. It comprised a slip hook attached to a cross-wire stretched between the rear undercarriage struts. From this hook, a wire ran down and aft at an angle of 45 degrees to an anchor point on an eye-bolt on the deck of the turret platform. A lanyard with wooden toggles to allow a firm grip was attached to the slip hook. When the pilot signalled that he was ready and the bridge gave the order to launch, a firm pull on the lanyard released the hook and the aircraft flew off. Then, as now, the decision to launch rested with the captain, who took full responsibility for everything that happened in his ship. It is indicative of the importance placed on aviation in general and the safety of

the pilot in particular that it was invariably the second-in-command, or executive officer, who worked the quick-release device.

The same platform was then dismantled and reassembled on Y turret aft, from which Rutland took off successfully in the same aircraft on 9 October 1917. The platform was rigged so that the aircraft took off over the rear of the turret, as it was thought that this would reduce the amount of training necessary because the 'felt wind' was often forward of the beam. Experience was to show this technique to be unnecessary, and only five battle cruisers, *Repulse*, *Renown*, *Lion*, *Tiger* and *Princess Royal*, were so modified. In all other ships the platform was mounted to face toward the barrels. This second trial launch

Flight Commander Donald takes off from Q turret of HMAS *Australia* on 7 March 1918. The ship in the background is HMS *New Zealand*.

A Sopwith Pup takes off from a turret platform. Engine torque has caused the aircraft to veer significantly to the left as it nears the end of the deck, and right rudder has been applied to correct it.

(AUTHOR'S COLLECTION)

was also successful. Having shown that light, high-performance fighters could fly off a turret platform, the next advance was the addition of an extension over the gun barrels to allow heavier two-seat reconnaissance aircraft to fly off capital ships in order to spot their fall of shot at long ranges. The aircraft selected was the Sopwith 1½ 'Ship' Strutter with two seats and a W/T installation powered by a wind-driven generator. The first extension was fabricated from steel wire rope and was fitted to B turret on HMS *Repulse* in March 1918. On 4 March 1918 Flight Commander D.G. Donald RNAS attempted to take off in Ship Strutter 9744, but found the wire extension to act like a 'sprung mattress' [6] which hit and shattered the propeller during the short take-off run. The aircraft ditched and Donald was lucky to escape with minor bruises. He was rescued by a sea-boat from the destroyer *Rival*.

Subsequently a more practical extension was fitted to Q turret of HMAS *Australia*, using two-inch planks attached to angle-irons strapped to the barrels. The planks at the junction between the original turret platform and the extension were made quickly

removable to permit elevation of the guns. Given reasonable warning of action, the remainder of the extension could be dismantled, removing the risk that it would disintegrate when the guns were fired. The basic platform on the turret roof was fabricated from metal sheeting and could be left in place with reasonable prospects of survival. Donald launched successfully from this ramp on 7 March 1918 into a wind over the deck of 20 knots. The turret platform proved an effective and reliable method for launching the aircraft that the Grand Fleet needed in 1918, but it was still a 'one-shot' system. In the short term this was acceptable, since reserves of aircraft were available ashore to replace those that ditched, but by late in the year there were not enough and French-built single-seat Strutters were procured and modified to Ship Strutter standard to meet the fleet's growing demands. In major operations reconnaissance aircraft would be flown off in small numbers to find the enemy, together with fighters to escort them. When action was imminent, all serviceable aircraft would have been flown off their platforms, which would have then been dismantled to 'free' the guns. It was accepted that all these aircraft would have to ditch when they ran out of fuel, relying on destroyers to locate and rescue the aircrew as and when they could. Aircraft that were unable to take-off would have been pushed over the side because of the fire danger from the Avgas in their tanks. Unused Avgas in two-gallon tins would also have gone over the side before action was joined.

Light cruisers, the 'eyes' of the fleet, did not have power-operated turrets like the bigger ships and could not be fitted with turret platforms, but Gowan designed a turntable modification for the type of deck fitted on *Yarmouth* which enabled the deck forward of the small hangar to be turned into the relative wind, provided that it was forward of the beam, without interfering with the forecastle gun. The first flight from this improved deck took place on 8 December 1917, when a Sopwith Pup launched from HMAS *Sydney*. These platforms were relatively simple to install and practical to use. Further trial launches from *Sydney* were carried out in Scapa Flow on 17 December by Flight Sub-Lieutenant A.C. Sharwood RNAS, flying a Sopwith Pup. In 1918 Captain Dumaresq took command to gain experience of an Australian warship before becoming Commodore of the Australian Squadron. He insisted on his cruiser being equipped with one of the new Sopwith 2F.1 Ship Camels, and *Sydney* was at sea with N6783 embarked as part of a large British force operating against German minesweepers in the Heligoland Bight on 1 June 1918 when two enemy seaplanes attacked. Dumaresq was one of the Grand Fleet's most air-minded officers, and had his fighter at a high state of alert, using a bugle call to bring it into action.[7] Another Camel was launched from HMAS *Melbourne*, but lost sight of the enemy and returned, but Sharwood from *Sydney* kept the enemy aircraft in sight and chased them for over 60 miles.[8] He certainly damaged and probably destroyed an enemy aircraft in a confused dogfight in and out of cloud at the end of this chase. Like Smart he considered landing in Denmark and had five sovereigns sewn into his uniform jacket against the possibility, but he saw ships of the Harwich Force below him and ditched near the destroyer *Sharpshooter*. It was not the first time he

had ditched in a Camel, and his exit from the cockpit was helped by an enlarged 'cut-out' in the upper wing he had instructed his rigger to make. The aircraft was salvaged by the cruiser *Canterbury* but was not used again.

By November 1918 twenty-two cruisers had fixed or revolving platforms capable of operating fighters, and twenty-six battleships and battle cruisers had two turret ramps fitted and aircraft embarked. A further ten capital ships had platforms but had not yet embarked aircraft, and eight more were authorised to have platforms fitted, yet more evidence of the Royal Navy's desire to get aircraft to sea in large numbers. The big ships usually carried two aircraft, one 2F.1 Camel and one Ship Strutter, the heavier aircraft usually operating from a longer platform on B turret. New aircraft were taken to their respective ships by lighter and hoisted on board by crane, derrick or the gun barrels of adjacent turrets. While

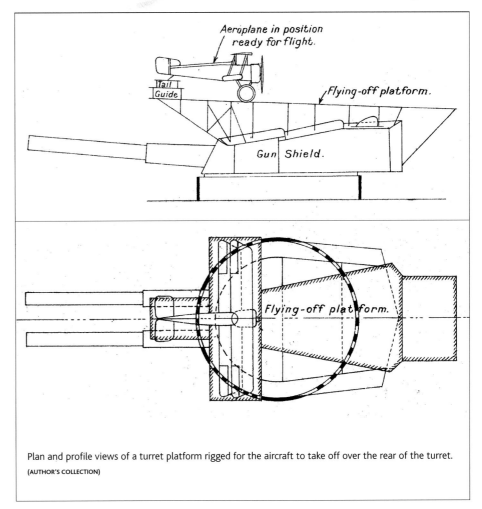

Plan and profile views of a turret platform rigged for the aircraft to take off over the rear of the turret. (AUTHOR'S COLLECTION)

A Sopwith 2F.1 Camel on the rotatable flying-off platform of HMAS *Sydney*. Mild steel side-panels are fitted on the sides to give the aircraft some protection at sea.

A view of the tiny flying-off deck and the bridge above it from HMAS *Sydney*'s spotting top. The white-painted squares on the forward corners were to show the pilot when he had run out of deck.

on board aircraft were protected by oiled canvas screens and lattice wind breaks which were unrigged before launch. Some cruisers extemporised mild-steel walls for the side-screens of their small hangars.

Both the Royal and United States' Navies investigated the possibility of assisted take-off using catapults. Captain Murray Sueter RN, the Inspecting Captain of Airships who had led the Airship Project at Barrow-in-Furness between 1909 and 1911, encouraged his officers to advance the theory of aviation. Together with Lieutenants Boothby and Paterson he took out Patent Number 3333 in February 1911 for a shipborne catapult which employed a dropped counterweight and a system of wires to accelerate the aircraft. It was not, however, taken forward. Significant early work on catapults was carried out by the US Navy, and as early as 1911 Glenn Curtiss, Captain Chambers and Lieutenant Ellyson experimented with a counterweight accelerator, but abandoned the concept in 1912 when they decided that a compressed-air catapult was a better option. On 31 July 1912 the first attempted take-off by a manned aircraft using a compressed-air catapult was a dramatic failure. It comprised a short-stroke piston driven by air from

a high-pressure accumulator which pulled a cable through a series of blocks and pulleys, known as the 'reeving'. This had an 'advantage' of 10:1, meaning that a piston stroke of 6 feet resulted in a movement of 60 feet at the end of the cable where it was attached to the trolley on which the aircraft was placed. The 'end speed' (the speed of the trolley relative to the structure of the catapult at the end of the track) was regulated by a valve controlling the pressure applied to the main piston as required by the weight of the aircraft and the speed needed for it to achieve flight. Because of the nature of the actuation, acceleration was immediate, not progressive, and only the 'slack' or 'stretch' in the cable protected the aircraft from the full shock of the initial kick.

The prototype catapult was designed by Chambers and built at the Washington Navy Yard under the supervision of Naval Constructor Holden C. Richardson. It was assembled at the Santee Dock of the US Naval Academy at Annapolis, Maryland, where a Curtiss Triad was used for the first live launch, flown by Lieutenant Ellyson USN. A small trolley was fitted to the parallel rails of the catapult track and the aircraft was hoisted on to a flat platform on top of it, the rear end of which was built up to provide rearwards restraint for the flat-bottomed central pontoon float. No restraint was provided against side loads or aerodynamic lift during the launch. On this first attempt the rapid increase of airflow over the wings produced lift so suddenly that Ellyson was unable to prevent the nose from pitching up and the aircraft left the catapult in a pronounced nose-up, fully stalled attitude. In the ensuing crash the Triad was damaged, but the fortunate pilot escaped with no serious injury.

Following this failure, the catapult was returned to Washington Navy Yard and modified with a valve to reduce the starting jolt and ensure that the maximum thrust was not developed until approximately one-third of the piston stroke. Other refinements included a 'buffer' to prevent the trolley from leaving the end of the rails and, most importantly, fittings to hold the aircraft on to the trolley until the end of the run.[9] The rebuilt Triad, again flown by Ellyson, was successfully launched from the modified catapult installed on a former coal barge anchored in the Anacostia River near the Washington Navy Yard on 12 November 1912. The end speed achieved by this 40-foot catapult was approximately 30 knots and, in all essentials, it was the first effective aircraft catapult

and embodied all the principles that were to govern development for four decades to come.

The Royal Navy continued to be interested in catapult development and, also in 1912, Commander Samson with J.H. Narbeth attempted to devise a catapult that would not produce the shock effect inherent in hydraulic or pneumatic designs. Their solution was a threaded shaft turned by an electric motor [10] to propel a 'nut' to which an aircraft's axle could be attached by a quick-release clip. A growing rate of acceleration was to be provided by increasing the pitch of the screw thread, and when the aircraft reached flying speed the pilot would release the attachment and the freed 'nut' would be decelerated by reversing the pitch of the screw thread. In this way the actual shaft speed would remain constant for a given end speed. This ingenious idea was patented in 1912 but, like the earlier counterweight proposal, not progressed further. By 1914 the RNAS was considering the development of a pneumatic cata-pult, but the outbreak of war absorbed all the technical personnel who could have worked on such a system and the idea lapsed.

Lack of funding slowed catapult development in the USA, but Richardson continued to work on designing a practical system. After a long series of

Turret platforms continued in use after 1918, until aircraft weights increased to the point where they were no longer practical. Here a Fairey Flycatcher is trained into wind on HMS *Hood*'s B turret, although its engine covers are on and it is not manned.

(AUTHOR'S COLLECTION)

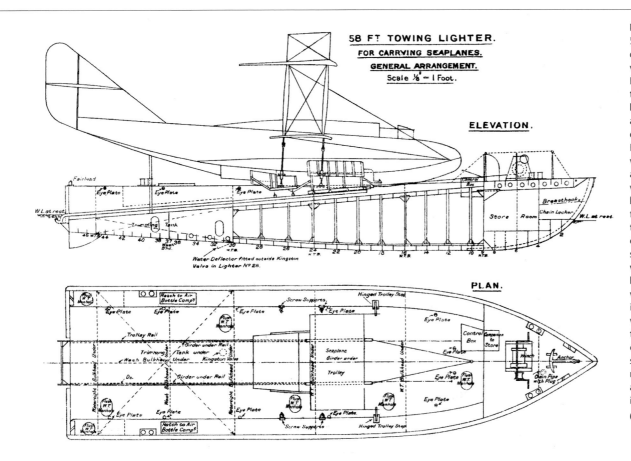

58 FT TOWING LIGHTER.
FOR CARRYING SEAPLANES.
GENERAL ARRANGEMENT.
Scale ⅛" = 1 Foot.

ELEVATION.

PLAN.

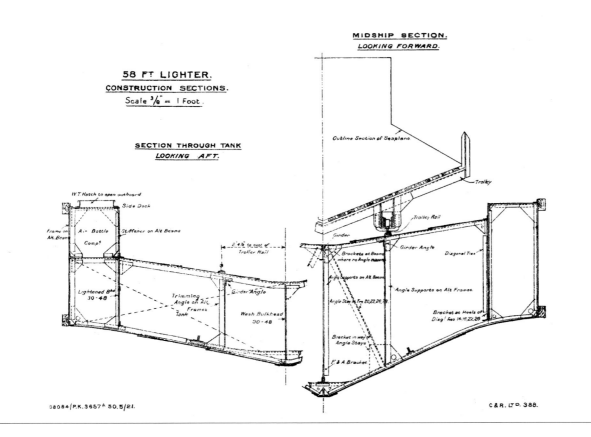

58 FT LIGHTER.
CONSTRUCTION SECTIONS.
Scale ⅜" = 1 Foot.

MIDSHIP SECTION.
LOOKING FORWARD.

SECTION THROUGH TANK
LOOKING AFT.

Plan and profile views of the 58-foot lighter as originally designed. It was a complex vessel, not unlike a modern LPD in operation. Trimming tanks aft were flooded to lower the stern and the aircraft trolley run to the rear on its two rails. The Felixstowe F2B flying boat was taxied on to the trolley and secured in place with wire cables connected between the lower wing and the trolley. The water in the tanks was then blown out by compressed air, raising the stern, and the aircraft was winched forward to the lighter's centre of gravity, where the trolley was locked in position. The flying boat was launched by reversing the process. The lighter had a crew of four who used the store-room forward as rudimentary accommodation at sea; the aircrew remained in their flying boat.

(AUTHOR'S COLLECTION)

disappointing material failures, a prototype catapult was erected on another former coal barge, number 214, at Pensacola in Florida, the site of the US Navy's first air station. On 16 April 1915 Lieutenant P.N.L. Bellinger USN, Naval Pilot Number 8, was successfully launched in a Curtiss AB-2 flying boat. Subsequent trials continued to be successful, and at the end of October 1915 the catapult was dismantled and re-erected on the quarterdeck of the armoured cruiser *North Carolina*, making her the first ship in the world to be fitted with an aircraft catapult. On 5 November 1915 a Curtiss AB-3 flown by Lieutenant Commander H.C. Mustin USN, Naval Pilot Number 11, was launched over the stern while the ship made bare steerage way in Pensacola Bay. The value of the catapult was readily apparent. It was shorter than the tracking that would have been needed to allow the same aircraft to carry out a free take-off and, with a height of only four feet, it could be fixed to the quarterdeck without interfering with the guns' arcs of fire. An improved, more powerful version installed in *North Carolina* in June 1916, however, forfeited this advantage. To gain a longer track it had to be mounted clear of the crown of the quarterdeck turret, and was raised to a height of about twelve feet, and the supporting framework interfered both with the elevation and training of the turret. The catapult track itself was of minimal depth, though, and installation in the deck of a new ship built to operate aircraft would leave only the trolley itself above the deck, running in a slot.

British interest in catapults revived in 1916, and the Admiralty invited bids for hydraulic, electric and compressed-air types from industry. The specifications called for the ability to launch a 5,000lb aircraft at 55 knots in a distance of 60 feet with an acceleration of no more than 2.5g. The hydraulic and electric types were not taken up, but in late 1917 two compressed-air prototypes were offered for test. The first was designed by R.F. Carey and manufactured by Waygood-Otis, a firm that specialised in the manufacture of lifts in peacetime. It was installed at an airfield at Hendon on the north-west outskirts of London. The second was designed and built by the engineering firm of Armstrong Whitworth and was fitted to a converted

steam hopper commissioned for the purpose and appropriately named HMS *Slinger*. The first launch at Hendon took place in October 1917, when Flight Commander R.E. Penny RNAS successfully flew an Avro 504H which had been specially strengthened to withstand the shock of catapult launch, believed to be the first aircraft in the world to be so modified. The first launch from *Slinger* had already taken place while the ship was alongside a jetty on the River Tyne. Her catapult was a steel box girder 60 feet long and slightly inclined towards the bow; the aircraft were mounted on a trolley running on rails propelled by a compressed-air system operating a series of wires. At first unmanned aircraft and dead weights were launched, but trials continued into 1918 under the supervision of Wing Commander Harry Busteed RNAS at the Isle of Grain Experimental Aircraft Depot. These experiments did not lead to any immediate operational use, as both catapults were felt to be too cumbersome and bulky for shipboard installation and, in the short term, they offered no advantage over the platforms being fitted to some of the larger warships. After the war, when aircraft weights increased significantly, Royal Navy interest in catapults revived and further development was undertaken. This will be described in a later chapter.

In any fixed catapult the relative wind, the resultant of the vectors of ship speed and surface wind direction and speed, would have to be in line with the catapult at the moment of launch, but if a turntable arrangement could be designed the ship would have greater freedom of manoeuvre and the catapult would not be limited to the clear areas forward and aft. It would be some years yet before such a catapult was perfected. The development of turret platforms by the Royal Navy had offered a means of flying-off both fighters and reconnaissance aircraft that was both cheaper and tactically more viable than the fixed installation catapult. By 1918 the rotating platforms being fitted in large numbers of cruisers offered a simple means of launching a defensive fighter without interfering with the ship's gun armament. In consequence, when the United States entered the First World War in 1917, the USN decided to remove the catapults from the three armoured cruisers, *North Carolina, Seattle* and *Huntington* that were by then so fitted. In 1918 the Battle Squadron which joined the Grand Fleet was fitted with British-designed turret platforms rather than catapults.

One other method of launching aircraft at sea deserves mention. Lighters, to be towed by destroyers, had been built to carry flying boats across the North Sea in order to extend their radius of action, following a suggestion by Wing Commander J.C. Porte RNAS in 1916. They were complicated vessels designed to be towed at speeds in excess of 30 knots and with pumping and flooding arrangements capable of lowering them in the water to make it easier to float Felixstowe flying boats on to them. A small cabin in the bow gave room for an operating team of four to winch in the boat and float it clear when necessary. Wing Commander Samson was asked for ideas in 1918 on how best to operate fighters from destroyer flotillas, the ships themselves being too small to fit flying-off decks. He conceived the idea of fitting wooden decks on to several of these lighters, each to be complete with tail trestle and hold-back, and towed at high speed into wind. The concept was practical but was made over-complicated by the decision to fit wooden skids, rather than wheels, to N6623, the 2F.1 Camel selected to evaluate the idea. These were to run within troughs to maintain directional stability. Samson carried out the first take-off from a deck fitted to lighter H3 towed by HMS *Truculent* off Orfordness on 30 May 1918. The deck was built level with the lighter's upper deck at rest, but unfortunately at high speed the lighter assumed a pronounced bow-high, stern-low attitude that gave the Camel an uphill run. It failed to gain flying speed and ditched over the bow of the lighter, which then ran over aircraft and pilot. Samson was rescued but the aircraft was lost. Lighter H3 was then rebuilt with a deck that was higher at the stern while at rest but level or slightly nose-down at speed. After a series of fast runs with ballast weights, another launch was attempted on 31 July 1918 by Flight Sub-Lieutenant S.D. Culley RNAS.[11] For this trial 2F.1 Camel N6812 was used, which had a wheeled rather than a skid-type undercarriage, and the troughs were removed from the deck. It was entirely successful and Culley got safely airborne, several lighters afterwards being converted for this role and used operationally.

Appropriately, it was Culley who scored the only 'kill', with 2F.1 Camel N6812, launched from a lighter on 11 August 1918. At 08:58 he took off with a run of only 5 feet, under tow from the destroyer *Redoubt* at 30 knots, and took an hour to climb to 18,000 feet in order to intercept and destroy the Zeppelin L53. He then descended to 6,000 feet [12] and located *Redoubt* at the briefed rendezvous off the Terschelling Bank, carrying out the inevitable ditching just ahead of the ship. The aircraft was not only salvaged but retained, and now forms part of the collection of the Imperial War Museum at Lambeth in London. Despite this limited success, fighter-carrying lighters were another short-term, one-shot system with no future.

HMS *Furious*

The world's first deck landing by a Service pilot in an operational aircraft on to a warship under way: Squadron Commander Dunning's landing on HMS *Furious* in Sopwith Pup N6543 on 2 August 1917. A triangle of white paint on the starboard extremity of the starboard lower aileron marks the individual aircraft, which has not yet had 'grab handles' sewn on to the wings and fuselage for the handling party to hold on to.

(AUTHOR'S COLLECTION)

The Grand Fleet Aircraft Committee's recommendation that *Furious* be completed as a second large, fast seaplane carrier was forwarded to the Admiralty, with Admiral Beatty's support, on 7 February 1917. By 18 March it was endorsed and a sketch design for the modification, with a flying deck built over the forecastle, had been laid before Board Members and approved. Originally designed as a 19,100 ton battle-cruiser[1] capable of 31½ knots, she was to have had two single turrets with 18-inch guns, one forward and one aft, but only the after one was installed. The forecastle barbette was plated over and a hangar 120 feet long, 57 feet wide and 18 feet high was built over it. A flight deck 228 feet long was constructed over the forecastle, the after part forming the hangar roof. Aft of the deck was a hatch through which aircraft were hoisted from the hangar by topping lifts attached to two derricks, one to port and one to starboard. Aircraft on deck near the hatch could, if necessary, be protected from wind blast by wooden palisades, attached vertically to the outboard hangar sides in metal brackets. In use they were slid vertically upwards and locked in position; when not in use, they were slid down, the tops being flush with the deck edge.

The take-off 'runway' was 160 feet long by 57 feet wide, narrowing to 36 feet forward of the hangar roof, with a slotted trackway along the centreline. This contained the 'anchor slot' for the four-wheeled trolley that allowed float-fitted Short 184s to take off from the flight deck. The 'anchor' ran inside the slot during take-off and was stopped by a wooden buffer at the end of the run, retaining the trolley for further use, an advance on the 'total loss' system used in *Campania*, but in some respects the arrangements in *Furious* were not as good as those in the earlier conversion. Squadron Commander Richard Bell Davies RN was the senior flying officer in *Campania*, and learnt in conversation with the senior air officer in *Furious*,[2] that the derricks were too short and the booms placed too low on them. Instead of reliable steam winches for working the derricks, she had electric bollards which were violent in action and liable to trip the overload switch at the slightest provocation. The ship itself was a big improvement, however. She provided a steadier deck and higher speed, which allowed flying-off by all embarked aircraft types, even in calm conditions. The biggest weakness was the relatively light flight deck structure, which prevented the ship from being driven hard into even moderate seas, negating some of the advantage of her high designed speed.

Furious joined the Grand Fleet at Scapa Flow on 6 July 1917, commanded by Captain Wilmot S. Nicholson RN, a non-aviator who wanted to see his ship perform well in its new role. The air group comprised three Short 184s and five brand new Sopwith Pups which had been delivered to the shipyard in June. She was a 'stop-gap' that could be introduced to service quickly with a viable number of aircraft, but her senior RNAS officer was impressed by the ship's speed and flying-off deck. Squadron Commander E.H. Dunning DSC RNAS was to earn a place in history as the first man to land an operational aircraft, Sopwith Pup N6453, on an operational warship.[3]

The Pup's landing speed was about 45 knots; the stalling speed was slightly less, the exact figure depending on the aircraft's weight at the time. Given sufficient ship's speed into an adequate wind, the speed of approach relative to the deck would be very slow. Taken to an extreme, 25 knots of ship speed into a 20-knot wind would allow a skilled pilot to hold the aircraft in a stationary hover over the deck. A wind over the deck that close to the aircraft's stalling speed would be dangerous after the aircraft landed, however, since any increase in wind speed due to a gust or reduction in aircraft weight, such as the pilot stepping out of the cockpit, would result in an uncontrolled take-off. An approach speed up to 10 knots greater than wind speed was ideal to cater for gusts and safety after coming to rest.

Dunning's landing was all the more remarkable when one looks closely at the aircraft and its engine control. The Pup was light, manoeuvrable and described by many pilots as a delight to fly. Its wing loading was a mere 5lb per square foot,[4] so it would have been tossed about in any air turbulence, but there can have been few other aircraft that would have given pilots the confidence to fly within a few feet of a moving ship's structure, especially ahead of it. The 80hp Le Rhone 9C rotary engine did not have a throttle control that would be familiar to a modern pilot[5] and its manipulation needed to be as much a part of the pilot's handling skill as the primary flying controls, since it operated over a very narrow range of revolutions and the nearest equivalent to the control we know as a throttle was a lever that adjusted the fuel/air mixture and set the engine running as smoothly as possible. With differing conditions of height, speed and turning forces it needed constant adjustment. 'Instant' control of engine power was achieved by means of an ignition thumb switch on top of the control column with which the pilot turned the engine on and off,[6] producing the characteristic 'blipping' sound associated with aircraft of the period.

Dunning made several dummy approaches to *Furious*' deck while the ship lay head-to-wind at anchor in Scapa Flow. He flew low left-hand circuits close to the ship, controlling his height with the elevators and his speed by 'blipping' the ignition on and off. Some turbulence would have been encountered as he passed the superstructure and a 'cliff-edge' effect[7] as he ruddered across the deck in a flat or 'S' turn. He may also have used a 'side-slipping' technique in which the nose was canted off the centreline with rudder while bank was applied with opposite aileron, giving a good view of the deck. Whichever technique he used, the controls would have been centred for the actual landing, with the pilot aiming for a 'three-point' attitude in which the wheels and tailskid would touch the deck together after the aircraft was lined up with the centreline. On at least one approach he had actually put his wheels on to the deck, and he obtained permission for an attempted 'full-stop' landing to be carried out on 2 August 1917. On that day the ship got under way in Scapa Flow, steaming at 26 knots into a 21-knot natural wind, giving a steady wind over the deck of 47 knots coming from directly ahead.[8] This was slightly greater than the ideal, and meant that Dunning needed to 'overtake' the landing area and touch down at above stalling speed. It also meant that the aircraft would be unstable on deck, having to be firmly held down as the pilot stepped out until the ship slowed down. Over the deck itself Dunning was

in relatively smooth air, holding the aircraft's attitude with the elevators and 'blipping' his engine off frequently to descend gently on to the deck. He would not have wanted to drop with a high sink rate, as a bounce near flying speed would render the aircraft uncontrollable until it fell back to the deck or could be flown away. 'Eye-level', about ten feet[9] higher than the deck, was the ideal height to move over. Any higher and the deck would have been partly obscured, making it difficult to see the space on to which he was descending; any lower and he risked touching the deck edge with his wheels or tailskid. This is consistent with the images of the handling party reaching up to grab the Pup as it steadied over the deck. Dunning touched down at 11:10 on the hangar roof area, the widest part of the deck just forward of the hatch, bounced gently once and was held firm by officers posted to keep the aircraft on deck. The proceedings were watched by a number of Grand Fleet flag officers on the bridge. Five and half years after Ely, an operational aircraft flown by a naval pilot had landed on an operational warship. The way forward using high-performance aircraft that could both take-off from and land on an aircraft carrier with a large flight deck was clear. The ship's pilots were delighted, because taking off from the deck was already an 'everyday' event and their Squadron Commander had shown that landing appeared to be a practical proposition too.

Unfortunately Dunning's later demonstrations, carried out on 7 August, were not as successful. He intended to carry out one further landing himself and then let other pilots, starting with Flight Commander W.G. Moore RNAS, his second-in-command, make a series of landings to show that they were not 'stunts' but something that could be re-peated regularly by a variety of pilots. Dunning used the same Pup, N6453, that he had flown five days before, but this time it was at operational weight with a Lewis gun mounted forward of the cockpit. Strops were sewn on to the trailing edge of the lower wing and the underside of the fuselage to help enable the handling party of officers to grab and restrain the aircraft. They were somewhat over-enthusiastic on Dunning's first approach of the day, however, and

Sopwith Pups ranged on HMS *Furious'* flying-off deck with some of the wind-breaks raised. The narrowness of the deck forward of the hangar is evident.
(AUTHOR'S COLLECTION)

actually pulled the aircraft down on to the deck, but were unable to prevent a gust blowing it backwards into the hatch-coaming, which damaged the elevators. On stepping out of the aircraft Dunning briefed the handling party that they were to wait until the aircraft's wheels were on the deck before grabbing it. The aircraft needed to be repaired before it could fly again, and he went over to Pup N6452, which Moore intended to use, and said: 'Come out of that Moore, I'm not satisfied with that run and I'm going again'.[10] He took off at 13:30 and flew three approaches before making his last at 14:00.

This time he came in too high and touched down at the forward end of the hangar roof, where the flying deck narrowed, well forward of the 'eye line' painted across the deck that showed the ideal cockpit position on landing. That far forward the 'cliff-edge' effect would have been a significant factor, especially in the prevailing gusty conditions. Accounts differ as to what happened next, but as the Pup touched the deck the handling party started to grab it. Dunning waved them away and 'blipped' the engine on to fly away, but it choked and lost power. Photographs show the aircraft well forward over the deck with its port wing lifting slightly and both ailerons and rudder deflected to the left as if to counter a roll and swing to starboard, but with the wheels still astride the centreline. The most probable cause of the aircraft's departure from controlled flight was a gust from fine on the port bow, causing 'cliff-edge' effect which got under the port wings and lifted the aircraft, semi-stalled, off the deck and literally blew it over the starboard side of the ship. With no engine power, Dunning stood no chance of recovering the situation and ditching was inevitable. There was no launch or trawler in attendance, and *Furious* had no sea-boat

Hoisting a Sopwith Pup through the hatch from HMS *Furious'* hangar, a manoeuvre that was difficult in calm weather and extremely difficult with any ship motion causing the lifting tackle to swing.

(AUTHOR'S COLLECTION)

A Sopwith Pup is ferried out to HMS *Furious* in Scapa Flow from the naval air station at Smoogroo in the Orkney Islands. It is about to be hoisted aboard from a makeshift raft constructed from aircraft floats.
(AUTHOR'S COLLECTION)

ready, surprisingly, given the hazardous nature of the trial. It took her twenty minutes to get back to N6452, which had remained afloat. It was hoisted back on to the deck, where Dunning was found to have drowned after being knocked unconscious when the aircraft hit the water.

After Dunning's loss no further landings were made, but Flight Sub-Lieutenant W.D. Jackson RNAS and Flight Lieutenant F.M. Fox RNAS carried out a number of 'experimental approaches' in October. Squadron Commander F.J. Rutland RNAS was appointed to succeed Dunning after a few weeks in which Moore had led the air group. Characteristically, he tried out Dunning's landing technique, and reported:

'I came in [with my wheels] about four feet above the deck and my wing tip within two feet of the conning tower. "Blipping" my engine, I landed only a couple of fuselage lengths from it. I sat there for perhaps ten seconds with the tail up, literally flying the plane with my wheels on the deck. Then I flew off, landing at Smoogroo ashore.'[11]

He subsequently reported to Captain Nicholson that: 'With training, any good pilot can land on the flying-off deck of *Furious* but I estimate the life of a pilot will be approximately ten flights. Under sea conditions, tests would be needed to determine whether this average would be appreciably less.' Surprisingly, he made no comparison between this rather pessimistic prediction and the expectancy of pilots who had to ditch at the end of every sortie. Reluctantly, the Grand Fleet accepted that *Furious* would remain a 'one-shot' carrier.

The positive outcome of these early landings on *Furious* was the recognition that landing aircraft on ships represented the best way forward and that 'one-shot' flying-off decks were a 'dead-end' technology. After *Furious* had joined the fleet the Admiralty approved a more extensive conversion to a cruiser that was still under construction, the *Cavendish*, name-ship of a new class. She was originally to have had nine 7.5-inch guns in single mountings on a 9,800-ton hull which was 605 feet long and capable of 30½ knots. Her conversion into an aircraft carrier entailed the suppression of five guns, only the extreme fore and aft and two beam mountings being retained. A hangar was erected forward, where B mounting had been, with space for six folded aircraft, over which a flying-off deck 106 feet long was constructed. Abaft the two funnels a landing deck 193 feet long by 57 feet wide was constructed on a raised platform. The deck was the first to be designed based on the experimental work at the Isle of Grain, and she was the first ship in the world built both to launch and recover wheeled aircraft. She was re-named *Vindictive* to keep the name made famous in the attack on Zeebrugge in the active fleet.

The Grand Fleet Committee discussed the implications of Dunning's landings on *Furious* on 18 September 1917 and recommended that a landing deck should be added aft of the funnel in place of the after 18-inch gun and turret. It was to be similar to the deck already approved for *Vindictive* and was to be capable of landing-on both Pups and Ship Strutters. Since the drawings for the latter ship had already been prepared, the extra design work was minimal and Admiralty approval for the work was given by the end of October. *Furious* left Rosyth for the Tyne on 14 November 1917 to have the work carried out after a brief spell of operational service.

Enthusiasm for the new scheme was not universal, and Captain Nicholson, briefed by his pilots, expressed doubts about the ability of light aircraft such as the Pup to be able to land in the turbulence and funnel gases aft of the central superstructure.[12] Admiralty opinion was that the superstructure was 'minimal' and could 'easily be streamlined'. Actual experience was to prove the captain right and leave a lasting impression about the importance of smoothing the airflow over a carrier deck on British carrier designers. While *Furious* was in the builder's

hands the opportunity was taken to incorporate a number of detail improvements that the Royal Navy's rapidly increasing store of aviation experience had shown to be important. More aircraft workshops and stores were created, and a second hangar was installed under the landing deck. This was 116 feet long by 33 feet wide and 15 feet 6 inches high and capable of containing six folded aircraft, increasing the number that could be stowed to fourteen.

A lift 48 feet long by 18 feet wide, designed by Waygood-Otis, replaced the forward hangar's hatch, and a similar one was built into the after hangar. As in all subsequent British aircraft carriers they formed part of the flight deck when in the 'up' position, leaving a gap in the hangar deck. The forward lift was hydraulically powered and the after one electrically powered for comparison. The hydraulic-powered version was preferred. Both were capable of lifting a working load of three tons and moved at a rate of 40 feet per minute. The derricks were retained to recover seaplanes if necessary. The lifts not only speeded up the process of ranging and striking down aircraft, but allowed movements in adverse weather, since there were no longer concerns about aircraft hanging from a rope attached to a derrick being hoisted slowly through a narrow hatch. The aircraft could be secured to the lift platform and held secure by the handling party as it was moved off it. Two walkways, one either side of the superstructure, connected the two flying decks. Each was about 170 feet long and 11 feet wide and would not have been easy to use in rough seas. The landing deck was 284 feet long and 70 feet wide, constructed 26 feet above the upper deck as superstructure with space between the roof of the hangar and the underside of the flight deck. It was hoped that air would pass under, as well as over, the deck in order to minimise turbulence, but the idea was subsequently found to make no difference. The rear of the deck ended 75 feet forward of the ship's stern. Another positive feature was opening the after hangar on to the quarterdeck to allow seaplanes to be moved on to and off the water from this lower level, obviating all the swing problems that had plagued the high-sided *Campania*. This feature was repeated in the Royal Navy's first

Dunning's third landing on HMS *Furious* on 7 August. This aircraft, N6452, did not have the triangle of white paint but did, by then, have 'grab handles' sewn on to it, one of which is visible on the trailing edge of the starboard lower wing. The aircraft is a long way forward of the widest part of the deck, but its wheels are only just to starboard of the centreline. The port wing is rising, probably because of 'cliff-edge' effect, but opposite aileron and left rudder have been applied to correct it.

(AUTHOR'S COLLECTION)

Pup N6452 going over the starboard side of the deck of HMS *Furious* out of control.

(AUTHOR'S COLLECTION)

generation of true aircraft carriers.[13]

While *Vindictive* and *Furious* were fitted with landing platforms, experiments on deck landing were continued at the Isle of Grain Experimental Establishment. The engineering firm Armstrong Whitworth proposed a transverse arrester wire system, similar in concept to that used by Eugene Ely in 1911, in which a wire was stretched across the deck, to be caught by a hook suspended below an aircraft and aft of its centre of gravity. Deceleration was achieved by paying out the wire from drums controlled by an electric motor, and the aircraft was to be held steady by the tension in the wire until the hook was lifted clear when the handling party took charge of it. A dummy deck 200 feet long by 60 feet wide had been used at the Isle of Grain to test arrester gear in 1916,

successfully evaluating a number of systems. Among these was an arrangement of three transverse wires, twenty feet apart with 30lb sandbags at their ends. The bills of aircraft tail hooks for this trial were unusually large as they were intended to pick up all three wires, each adding to the gradual rate of retardation, rather than giving a single 'snatch' load. The landing rate with this arrester gear would have been slow, since the transverse wires had to be reset by sailors after every landing.

The alternative scheme, and the one that was actually adopted, involved the use of a number of parallel fore-and-aft retaining wires anchored and held taught at each end by strong-points in wooden ramps which held the wires some inches above the deck. They covered a rectangular area of deck

A skid-equipped Sopwith Pup is buffeted by turbulence as it lands on HMS *Furious'* after deck during the landing trials in March 1918. The vertical ropes of the barrier are visible in the foreground.

forward of the ideal touchdown point and were to be engaged by hooks fixed rigidly to the spreader bar between the aircraft's wheels. After landing the pilot had to steer into the wires to engage them. The hooks went through several modifications, and were complicated by the addition of hinged locking tabs that prevented the wires slipping out after engagement. They also made it difficult and slow to extricate the aircraft after it came to rest. The rigid structure transmitted the shock of landing into the airframe and contributed significantly to drag. Torpedo strike aircraft could not be fitted with the hook bar because the torpedo was mounted between the wheels. They were heavy enough not to need retaining, however.

The fore-and-aft gear, first proposed and subsequently developed by Squadron Commander H.R. Busteed RNAS at Grain, was formally adopted and installed in *Furious*. As a 'last-ditch' safety measure, a rope barrier was strung across the forward end of the landing deck in a structure like football goal-posts, to prevent aircraft which both missed the wires and failed to stop from crashing into the aft end of the superstructure. The Grain experiments also led to a change of undercarriage for the Pup for use with the 'Busteed gear', as it was at first known. Several aircraft were refitted with skids rather than wheels,[14] which were believed to reduce the tendency to bounce on landing. They were not sprung or fitted with any form of shock-absorber, and tended to break rather than bounce if they hit the deck hard. Directional stability was reduced on take-off, however, and the concept was not a success.

A Pup is stopped in HMS *Furious'* retaining wires with a broken skid undercarriage. The boards used to keep the wires up off the deck can be seen knocked flat behind the aircraft. Resetting them was difficult and time-consuming.
(AUTHOR'S COLLECTION)

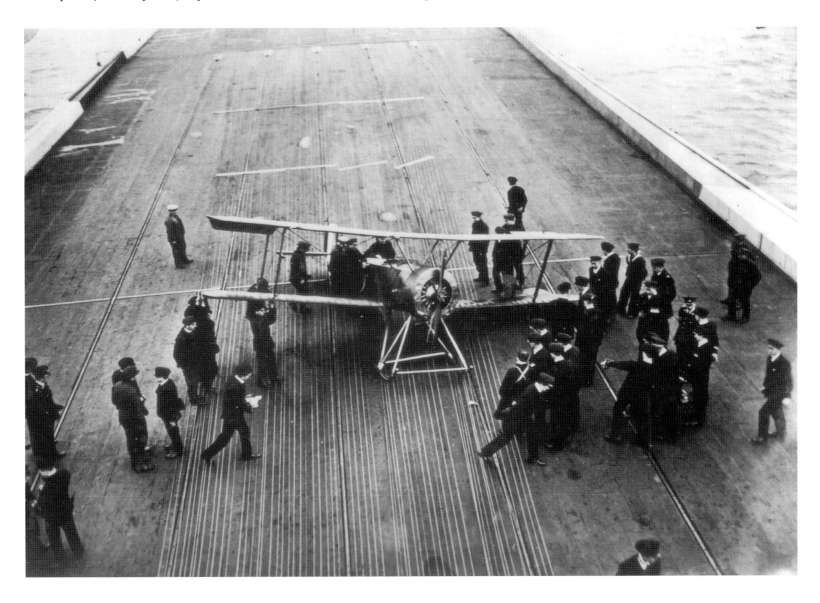

HMS *Furious* recommissioned on 15 March 1918 and began flying trials on 25 March. The first four 'passes' at the landing deck showed immediately where the problem lay, and that the captain and his pilots had been right to anticipate problems with turbulence. The Busteed retaining gear did not work on the first three occasions when aircraft made contact with the deck, and several Pups were written-off as they 'dropped on to the deck like shot partridges'.[15] Two of the aircraft went into the safety barrier, one of them at 30 knots in spite of a relative wind measured on the bridge at 30 knots from ahead. It was not measured on the landing deck, however, and one of the early lessons was that there were considerable variations in the airflow over a warship. During the fourth approach the wind over the deck appeared to be blowing from dead astern, despite the ship steaming at 22 knots into a 10-knot surface wind. The turbulence over the stern was so bad that the pilot was lucky to regain control and overshoot to port. The turbulence created by funnel gases

appeared to flow 20 to 30 feet above the deck, but was predictable. The completely unpredictable turbulence over the protruding quarterdeck was more serious. It was caused by the interplay between the two air streams along the sides of the hull and the blunt after end of the landing deck. The disturbed air extended 30 feet either side of the hull and for approximately 300 feet aft of it. When trials were resumed on 27 March an attempt was made to reduce this turbulence by stretching a canvas awning between the after lip of the flight deck and the stern, but this had little effect. The early landings had failed because the aircraft approached just above stalling speed and were barely controllable as they entered the turbulent air just aft of the deck. Turbulence had been predicted by windtunnel tests of ship models in 1916, but its severity came as a surprise. It may be that the tunnel tests failed to appreciate the flight paths, relative to the deck, that pilots would follow, and thus failed to indicate the impact the airflow would have on actual landings.

A Sopwith Pup embedded in the rope barrier abaft HMS *Furious'* funnel. Most boards have been knocked flat by its passage, but one to the right is still upright, showing how high the retaining wires were set above the deck.

(AUTHOR'S COLLECTION)

A Sopwith Ship Strutter takes off from HMS *Furious'* flying-off deck in 1918.
(AUTHOR'S COLLECTION)

A skid-equipped Sopwith Pup approaches HMS *Furious'* aft landing-deck. It has not yet been affected by turbulence.
(AUTHOR'S COLLECTION)

HMS *Vindictive*, with her short flying-off deck and landing deck aft. The prospect of a single ship able to mount both a heavy cruiser gun armament and flying facilities caused intense interest but soon proved completely impractical.

(AUTHOR'S COLLECTION)

Squadron Commander Rutland made two unsuccessful attempts before his first successful landing. With the ship steaming at 28 knots and virtually no natural wind, he crossed the stern just above flight-deck level and just above stalling speed, 'wallowing' in turbulence which he admitted to underestimating.[16] The skid undercarriage broke on impacting the deck. On 27 March he approached steeply in a nose-high attitude from the starboard side, hoping to avoid the turbulence at the after end of the deck and pass through the funnel smoke with minimal forward travel. Relative to the deck, therefore, the aircraft had a considerable rate of descent, as well as crossing momentum from right to left. It bounced and skidded to port without engaging the wires and stopped with one wing over the deck edge. On a split-second decision, Rutland jumped clear and dived fifty feet into the sea. The aircraft did not in fact go into the water, but caught on a torpedo tube fitted two decks below the flight deck and hung there. Rutland used a cushion to help him stay afloat and was picked up by sea boat twenty minutes later, when

the ship turned back to him.

Not all landings ended in failure, and some variations were tried. Transverse arrester wires with sand bags, like those evaluated at Grain, were rigged across the fore-and-aft wires. The complicated result was time-consuming to rig and difficult to move aircraft across, but did allow faster, better-controlled approaches with a hook down. The transverse wires stopped forward momentum and the longitudinal wires kept the aircraft on deck. Two Sopwith Pups landed successfully using this technique on 19 April 1918, watched by the First Lord of the Admiralty. In both cases the ship was steaming at low speed, lessening the problem of funnel smoke, and the wind over the deck was between 21 and 26 knots. One successful landing was carried out with only 10 knots of wind over the deck and almost no turbulence. The aircraft was manhandled to the forward deck, took off and landed safely for a second time.[17] Officers from *Furious* made several suggestions for improved arrester gear[18] but, with the completion of *Argus* imminent, none was felt worth acting upon. The concept of both longitudinal and transverse wires was not popular, as the latter tended to get caught up in the former and the resulting tangled mess took some minutes to sort out and reset. The second Pup, piloted by Squadron Commander Gallehawk RNAS, landed against a 'negative' while the ship was still turning into wind, but encountered no turbulence and was stopped successfully in 65 feet by the combined effects of the arresting and retaining wires.

The consensus among the pilots was that landing on the after deck was more dangerous than the experiments on the forward deck had been. Squadron Commander Busteed tried himself in a Pup appropriately named *Excuse Me* while the ship was at anchor. He hit the barrier hard and was lucky to get away with cuts and bruises. The trials were abandoned and no further attempt was made to land aircraft on *Furious* during 1918, but she did continue in use with the Grand Fleet as a 'one-shot' carrier with the extra aircraft that the second hangar and after deck 'real estate' made available. On 17 June 1918 two German seaplanes bombed a force in the North Sea which included *Furious*. Two Sopwith 2F.1 Camels were launched from deck alert and shot down one of the

Profile and plan views of HMS *Furious* as completed, showing the deck on which Squadron Commander Dunning landed.
(AUTHOR'S COLLECTION)

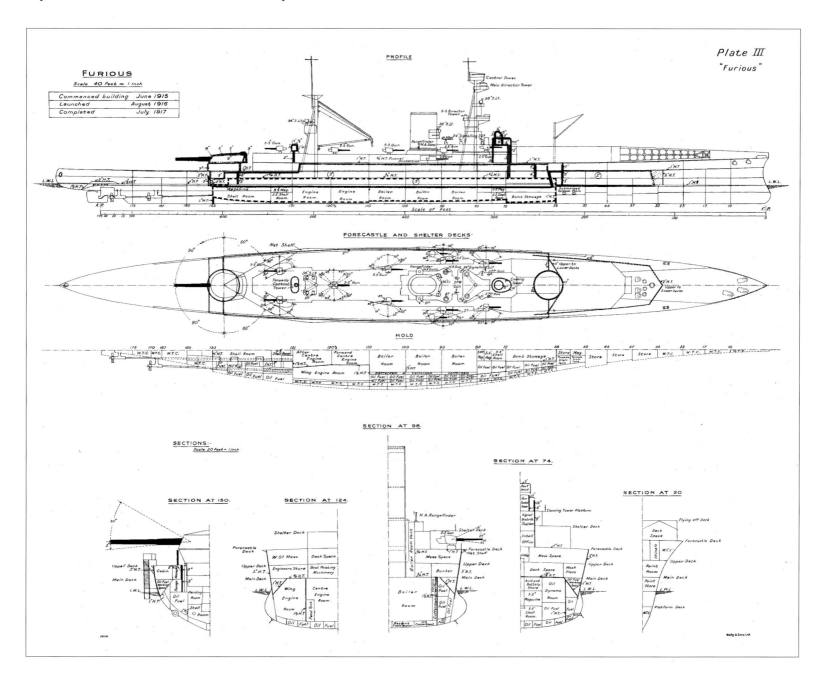

Squadron Commander Dunning's
Sopwith Pup being recovered by
HMS *Furious* after the fatal
ditching on 7 August 1917.
(AUTHOR'S COLLECTION)

attackers, but only after they had completed their attack. One effect of this incident was to convince the Admiralty that strikes against enemy air bases ashore from aircraft carriers were the best method of dealing with them. In consequence a squadron of 2F.1 Camels was formed to be trained in strike warfare. Seven aircraft were embarked in *Furious*, and on 19 July 1918 they attacked the German naval air station at Tondern, destroying the Zeppelins L54 and L60 in their hangars. Another hangar, which turned out to be empty, was also destroyed. Each aircraft carried two 50lb bombs in addition to its front guns, and attacked low from the sea, achieving complete surprise. They could not land back on 'mother', but three managed to ditch near the fleet. Three others landed in Denmark and one was lost without trace. This was the first successful carrier air strike in history.

Intended as an interim solution, *Furious* formed the link between the seaplane-carrying conversions and the first true carrier, *Argus*. The failure of the various landing trials carried out on her decks can be put down to a lack of appreciation of the effect of turbulence over flight decks, but did lead to the redesign of the superstructure intended for the first-generation carriers *Argus*, *Hermes* and *Eagle*. From 1918 aircraft carrier models were investigated in the windtunnel at the National Physical Laboratory, and areas needing improvement were recognised. The abrupt, flat 'lip' at the after end of *Furious*' landing deck was found to generate much of the turbulence that had been found in the 'real world' during the landing trials. By rounding the after end of the flight deck down and narrowing the sides right aft on a model in the windtunnel, the airflow was smoothed and the turbulent effect virtually eliminated. British designers carried the remedy to extremes, however, and in *Eagle*, then under construction, the after round-down was designed to extend forward for 63 feet which, together with the narrowing of the deck, significantly limited the number of aircraft that could be ranged on the after part of the flight deck.

HMS *Argus*

Fairey IIID S1092 is hoisted on to the water with its engine running. Aircraft carriers were expected to operate their aircraft as seaplanes when they were at anchor or in harbour. They were pushed out of the opening at the after end of the hangar on to the quarterdeck, where they were prepared for flight before being lowered by one of the two, port and starboard, cranes. The 'drop' to the water was much less than in the early seaplane carriers, so the aircraft were less at risk from swinging into the ship's side. The concept was practical but seldom used. This IIID operated with 441 and then 422 Flights embarked in HMS *Argus* between March 1927 and May 1928.

(AUTHOR'S COLLECTION)

HMS *Argus* was the culmination of the Royal Navy's pioneering efforts to develop a true aircraft-carrying warship, capable of launching and recovering aircraft in the open ocean. To speed her construction, the incomplete hull of one of two liners laid down in June 1914 for the Italian Lloyd Sabaudo Line, to have been named *Conte Rosso*, was purchased by the Admiralty in August 1916. As work progressed and experience grew, her design evolved from a seaplane carrier, similar to *Campania*, to a flush-deck carrier.

J.H. Narbeth led the design team and maintained the principle that a mercantile hull would be better adapted to the role than one designed from the outset on warship lines. Two proposals influenced his thinking; the first was that put forward by Squadron Commander Hugh Williamson in 1915, which envisaged a ship with a continuous flight deck, athwartship arrester wires, and the bridge and funnel arrangements grouped into an 'island' to starboard of the flight deck amidships.[1] An alternative proposal for a flush-decked carrier with no superstructure at all was put forward in 1916 by Lieutenant Gerard Holmes RNVR, who had been a naval architect for the Cunard Line, which had carried out the early seaplane carrier conversions and who had served in *Riviera* before joining the Air Department at the Admiralty. Key to his concept was a system of trunking funnel smoke aft in two horizontal ducts under the flight deck. Narbeth used Holmes' ducting in *Argus* because her machinery was a relatively low-powered mercantile installation. The application had distinct disadvantages, however, in that the ducts occupied the space between the hangar roof and the flight deck aft of amidships, preventing the installation of lifts. Despite the influences others may have brought to bear, the design was very much Narbeth's own.

Although the flight deck was continuous, it was originally intended to be operated as a flying-off area forward, connected by a passageway between two small 'island' superstructures, to port and starboard of the centreline, to a landing area aft. The islands would have contained the control positions and navigating offices, with the compass platform on a 'bridge' joining the two twenty feet above the deck. Aircraft would have been pushed between the two

decks but were not, at first, expected to pass through at speed under their own power. Such an arrangement would soon have proved impractical. Some of the earliest windtunnel tests ever carried out on a structure other than aircraft were carried out on a model of *Argus* in November 1916 at the National Physical Laboratory.[2] These showed that the landing

HMS *Argus* in November 1918, while preparing for the planned attack on the German High Sea Fleet in its harbours, with Sopwith T.1 torpedo-bombers on the flight deck. The 'splinter' paint scheme was designed to confuse enemy range-finders, but had the negative effect of making the ship more obvious. (AUTHOR'S COLLECTION)

deck could be subject to turbulence, but no changes to the design were made until the failure of the *Furious* trials in 1917 showed just how great the impact of turbulence could be on aircraft operations. In consequence the superstructures were removed and the ship completed to a flush-deck design. From the air she resembled an inverted flat-iron, and was known throughout her service as the 'floating flat-iron'. There is no evidence to show that the removal of only one island was considered, and the flush-deck approach may have been an over-reaction to the failure of the landing trials on *Furious*. The importance given almost immediately after completion to the trial installation of a dummy island might indicate that Narbeth regretted the complete removal of superstructure.

The key features of the design were the flight deck, the hangar beneath it and the workshops and magazines designed to support embarked aircraft. The flight deck was 550 feet long and 85 feet wide, with a narrow section one third of the way aft from the bow to give forward visibility from the control positions re-sited under the deck and arcs of fire for the 4-inch anti-aircraft guns mounted either side at the after end of the forecastle. The flight deck was built as superstructure supported by a steel lattice framework with 14 feet 6 inches clear space between the roof of the hangar and the deck. Into this the two funnel ducts were led. To reduce the wild heat they generated the ducts were surrounded by tubes through which cool air was blown by fans. This arrangement had the secondary effect of preventing a 'back draught' if there was a strong following wind blowing into the horizontal ducts. The smoke was exhausted aft, just where aircraft crossed the after part of the deck to land. The whole system was complicated, unpopular with pilots, limited the places where lifts could be installed, and inefficient. It was not repeated. There were expansion joints in the unpainted, mild steel deck to ensure that the hull's longitudinal bending moments did not cause distortion. In July 1918 the decision was taken to install fore-and-aft retaining wires like those fitted in *Furious*, although they were not to be fitted until after an initial assessment of deck landing so that their position on the flight deck could be optimised.

Argus's first senior air officer was Commander Richard Bell Davies VC RN, an ideal choice after his previous experience as air commander in *Campania* and *Furious*. Although he never transferred to the newly formed Royal Air Force (RAF), in late 1918 he held the temporary 'flying rank' of Lieutenant Colonel RAF. The ship commissioned at Beardmore's Dalmuir Yard on 14 September 1918 and began flying trials in the Firth of Forth on 24 September. They were carried out in three phases[3] by two pilots, Bell Davies himself and Captain L.H. Cockey RAF, using aircraft from the Grand Fleet's air base at Turnhouse, later to become Edinburgh International Airport. The first phase was to carry out a number of flights close to the ship in 1½ Strutters while she was under way to evaluate the airflow near the deck and to decide on the point at which aircraft could most easily land. From this, the ideal location for the retaining gear could be calculated[4] before its installation. The second phase was to carry out a series of landings to find the

HMS *Argus* fitted with a wood and canvas island mock-up in October 1918. It proved successful and was popular with pilots, who used it judge height and position over the deck on landing. The small compass platform is in the raised position, visible just to the left of the 'island'.

(FLEET AIR ARM MUSEUM)

optimum speed for landing-on and to discover at what speed the aircraft would enter the retaining gear when it was installed. Many landings were required to define 'best practice' and to confirm that the technique was repeatable by average squadron pilots. The last phase was to install and set up an improvised version of the retaining gear and taxi into it after landing. On the first day of trials there was a gusty wind with a mean speed of 22 knots, into which *Argus* steamed at 15 knots. Bell Davies carried out the first landing and a total of six more were carried out by both pilots. After each landing they taxied up the deck and took off using a short deck run. Red lines were painted fore and aft to show the pilots where the inboard edges of cut-away portions of the deck lay so that they could line up for take-off without the risk of putting a wheel over the edge. Later in the day a further six landings were made with a ship's speed of only 6 knots into similar wind conditions. Both the taking-off and landing of front-line aircraft on a ship had become a matter of routine.

In his subsequent report[5] Bell Davies noted that there was very little turbulence, even over the stern on final approach. On take-off there was occasional cliff-edge effect from the cut-away areas of the deck that caused 'a slight bump' to be felt as the aircraft passed them. Both pilots had tended, at first, to land well forward, but as they gained experience they were able to judge a point closer to the stern. The aircraft flew left-hand circuits because their rotary engines made the nose rise in a left turn and drop when turning right owing to the gyroscopic effect of the rotating cylinders. Left-hand circuits were the more controllable option, as predicted by Hugh Williamson in 1915. Human anatomy was also a factor, since pilots found it easier to deflect the control column to the left.[6] The two pilots quickly discovered that, in a long straight approach from astern, the aircraft nose tended to obscure the deck, making it difficult to judge height exactly. They found that by flying a tighter circuit with a continuous turning approach on the quarter, followed by a short, straight final line-up, they could keep the deck in view and produce a more controlled, accurate deck landing. The aircraft often landed with slight drift on and were not lined up on the centreline when their wheels touched the deck, but it proved easy to straighten up and move on to the centreline within twenty or thirty feet after

A unique but unfortunately poor-quality image of HMS *Argus* landing-on a Sopwith 2F.1 Camel during flying trials in October 1918. Pictures of the first deck landings are, unfortunately, rare. The aircraft is well above the after end of the flight deck, on what appears to be a 3 degree glide slope.
(AUTHOR'S COLLECTION)

HMS *Argus*'s hangar, looking aft from a point just aft of the forward lift. The aircraft are Sopwith T.1 torpedo-bombers, and the one to the left is on the after lift platform. By later standards the hangar looks high but narrow and cramped.

(AUTHOR'S COLLECTION)

Another hangar view, this time looking forward from a point just aft of the after lift. Aircraft N6982 and N6977 are both Sopwith T.1s allocated to HMS *Argus* in the week ending 14 November 1918. Both were damaged and written off charge in December. The former is on the lift platform.

(AUTHOR'S COLLECTION)

Some idea of HMS *Argus*'s original design features can be gained from this photograph of a windtunnel model taken in November 1916. After the turbulence experienced in HMS *Furious*'s 1918 landing trials the two islands, both of which had been installed by the shipbuilder, were removed to give a flush deck with no obstructions.
(AUTHOR'S COLLECTION)

landing. Both pilots agreed that better landings were carried out with a lower wind over the deck. They were comfortable 'hitting' the deck about 150 feet forward of its after extremity and taxiing forward a further 30 feet to get the aircraft centred and under control. Bell Davies felt that the further forward the retaining gear could be installed the better; aircraft taxiing forward after landing 'were under perfect control, and could be steered easily on to the retaining gear'. Landings were carried out over a relatively wide range of airspeeds, and hitting the deck at minimum speed, close to the stall was not considered essential as the lightweight aircraft were easy to control on deck, even after fast approaches. Bell Davies noted that with a felt wind of 25 knots there was no need for arrester gear as the wind resistance would bring aircraft quickly to a standstill.

Phase two of the flying trials was carried out on 26 September 1918 in the Firth of Forth. A line was painted athwartships across the deck to mark the proposed position of the after ramp of the retaining gear, and the first run was carried out at a ship's speed of 15 knots into a steady 7-knot wind. Seven landings were made, during which the pilots were able to move their point of landing further aft to an average point 100 feet forward of the after edge of the flight deck. The landings confirmed the opinions formed on 24 September and no difficulty was experienced steering the aircraft on to the line at moderate speed under good control. Three further landings were carried out at a ship's speed of 17 knots, then another eleven at 19 knots. Landing skills continued to improve with practice, and both pilots agreed that 25 knots wind over the deck gave the best conditions. On the successful conclusion of this day's trials *Argus* was taken into Rosyth Dockyard, where temporary retaining gear was fitted. It comprised fifty-four wires[7] spaced 9 inches apart rigged fore and aft between two ramp structures, the high points of which were 100 feet apart. The after one was installed just aft of the after lift, and the forward one just aft of the forward lift. Both were 40 feet 8 inches wide and 15 inches high. The wires were held off the deck by tension over the ramps between the anchor points and a 'fiddle bridge' at the halfway point. The ramps were made of wood, with shot mats placed over the after slopes. The after ramp was 17 feet long and triangular in section; the forward one was 42 feet long with a 24-foot flat section between the sloping sections at each end. The centreline of the retaining gear was to port of the flight deck centreline to allow space for a dummy 'island' to be erected on the starboard side of the deck amidships as part of the flying trials to evaluate its impact on airflow over the deck. The retaining gear covered the after lift and would have prevented its use, but it had not yet been set to work and was inoperable during this phase of the trials. The gear had the effect of dividing the flight deck into a take-off deck forward and a landing area aft, divided by the clumsy ramps and the space between them. The definitive retaining gear, to be fitted after the trials, needed ramps that lowered flush with the deck in order to range aircraft over them and restore the advantage of an unobstructed flight deck. They also needed to be lowered for deck landing practice, as Bell Davies had noted that aircraft that were not to carry out a 'full stop' landing only needed to touch the deck and 'roll' into a take-off for a further circuit. The gear was cumbersome, and though it served its early purpose it made it difficult to move the aircraft after landing.

Phase 3 was carried out on 1 October, and the first

'retained' landing took place with the ship steaming at 15 knots into a wind that gusted between 14 and 16 knots. A hand-held anemometer in the landing area of the deck gave an indication of 26 knots wind over the deck. The aircraft landed well aft and taxied forward at low speed, moved up the after ramp and dropped into the retaining gear, all the wires between the hooks being caught. Engine thrust kept the aircraft moving forward until it came to rest on the after slope of the forward ramp. One sailor was placed at each wingtip and another at the tail and, when they were ready, the engine was switched off. The slope of the ramp and wind pressure moved the aircraft back a few feet, but the men controlled it and held the aircraft firmly while the wires were lowered so that it could be extricated and moved forward. On the second approach of the day the aircraft dropped low on final approach and encountered considerable

A Parnall Panther two-seat spotter/reconnaissance aircraft lands into HMS *Argus*'s retaining wires during the Atlantic Fleet's Spring Cruise in 1921.

(AUTHOR'S COLLECTION)

A Sopwith T.1 instructional airframe with a torpedo in place, showing why an axle fitted with hooks could not be inserted between the wheels. The T.1 was heavy enough not to need retaining gear when it came to rest on landing.

(AUTHOR'S COLLECTION)

turbulence level with the flight deck. On what had become the normal approach path the aircraft had been above this turbulent area and had landed in a relatively smooth airflow. A second circuit was flown, and resulted in a successful landing with the ship making 11 knots into a wind that had strengthened to give an anemometer reading of 25 knots. This time the aircraft came to rest on the after slope of the forward ramp, where it was firmly held in place by the wires. On the third approach the ship reduced speed to 4 knots and the anemometer read only 12 knots. This caused the pilot to misjudge his approach, and he was too high on the final turn, having to fly a second circuit. The engine was switched off just before the landing was made 100 feet forward of the after edge of the deck, and the aircraft ran forward along the deck 'at good speed'. It bounced some feet into the air after hitting the after ramp and fell into the wires, which were caught as the hooks made contact. It tried to bounce again, but was retained and pulled back to the deck by the wires in the manner intended. Significantly, only three landings were achieved on this day.

The trial had proved that landing-on aircraft similar to the 1½ Strutter was 'a very easy operation' with wind speeds over the deck of between 20 and 30 knots, provided the aircraft was landed sufficiently far aft of the retaining gear to 'straighten up the machine and regulate the speed'. No arresting apparatus was required with wind speeds of 25 knots, or greater, over the flight deck. Bell Davies recommended that pilots would need practice to gain and maintain deck-landing skills and that, in order for them to do so, the retaining wires needed to be capable of laying flat. The after anchor point of the wires should be attached to a ramp that was less steep than the temporary one fitted at first in *Argus*, to cater for occasions when the wind speed over the deck was low or the aircraft speed on deck into the wires was high. Overall, the trials had shown that deck landing on *Argus* was a practical everyday possibility and that the retaining system was 'entirely effective', although it was cumbersome to use. Again, it was noted that torpedo-carrying aircraft such as the Sopwith T.1 would have to land-on without being retained, as there was no axle between the wheels.[8] Since the T.1's

HMS *Argus* in 1938, after reconstruction as a trials and training carrier. The flight deck forward was enlarged and fitted over a more robust structure to support the weight of an hydraulic catapult. The prominent palisades were to stop aircraft being blown over the side before handling parties could secure them as they came to rest after landing.

(AUTHOR'S COLLECTION)

empty weight, without aircrew, fuel or weapons, was nearly a ton greater than that of the 1½ Strutter,[9] it was already arguable that the newer aircraft was no longer a lightweight and did not need to be retained when it came to a halt. In subsequent correspondence[10] the ACA stated that these trials were most satisfactory, showing great promise for the future. In correspondence with Captain Nicholson of HMS *Furious* he noted that the cut-away portions of the deck adversely affected flying operations, both in restricting the width of deck available for take-off and in creating 'cliff-edge'-effect turbulence. It was recommended that they be filled in eventually, perhaps by awnings in the short term.

On 4 October 1918 *Argus* returned to Rosyth Dockyard to have a 'dummy' island fitted on the starboard side amidships. Originally it had been intended to mock-up the island intended for *Eagle*, with two funnels and a tripod mast. The structure

actually fitted was somewhat simpler, however, resembling a rectangular box with a single large funnel shape and no mast. A further set of flying trials, with the island in place, began on 22 October with a smoke generator at the after end of the island. This showed that the actual airflow over the flight deck closely matched the simulations carried out earlier in the National Physical Laboratory wind-tunnel. Two Sopwith aircraft from the Grand Fleet pool were used, a Pup and a 2F.1 Camel, and they began by flying past the ship from a number of different angles[11] before attempting to land. Unfortunately, the more experienced pilot in the Camel suffered an engine failure and ditched, and the Pup pilot was concerned about turbulence and approached much too fast during his early approaches. The first successful landing with the island in place took place on 24 October, and thirty-six more successful landings were carried out before

narrow deck would have limited the wingspan of aircraft she could operate. The ship was controlled from a bridge structure under the flight deck about one third of the ship's length from the bow. The compass platform was in a structure to starboard, connected to a standby platform to port by a passageway under the deck. Visibility ahead and round to two points abaft the beam was helped by the cut-out portions of the flight deck. The port platform was used as a flying control position, known in the RN as 'Flyco', where Commander Air ran the deck and controlled aircraft in the local vicinity. When flying was not in progress the ship was conned from a charthouse raised hydraulically above flight deck level which was accessible from the cross-deck passage amidships. I have heard verbal evidence of at least one occasion when an hydraulic failure while in pilotage waters led to the charthouse sinking below deck level with the captain, navigating officer and officer of the watch trapped in it. Wireless telegraphy and signal masts were fitted at the deck edge and were lowered to the horizontal, outboard of the deck, during flying operations. The whole arrangement was not ideal, and was only ever repeated in the rebuilt *Furious*. Personnel on both bridges had to be aware that aircraft that swung on take-off could put a wheel into them with spectacular results.

The retaining gear created problems. It took a long time to rig and, when the wires were 'up', aircraft could not be manoeuvred or take off over them. The after ramp sometimes caused aircraft to bounce or slew sideways into the wires, causing damage to the undercarriage.[12] The location of the wires was modified between December 1918 and March 1919, after the first series of flying trials. The ramps were removed and, instead, the after lift was lowered slightly to form a 'depression' or 'well' in the deck 15 inches deep. When it was up, the wires lay flush with the deck and aircraft could be wheeled over them, when it was lowered, the axle hooks would engage the wires and hold aircraft on the deck. A wooden ramp 10 feet long and the full width of the lift was placed at the forward end of the 'well' thus formed to prevent undercarriages being damaged by hitting the vertical forward lift-well bulkhead after a fast

trials ended. Contrary to the fears expressed by some doubters, the island caused very little turbulence over the deck, and actually helped pilots to land by giving them a vertical reference against which to judge their height and position relative to the ideal landing point. As long as the wind over the deck was kept from right ahead to within a few degrees on the port bow, there was no serious turbulence over the deck. If the wind was allowed to shift to starboard, turbulence over the deck made it impossible to land. This was acceptable and offered the best solution from the points of view of deck landing, ship control and getting rid of funnel smoke in the least problematical manner. The decision was taken to complete *Eagle* and *Hermes* with islands although, surprisingly in the light of the trial reports, no consideration was given to fitting *Argus* herself with a permanent structure. Perhaps the complication of re-routeing the smoke ducts would have been too difficult to justify the expense and her landing. The side bulkheads of the lift remained a danger for aircraft that entered the well close to the edge or slewing at an angle. Since the retaining gear was now off the centreline to starboard and was both narrower and shorter, a higher degree of pilot skill was demanded to engage it. Lowering the after lift 15 inches created the same effect as having ramps that could be lowered flush with the deck and, with the lift up, aircraft could be ranged or even take off over the wires. Keeping them permanently rigged, however, kept the after lift out of action, and it was not in the ideal place for a retaining gear well. If pilots landed too far aft or too slowly, or both, they might stop before being retained by the wires and be blown over the side by a gust. If they landed too far up the deck or too fast they risked stopping abruptly and having the undercarriage demolished by the lift's vertical surfaces. Landing was also complicated by the fact that pilots had no means of knowing whether their hooks had engaged the wires or not, since there was no marked rate of deceleration. If a pilot thought that his hooks had not engaged and 'blipped' his

engine to full power with a clear deck in front of him to take off, the aircraft could be wrecked if it was, in fact, retained by the wires. Following pilot reaction to the second set of trials, the gear was modified again in April 1919, the well under the wires being moved aft of the after lift and widened to 58 feet, most of the practical width of the deck. Because it was now over the smoke ducts, the depth of the well had to be reduced to 9 inches. At the same time it was decided that the after lift was of little practical value, and it was permanently locked at flight-deck level, leaving *Argus* with only the large, forward lift. Another inherent danger was discovered after a bounce following a high-speed entry into the gear, when an aircraft wheel fell on to a wire, which acted like a spring and bounced it sideways, causing the undercarriage to collapse. Further trials with a 1½ Strutter in April 1919 showed that the shallower well was acceptable, and it was enlarged and made into a permanent fitting by October 1919.

The lightweight aircraft in service in the years immediately after the end of the First World War were

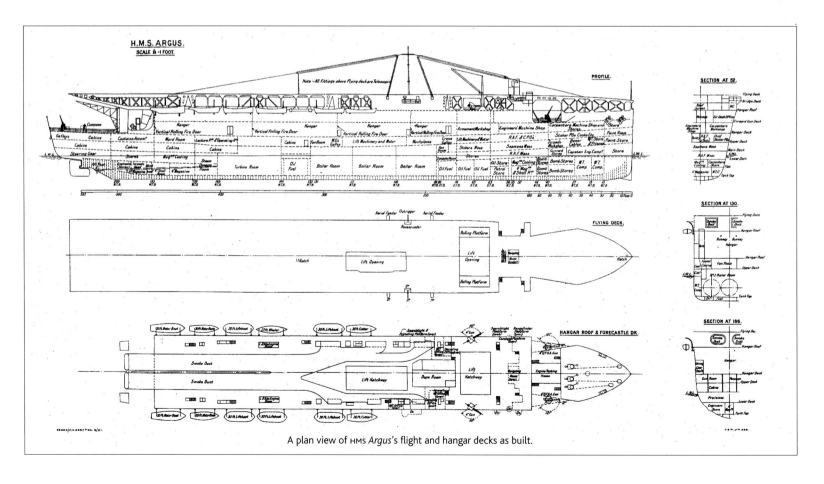

A plan view of HMS *Argus*'s flight and hangar decks as built.

not easy to operate at sea. Rotary engines tended to overheat without airflow through them, and could not be run on deck for more than two or three minutes before launch. Unfortunately they could take as long as ten minutes to start, and during that time the ship had to be into wind, ready for an almost immediate take-off. In the 1921 spring cruise with the Atlantic Fleet, *Argus* took forty minutes to fly-off two aircraft and land-on one while steaming into wind in a direction that took her away from the main part of the battle fleet. On another occasion recovering three aircraft took twenty-five minutes steaming into a similarly unfavourable wind. The reduction of the time interval between aircraft being launched and recovered became the biggest issue to resolve for several important reasons. The most obvious was that the carrier was intended to operate closely with the battle fleet for protection against enemy cruisers and to help pilots locate the ships they were spotting for

or protecting. If the carrier literally disappeared out of sight over the horizon, her integration with fleet manoeuvres became difficult. The Royal Navy had used wireless direction finding extensively during the recent war to detect and localise enemy forces at sea. In consequence it operated a silent emission control policy itself to avoid detection, and relied on visual signals such as lights and flag hoists for tactical communication. If the carrier could not 'see' the flagship it could not 'read' instructions, and 'link-ships' had to be stationed to relay messages to her. Worse, if she spent time away from the main body, escorts had to be detached to protect her, weakening the battle fleet's escort force, a process that later became known as 'bulging' the screen. As the first ship of her kind to go to sea, *Argus* taught the Royal Navy invaluable lessons about how to integrate the operation of aircraft into its tactics.

The risk to the early naval aircraft posed by strong

A Sopwith 2F.1 Camel on the forward lift of HMS *Argus* in December 1918.

(AUTHOR'S COLLECTION)

HMS *Argus* shortly after completion, with her ship's company manning the side.
(AUTHOR'S COLLECTION)

or gusting winds over the flight deck led the Royal Navy to believe that they could not be kept on deck, but would have to be kept in a hangar most of the time, being ranged on deck shortly before launch and struck down immediately after landing. This equated to practice ashore, where aircraft were kept in hangars and wheeled out shortly before flight, and there is evidence that, in her early years, *Argus* was operated as an airfield that moved.[13] The hangar, therefore, was seen as one of the most important aspects of the design. Narbeth was influenced by the petrol-vapour fire that had contributed to the loss of *Ben-my-Chree* in 1917 and isolated the hangar from the rest of the hull by air-locks. In the event of fire it could be subdivided into four sections by three fire-resistant roller curtains in the deck-head. The hangar was by far the largest worked into a warship to date, and was 330 feet long with a clear width of 48 feet and up to 68 feet between frames. It had a clear height of 20 feet and was fitted with an overhead gantry system so that serviceable aircraft 'blocked' into a corner by others that were unserviceable could be lifted up and carried towards the lift over them. This ingenious

method of solving bottlenecks grew less practical as aircraft increased in size, and has never been repeated. At the after end of the hangar a steel roller-door gave access to the seaplane operating area on the quarterdeck. Cranes were sited against the after hangar bulkhead to lift them from this low platform on to and off the water with no great risk of them swinging. Although the primary purpose of this ship was to operate aircraft from the flight deck, the potential for operating seaplanes while moored in harbour was still thought to be significant, and was not written out of naval staff requirements for another twenty years. The hangar deck was completed like the flight deck in unpainted mild steel, but with the addition of slip-resistant metal strips to give sure footing for the large number of mechanics working in the space. Quantities of first aid fire-fighting equipment, including hand-held extinguishers and sand boxes, were provided at intervals so that an outbreak could be contained and brought under control.[14] Care obviously had to be taken to ensure that aircraft were not stowed under the fire curtains, which might have prevented them being lowered in an emergency.

HMS *Argus* alongside in Beardmore's yard during July 1918, two months before completion. The charthouse is in the fully raised position.
(AUTHOR'S COLLECTION)

HMS *Argus* in the Clyde during trials in September 1918, with funnel smoke exhausting aft from under the round-down. The aircraft approach path was above the smoke, but it must have made flying on to the ship an unpleasant experience nonetheless.

(AUTHOR'S COLLECTION)

As in *Ark Royal*, it was thought that a bulk fuel installation with pipes taking Avgas to refuelling points in the hangar or on deck was likely to leak with potentially catastrophic results, so aircraft fuel was provided in the familiar two-gallon tins at first, 4,000 of which could be stored in a hold forward of the hangar, which had its own ventilation and was surrounded by void spaces filled with water. The forward lift was unusual in that it was wide enough to strike down aircraft with their wings spread and had roller shutters on either side of it that could cover the hole when the lift was at hangar-deck level to allow aircraft to take off. This is another design feature that has never been repeated, although I can think of many occasions when it would have proved useful.

Workshops with easy access to the hangar were installed forward, under the take-off area of the deck on top of the original liner forecastle. These included facilities for carpenters and engine fitters, tyre bays, metalworking shops and instrument repair offices intended to support a wide variety of the aircraft that could, potentially, be embarked. An open space immediately under the deck had fittings, including electrical connections, that allowed engines to be locked in position, run-up and tested before being fitted to aircraft. Weapons, including torpedoes and

bombs up to 112lb were stowed in deep magazines forward, in what had been the liner's hold. There were no bomb lifts and weapons were brought up to the hangar by chain hoists through vertical hatches. Ready-use bomb stowage was built into the hangar sides in the after part of the hangar. The inability to range aircraft from anywhere but the forward end of the hangar always proved a limitation.

Argus was a considerable improvement on the Grand Fleet's *ad hoc* collection of 'one-shot' seaplane carriers, and was well suited to operating aircraft in small numbers over a prolonged period in daylight. In November 1918 she embarked Sopwith T.1 torpedo strike aircraft and worked up with them for an attack on the German fleet in its harbours. The contemporary view was that a faster launch rate could be achieved using a large number of small carriers, rather than a small number of large carriers. Given the state of the art in 1918 this was a reasonable assumption, but the Admiralty refused to order the eight mercantile conversions that were requested by the Grand Fleet and, at best, *Argus*, *Furious* and *Vindictive* would have been used for the strike, with as many aircraft as possible recovering to *Argus* and the remainder ditching close to the fleet's destroyers. In the event the Armistice came before the strike could take place.

Navigating over the sea was a specialist science requiring skill and practice. There was nothing on which a 'fix' could be taken, so aircraft 'took departure' from the carrier using the briefed latitude and longitude and flew accurate speeds and headings which allowed the observer to maintain a 'dead reckoning' plot of the aircraft's position. Accuracy was essential, both to enable 'mother' to be located at the end of the sortie and to ensure that the position of an enemy force located was transmitted as nearly as possible in the correct place for the fleet to intercept. Wind over the sea differed with height and time, so accurate observations were taken at regular intervals using smoke and flame floats and a specialised 'drift sight'.[15] Aircraft without observers were expected to operate largely within visual range of the fleet or to be led by an aircraft which did have an observer. Once the carrier was located, returning aircraft orbited overhead until it was seen to turn into wind. Once the captain gave permission for aircraft to land on, the 'affirmative' flag was run out on to a yard on a horizontal mast close to the position of Commander 'Air'[16] in Flyco and left displayed while the recovery was in progress. If aircraft of different types from different units were airborne, numeral flags could be run out to the yard to indicate whether fighters, reconnaissance, strike aircraft or all types were to land. If the recovery was to stop, the 'negative' flag was run out and the others struck.

A typical sortie entailed the aircraft being prepared in the hangar and ranged on deck fully fuelled and armed. The Grand Fleet plan for a torpedo strike on the German High Sea Fleet in its harbours in 1918 anticipated aircraft being launched in flights of five at a time,[17] and this may be taken as the maximum 'deck-load' range considered practical at the time. Subsequent flights of five would be prepared in the hangar as each range was launched, and a total air group of about twenty three[18] would have been possible. Aircraft were spread as they came on to the lift, and care had to be taken as the lift reached flight-deck level that the deck-handling party was ready for them in case they were caught by a gust. Once under control by the handling party they were pushed aft

and chocked. Pilots and observers were briefed about their sortie by the captain and senior aviation officer on the bridge, but ratings such as telegraphists or gunners went straight to the aircraft. Aircraft were lined up on the flight deck centreline and started by swinging their propellers, a process that did not always succeed at the first attempt. An engine might have to be turned over by swinging the propeller several times to clear Avgas that had flooded the cylinders before another attempt to start and, while this happened, the ship would remain steady into wind and the 'chock-man' lay alongside each wheel, holding the chocks in place. Aircraft had no brakes, and only the chocks prevented them from rolling forward once the engine was started. Then as now, the decision to launch rested with the captain, and when he gave his permission the senior aviation officer placed an 'affirmative' flag by his control bridge on the port side forward. His deputy would be on deck, near the range, and when each pilot indicated that he was ready he would order away the chock-men, allowing the aircraft to roll forward to reach take-off speed. The aircraft immediately behind would be buffeted by propeller wash, making their chock-men's job more difficult. They would be ordered clear in turn, and subsequent aircraft would roll forward one at a time. The ship would be free to manoeuvre once aircraft were clear of the deck, but would be constrained again when more were ranged.

Once airborne, fighters operated close to the fleet and might well stay in visual contact. Strike and reconnaissance aircraft operated further away, navigating with sufficient accuracy to find the ship at the end of their sortie, perhaps three hours after launch. The captain had a responsibility to place the carrier where the aircrew had been briefed that it would be for the recovery. This could be 60 nautical miles[19] from the launch position and was considered to be another reason for the carrier to stay close to the battle fleet as the major warships with their escorting cruisers and destroyers covered a large area of ocean, more easily intercepted by returning aircrew. Politically, the Royal Navy was not allowed to evaluate the use of carriers as a long-range strike force, as the Government had entrusted that capability to RAF bombers based ashore.

Pilots judged their own timing once the ship was ready to start the recovery, and flew a circuit at about 200 feet, turning on to final approach and descending slightly to be lined up with the deck, above its after end at a speed which was comfortably above the stall. Individual pilots formed their own techniques, but the ideal landing point was marked with a circle about 100 feet forward of the after end of the deck, and most landed near it. Ship speed and wind over the deck were variables that needed to be compensated for; high wind over the deck tended to make pilots go low with a more drawn-out approach, and low wind over the deck made them go high with an approach speed that was faster, relative to the deck. If an aircraft was seen to be 'stuck' in the retaining wires, those still airborne circled until the deck was clear. Once an aircraft stopped in the wires and was grasped by handlers, the pilot switched off the engine and the wires were prised clear to allow it to be manhandled, still spread, on to the lift. The wings were folded as it was struck down into the hangar. Only when the lift was back at flight-deck level could the next aircraft land on, a process that took up five minutes. Long recoveries meant that aircraft had to return with a considerable percentage of their fuel remaining in the tank. Pilots had to land accurately and consistently in the right place to pick up the retaining gear, and handlers had to move the aircraft on to the lift and off it quickly once it was folded.[20] When the recovery was complete, the deck was clear but the aircraft which had just landed were all at the forward end of the hangar and a 'shuffle' might be needed to range the armed and fuelled aircraft from behind them. Handling parties at the time comprised a mixture of RAF mechanics and RN seamen detailed to work on the flight deck from the ship's pool of men. Both groups changed frequently, were trained and paid differently and had different conditions of service, facts which were not conducive to standardisation of technique.

After the Armistice *Argus* joined the Atlantic Fleet and continued with a programme of trials, the only aircraft carrier in the world for the first four years of her life. Experiments with the retaining gear continued until October 1919, when the ship was accepted for operational service. She took part in the Fleet's Spring Cruise, which began in January 1920, with an air group embarked that comprised eight 1½ Strutters, four 2F.1 Camels, two D.H.9As and two Fairey floatplanes for operation in harbour. The exercise programme emphasised air operations with the fleet[21] and saw aircraft used to scout for enemy warships and to observe gunfire from the fleet flagship, HMS *Queen Elizabeth*. Aircraft W/T sets demonstrated a useful range of up to 50 miles but lacked power to overcome jamming or interference on their frequencies. In his Report of Proceeding, the C-in-C noted that more-powerful sets would help the fleet to obtain radio fixes on aircraft for their own safety if they ditched and to provide accurate fixes when they were in contact with the 'enemy'. Progress was made with deck landing as the ship operated in the open Atlantic Ocean for the first time. The flight deck was high above the water and amplified any ship motion. When she pitched, pilots tended to approach high for fear of hitting below the after-edge of the flight deck, and there were three instances in which aircraft were blown over the side before they engaged the retaining gear.[22] A conference was held on board on 13 May 1920, at which it was decided that aircraft should land directly into the retaining gear so that they would be held from the moment of touchdown. To facilitate this the well was extended to 300 feet in length, with a shallow ramp of 60 feet at either end. It was found possible to make it 16 inches deep. The forward ramp was powered so that it could be lowered flush with the deck to allow aircraft to take off over it or be manoeuvred on deck. The after ends of the wires were supported by an 18-inch slotted hurdle which was power-operated. Between the two suspension points, hinged flaps 15 inches high were placed at intervals of 50 feet to hold the wires clear of the deck. When knocked flat by an aircraft being retained, these had to be reset by hand. The after end of the flight deck was rounded down both to incorporate the after connections for the wires, which stretched over the curved surface, and to reduce the risk of damage to aircraft that came over the stern slightly below flight-deck height. Another new feature was installed in 1920. This comprised two power worked palisades, one on either side of the central portion of the flight deck, intended to prevent aircraft that did not engage the retaining wires from being blown over the side. These could be lowered flush with the deck or raised to a 45-degree angle.

Argus participated in the Atlantic Fleet's 1921 Spring Cruise with an air group of ten Parnall Panther spotter/reconnaissance aircraft and three Fairey IIIC seaplanes. The fleet commander, Admiral Sir Charles Madden, reported that the improved retaining gear had proved successful,[23] with thirty-one out of forty-five landings in bad weather being carried out successfully. Of the balance, only two incidents were serious and these were attributed to the inexperience of the pilots. Since deck operations had become a 'normal' process, attention concentrated on the tactical implications of carrier operations, and attempts were made to see how the time spent by the ship steaming into wind could be reduced. Landings were attempted without the ship being fully into wind, but it was found that wind on the bow created a considerable cliff-edge effect and blew aircraft across the retaining gear, causing damage to their undercarriages. In one instance a Panther's lee wing was forced under the wires as it drifted sideways, causing it to tip on to its nose. The ship had to be accurately steered into wind if aircraft were to land safely.

Argus proved to be successful in providing the localised air needs of the fleet, but it is important to see her operational use against a background of change. Before 1918 the RNAS had employed both ship- and shore-based aircraft, using whichever was most appropriate to achieve the operational aim. After the RNAS was subsumed into the RAF the new Service would not allow its shore-based aircraft to come under naval orders and sought to use aircraft in a form of 'substitution warfare'[24] under an Air Officer Commanding (AOC) who directed his own operations from ashore. Although jointly administered when disembarked, carrier-borne aircraft were under the tactical control of the fleet commander while they were at sea and, as the only aircraft he had, they had to provide all his airborne needs. Thus the existence of the RAF had a pernicious impact on naval warfare at the outset which took many years to correct. Future aircraft carrier development required the agreement of four bodies representing the operational and technical sides of the RAF in addition to their equivalent bodies in the RN. Since the RAF saw carrier-borne aircraft as a phenomenon that was secondary in importance to its own land-based operations, it had the effect of stalling development and 'freezing' deck operations to those used in the new *Argus*. She was a prototype, and demonstrated the drawbacks common to all new and complex systems. The carriers that followed her all benefited from *Argus*, and it is fair to say that she represented the baseline from which every subsequent carrier design and operational technique has evolved.

USS *Langley*

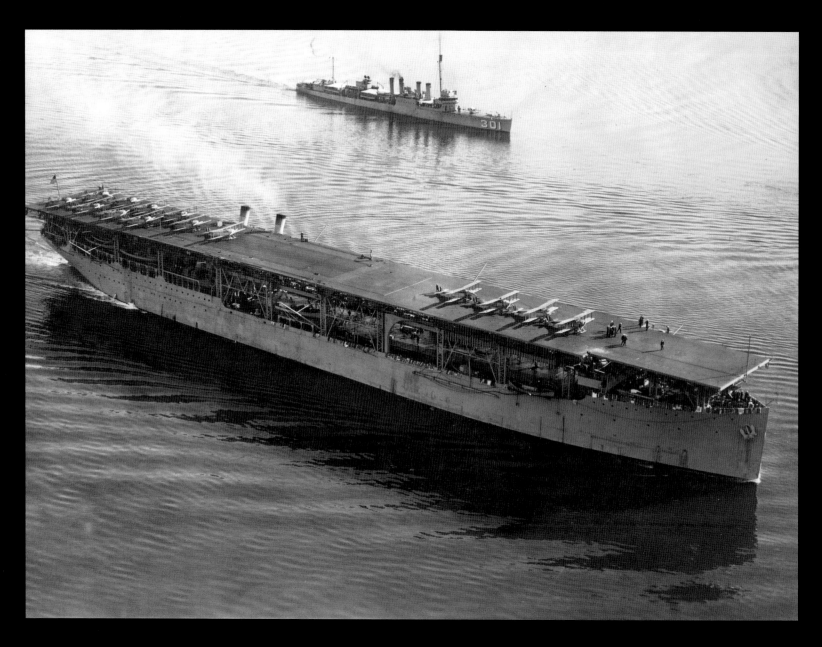

The USS *Langley* off San Diego in 1928 with her
expanded air group ranged on deck. The two funnels on
the port side aft are in the raised position, and would be
lowered to the horizontal during flight operations.
(US NAVAL HISTORICAL CENTER)

US Navy officers serving in Britain during the First World War took a close interest in the development of naval aviation. Their own Service lagged behind British development when America entered the war in 1917, and Royal Navy constructor Stanley Goodall[1] was lent to the USN Bureau of Construction and Repair. He took with him a number of warship plans, including those for the aircraft carriers *Eagle* and *Hermes*, which were in the early stages of construction. He was also able to summarise British operational doctrine and informed the General Board that:

> Air fighting has become a feature of naval operations and the tactical movements of a fleet before an engagement opens will, most probably, be governed by information obtained from air scouts. A series of fights between opposing aircraft will most likely be a preliminary to a fleet action. A fleet should, therefore, be attended by reconnaissance and fighting machines …

The General Board accepted this philosophy and, with the evidence of the large number of aircraft carriers being built or converted by the Royal Navy, pressed for the construction of large and capable ships in 1918.[2] Design work continued after the war's end, but Congress refused the necessary funds and only allowed the conversion of the collier USS *Jupiter*, originally completed in 1912, into an experimental aircraft carrier. Design work was completed in July 1919 and she entered Norfolk Navy Yard in March 1920, emerging on 22 March 1922 as the US Navy's first aircraft carrier, renamed USS *Langley*, CV 1. By then the British *Argus* was over three years old and *Eagle* had run trials with a starboard-side island structure.

Langley was an austere conversion, with a parallel-sided flight deck built on to a lattice-work structure over the former upper deck. The original bridge was retained under the deck with little modification. As a collier she had a large internal volume, divided into six holds. The foremost of these was modified for use as an Avgas storage tank, and the fourth contained machinery that drove the single lift in the upper half, immediately under the lift platform. A magazine for air weapons was installed beneath the machinery in the bottom half. The remaining four holds, two forward and two aft of the lift, were used to stow dismantled aircraft.[3] Funnel smoke was discharged through a short, single funnel on the port quarter, close to where the original, vertical smokestack had been sited. The new funnel folded aft during flying operations, but this arrangement never proved satisfactory and she was refitted with two funnels which hinged outboard to port in about the same position. The original superstructure was retained aft of the holds and provided accommodation for both officers and men and a large sick bay, known as a hospital in the USN. *Langley* had turbo-electric drive, giving her a maximum speed of 15 knots clean, more usually 14 knots some months out of dry dock. She could reverse the direction of drive of her two electric motors to develop full power astern, with the effect that, in theory, aircraft could land over the bow as well as over the stern, although the position of the retaining gear, aft of the lift, was not ideal for landing from forward to aft.

Langley had no hangar and the former upper deck was completely open at the sides. The flight deck had the appearance of a 'cover' over the ship, and led to her being nicknamed the 'covered wagon'. Rails were fitted centrally under the flight deck, and on these ran two three-ton travelling cranes, one forward of the lift and one aft. Each one had a swivelling section to allow the purchase to plumb the lift when it was in the down position[4] and to lift aircraft that were not central under the rails on the working deck or in the holds. Aircraft components were raised from the holds by the travelling cranes and placed on the working deck, where they were assembled and prepared for flight. When ready, they were taken to the flight deck on the single lift, which opened just forward of the centre of the flight deck. One other interesting feature of the conversion was the installation of a box-shaped pigeon loft on the former quarterdeck or fantail right aft.[5] Two masts to support W/T aerials and yards for flag hoists were fitted on the port side of the flight deck, from where they could be lowered to port during flying operations. Two conventional cranes were fitted, one either side amidships, to lift seaplanes from the working deck on to the water and back again when the ship operated at anchor.

Two parallel catapults were fitted in the flight deck forward. These were similar to those that had been fitted to the armoured cruisers; each was 94 feet long and capable of launching a 6,000lb aircraft at an end-speed of 55 knots. They were replaced by two AIII compressed-air types in 1925, but these were, in turn, removed without replacement in 1928. Fore-and-aft retaining wires, very similar to those fitted on *Argus*, were installed. *Langley*'s first take-offs and landings took place in October 1922, and in the months after that athwartship arrester wires were installed to arrest aircraft fitted with tailhooks. The 'criss-crossed' wires must have been extremely difficult to walk across, and doubtless hindered the manoeuvring of aircraft on the flight deck.

The unusual stowage arrangements below the flight deck significantly affected the way *Langley* operated her aircraft and, at first, a series of flying trials developed at a leisurely pace. Aircraft were hoisted on to the working deck and assembled by their fitters and riggers. The open sides allowed aircraft engines to be run-up, tested and warmed before the machines were taken on to the flight deck, where space was at a premium. When the lift platform was fully down it stood about six feet above the level of the working deck, and aircraft could not be placed on it except

by use of the overhead cranes. The process of getting aircraft on or off the lift could take as long as 12 minutes,[6] to which at least two more should be added for the lift to complete its journey up or down. Once on deck, aircraft were ranged aft and chocked while the ship turned into wind. No more than eight aircraft were embarked at first, taking off singly. The catapults were seldom used because they took time to load. On recovery, aircraft would fly back to the ship and orbit overhead until she turned into wind and the 'affirmative' flag was broken out on the horizontal mast to port. They flew left-hand circuits to land on a clear deck with a long final approach just above flight-deck level. Once the aircraft was safely retained it was pushed on to the lift, folded and struck down. The next aircraft could not land-on until the lift was back at flight-deck level. As in the Royal Navy, the need for a clear deck limited the radius of action to which aircraft could operate, since they would have to return with a considerable proportion of their fuel to wait for the aircraft ahead. The clear deck was similar to the technique used by the RN, but in British ships the aircraft could be pushed off the lift into the hangar, a process that took five minutes or less; considerably shorter than the time needed for the crane to clear the lift in CV 1. Until something could be done to speed this process *Langley* could not be

An Aeromarine 39-B lands on the USS *Langley*, CV 1, in 1922, shortly after her conversion. The ship is at anchor with little wind and a flat, calm sea. The aircraft is carrying out a flat approach and is landing well aft.

(US NAVAL HISTORICAL CENTER)

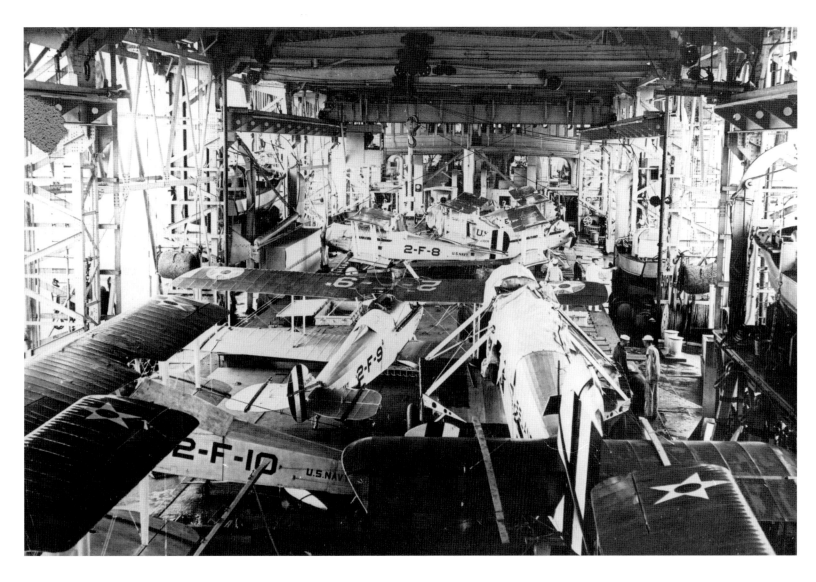

considered an effective carrier, although she joined the Battle Fleet in November 1924. In February 1925 she embarked VF-2, the first USN squadron trained to operate from a carrier, and in March she was the first carrier to take part in USN fleet exercises.

By then, Brigadier General 'Billy' Mitchell of the US Army Air Corps (USAAC) was promoting the concept of a unified air service like that in the UK. He made a series of public statements criticising the USN's ability to operate its own aircraft, and was eventually court-martialled after accusing both the Army and Navy of 'incompetency, criminal negligence and almost treasonable administration of the national defence', after which he ceased to be a factor. He failed in his objective, but did have the beneficial impact of obliging the USN to demonstrate before Congress that aircraft formed a vital part of its fighting

capability, and that the Service was capable of managing them. A Bureau of Aeronautics (BuAer) was formed in 1921 under Rear Admiral William Moffett, charged with 'all that relates to designing, building, fitting out and repairing naval and marine corps aircraft'.[7] The BuAer worked with the Naval War College and the operational fleet to evaluate the best use of carriers in a series of 'war games' through the 1920s that proved to be valuable in stimulating progress and tactics before sufficient ships and aircraft became available to evaluate them 'for real'. The critical year was 1925, during which President Coolidge set up a President's Aircraft Committee chaired by an eminent lawyer, Dwight D. Morrow, to advise on the best way forward. The 'Morrow Board' took extensive evidence, much of it the work of Moffett and his staff, and rejected calls for a unified

Dismantled and complete aircraft packed densely in the uss *Langley*'s open-sided working area below the flight deck during the 1920s, looking from aft to forward. Boats are stowed on both sides, and the height of the flight deck over the original upper deck, so that aircraft can be hoisted over others on deck, is interesting.
(US NAVAL HISTORICAL CENTER)

air service. Further, it recommended that only pilots should be given command of aircraft carriers and naval air stations. This encouraged many senior officers, some of them in their late forties or even early fifties, to become pilots or observers, among them the future Admiral 'Bull' Halsey. Aviation training for mature officers was necessary at the time because none of the Navy's early fliers was yet senior enough to command a carrier. Commander John H. Towers, Naval Pilot Number 3, for instance, would not become a captain for another ten years.

One of the most outstanding figures in the early development of naval aviation came out of the group trained as air observers in 1925. Captain Joseph Mason Reeves USN was 53 when he joined the Naval Aviation Observer's course at Naval Air Station (NAS) Pensacola in Florida. He had been selected by the Chief of Naval Operations (CNO), Admiral Edward W. Eberle, to be appointed first Commander Aircraft Squadrons Battle Fleet (ComAirBatFlt), and was well qualified for the post. He had served with Eberle with distinction as an engineering officer in the battleship *Oregon* during the Spanish American War, and subsequently specialised in gunnery. His forceful leadership produced record-breaking gun crews in the battleships *San Francisco*, *Wisconsin* and *New Hampshire*.[8] In 1925 there was considerable argument over the administration of aircrew officers' appointments between the new BuAer and the Bureau of Navigation (BuNav), which had, until then, been responsible for all officers' personnel matters. Reeves had served in BuNav and brought knowledge and careful consideration to the resolution of this important question. In early 1925 he was the Head of the Tactics Department at the Naval War College, and had a reputation as an innovative thinker who was keen to evaluate new ideas, including the use of both submarines and aircraft. To complete his credentials, *Jupiter* had been his first sea command, with orders to evaluate her then new turbo-electric drive.

Reeves completed the aviation observer's course on 3 September 1925 and was pronounced 'ready for duty involving actual flying in aircraft, including airships, balloons and airplanes'.[9] He was promoted commodore and assumed command of the Battle Fleet's aircraft squadrons and the USS *Langley*, based in San Diego, California, in late September 1925, at the height of the national debate about the future of military aviation. While Admiral Moffett could place extensive theoretical arguments about the importance placed on aviation by the navy, it was up to practical sailors to prove the case in the air over the sea. Reeves was the ideal man to do so, and understood the concept that to be effective at sea aircraft needed to be concentrated in significant numbers. He was surprised to learn on assuming command of *Langley* that she had never operated more than eight aircraft. If he was to provide air superiority over the battle fleet he needed to do better, but for the first few weeks of his command he observed operations and noted techniques. In November 1925 he called officers under his command to a meeting in the auditorium of their shore base at NAS North Island and laid down the principles on which naval aviation was to be developed. His audience, some of whom had considerable flying experience, were shocked when Reeves stated bluntly that they had demonstrated 'no conception of either the capabilities or limitations of the naval air force', and followed that blunt appraisal with a series of sharp questions. What were the most efficient methods of launching aircraft? How best to recover them and handle them on deck? What were the ideal tactics to be employed by the various types of aircraft employed on scouting, fighting, bombing and torpedo attack, and how would they affect flight-deck operations? What was the best that an air group embarked in *Langley* could deliver as part of the battle fleet? In adopting this approach Reeves broke new ground and, after voicing his list of questions, Reeves told his officers that he did not know the answers. To discover them, *Langley* and the fleet squadrons would have to become a 'school' that would learn its lessons on the flight deck and in the air.[10] His staff produced a booklet entitled *A Thousand and One Questions*, listing all of Reeves' original questions and others that occurred to them after his address. Not all of Reeves' officers agreed with him, and some believed that his ideas were downright dangerous. As results were achieved, however, they began to realise that they were 'writing the manual' of carrier warfare and

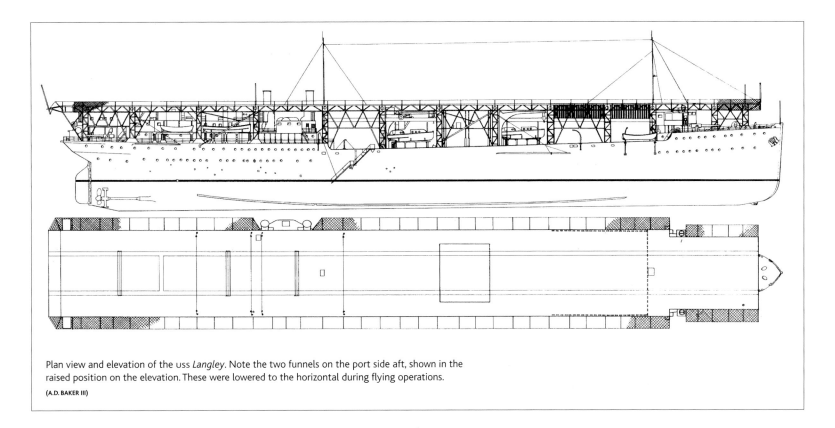

Plan view and elevation of the USS *Langley*. Note the two funnels on the port side aft, shown in the raised position on the elevation. These were lowered to the horizontal during flying operations.

(A.D. BAKER III)

literally inventing the tactics that the whole US Navy would use in future.

The Royal Navy had taken seven years to reach the point in 1918 where aircraft could operate with reasonable success from a carrier at sea with the fleet. On 'All Fools' Day', 1 April 1918,[11] it had been robbed of virtually all its aviation experts and, with the end of hostilities against Germany, embarked flying had become virtually trapped in the prototype stage. The open hostility of the new Air Ministry toward the tactical use of aircraft at sea placed a 'dead hand' of inertia over progress. In the United States the situation was very different, and men such as Moffett and Reeves were encouraged to demonstrate not just that aircraft could be flown off carriers, but that the whole spectrum of naval aviation could be absorbed into the fleet's tactics to stimulate a revolution in naval war-fighting. It was an exciting period, and when Reeves wrote the orders for the aviation aspects of the fleet exercises planned for January 1926 he increased the size of the air group from eight to fourteen aircraft. A number of senior pilots protested that this would be dangerous and could not be done, but Reeves proved them wrong.

On the first day at sea with the enlarged air group, *Langley* turned into wind and launched six fighters of VF-2, led by the unit's commanding officer, Lieutenant 'Spig' Wead USN, to intercept a theoretical bombing attack. Minutes later a further six fighters were launched to demonstrate that the carrier could get a tactically significant number of aircraft into the air quickly. Reeves drove his men to do better every day, and did more than just watch them. He frequently took charge of the flight deck himself with a stop-watch in one hand, standing on the ladder that connected the bridge to the flight deck. He oversaw the ranging of aircraft into a tightly-packed group, the forward end of which was dictated by the foremost aircraft's minimum requirement for a take-off run. He calculated the ship's heading and speed required to give the optimum wind over the deck, and ordered the watch-keeping deck officers to achieve it. The ship's air officer was placed ahead of the range and, on signals from Reeves, he ordered the aircraft to start engines and lashings to be removed. On a further signal from Reeves the air officer started the launch, with subsequent aircraft taxiing on to the centreline and rolling forward as the one ahead lifted clear. The operation of aircraft from a carrier is a problem of space and time, and Reeves was the first man to realise that making the maximum use of both would improve the weapons system. Ten years earlier Goodall had stated the British view that fleets should be 'attended' by aircraft-carrying ships. Reeves showed that aircraft were not an attendant force but an essential element of warfare, without which no navy could expect to operate effectively and his views were accepted by the USN's General Board.

By April 1926 the 'covered wagon' was regularly operating twenty aircraft from her flight deck, an achievement made possible by changes in equipment, concepts and technique. First to go was the retaining gear, which Reeves believed to be cumbersome, over-cautious and unnecessary as the weight of aircraft increased. Apart from making aircraft movement difficult, the wires had continued to damage aircraft that entered them with sideways drift, and after their removal the number of deck landing accidents decreased. On the other hand, the athwartship arrester wires, tried by the Royal Navy in 1917 but rejected, were found to be extremely effective. Once arrested, aircraft remained steady until the handlers had charge of them, fulfilling the purpose for which the retaining gear had been installed. Wire pull-out was constant for a given weight of aircraft, with the retarding force being provided, in the first models, by friction drums.

With the help of *Langley*'s executive officer, Commander Towers, Reeves reduced the tasks required of sailors on the flight deck into a number of specific functions. Groups of men were then trained to perform these tasks quickly and efficiently in response to hand signals, the noise on deck being too loud for verbal instructions to be comprehended. Tasks included the engineers who worked the wires, mechanics who maintained the aircraft, the 'hook-men' who pulled the hooks clear of the arrester wires after landings and the handlers who pushed aircraft quickly and accurately into their allotted positions on deck. In charge of all were the marshallers, who wore yellow shirts so that they could be seen easily by pilots and the command team. Coloured shirts were

introduced for other groups so that their work could be seen and comprehended at a glance. Coded colours included blue for the handlers, purple for the fuelling party, white for engineers, brown for aircraft mechanics and green for the hook-men. To improve efficiency still further, handlers were divided into numbered teams with the numbers painted conspicuously on their shirts so that the same men always worked together under the same petty officer. Handlers were absorbed into a specialised Aviation Branch, which gave their work stability and formalised training. The number one 'yellow-shirt' was the flight control officer, who had charge of the deck. Once recovery times were reduced, these officers were instrumental in speeding launches by using their marshallers to move aircraft out of the range and on to the centreline for him to take control. When each pilot was ready he saluted the control officer, who signalled each launch with a chequered flag dropped to the deck.[12]

The most radical of Reeves' innovations was the barrier. Good drill had reduced the time taken to strike aircraft down and get the lift back to flight-deck level for the next aircraft to land on, but it was still not acceptable. He noted that, owing to the cumbersome arrangement on the working deck, the only place for aircraft that were not airborne was on the flight deck, from where they could be launched quickly. He wanted a safe parking area, and achieved this by having a barrier of steel wire rope constructed, supported on either side of the deck by collapsible metal stanchions. When raised, this prevented aircraft that missed all the arrester wires from rolling forward into aircraft in the new deck park. In use it was manned by an operator in the port catwalk. As soon as he saw that the next aircraft to land had caught a wire he would drop the barrier, allowing the aircraft to taxi briskly forward into a tightly parked area on the forward part of the flight deck, known to the marshallers as 'Fly One'. As soon as the aircraft had passed over the barrier it was raised to allow the next aircraft to land on. With the introduction of the barrier and the new techniques it allowed, aircraft could back each other up much more closely, and the landing interval reduced from 3½ minutes to 90

A Boeing F-4B of VF 5B lands on the uss *Langley* in 1931. The arrester wires are in the raised position but the aircraft's hook is only inches below the housed position. It has probably hit the deck and bounced up, a common problem before hydraulic dampers were introduced to keep them in the 'down' position.
(AUTHOR'S COLLECTION)

seconds. This was still too slow for Reeves, who wanted that time halved. The improved operating times meant that *Langley* was able to increase the diversity and number of missions flown by her aircraft, transforming her into a carrier that could realistically be declared operational.

Langley sailed for a fleet concentration off Puget Sound, Washington, in August 1926 with thirty-four aircraft embarked,[13] including two new Curtiss F6C-2 Hawks fitted with arrester hooks for carrier trials. These single-seat fighters had a maximum weight of 3,170lb, 1,000lb greater than that of the Sopwith 1½ Strutter two-seat scout that had carried out the first landing on *Argus*. Commander Towers recorded that *Langley* was a 'perfect mass of men and aeroplanes', and that it was 'almost impossible to walk about the decks on account of the congestion'.[14] Flying started on 7 August 1926; by then, launch intervals averaged 15 seconds and landing intervals were still an unacceptable 90 seconds. On 9 August VF-1 set a record of 127 sorties in a single day,[15] a feat that meant most aircraft flying four sorties, and some of them more. No British carrier came near this record until the Second World War.

By 1929 improved aircraft design was able to make a contribution to improved deck operations. The aircraft embarked in *Langley* in 1926 had no brakes and tailskids rather than tailwheels. The skid had to be lifted into a steerable 'box on wheels' to enable the aircraft to be pushed and spotted on deck. The lack of brakes meant not only that aircraft had to be held, chocked or lashed down at all times when on deck, but also that they had a slow acceleration out of the range when a pilot opened his throttle to take off. The provision of brakes and a tailwheel that could be unlocked by the pilot to help him turn while taxiing made an enormous difference. Brakes meant that aircraft could run-up to full power before starting the take-off roll, decreasing the length of the take-off run and increasing the size of the range that could

An Aeromarine 39-B approaches the uss *Langley* during deck-landing practice in October 1922. The handling party in the starboard catwalk look on as the aircraft crosses the after end of the flight deck following a very flat final approach. The hooks intended to engage the retaining gear are visible on the axle between the aircraft's wheels. (US NAVAL HISTORICAL CENTER)

be launched from behind the minimum deck run. The tailwheel enabled pilots to manoeuvre accurately on deck under marshallers' control, making deck operations quicker. Bigger running ranges made the chock-men's task more dangerous. When the lashings were removed as the ship turned into wind they lay alongside the main wheels, one man to each wheel, holding chocks in place both in front of and behind the tyre. When the officer in charge of the deck gave

the signal to remove chocks they had to run clear in the shortest possible time, dragging their two chocks by their lanyards while avoiding other aircraft and their whirling propellers. A mistake could easily be fatal, but their reactions were another factor in the time taken to launch aircraft.

Another innovation in the late 1920s was the deck landing control officer or 'batsman'. At first every pilot had judged his own approach to land, flying a

The first aircraft taking off from a deck-load strike ranged on the uss *Lexington*, CV 2. At first uss *Lexington* and uss *Saratoga* were thought to be too big, but experience soon showed the importance of large air groups.
(AUTHOR'S COLLECTION)

standardised left-hand circuit to line up a few hundred feet aft of the deck, then closing the throttle just short of the deck to glide into the wires. This caused a spread of landing points that was greater than strictly necessary. By advising pilots of their position relative to an ideal approach path it became possible for every approach to be made as close as possible to the ideal, reducing the spread of landings and shaving seconds off the recovery interval. He also reduced the number of aircraft that went into the barrier after a badly judged approach. Batsmen wore a brightly coloured coverall and held brightly coloured bats at arms' length, and rapidly became 'icons' of carrier aviation. Their signals were advisory, raised bats like a 'V' signalling 'you are high'. An inverted V signalled 'you are low'. The responsibility to do something about it remained with the pilot in the cockpit, and it was a matter of discipline and pride to engage the target wire. Since they watched every recovery, batsmen were able to debrief pilots after particularly good or bad landings.

Reeves was promoted admiral and eventually commanded the US Fleet, the first 'air' admiral to do so. Although criticised by some of the early pilots as a 'Johnny-come-lately' because of his lack of actual flying time, Reeves achieved more than any other individual of his era in the development of flight-deck operating technique. He was fully aware of the importance of the capability he had created and demonstrated. In a letter to Admiral Moffett dated 4 October 1928, for instance, he admitted hiding *Langley*'s operational capability during a visit by Vice-Admiral Fuller of the Royal Navy.[16] 'Of course I did not tell Admiral Fuller that we operated not twenty-four but thirty-six aircraft and could operate forty-two and, possibly forty-eight airplanes from the *Langley*'. Fuller would have been 'conditioned' by the RAF view that only a handful of aircraft were needed in carriers, their operation posed almost insuperable difficulties and land-based aircraft would soon be able to perform their missions.

After *Langley* came the big conversions *Lexington* and *Saratoga*. Their hulls had become available when the Washington Treaty terminated their construction as battlecruisers. They had large, distinctive funnels

and starboard-side islands that had more in common with British carriers than *Langley*, but were built on an altogether larger scale. They did not complete until 1928 and benefited from all the experience gained to date, including arrester wires and barriers. Using Reeves' techniques they were capable of embarking in excess of 100 aircraft, but their completion had been delayed by his insistence that aircraft were to be refuelled and rearmed on the flight deck from a number of points, rather than in the hangar. The first big test of the new ships was Fleet Problem IX in January 1929, which took place off Panama. During this exercise Reeves commanded the fleet's air squadron from USS *Saratoga* and detached from the main force to launch a strike on the Panama Canal by a force of seventy aircraft from a range of 140 miles. Many of them used the new 'dive-bombing' technique to attack the locks, and caught the defenders completely unawares. This showed that carriers had the potential to act as the centrepiece of powerful mobile forces which Captain E.E. Wilson USN, Reeves' Chief of Staff, described as America's first 'strategic air force'.[17] Admiral Pratt the Commander-in-Chief of the US Fleet felt that the attack had not been sufficiently realistic to prove the capability of carrier air strikes, but believed that it boosted the aviators' morale and showed carriers to be credible operational (as opposed to 'attendant') warships. The weakness of aircraft carriers lay in the enormous quantities of Avgas and ammunition they carried in their lightly armoured hulls. War games continued to be carried out at the Naval War College, and the Class of 1930 noted that aircraft carriers 'combine great power with extreme vulnerability'.[18] Simulations continued to highlight this dichotomy into the 1930s, and showed time after time that the fleet with a carrier force that struck first invariably emerged the winner. This confirmed the view that aircraft were needed in large numbers to find and annihilate the enemy before he could strike, and this thinking was to colour USN tactics in the Pacific War.

Progress

A typical running range on HMS *Courageous* in 1933. About 20 aircraft, just under half the air group, was the most that she could range because of the small flight deck; far fewer than the big USN carriers. The handlers are a mixture of RN and RAF personnel, and the position adopted by the 'chock-men', with their backs to the wheel, is interesting. These aircraft had no brakes, and each aircraft needed wingtip handlers to help the pilot line up for take-off. The aircraft in the foreground is Hawker Nimrod S1624, which was allocated to 404 Flight and then 800 Naval Air Squadron in *Courageous* in 1932/33.

(AUTHOR'S COLLECTION)

The naval aviation pioneers who transferred to the RAF had a new focus after 1918 and soon lost touch with post-war naval developments. They were actually banned by the Air Ministry from maintaining direct contact with the Sea Lords on matters of policy or the evolution of air tactics. Thus the way forward had to be found through a series of formal inter-Service committees. Following the success of the first landing trials in *Argus* and, recently, in the incomplete *Eagle* to evaluate the 'island' concept, a naval staff meeting was held on 23 July 1920 to plan the way forward.[1] The Chairman was the Assistant Chief of the Naval Staff (ACNS), Rear Admiral Chatfield,[2] and other attendees included Captain F.C. Dreyer RN, Director of the Gunnery Department, Sir Eustace Tennyson d'Eyncourt, Director of Naval Construction (DNC), and J.H. Narbeth, the carrier expert within that department. There were two representatives from the Air Ministry, Air Commodore Vyvyan RAF, formerly Director of Air Services in the Admiralty, and another former RNAS senior officer, Air Commodore J.M. Steele RAF, now the Director of Air Operations and Intelligence.

On the basis of the flying trials in *Eagle*,[3] the Committee decided that six was the largest number of aircraft that could be launched from or recovered to a carrier in a single evolution. This number was accepted as the optimum size for each embarked flight, a number of flights embarking to constitute air groups, which varied in size depending on the parent carrier. The Committee also decided that three carriers were needed for operation with the Atlantic Fleet, with a further two for deployment to overseas stations and to maintain numbers at home while ships were in refit. This meeting had significant consequences, as it ensured Air Ministry support for the completion of further carriers and motivated British demands for the total carrier tonnage put forward at the Washington Naval Conference. In 1921 the Admiralty set up a permanent committee to co-ordinate the work of constructors, engineers and aviators, known as the Joint Technical Committee (JTC). The first Chairman was J.H. Narbeth and the Secretary was W.A.D. Forbes, another carrier specialist within DNC.

Two advisory bodies were set up by the Air Ministry during the 1920s, the Advisory Committee on Fleet Air Arm Aircraft, and its Technical Sub-Committee. Most of the members were drawn from the RAF and Air Ministry, and these provided technical knowledge and direction, but there was RN representation, usually by junior officers with little staff experience. A comparison of these committees' views with contemporary work in the USA reveals their main defect as a failure to take a broad view of requirements.[4] For example, they often sought to put forward an existing RAF aircraft type to meet a naval requirement, but viewed any necessary modifications as 'a detraction and hindrance to normal aircraft development'. In other words their aim was to design an 'ideal' aircraft and then modify it to fly from a carrier. The USN was able to focus singlemindedly on the need for practical design, and procured aircraft that were intended from the outset for shipborne use. Aircraft that failed to operate efficiently from the deck were regarded as deficient and unworthy of production. The Air Ministry's failure to comprehend the Admiralty's needs is shown starkly in a contemporary analysis of design which stated: 'Whatever their function, naval aircraft were expected to satisfy certain special requirements which the Admiralty regarded as essential for naval purposes, but which often ran counter to the dictates of good design. To begin with, all carrier-borne aircraft had to be adjusted to the naval architecture of aircraft carriers'.[5] The Air Ministry belief that naval aircraft fulfilled a secondary purpose which could be met by superimposing naval features and equipment on aircraft designed for very different land-based functions was not a recipe for success. The secondary effect of this attitude was to give aircraft manufacturers the impression that the development of naval aircraft was difficult and of little value, contrasting strongly with the strong relationships developed between navies and industry in the USA and Japan.

Air Ministry opposition impacted on the number of aircraft that could be embarked as well as their design quality, and revealed little interest in flight-deck developments that could significantly improve

Hawker Nimrod S1624 of 800 Squadron, coded 510, takes off from HMS *Courageous*.
(AUTHOR'S COLLECTION)

HMS *Furious* serving with the Home Fleet in 1926/27. She still has fore-and-aft retaining gear fitted, but the four sets of boards are flat, leaving the wires flush with the deck for aircraft moves and take-off. Note the after anchor point for the wires just forward of the after lift under the raised section of deck. Two Blackburn Blackburns are being ranged. One is still on the forward lift, and wind breaks are raised to protect it. 'Flyco', the flying control position, is by the white 'T' at the port forward part of the upper flight deck. The horizontal masts near it were used for flag-hoists to indicate landing priorities. There is considerable staining on the flight deck aft from the vents used to 'smoke-up', and the ship's side is painted black to mask the staining from 'smoking-down'.
(AUTHOR'S COLLECTION)

Looking back at HMS *Furious* after take-off. The parallel lines painted on the deck were to help pilots line up for take-off and landing; the circle just visible under the range of aircraft showed the ideal landing point. The horizontal mast by 'Flyco' has a single flag hoisted to indicate take-off in progress. Palisades are in the raised position and there is a mixture of RN and RAF officers in 'Flyco', all with their caps on despite the wind over the deck.
(AUTHOR'S COLLECTION)

Hawker Nimrods of 800 Squadron land on HMS *Courageous*. Only one arrester wire is rigged, and the first aircraft has already begun to overshoot; it is already high over the landing circle and the single wire. There is a lack of urgency among most of the handling party, but the second aircraft is still 'in the groove' to land-on. Note the waterproof oilskin coats hung in the palisades and the 'plane-guard' destroyer just visible aft.

(AUTHOR'S COLLECTION)

the ability of aircraft carriers to operate larger and more effective air groups. Admiralty requirements for aircraft were frequently questioned on the ground of cost, which was paid from the Naval Vote, despite the aircraft being administered by the Air Ministry. 'Technical difficulties' were used as a barrier when the Admiralty asked for aircraft to operate from the new carriers *Courageous* and *Glorious*, the Air Ministry stating that the number requested 'could not be efficiently operated' from the two ships,[6] and forcing the Admiralty to offer 'proof' that they could. Worse, during preparations for a disarmament conference in 1930 the Air Ministry proposed that the number of aircraft embarked in carriers should be cut by half, with the balance provided from the general resources of the RAF 'if thought to be operationally necessary'.[7] A proposed exchange of Naval Air Squadrons with RAF units to demonstrate the practicability of embarking RAF units was eventually cancelled, and the Air Ministry was forced to admit that such a scheme, driven by an unreasoning belief in the

'ubiquity' of air power, was utterly impractical.

It has been said, mistakenly, that the Royal Navy lost its way with regard to aviation after the amputation of its air service in 1918, and that the Sea Lords were, somehow, averse to the development of aircraft carriers. Facts show the exact opposite, and by 1925 the Royal Navy had four carriers in commission,[8] the US Navy only one and the Imperial Japanese Navy (IJN) one. Whereas the USN relied on wargaming ashore, the RN was able to use sea trials to expand its understanding of what embarked aircraft could achieve using aircraft in realistic conditions. In the 1920 trials, for instance, aircraft of the specially commissioned '*Eagle* Flight' carried out 143 deck landings[9] on the partly completed carrier with only twelve minor accidents. The latter part of the trial sought and found bad weather in the Pentland Firth and proved that aircraft could continue to operate in adverse weather conditions. Some of the types flown were 'land' types such as the Bristol Fighter or D.H.9A, which proved unsuitable and underlined the need for specialised aircraft. By 1925 the fleet required a total of 150 carrier and shipborne aircraft, and the requirement for ships, aircraft and the training of naval aircrew had to be accepted by the Air Ministry following the Trenchard/Keyes Agreement of 1924.[10]

The Royal, United States and Imperial Japanese Navies studied the impact of aircraft on war at sea, but their different experience led them along divergent paths to solutions. All appreciated that the only ship-killing weapon yet evolved for aircraft was the locomotive torpedo, and that the heavy aircraft needed to carry them lacked the performance to evade the anti-aircraft fire they were likely to encounter. Thus an attack on a battle fleet by torpedo-carrying aircraft would either need to be on such a large scale that it could absorb heavy casualties in order to inflict the number of hits required to achieve success or, if numbers were not an option, some form of stealth would be needed to achieve hits without crippling losses. With two large-deck carriers under construction, the USN War College looked towards attack on a large scale and the aircrew themselves evolved dive-bombing as an alternative, less vulnerable but accurate method of hitting and damaging ships, although in 1930 aircraft that could dive steeply were incapable of carrying bombs large enough to sink armoured warships. With torpedo strike forces limited to a six-aircraft flight in each carrier, the RN evaluated stealth tactics. HMS *Furious* emerged from her conversion to a flush-decked design in 1925 as the largest carrier in the Royal Navy. She was chosen to carry out the first experimental night landings in 1926.

Night flying training for aircrew was carried out at the RAF airfield at Gosport, near Portsmouth in Hampshire. The JTC had designed and installed a comprehensive system of lighting around *Furious*'s flight deck that was intended to give pilots visual cues similar to those used for a 'normal' day landing. It comprised twenty concave 'posterlites'[11] down each

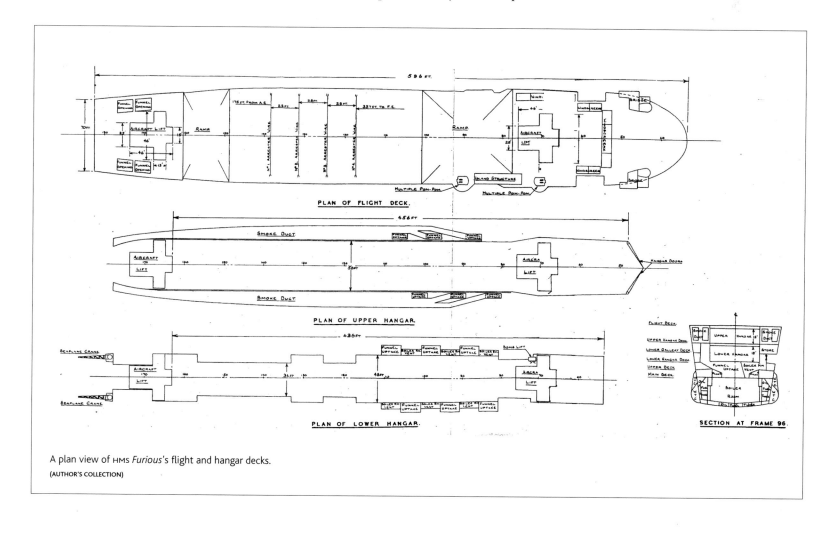

A plan view of HMS *Furious*'s flight and hangar decks.
(AUTHOR'S COLLECTION)

side of the flight deck, spaced six yards apart and standing two feet above the deck edge. The height above the deck allowed the light to be angled slightly downwards so that the source of light could not be seen at any great distance by other ships, but was not so great that the wingtips of aircraft near the deck edge were at risk. These threw a 'wash' of soft white light over the deck and the exact edges of the deck were indicated by fifty-eight amber lights spaced closely around the round-down aft and a further eighty-four fixed around the forward edge of the flight deck. None of the lights was fitted with a dimmer at first and trial reports called for this defect to be remedied. The ship's own torpedo unit, 462 Flight, was ordered to carry out the trial, and the pilots were the Flight Commander, Flight Lieutenant Boyce AFC RAF and Squadron Leader Howe RAF from the Torpedo Trials Unit at Gosport. The Blackburn Dart had no 'blind-flying' instruments and pilots relied on the night being clear with a visible horizon. On 5 May 1926 HMS *Furious* was anchored at Spithead, the sheltered water between Portsmouth and the Isle of Wight, and the two pilots flew over her to get accustomed to the flight-deck lighting.

Fortuitously she lay with her bows pointed into a light westerly breeze, and Squadron Leader Howe felt so confident after several low passes that he flew a circuit and rolled his wheels on the deck before selecting full power to fly back to Gosport. The Dart had a Napier Lion engine, with its power output controlled by a conventional throttle. It was thus much easier to handle than the Sopwith Pup that had carried out the previous 'notable' landing on *Furious* nine years earlier.

On the next night, 6 May, the ship was under way to the south of the Isle of Wight and the two pilots joined her for a series of 'full-stop' landings.[12] Neither aircraft was fitted with wireless, and they relied on finding the ship in her briefed position, identifying her by the unique deck lighting. A green light gave permission to land once she was steady on the flying course. The first to land-on was Flight Lieutenant Boyce in Blackburn Dart N9804, achieving the world's first night deck landing.[13] The aircraft weighed approximately 4,200lb and came to rest in 170 feet. It was designed to carry a torpedo on the fuselage centreline and thus had no axle on which to fit hooks. It made no use, therefore, of the retaining gear and,

A Grumman F3F–3 of VF 5 catches a wire on the USS *Yorktown* in December 1938. This was the last biplane fighter to be procured for the USN.
(AUTHOR'S COLLECTION)

with no brakes, it relied on friction and the headwind to roll to a stop. Once safely on deck it was pushed aft and the wheels were chocked until Boyce ran-up to full power and gave the signal that he was ready to take off. After the first landing Boyce and Howe carried out alternate landings until both were happy that they had worked out a satisfactory night landing technique.

Night deck landings tend to concentrate the mind more than those by day as there are fewer visual cues. It is essential, therefore, to follow careful procedures that keep pilots in a well practised 'groove' which differs little in principle today from the circuits flown by Boyce and Howe in 1926. The Dart was fitted with navigation lights visible externally to a distance of several miles; red to port, green to starboard and white aft. As with ships' navigation lights, the red and green were visible from dead ahead to 'two points' (22½ degrees) abaft each beam, and the white was visible in the remaining arc through the stern. Such

cockpit instruments as the aircraft had were illuminated by small torch lights fitted on either side of the instrument panel and adjustable so that individual pilots could set them up exactly as they wanted. It was essential that these were dimmable so that the minimum amount of light necessary was used. If not, it was difficult for the pilot to adjust his night vision to objects outside the aircraft. As pilots' eyes grow accustomed to the dark outside, most find that they continually turn down the brightness of cockpit lighting to keep it at an acceptable level.

Circuits at night were flown using both instruments and outside visual cues. Once the pilot lined up on deck with the engine giving full power, he signalled the FDO either with his navigation lights or a torch and was cleared to take off. As the aircraft rolled forward he looked outside at the deck to check acceleration and line-up. This was not easy in *Furious*, without an island to give depth perception, but the horizon on a clear night helped. As the aircraft passed

A DLCO in action on HMS *Unicorn*. He is holding his bats level, showing that the approaching aircraft is lined up straight and on the ideal glideslope. Note the 'affirmative' signal on the plate just above the 'pom-pom' mounting on the deck aft of the island.

(AUTHOR'S COLLECTION)

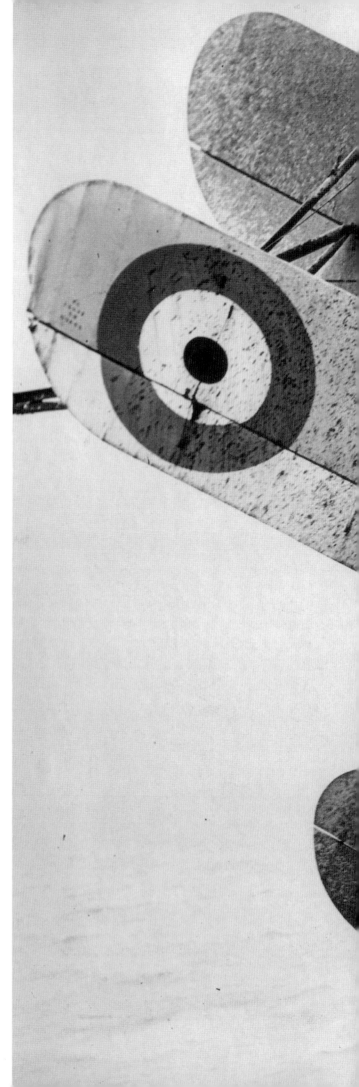

A Fairey Flycatcher hangs precariously over the side of HMS *Furious*. The propeller is broken and oil from the shock-loaded engine has sprayed all over the wings and fuselage. Note the men working to recover it in the catwalk above.

(AUTHOR'S COLLECTION)

the amber lights at the forward end of the flight deck the pilot looked inside the cockpit, holding the aircraft in a climbing attitude with a positive rate of climb on the altimeter, climbing straight ahead to the briefed circuit height of 400 feet. As it was reached he throttled back, levelled off and settled at circuit speed. When happy that the aircraft was stable, he looked out at the horizon and turned to port through 180 degrees on to the downwind leg, aiming to see the floodlit line of the flight deck in line with the port lower wingtip. If the wingtip appeared to cover the deck he was too close; if significantly short of it he was too far out. In either case heading was adjusted to make the final turn from the right place. Once the wingtip passed astern of the deck, power was reduced to make a descending turn to port. Eyes were out of the cockpit at this stage, looking at the deck to judge height and rate of turn, with occasional glances in to check airspeed. The deck appeared as a white rectangle and would give the pilot vital clues known as a deck 'picture'. As he completed the final turn the deck stretched away in front of him and the correct line-up would be relatively easy to judge. If the view over the nose showed a lot of runway, tending towards a 'plan view', the aircraft was too high. If it showed less, tending towards a thin line of light, the aircraft was too low. In the latter case throttle was used to adjust height and the elevators to select and maintain a suitable speed. In the former it was better to go round for another circuit as, with the throttle already closed, speed would rise if the pilot sought to descend too steeply to the ideal glide path. With good judgement and experience the throttle could be set closed at the end of the downwind leg and not adjusted again as the aircraft was flown neatly around the finals turn to an ideal landing spot about one third of the way forward of the after round-down. The deck appeared small and distant at first but, in the final stages of the approach, it seemed to get rapidly bigger as the wheels thumped on to the deck. As the aircraft rolled to a standstill the pilot kept his eyes out, aiming to keep the aircraft straight on the centreline and looking for the handlers as they grabbed the wingtips. Once parked aft, engine pressures, temperatures and the fuel state could be

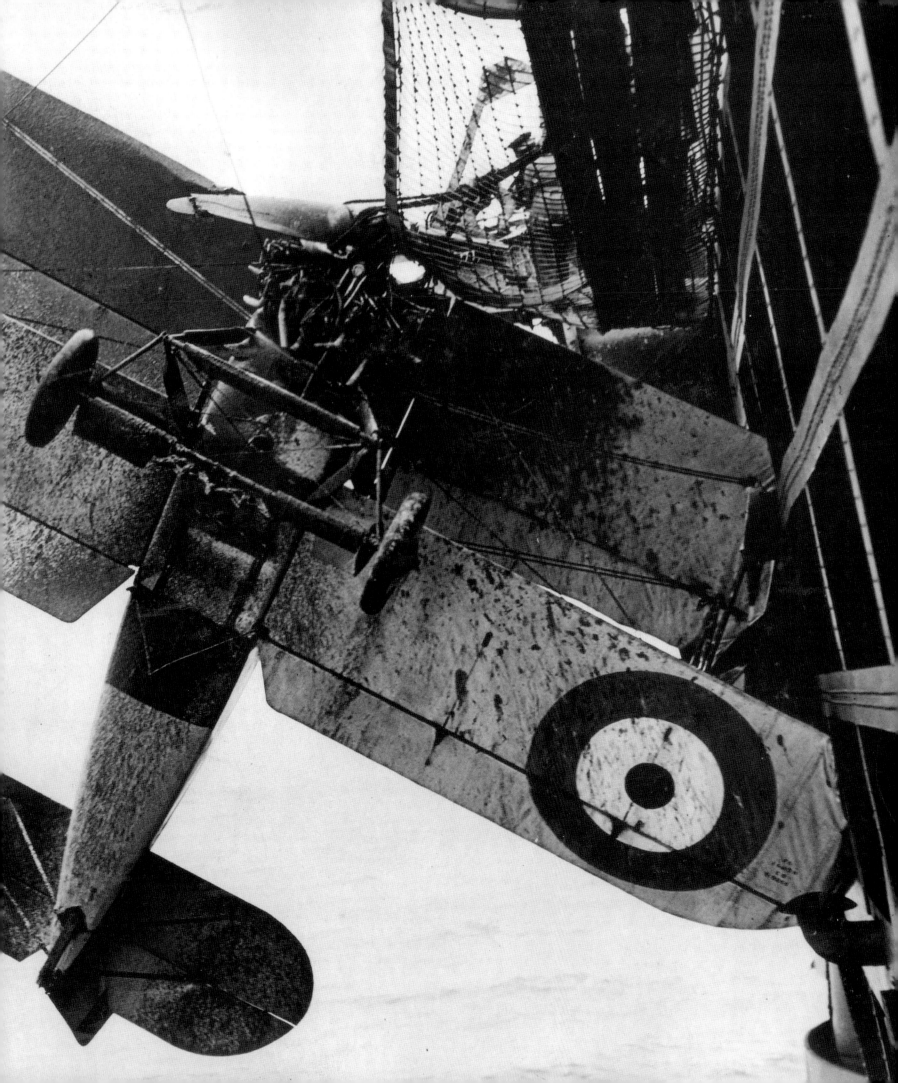

A single Hawker Osprey takes off from HMS *Eagle*. As no aircraft are taking off after it, the after chocks remained in place where it rolled forward from them. The mixture of RN and RAF personnel on deck is typical of the 1930s.

(AUTHOR'S COLLECTION)

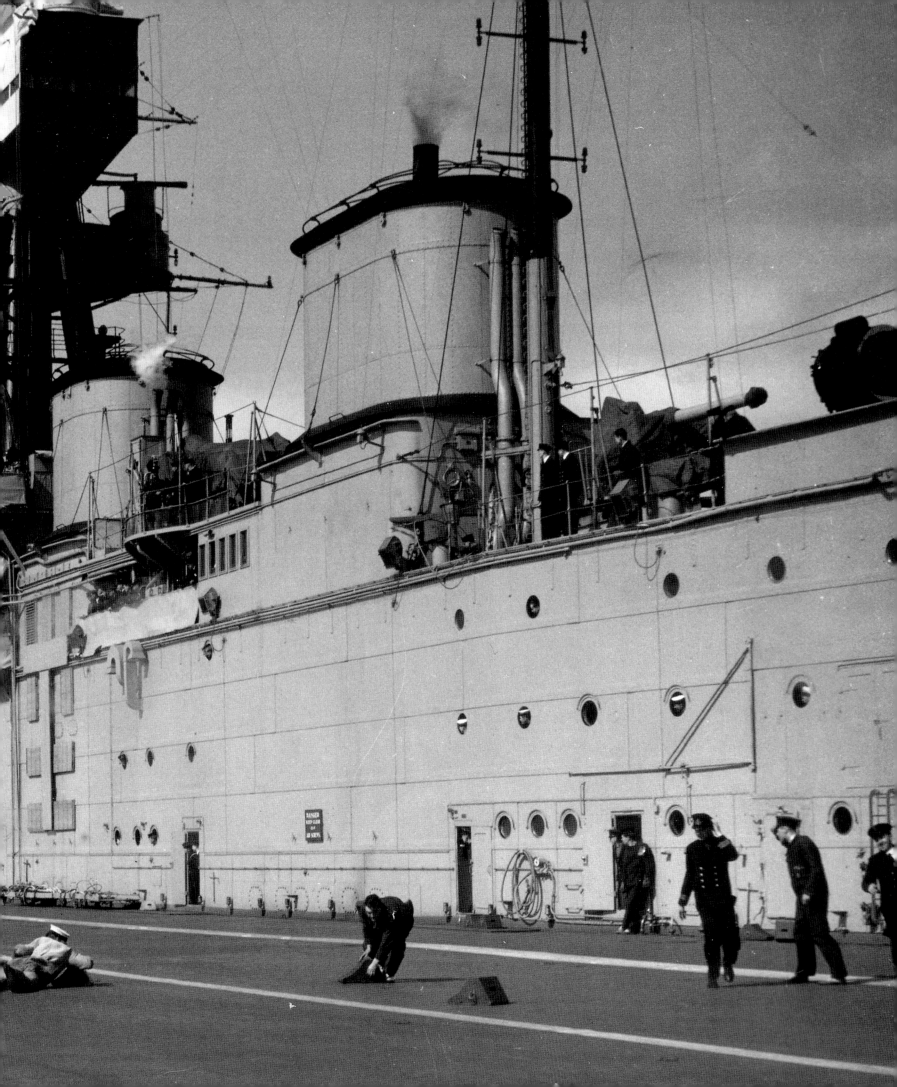

checked and the whole process repeated. Night deck landing proved to be a practical proposition, and 462 Flight carried out a series of night operations from *Furious* in Scottish waters during July 1926. From then onwards RN torpedo aircraft specialised in night strike operations both to minimise potential casualties and as part of a wider ambition to make the battle fleet capable of night warfare after the lessons of Jutland were assimilated.

The RN continued to think of aircraft as fragile machines that needed protection against the elements when not flying, and so, unlike the USN, regarded the number of aircraft that could be fitted into the hangar as the yardstick that determined the number of aircraft a ship could operate. After its experience with *Langley* the USN regarded the number that could be operated from the deck as the key factor, and hangars were used mainly for maintenance and repair. The rebuilt *Furious* was stripped to her original upper deck and fitted with two hangars, one above the other, alongside which ducts carried funnel smoke to the stern, restricting hangar width and making the ship's internal spaces uncomfortably hot aft. At flying stations funnel smoke was discharged from vents on the ship's side just forward of the quarterdeck, a process known as 'smoking down'. When there was no flying it was exhausted through grilles at the after end of the flight deck, known as 'smoking up'. Soot from both stained the grey ship's side, and for most of her life, the aftermost 100 feet of the ship up to flight-deck level was painted black. The main flight deck was 576 feet long, formed the roof of the upper hangar and was the upper strength deck. Doors at the forward end of the upper hangar opened on to a lower flight deck 200 feet long which sloped down towards the bow, reminiscent of the take-off decks in *Campania* and her own first incarnation. It was intended to allow fighters to get into the air quickly from the upper hangar to defend the fleet if the main deck had aircraft parked on it or a recovery in progress. While it worked with early lightweight fighters such as the Fairey Flycatcher, the lower deck was not a practical success and was seldom used. The blast effect of the open hangar doors as the ship turned into wind, despite the presence of a retractable

wind break on the deck, would have been unpopular and had the potential to cause significant damage to anything parked or stored in the upper hangar. *Furious*'s two near-sisters *Courageous* and *Glorious* were converted into aircraft carriers from 1925 and 1927 respectively when funds became available. Both were generally similar to *Furious* but had a small island which incorporated a funnel. Without the unsuccessful smoke ducts fitted in the latter, both had somewhat wider hangars which allowed 48, rather than 33, aircraft to be stowed in them.

The development of aircraft brakes in 1927 enabled significant improvements in deck operation. Aircraft with brakes could use them to stop in a shorter distance after landing and, as important, gave the pilot better control over his aircraft, allowing him to taxi to a specific point and hold the aircraft with engine running without chocks or lashings. Just before take-off the pilot could run the engine up to full power against the brakes before releasing them to start rolling forward. Previously, a certain amount of momentum had been lost because the aircraft rolled forward when the chocks were removed before achieving full power. In effect the brakes performed a function similar to the hold-back used on the cruiser and battleship take-off platforms. Aircraft with brakes could be parked in a denser range aft, moving forward and stopping on the centreline for seconds before starting the take-off roll. Instead of being ranged in a straight line along the centreline, aircraft could now be 'herring-boned' in groups of three, effectively tripling the number of aircraft that could be ranged in a given area of deck. Even more could

HM Ships *Furious*, *Courageous* and *Eagle* demonstrate the Royal Navy's multiple-carrier operational capability during a fleet exercise in the Mediterranean in the 1930s. (AUTHOR'S COLLECTION)

A Blackburn Ripon runs-up against the chocks on a wet flight deck in 1930. The rivets stand out clearly on the unpainted deck.

(AUTHOR'S COLLECTION)

be ranged in line abreast if they were tightly packed with wings folded. On taxiing on to the centreline they could be spread, locked and checked by handling parties in seconds before the pilot was given the order to take off. The forward end of the range was dictated by the minimum deck run needed by the first aircraft to get safely airborne. By 1930 the narrow after deck design of the prototype carriers, intended to create an optimal airflow, was proving to be a limitation on the size of strike that British carriers could fly-off in a single range which, in turn, began to limit the Fleet Air Arm's fighting capability. The greater control on deck that aircraft brakes gave pilots led to the removal of the unpopular retaining gear from all British carriers from 1927 onwards. The 'humps' at either end of the 'well' were retained because their removal would have been complicated and expensive and it was felt that they helped smooth the airflow. For some years aircraft landed on to bare decks with no form of retaining or arresting gear, although the palisades were retained alongside the landing area.

A report on the progress in deck landing achieved in the USS *Langley* was received in the Admiralty from the Air Attaché in Washington dated 1 March 1927.[14] It stated that while the ship had been fitted with longitudinal wires similar to those used by the British to retain the aircraft, she was now using cross-deck wires attached to friction devices instead, which were engaged by aircraft tailhooks lowered by a control in the pilot's cockpit. When the hook was dropped, an elastic stay held it down and prevented 'hook bounce' when the bill impacted the deck, making it more likely that it would pick up a wire. The report noted that the system appeared to be most effective in use. News of USN progress stimulated considerable interest within the Admiralty, and a 1929 Paper from the Intelligence Department[15] gave more information, including the details that arresting wires had been evaluated ashore at NAS Lakehurst, New Jersey, in *Langley* and in the new *Saratoga*. It noted that since January 1929 over 2,000 arrested landings had been carried out in the latter with a marked reduction in the landing interval and a most positive reaction from the commanding officer. The Naval Air Division

A Fairey IIIF of 824 Squadron over HMS *Eagle*, which is painted in the China Station colour scheme with a white hull and buff island. The athwartships white line aft of the after lift marked the limit of the usable deck for ranging aircraft or landing-on. The short white line forward of the after lift marks the centreline of the lift and deck, and was used as a reference mark for manoeuvring aircraft. The longer lines were references for pilots on landing. *Eagle* had no arrester wires at this time; they were fitted in 1936.

(AUTHOR'S COLLECTION)

(NAD) pointed out[16] that athwartship, or transverse, arrester wires, using sandbags at either end of the ropes to give retardation, had been tried at the Isle of Grain and in *Furious* in 1918 but rejected as being too cumbersome to reset after each landing. The British had failed to grasp the fact that, while the lightweight aircraft used for the early trials needed no retardation, their heavier successors were likely to. The officers who carried out the *Furious* trials had failed to notice that transverse arrester wires effectively held an aircraft in position until handlers took hold of it and released the hook, thus they could usefully fulfil the role of retaining aircraft after landing. It was, perhaps, unfortunate that transverse wires had only been tried at sea in conjunction with fore-and-aft wires, and that too much importance had been ascribed to the latter. The USN had seen the latent potential of transverse arrester wires on *Langley* and solved the resetting problem by using mechanical retardation rather than dead weights. The American system offered such clear evidence of improvement that NAD sought proposals from DNC and the Engineer-in-Chief for a practical British system of arresting wires.

The subject was placed on the agenda for the sixty-sixth meeting of the JTC, which took place on 29 November 1929. DNAD stated his belief that a British arresting gear should be designed and evaluated so that it could be fitted quickly to aircraft carriers. The recently removed retaining gear came in for considerable criticism owing to the delay it caused in flight-deck operation and the 'extensive damage' it caused to aircraft. It was also noted that the French carrier *Bearn*, which had been designed with British assistance, was operating successfully with a system of transverse arrester wires and sandbags identical to that tried and rejected in *Furious*. After general agreement that a system of transverse wires was worth evaluating, the meeting failed to agree on the detail of how best to do so. The Admiralty view was that initial trials would be best carried out ashore in a facility like the former RNAS Isle of Grain and the USN flight deck trials unit at NAS Lakehurst. The Air Ministry view was that trials ashore would incur 'much delay and expense waiting for suitable winds in the

absence of a revolving deck'. The meeting came to no immediate conclusion and recommended that the question be deferred for further consideration, but DNC did take positive action and state that, given data about carrierborne aircraft by the Air Ministry, design proposals would be raised. On 18 February 1930 the Department wrote to the firm of Clarke Chapman, requesting it to design a new type of arresting gear using transverse wires wound on to brake drums, and suggested that 'electrical force' be used to provide retardation. The request[17] explained that the initial force acting on the aircraft tailhook 'should not be excessive as inertia shocks on the aircraft must be avoided. The braking force should rise to a maximum and continue more or less constant'. Wires were to be 30 to 40 feet apart, with a pull out of 'about 200 feet', and capable of arresting aircraft between 3,000lb and 9,000lb weight at landing speeds, relative to the deck, of between 25 and 70 knots. The higher figures show that DNC was intending that the gear would remain useful into the foreseeable future. Resetting the wires for further landings was to be achieved by hand or by electric motors, and for trial purposes it was proposed to lead both ends of some wires to a single brake drum and others to independent winches so as to check 'which system is better for "off-centre" landings and landings at an angle to the fore and aft line of the ship'. Once designed by Clarke Chapman the gear was to be manufactured by Portsmouth Dockyard, and the Admiralty still hoped to carry out trials in an airfield ashore but, since 1918, had none under its own control.

Once the design drawings were received in the Dockyard's Construction Department, DNC tasked it to carry out experiments 'to determine the lightest possible weight of the moving parts', and as a consequence the production components were considerably lighter than those proposed in the design. In a letter to DNC dated 26 July 1930 Mr Forbes, manager of the Construction Department at Portsmouth Dockyard, noted that the Air Ministry still objected to trials ashore but the Admiralty insisted that they were necessary. The impasse was discussed at length during the sixty-ninth meeting of the JTC on 31 July 1930, and subsequently the Royal Aircraft Establishment (RAE) wrote to DNC, stating that it had been instructed by the Air Ministry to carry out shore tests of the arresting gear at its establishment at Farnborough in Hampshire. The argument over where and when shore trials were to be conducted have been explained in some detail, as it illustrates the Admiralty's frustration at not having direct control of its own aviation development.

Installation of the prototype arresting gear at an airfield ashore could not have been very difficult, because trials started at RAE Farnborough on 16 September 1930 using a Fairey IIIF reconnaissance aircraft with a landing weight of 6,000lb. To start with, the aircraft taxied into the gear at increasing speeds, and some difficulty was encountered with hook bounce, which caused it to miss the wire. When it did engage there was considerable 'tail slam' at first as the aircraft came to a stop, but by controlling the drum brakes at the end of the run this was eventually eliminated. The fitting of a single wire to two separate winches was not found to be an ideal solution, as the two did not completely synchronise. After a number of small adjustments, further trials were carried out on 25 and 26 September. These proved successful and demonstrated a pull-out of 117 feet at landing speeds up to 45 knots with a deceleration of 0.8g, comfortably inside the maximum of 1.0g set by the Air Ministry. Tests at speeds higher than 45 knots could not be demonstrated because the aircraft took off before engaging the wire. Following the success of these trials, DNC took action on 6 October 1930[18] to order a winch-type arresting gear to be fitted in HMS *Courageous*. Patents for winch-type arresting gear were applied for in the name of the Director, Sir Arthur Johns, and Mr Forbes.[19]

In April 1931 the initial sea trials in *Courageous* were given unfavourable reports and the Commanding Officer considered the equipment unsuitable for ship use. After some correspondence on the subject DNC took the view that the ship's officers did not realise the potential importance of satisfactory arresting gear,[20] and further trials were necessary to refine the gear. Work continued on a new hydraulic gear designated the Mark III, but the insistence of the Air

Ministry on a 1.0g deceleration limit remained a problem, because arresting a 6,000lb aircraft at 70 knots meant paying out 175 feet of cable from each winch. The Admiralty knew that the USN accepted considerably higher g forces, so a member of the DNC Design Department visited a number of aircraft manufacturers to get their view. As a result of their input the JTC agreed to raise the limit to 1.5g for future aircraft, but accepted that a limit of 1.0g must be retained for the Fairey IIIF. In July 1932 trials of the Mark I arresting gear were carried out successfully in *Courageous*. Landings by IIIFs and Hawker Ospreys and Nimrods were carried out with winds over the deck varying from 5 to 20 knots, and proved to be a matter of routine. The gear was then replaced by the Mark III[21] hydraulic system, and further trials were carried out in January 1933 which showed it to be an improvement. Seventy landings were carried out by Nimrods and Ospreys with winds over the deck recorded up to 25 knots. All the pilots preferred the gear to the Mark I, and noted a gradual application of retarding force with the tail falling gently, rather than slamming. Calculated valve settings were used which did not require constant adjustment. It took each wire 20 seconds to reset after it was removed from the aircraft hook.

In August 1936 DNC accepted the Mark III gear for operational service in all British carriers, with the designed capability to stop an 8,000lb aircraft entering the wires at 61 knots. Sea trials had never been able to reach these figures, however, and DNC pressed for a trial unit to be installed ashore from which accurate and complete data could be derived. Until such a facility was available, carefully monitored landings at very low wind speeds were carried out in *Courageous* to prove the system parameters. The Admiralty did eventually get its shore-based arresting gear trials and training facility, but not until it regained full control of its embarked aviation in 1939. A 'dummy deck' complete with arresting wires was built into the new RN Air Station at Arbroath in 1940 at cost of £17,000.[22] A second unit, intended mainly for training, was installed at RNAS Henstridge in 1943.[23] The JTC proposed fitting a 'crash' barrier in *Courageous* in June 1932 to allow a deck park

Fairey IIIFs over-fly HMS *Furious* in the early 1930s. One IIIF has landed-on and is about to be pushed on to the forward lift. Soot from funnel smoke is evident around the black-painted after hull. Note the palisades on either side of the deck by the area in which aircraft came to rest, which covered a large area until the introduction of arrester wires caused aircraft to stop in a 'standardised' distance.

(AUTHOR'S COLLECTION)

forward, in line with the now-standardised USN practice. The Air Ministry objected, however, and it was not until 1938, after years of argument and with the imminent resumption of full RN control over its air component, that the first RN barrier was installed in HMS *Ark Royal*. Its design differed from that in the USN in that it relied on heavy stanchions which were raised from a flush position on the deck to hold the barrier in place when an aircraft engaged it. The 'give' in the wire was the only effective 'pull-out', bringing the aircraft to rest in less than 40 feet. The USN barrier used lighter, collapsible, upright structures to hold the barrier in place, from which the wires detached after an engagement to give a longer, 'softer' pull-out that caused less damage to aircraft, but with the risk that aircraft might 'burst through' into the deck park in Fly 1. Both concepts had positive attributes to commend them, and the Royal Navy eventually used both types during the Second World War because of its mixed fleet of British- and American-built carriers.

Some developments that were applied to all aircraft were of particular importance to carrier-borne aircraft with their requirements for low landing speeds and short take-off runs. First in use was the slat, patented by Frederick Handley Page in 1919. This comprised a small aerofoil that sat just in front of the wing leading edge when deployed, and smoothed the airflow over the upper surface of the wing, allowing it to operate effectively at higher angles of attack and thus permitting lower landing speeds. By the 1930s a number of aircraft, including the Fairey Swordfish, were fitted with slats which activated automatically when airflow over the wing reduced pressure on the leading edge, allowing small springs to deploy the slats. A cockpit control allowed the pilot to lock the slats when combat manoeuvres might cause unwanted asymmetric extension. Another important development was the trailing-edge flap, which came into general use with the introduction of monoplanes with their thinner wings. These are deployable surfaces on wing trailing edges that reduce the stalling speed when extended by increasing the camber, and therefore the wing's maximum lift coefficient. They also increase the drag coefficient because they alter

the planform of the wing when extended, causing greater induced drag and, in some cases, increasing the wetted area of the wing, increasing parasitic drag. Trailing-edge flaps can be selected to give high lift with minimal extra drag for take-off, and high lift with more drag for landing.

The introduction of flaps on monoplanes led to the adoption, in the late 1930s, of a powered final approach in place of the glide approach generally used in the biplane era. This new technique required the pilot to slow the aircraft to a few knots above the calculated stalling speed by the end of the downwind leg and select full flap before starting the turn on to final approach. Speed was maintained by flying the aircraft in a 'three-point' landing attitude and using elevator to make fine adjustments; nose down for more speed, nose up for less. Height was adjusted with the throttle, using more power to reduce the rate of descent when below the ideal glide slope, and less power when high.

Throughout the 1920s Royal Navy carrier operations were in part tentative and experimental but had a growing operational capability. The RAF, in theory the repository of all British post-First World War aviation knowledge, was of little help, as it sought to impress politicians with its blinkered vision of strategic bombing.[24] Senior Royal Navy officers, very few of whom had aviation backgrounds, succeeded against considerable opposition in developing an effective carrier force. The following figures give some idea of the gradual improvement. In 1924 HMS *Argus* reported carrying out 108 deck landings, among which there were 33 accidents, most of a minor nature. Of these accidents, 26 per cent were deemed to be due to causes outside the control of the pilots. A year later, after the impact of renewed interest stimulated by the Trenchard-Keyes Agreement, there were 1,457 landings in all carriers, of which 802 were for training purposes, but the accident rate dropped to 6 per cent. During the next four years, progress was good and returns for the carrier force in 1929 show a total of 5,372 landings, of which only 237 were for training purposes, with an accident rate of only 0.6 per cent. The high figures for the latter year reflect the arrival of the larger *Furious* and *Courageous*

in the fleet and the dynamic energy of the Commanding Officer of *Furious,* Captain R.G.H. Henderson RN, who was subsequently appointed Rear Admiral Aircraft Carriers.[25]

The appointment of a flag officer to take charge of the carrier force had been considered for some years but it was, at first, considered to be unacceptable by the RAF. In December 1930 the First Sea Lord had proposed placing the carriers under the senior cruiser admiral but this found no favour with the fleet and he decided, instead that 'the only practical solution is the appointment of a Rear Admiral Commanding Aircraft Carriers. The development of fleet air work has made considerable progress since the constitution of the Fleet Air Arm in its present form in 1924, and has reached a stage when, it is considered, the conditions in the fleet governing its further progress should be reviewed.'[26] Prior to this the administration of the carriers, the sea training of personnel, the development of material and of the fleet's tactical air operations had been in the hands of different authorities. 'Although this system was at first adequate, experience has shown that it is not sufficient to maintain the progress which might be made, nor capable of meeting the present and future needs of the fleet.'[27] The Admiral's duties included direct command of the carriers of the Atlantic Fleet and responsibility as adviser to the Commanders-in-Chief of other fleets on aircraft carrier matters including the organisation and training of personnel and the co-ordination of exercises. He was also required to prepare a common doctrine for the tactical employment of aircraft by the various fleets.

Henderson encouraged officers of every rank and from every ship in the fleet to visit carriers and fly from them as passengers to learn both the qualities of the aircraft and the need for integration with their crews. Short air courses, which survive today, were instituted for all young officers and changes were made in organisation and tactical method to improve the tactical capabilities of air units. Prominent among these was the introduction, in April 1933, of the system of squadrons which continues in use today.[28] Henderson believed that the Flights he inherited in 1931 were too small to be tactically viable and that the commanding officers, Lieutenants and Flight Lieutenants, were too junior to have their views taken seriously by flag officers and captains. There were also too few sea-going appointments for the more senior and experienced aircrew officers. The solution to all three problems was to form new squadrons with a nominal strength of twelve aircraft, each commanded by a Lieutenant Commander, or equivalent. Front-line squadrons, capable of embarking, were numbered in the 800 series and second-line units and float-plane flights were numbered in the 700 series. This change allowed the administrative work, as well as the tactical handling of aircraft to be put into the hands of more experienced officers, of which more were available since the training of naval pilots and observers had resumed in 1924. It was also key to enabling the co-ordination of larger numbers of aircraft in multi-carrier strike formations after *Courageous* and *Glorious* had joined the fleet.

Henderson made significant progress in the tactical handling of multiple carrier forces, later referred to as task forces and in the co-ordination of several air units to achieve a single task. In this respect the Royal Navy remained ahead of the USN which did not come adequately to grips with the problem until the early years of World War 2. These improvements included the flying off, forming up and concentration of squadrons from several aircraft carriers simultaneously and, as important, their orderly and safe return into several landing patterns for landing-on. Underpinning these improvements was the growing core of naval pilots and observers who could return to carrier flying for successive appointments after their training, giving back the benefits of their growing experience in terms of inputs to what were now known as carrier air drills or standardised operating procedures. The 'ubiquitous' RAF pilots that made up 30% of the Fleet Air Arm total tended to do one tour at sea before returning to the metropolitan air force, taking their experience with them in what was seen by the Navy as a 'skill drain'.

The 'personnel aspects' of the development of naval aviation in this period were of critical importance, especially with regard to training and development after the 'Inskip Award' ended the era

of dual control.[29] This change of organisation gave the navy a firmer grip on the means for solving its own problems, and the responsibility for doing so added greatly to the interest which all naval officers took in matters which had been outside their control since the end of the RNAS. The new administration brought with it new schools and shore establishments to meet technical needs. These were soon followed by the establishment of naval schools for operational flying training, including a torpedo training school, two observers' schools and an air gunners' school, a fighter training school and a deck-landing training school. The opening of these naval establishments resulted in intense and specialised study by their staffs of many problems that had previously gone almost untouched. They were not the modification of RAF dogma applied on an '*ad hoc*' basis, but a specialised treatment of naval problems that required naval solutions. The adoption of a naval deck-landing school, at first at RNAS Donibristle in Fife, then at RNAS Arbroath in Tayside, is a prime example. Soon after its creation, which coincided with the introduction of monoplanes into naval service, the Admiralty realised just how far ahead of RN practice the USN had advanced. It was recognised that a system like that used by the Americans to control deck landings by signals to the pilot from the deck was essential if an increasing wastage of both aircraft and personnel was to be avoided.

The system was introduced by the Admiralty from 1937, and differed from that in use in the USN, which used advisory hand signals from which pilots 'took advice' and remained responsible for their own safe landing. Under this system, the batsman's arms held level meant 'approach fine, come on'; arms raised indicated 'you are high' and arms lowered indicated 'you are low'. Under the RN system the signals were used to give mandatory orders which the approaching pilot had to obey, and it was the Deck Landing Control Officer (DLCO) or batsman's responsibility to get pilots safely on to the deck, having guided their approach from the turn on to finals and given the order to 'cut the throttle' at the right point over the arrester wires. His signals included the 'come on' with level arms, but raised arms meant 'go higher' when

A Blackburn Dart comes to rest on the forward lift of a carrier. The handling party around the lift is moving to grab the aircraft as soon as it stops, in order to strike it down into the hangar as quickly as possible to clear the deck for the next aircraft to land. (AUTHOR'S COLLECTION)

the approaching aircraft was low, and lowered arms meant 'go lower' when the aircraft was high. A bat pulled swiftly across the chest meant 'cut the throttle', and bats waved over the head ordered a 'wave-off' to climb away for another circuit. The greatest crime was to arrive late for a briefed recovery time, but the second, of only marginally less significance, was to land against a signalled wave-off by the batsman. Other signals could be given to indicate 'lined up left/right', 'hook not down', 'wheels not down', 'flaps not down',

'too fast' or 'too slow'. A sailor specially trained as a 'talker' supported the DLCO. His job was to examine every aircraft turning finals through binoculars to check that aircraft had wheels, flaps and hook down, calling the ritual incantation 'wheels down, flaps down, hook down' to the DLCO, and pointing out any that had not done so. He watched the aircraft right in to the wires and called which wire the hook caught, when the barrier went down, and when it was back up so that the next aircraft could land. 'Three

wire, centre, barrier down' would be a typical call, followed by 'barrier up'. The DLCO would have his eyes fixed on the next aircraft, 30 seconds behind the last, and would rely on the 'talker' to inform him whether to let the landing continue or order a wave-off. Every landing was graded, and a third sailor was trained as a 'writer' to jot down the DLCO's brief comments; 'high in close' written as HIC; 'lined up left' (LUL), and so on. The system of controlled deck landings was at first difficult to enforce among the small number of long-serving pilots who had extensive experience of landing without it, but its adoption as part of the training syllabus of the large number of new pilots coming forward resulted in an immediate and noticeable improvement in deck landing. The DLCO School also proved to be a focal point for knowledge on improving the design of aircraft to make them safer to deck-land within the competency of the average pilot.

CHAPTER 9

Different navies, different techniques

The USN sought to put the biggest possible flight decks on its carrier hulls. The wide deck of the uss *Lexington*, CV 2, can be seen here to have been taken as far forward as possible.
(AUTHOR'S COLLECTION)

By 1933 the Admiralty expected that, in wartime, reconnaissance aircraft would remain airborne throughout the time that the battle fleet was at sea, and that carriers, rather than catapult-equipped cruisers, represented the most efficient method of operating them. Aircraft were to be operated in small numbers both by day and by night to carry out naval tasks within the overall organisation of the fleet. No other task was allowed for them by the Air Ministry, and the Government believed, despite the lack of corroborative evidence, that long-range attack was the role of the RAF bomber force. The aircraft from battleships and cruisers were to be launched only when contact with the enemy was certain, and while there was still time to do so before the parent ships became engaged. Once they did, aircraft left on catapults represented a fire risk and would probably be jettisoned.[1] In the last minutes before battle started, carriers would launch spotters and fighter escorts for their action duties with other fighters to strafe the decks of enemy carriers to disrupt their operations. Torpedo aircraft would be held at readiness, but their use would depend on the distance of their targets from the carrier force and the certainty of their location. During a surface action the carriers were expected to remain available to

refuel and rearm aircraft, including those launched from battleship and cruiser catapults.[2] At this stage the Royal Navy considered its carriers to be vulnerable chiefly to attack by enemy cruisers and destroyers, rather than aircraft,[3] and the Admiralty produced several memoranda intended to clarify questions about their best tactical employment. These included 'Cruiser-borne Aircraft', produced in 1934, and series entitled 'Fleet Air Arm Tactics and Equipment', first produced in 1930, and 'Progress in Tactics', produced annually. While these focused attention on air matters they encouraged discussion from the fleet which, while it ensured operational input, took too much time to mature, a shortcoming that reflected the small size of the Air Department within the Naval Staff. A more forthright statement was produced as 'Air requirements in War', dated October 1938 but issued under the authority of an Admiralty Letter[4] in June 1939. This arrived too late to influence prewar training, but in time to influence early wartime strategy.

Lightweight single-seat fighters such as the Fairey Flycatcher, in service from 1923 to 1934, stood a good chance of intercepting attacks by the low-performance land-based bombers of the period after their initial, visual detection by destroyers in the

The Royal Navy's concept of separating the flying-off and recovery decks vertically rather than horizontally had theoretical merit but was soon made impractical by increasing aircraft weights and the need for longer take-off runs. HMS *Courageous* is seen in Plymouth Sound with her upper hangar door open, leading on to the flying-off deck. (AUTHOR'S COLLECTION)

screen. They had no radio or W/T installation and were expected to operate within sight of the fleet. In clear weather, airborne fighters could circle the fleet and intercept enemy aircraft at the limit of visual detection, but their ability to do so for protracted periods was limited by the amount of Avgas available. Since the reconstruction of *Furious*, British carriers carried their volatile aviation fuel in bulk stowage comprising cylinders built into larger compartments filled with water. While this markedly reduced the chances of explosion and fire, it also reduced the amount of fuel carried in comparison with USN and Japanese carriers, which both used large, unprotected tanks. The theoretical British requirement was for one month's supply of Avgas, assuming 60 flying hours for each torpedo-spotter-reconnaissance (TSR)

The Royal Navy improved its concept of flight-deck design with HMS *Ark Royal*, commissioned in 1938. Although the deck was flush and longer than that of HMS *Courageous*, it was narrow and tapered aft, severely limiting the number of aircraft that could be ranged for a single strike, and the possibility of maintaining a deck park.
(AUTHOR'S COLLECTION)

aircraft and 45 for a fighter. The greater the number of continuous patrols flown, the quicker the fuel would be used up, and the Royal Navy did not adopt replenishment at sea until 1944. The speed at which enemy aircraft could attack the fleet increased dramatically in the late 1930s with the development of monoplanes and 1,000hp aero engines. It became clear that even the new *Ark Royal* was not big enough to embark sufficient fighters, or carry enough fuel, to mount the number of Combat Air Patrols (CAP) needed if the fleet relied on visual detection of the enemy to intercept an air raid. In consequence the Royal Navy relied on gunnery to make enemy air

attack unprofitable and, instead of building repeat ships to the *Ark Royal* design, shifted to the armoured carriers of the *Illustrious* group. By then Germany and Italy were believed to be more likely opponents than Japan, and the principal threat was seen as coming from land-based bombers in the North Sea and Mediterranean. Making the single hangar into an armoured 'box' capable of absorbing hits from cruiser gunfire and aircraft bombs up to 500lb produced resilient ships that proved their worth in the Second World War but which proved difficult to modify after the conflict. At the time of the Munich Crisis in 1938, fleet tactics reflected a belief that fighter defence against large numbers of land-based bombers was not practical given the limited response time after visual detection and the limited number of fighters embarked. Trials using the radio-controlled target-ship *Centurion* seemed to indicate that level bombers only stood a chance of hitting a man-oeuvring warship if they attacked in formation at medium level. The extensive batteries of medium and light anti-aircraft guns fitted to the *Illustrious* group were expected to break up just this sort of attack. The lack of a fighter control system indicated that the Admiralty believed that the Air Ministry view that 'the bomber will always get through'[5] was the correct one.

The Air Ministry view that the only aircraft likely to be encountered over the open ocean would be bombers or 'inferior naval types' was not questioned by the Admiralty until it was too late, and the role of fighters was limited to strike support and the interception of low-performance shadowing aircraft outside the range of guns. Thus the Blackburn Skua should be seen not as a poor compromise between dive-bomber and fighter, but rather as an escort fighter capable of delivering a useful bomb load accurately against unarmoured warships, especially carriers, in support of the torpedo-armed strike aircraft. Its useful performance in combat against German bombers and reconnaissance aircraft was proved in the Norwegian Campaign of 1940. By USN standards[6] Lieutenant W.P. Lucy DSO RN, the commanding officer of 803 Naval Air Squadron in April/May 1940, was the first British 'ace' of the Second World War, with five 'kills' flying Skuas from

RNAS Hatston in Orkney and HMS *Ark Royal*.

Admiralty indecision about the need to operate a variety of aircraft from battleship and cruiser catapults led to another limitation on the performance of British naval aircraft. In the early 1930s it was considered desirable to embark fighters in catapult flights so that TSR aircraft could be concentrated in the carriers, and to give some protection to detached ships on the ocean trade routes. A number of cruisers embarked Hawker Ospreys because of their useful reconnaissance capability. As a consequence all naval aircraft were specified to have alternative float undercarriages and were strengthened and fitted with spigots for cradle-type catapult trolleys. Their dimensions had to be such as to fit between the arms of the cradle. Worse, all naval aircraft were specified to have a landing speed of about 60 knots to make deck landing easier. This was no great drawback with biplanes, but the design of a monoplane wing to achieve it had a crippling effect on high-speed performance, as the Air Ministry's experts should have pointed out. These were major limitations that had the effect of increasing weight and drag, which combined to limit fighting performance.

Radar revolutionised the ability of fleet fighters to intercept attacking aircraft before they got to the fleet. The Admiralty had been aware of it before 1939, and several sets were at sea before the war broke out,

but it seems not to have realised the impact it would have on fleet air defence until war experience made it obvious. Fortunately the Royal Navy proved able to improvise fighter control teams effectively and quickly to keep pace with the installation of air-warning radar sets in all carriers. It was ironic that the armoured *Illustrious* class entered service just as the installation of radar made the number of embarked aircraft a more important factor than passive protection. Another new installation that complemented radar was the homing beacon, which allowed single-seat pilots to 'home' on to their carriers without navigational assistance. First to be fitted was the British designed Type 72, followed by the superior USN YE Beacon. The two technological advances allowed high-performance fighters to operate at considerable distances from 'mother' and still return safely.

Throughout the interwar period the Admiralty saw torpedoes as the primary aircraft weapons because battleships were their principal targets, the Washington Treaty having allowed too few carriers, and aircraft, to prove beyond doubt that aircraft had displaced guns as principal instruments of naval warfare. The appearance of multipurpose TSR aircraft had the effect of increasing the potential striking power of the small British carriers without having to increase the number of embarked aircraft. Even if torpedo hits did not sink an enemy battleship

The reconstructed Japanese *Akagi* in 1940; one of only two aircraft carriers ever completed with port-side islands.

(AUTHOR'S COLLECTION)

The uss *Enterprise*, CV 6, was the epitome of pre-war USN carrier design, having a large, uncompromising flight deck designed to operate the largest possible air group with a permanent deck park.

(BY COURTESY OF A.D. BAKER III)

they would probably cause a reduction in speed, allowing the generally slower British capital ships to close to gunfire range. This was certainly the effect achieved by Swordfish from *Ark Royal* in the action against the *Bismarck* in 1941. Although the biplane Swordfish looked like a relic from the First World War, it was at least a practical aircraft capable of carrying a torpedo weighing a ton or the equivalent weight in bombs. Its low landing speed and easy handling made it straightforward to fly, and even the most inexperienced pilots could land on a pitching deck at night or in extreme weather conditions. Unlike the other carrier navies, the RN perfected a diving attack for torpedo aircraft, intended to confuse enemy gunnery, before levelling briefly to release the weapon.

Japan was recognised by the 1930s as America's most likely enemy. By 1940 both the USN and IJN had recognised carriers as fleet units capable of long-range offensive operations, but which were vulnerable to air attack. Both believed fighter aircraft to be the best form of fleet air defence, and embarked them in significant numbers. The USN developed a complementary policy of long-range reconnaissance using both shore-based flying boats under fleet command and carrier-borne aircraft intended to find the enemy carriers first and then to ensure their destruction with massive 'deck-load' strikes from the carriers. The USN concentrated on dive-bombing after 1930 because exercises showed this to be the best way of achieving a large number of hits that would at least disable the enemy carriers. Torpedoes were given less emphasis, as battleships were not the primary targets and the aircraft that carried them were less able to avoid anti-aircraft fire.

From 1930 onwards the USN learnt how best to operate aircraft carriers through practical experience rather than 'table-top' war games, and operating procedures developed a distinctive style. The bigger carriers showed the importance of size, and the diminutive *Ranger* was not repeated. The delay in completing *Lexington* and *Saratoga* to allow refuelling and rearming of aircraft to take place on the flight deck proved to be far-sighted, and the USN specialised in the operation of deck-load strikes that could be recovered and turned round in the minimum

amount of time for further operations. By 1939 the USN undoubtedly led the world in single-carrier operating technique, but lacked experience in multiple-carrier operations. Extensive training proved valuable, and although US carriers remained vulnerable to fire and blast damage in the hangar and on the light flight deck structures, damage control was of a high order. The manufacturing quality of both ships and aircraft was good, and the 19,800-ton *Yorktown* authorised in 1933 reflected all the experience gained by the USN to date, forming a link to the superb 27,000-ton *Essex* class built in impressive numbers during the Second World War, the best aircraft carriers of their era.

Different equipment led to interesting differences between British and American deck-landing techniques. British designers were undoubtedly too cautious about the airflow over a flight deck, whereas their American counterparts regarded carriers as a

suitable hull with the largest possible, rectangular platform placed on top of it regardless of aerodynamics. The biggest difference was in the application of aircraft design. USN aircraft flew a steep final approach at a speed well above the stall, and literally flew into the deck. Their undercarriages could accept this because they were robust, with long travel and good energy absorption which prevented them from bouncing or breaking. British undercarriages were not designed for the purpose and were generally inferior. To give examples, the Grumman F4F designed for the USN (Wildcat in FAA service) absorbed 75 per cent of the landing impact in the oleo and 25 per cent in the tyres, whereas the Supermarine Seafire absorbed only 20 per cent in the oleos and 80 per cent in the tyres. Thus 80 per cent of the impact energy in the latter was available for a bounce, and landing speeds had to be perfectly executed if the aircraft was not to bounce over the

Opposite: The USN concept of refuelling and rearming aircraft on deck paid handsome dividends in combat operations. A range of Grumman F4F Wildcats and Douglas SBD Dauntlesses are seen here, densely packed and with armourers reloading ammunition in their wings. They are too densely packed to start up, and would be moved forward before launch. Note the large roundels painted over the pre-war national markings early in the Pacific War.
(AUTHOR'S COLLECTION)

The Japanese carrier *Hiryu* in 1941.
(BY COURTESY OF A.D. BAKER III)

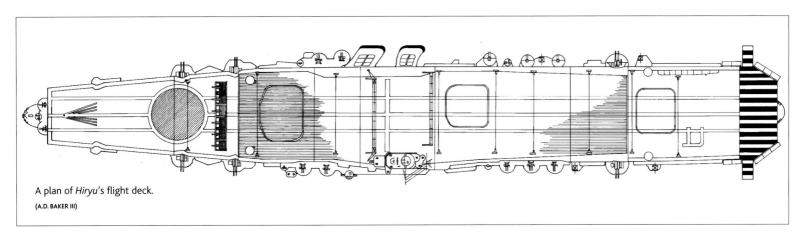

A plan of *Hiryu*'s flight deck.
(A.D. BAKER III)

The British armoured carriers were designed with relatively small flight decks to reduce the area of armoured plate required high in the hull, but this feature unfortunately limited the size of both strikes and deck parks that could be operated. Here HMS *Illustrious* is recovering a strike of Fairey Albacores in 1943. The single Seafire on the outrigger forward of the island appears to have suffered a port oleo collapse. (AUTHOR'S COLLECTION)

wires into the barrier. The higher approach angle of USN aircraft also allowed them to land safely nearer the stern, and their higher speed allowed a safer margin when they flew through any wake turbulence astern of the carrier.[7]

The limited potential of the RN's prototype carrier force two decades after its creation showed that it is not always best to be first in a new field, but, had it not existed, the Air Ministry may well have been able to 'strangle naval aviation at birth' before its potential had been demonstrated. The German Navy was an example of a failed carrier force. Two aircraft carriers were ordered and the *Graf Zeppelin* was launched in 1938. She incorporated many unique ideas for operating aircraft in rough weather, including a railway track that carried aircraft on trolleys from the hangar to the lifts, and from the lifts at flight-deck level to the two catapults forward. Plans for her completion were initially delayed by Luftwaffe opposition and then by naval staff concern over the vulnerability of carriers, given the sinkings of HM Ships *Courageous* and *Glorious*. The Germans lacked the determination shown by the British to make naval

aviation work[8] and a full understanding of modern sea warfare, but the near-appearance of *Graf Zeppelin* provides students of naval war with two 'what ifs'. What if a carrier battle group instead of *Bismarck* and *Prinz Eugen* had sailed into the Atlantic in May 1941? Worse, what if the Admiralty's determination to include aviation within the Royal Navy had been less and the RAF had succeeded, as the Luftwaffe did in Germany, in removing aircraft carriers from Britain's order of battle?[9]

Like the US Navy, the IJN was influenced, at first, by early Royal Navy progress. A British Naval Mission[10] had revealed the latest British carrier and aircraft designs to it as a former ally. The Washington Treaty created a major difference between the IJN and the western navies, however. Since it was only allowed 60 per cent of the tonnage of the British or US navies, the Japanese developed a large force of land-based naval bombers, which were not restricted by the treaty, to operate alongside the fleet at very long range from the mandated islands Japan owned in the Pacific. Unlike the Western air forces, the Japanese Army seems not to have opposed this aspect of naval

The Japanese aircraft carrier *Kaga* in 1930, two years after completion. The IJN took the British concept of short take-off decks a stage further, and completed *Kaga* and the contemporary *Akagi* with 'slip' decks for each of the two hangars. Aircraft can be seen parked on the lower take-off deck, and two twin 8-inch gun turrets are visible, one on either side of the upper flying-off deck. The short decks were not a success and the ship was rebuilt in 1934 with a flight deck that extended the full length of the hull, which was itself lengthened by the insertion of a 34-foot 'plug' to improve the ship's length to beam ratio. The diminutive island on the starboard side amidships was the first to be fitted to a Japanese carrier.
(AUTHOR'S COLLECTION)

The USS *Boxer*, CV 21, was completed on 16 April 1945, only 17 months after the Newport News Shipbuilding Company started work on her. She is seen here on 24 May 1945 with 89 aircraft of her air group on deck. By striking some down into the hangar and using the catapults to launch the first aircraft of a deck-load strike she could operate this impressively large number, but by 1945 the USN wanted even bigger ships with larger air groups. Note that, with so many aircraft ranged on deck, only the side lift is usable, a factor which influenced the USN to delete centreline lifts from future designs. These were the outstanding aircraft carriers of their generation and formed the 'backbone' of the USN's wartime fast-carrier striking force.

(A.D. BAKER III)

aviation since it was, for much of the 1930s, absorbed with its own tactical aircraft requirements fighting in China. The IJN bombers were trained to act as part of the fleet and to attack ships. Their biggest success was the sinking of HM Ships *Prince of Wales* and *Repulse* off the east coast of Malaya in December 1941. British influence showed most in carrier design, the reconstructed capital ships *Akagi* and *Kaga* both being fitted with 'slip' decks like the British battle-cruiser conversions. Deck operations resembled RN practice at first, with aircraft being struck down into the hangar after landing and air group size being equated to hangar stowage. Thus the big Japanese carriers carried significantly fewer aircraft than their USN counterparts. Like the Royal Navy, the IJN began to use deck parks after 1940, but after the lost battles of 1942 the IJN lacked the replacement aircraft to fill its carrier decks and failed to train an adequate number of pilots.

The IJN developed its own distinctive procedures as experience grew. Like the other major navies it recognised the importance of an early 'knock-out' blow against an enemy carrier force, and rebuilt the early ships *Kaga* and *Akagi* with the 'slip' decks replaced by an enlarged flight deck and hangars. Emphasis was placed on the ability to outrange an opponent, and a series of lightweight carrier-borne aircraft with long range that could strike at ranges up to 350 nautical miles were developed.[11] Their USN counterparts were limited, in general, to about 100 nautical miles less. A major Japanese weakness was the need to strike aircraft down into the hangar to be refuelled and rearmed, a time-consuming process in which the operating speed of the lifts was a critical limitation that was to prove disastrous at the Battle of Midway in 1942. Surprisingly, most Japanese carrier-borne aircraft had wings that only folded at the tips, since heavy wing-fold structures nearer the root were felt to be too heavy, compromising long-range performance. The hangar heights of Japanese carriers were deliberately kept low to minimise top-weight and improve stability. Thus, perhaps, Japanese aircraft lacked folding wings because there was insufficient space for the wings to fold, limiting the number of aircraft that could be struck down into the hangar.

Two Japanese carriers, *Akagi* and *Hiryu*, had port-

side islands, the only ships of their kind to do so. It is possible that they were intended to allow two carriers, with port and starboard handed visual circuits, to operate in close proximity, but there is no firm evidence for this. Like US carriers, the Japanese had flight decks of wooden planking laid over steel plates, but, unlike them, the planks were laid fore and aft. In US ships the Oregon pine planks were laid athwartships, interspersed by metal channels into which lashings could be secured.

Japanese take-off and landing procedures were significantly different, and were controlled by an air operations officer from a platform on the after end of the island. Aircraft were ranged aft, chocked and lashed, and engines were started before turning into wind. When the ship was steady into wind, a white flag with a central black ball was hoisted, the executive signal for the flight deck officer to order away chocks and lashings. The executive signal to start launching aircraft was a white flag at the masthead, and when it was close-up aircraft would begin to take off at twenty-second intervals.[12] No Japanese aircraft carrier was fitted with catapults, and the length of deck required for a rolling take-off by the foremost aircraft always dictated the size of the range. Barriers were adopted after the USN but before the British.

Aircraft waiting to recover joined a right-handed pattern to starboard of the ship until she was into wind. The carrier signalled that it was ready to begin the recovery by hoisting a black 'ball' at the masthead, beneath which were two numeral flags indicating the wind speed. Pilots joined the visual circuit by turning ahead of the bow at 700 feet and continued downwind to a point on the port quarter where they turned finals to line up about 700 yards astern, still at 700 feet. The IJN never used batsmen, but had a group of red and green lights, known as 'landing guidance lights', positioned on either side of the deck, each rather like the Royal Navy sector lights. When he had both sets in view the pilot was correctly aligned with the deck and, to help him when close in, outrigger platforms were built out from either side of the round-down at the extreme after end of the deck. These were painted conspicuously red and white, and helped pilots line up with the centreline,

even when the nose of their aircraft obscured the deck itself. This was a very different technique from the Royal Navy's continuous turning approach and, since it involved flying a larger circuit, it was slower and added to the IJN's slow turn-round time between sorties. Once lined up astern of the deck, pilots judged the correct glideslope by descending with the green light appearing immediately over the red. If only the red could be seen, the aircraft was low, and if the red appeared over the green it was dangerously low. If the green appeared to be at some distance above the red, the aircraft was high. Although there was no batsman as such, a sailor was positioned on the port side aft to make signals to pilots with hand-held flags if instructed to do so by the air operations officer. A red flag constituted a 'wave-off', requiring pilots to go round for another circuit; a white flag with a letter H was meant to tell pilots that they had not lowered their tailhook, but with the wind straight down the deck, both flags blew toward the aircraft and were difficult to discern. Often they were waved from side to side to make them more obvious.

The Royal Navy provided considerable assistance to the French Navy in the design and completion of the carrier *Bearn* on an incomplete battleship hull in 1927. She was slow, not a great success, and lack of funds prevented any further French carrier construction until after the Second World War. The flight deck was lightly armoured and, like the British conversions, she had two hangars. Her three lifts were unique in that the platforms did not form part of the flight deck but were normally kept at upper hangar deck level, the apertures in the flight deck being closed by 'clamshell' doors which served as side windbreaks when open with the lift platform at flight deck level.[13] Aircraft capacity was officially stated to be 40, but this figure included a number held in dismantled reserve in the workshop and storage area of the lower hangar. The maximum that could reasonably be operated from the deck was 25. Transverse arrester wires using sandbag weights were used in trials, followed soon afterwards by electrically controlled units similar to those adopted by the USN.

Flight from ships other than carriers

The USN resumed development of aircraft catapults after 1918, and a prototype compressed-air model designed by the Philadelphia Navy Yard was authorised in January 1921. Designated the Type A Mark 1, it was mounted on a turntable at the yard for development work. The first aircraft to be launched was a Curtiss N-9 seaplane piloted by Commander H.C. Richardson USN, the Service's catapult pioneer.[1] A second A1 catapult was fitted to the battleship USS *Maryland* and a successful launch was carried out by a Vought VE-7 piloted by Lieutenant A.C. McFall USN on 22 May 1922. The Secretary of the Navy had, by then, been so encouraged by the potential demonstrated by the catapult mounted ashore that, in April 1922, he authorised the equipping of all US battleships and cruisers with catapults. By the mid-1920s virtually every USN battleship was fitted with a catapult, and some had two. The *Omaha*-class cruisers completed between 1923 and 1925 were the first warships built with catapults.

The compressed-air catapult had proved a success, but the USN went a step further in 1922 and began development of a catapult that used slow-burning cordite as the motive power. This had the advantage that the charge could be varied according to the weight and payload of the aircraft being launched. By eliminating the time it took to recharge the compressed-air accumulator it also meant that consecutive launches could be carried out more quickly. The first aircraft to be launched at sea by a cordite catapult was a Martin MO-1 piloted by Lieutenant W.M. Fellers USN from the USS *Mississippi* at Bremerton, Washington, on 14 December 1924. Again trials proved successful, and slow-burning cordite catapults were widely fitted but never entirely replaced the compressed-air type.

In the Royal Navy the increasing weight of operational aircraft meant that the flying-off platforms that had been widely fitted to battleships and cruisers in 1917/18 were no longer viable, and catapult development resumed in 1922. Two competitive designs were ordered; the first was designed by Carey, used a compressed-air piston to operate a system of pulleys and wires and was built in prototype form at Chatham Dockyard. The second was designed and built at the RAE at Farnborough, Hampshire. The latter was also powered by compressed air, but transmitted the force with a series of telescopic pistons connected to a trolley on which the aircraft was mounted.

The prototype Carey catapult was installed in the cruiser HMS *Vindictive* in 1925, by which time her flight decks had been removed but she retained the hangar forward of the bridge. A crane was installed to lift aircraft on to the catapult, out of the water after landing and into/out of the hangar through a hatch in the deck-head. The first launch was carried out on

30 October 1925 by Wing Commander Burling RAF in a Fairey IIID seaplane, and subsequent trials used both these aircraft and float-fitted Fairey Flycatchers. The Carey catapult was capable of launching aircraft at a maximum weight of up to 12,000lb at 45 knots, and proved a useful addition to *Vindictive*'s equipment. She subsequently served on the China Station with a squadron of six Fairey IIIDs embarked, using them to locate pirates. The RAE catapult was first mounted ashore on a turntable at Farnborough. The telescopic pistons were mounted within a girder structure 50 feet long, 3 feet high and 3 feet wide.

The first 'shots' proved capable of firing dead weights of up to 7,000lb at 55 knots in a travel of 34 feet with an initial acceleration of 2g. Because of concerns about the ability of pilots to withstand such a g-loading, unmanned aircraft were launched at first, with live sheep strapped into the cockpit, and it was not until they were found to have survived the experience that aircraft were launched with pilots. A prototype RAE catapult was fitted to the cruiser *Frobisher* in 1927. By then the USN success with slow-burning cordite was noted, and the RAE was tasked to modify one of its prototypes to use a cordite charge

HMS *Vindictive* with the prototype Carey catapult mounted on the hangar roof in 1925.

(AUTHOR'S COLLECTION)

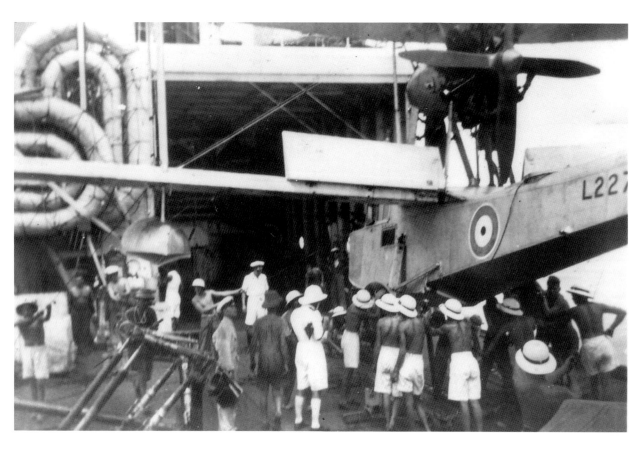

Top: A Supermarine Walrus is prepared for flight after removal from its hangar in a *Southampton*-class cruiser on the China Station in the late 1930s.

Right: Launching a Walrus from the 'Colony'-class cruiser HMS *Bermuda* in 1943. The catapult has been extended beyond the ship's side and the arms of its cradle have just dropped as the aircraft has flown clear.

(AUTHOR'S COLLECTION)

Left: A Walrus taxiing under the Thomas Grab, which has been swung out to starboard of its parent cruiser. The 'hooker-on' is ready on the upper wing and the officer-in-charge of the recovery is standing on the catapult extension. The amount of spray thrown up by the choppy sea emphasises the importance of the Walrus's enclosed canopy.

Below left: A delightful fusion of technology; the parent cruiser is at anchor and the Walrus has landed some distance clear. A 27-foot 'Montague' whaler is towing it under the Thomas Grab for recovery.

Below: A Walrus being hoisted inboard. The engine has been stopped and, without hydraulic pressure, the undercarriage has dropped. Steadying lines are being held by the handling party on deck.

(AUTHOR'S COLLECTION)

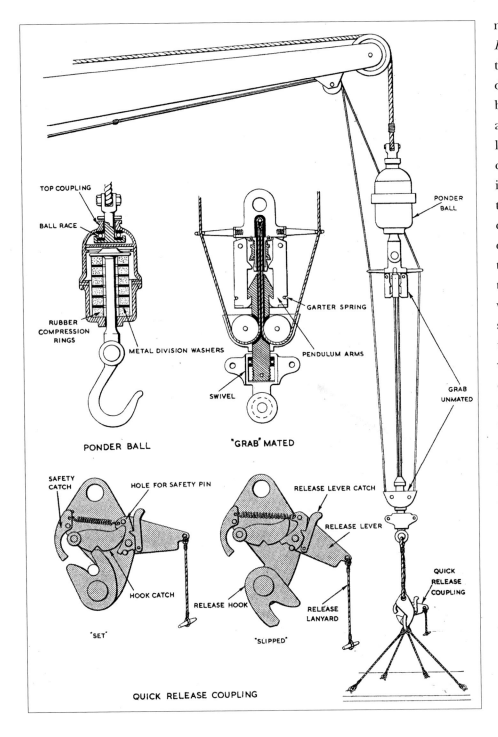

TOP COUPLING

BALL RACE

RUBBER
COMPRESSION
RINGS

METAL DIVISION WASHERS

PONDER BALL

GARTER SPRING

PENDULUM ARMS

SWIVEL

'GRAB' MATED

PONDER BALL

GRAB
UNMATED

SAFETY
CATCH

HOLE FOR SAFETY PIN

RELEASE LEVER CATCH

RELEASE LEVER

HOOK CATCH

RELEASE HOOK

'SET'

RELEASE
LANYARD

'SLIPPED'

QUICK
RELEASE
COUPLING

QUICK RELEASE COUPLING

Details of the Thomas Grab, quick-release hook and strop. (AUTHOR'S COLLECTION)

mounted on the quarterdeck of the battle cruiser HMS *Hood*. Both could launch a Hawker Osprey, but only the latter could launch a Fairey IIIF. One version was designed to be folded at the mid point so that it could be stowed in the limited space between ships' funnels and extended when trained on to the beam for launch. From 1928 the Royal Navy standardised on cordite-powered catapults and newer ships used installations fixed into the deck athwartships rather than mounted on turntables. Some of the light cruiser classes were too small for these, however, and continued to mount lightweight catapults on turntables. Battleships had sufficient beam to take the full length of the catapult, but cruisers were fitted with catapults that were extended beyond the ships' side just before launch, such as the D1H type fitted to the *Southampton* and *Cumberland* classes. In this version aircraft were stowed in hangars on special cradles, on which they were wheeled aft to be loaded on to a launching trolley which was mounted on a turntable. This allowed it to be positioned facing forward to receive the aircraft and then rotated to port or starboard for launch; the catapult could be used in either direction. Later systems, such as that used in *King George V*-class battleships and *Fiji*-class cruisers, actually stowed the aircraft on launch platforms which connected to the catapult mechanism when the aircraft was ranged. Battleships could carry up to five aircraft; four stowed in hangars and one on the catapult. Cruisers, with their smaller hangars, typically carried up to three. The Royal Navy operated a large cruiser force and used a variety of aircraft types in catapult flights, but by 1939 most were equipped with the Supermarine Walrus. It had originally been specified by the Royal Australian Navy (RAN) and viewed with indifference in the UK, but its trials[2] showed it to be an outstanding aircraft, capable of operating in moderate to rough sea conditions, and it was purchased in large numbers. Some light cruisers could not operate such a large aircraft and operated the Fairey Seafox light spotting seaplane, and a few flights operated float-equipped Swordfish.

In a typical sortie from a battleship catapult the Walrus was pushed out of the hangar by a handling

as the motive power. This proved successful and it was subsequently fitted operationally to the heavy cruiser HMS *York*.

The RAE continued to develop catapults, and eventually produced a family of variants that could launch aircraft weighing from 5,000lb to 7,000lb, both at an end-speed of 55 knots. An example of the lighter type was fitted amidships in the heavy cruiser HMS *Kent*, and an example of the heavier type was

party of Flight ratings and the trolley fixed on to the catapult with the help of the catapult crew. The aircraft was 'very high off the deck on its launching gear'[3] and the crew needed a ladder to gain access through an open hatch in the glazed roof of the pilot's cockpit. The pilot checked that everything was securely stowed and the aircraft ready for flight before strapping in. Once the aircraft was on the trolley in the launch position it was held by 'haul-back' cables until just

before launch while ratings spread the wings and loaded any weapons required for the sortie on to the wing racks. The opportunity was taken to top-up the fuel tanks in the upper wing, if necessary, to their maximum content of 155 gallons. The fitter and rigger climbed on to the lower mainplane and fitted the starting handle into place on the engine nacelle with its aft-facing 'pusher' propeller. They cranked the handle at increasing speed as the pilot switched the two

HM Submarine *M2* with the tiny Parnall Peto reconnaissance aeroplane on its catapult trolley for maintenance. The girder-like crane arm is visible mounted on top of the hangar, the door of which is open.
(AUTHOR'S COLLECTION)

petrol cocks on the starboard cockpit bulkhead to 'ON' while checking the controls for 'full and free movement'. When the whine of the inertia starter reached the familiar note the pilot shouted 'contact' and flicked the two magneto switches on the instrument panel upwards to 'ON', and the fitter let in the clutch to engage the starter. After a grinding noise the propeller turned and the Bristol Pegasus XXX radial engine fired, quickly settling down to idling rpm. The pilot raised the undercarriage, which would have lowered without hydraulic power, checked the position of the water rudder and set the tail trim for launch. The fitter handed the starting handle down into the cockpit, where it was stowed in case the aircraft came down in the sea and the crew needed to restart the engine. Once the engine was warmed up, the pilot switched each magneto off in turn to check that the 'mag drop' was within limits and then, with both back on, checked maximum rpm and boost pressure.

Meanwhile, the catapult crew tested it with a 'light shot' and the directing officer checked that the correct cordite charge for the aircraft weight had been delivered by the Gunner's Party. Two 'signal men' held up red flags to show that all was not yet ready, and two other sailors operated the 'transmitter' to pass messages between the catapult control position and the ship's bridge. The signal flag 'F' was clipped on 'at the dip' on the yard-arm on the side to which the aircraft was to be launched; port yard-arm for a launch to port. The directing officer carried out a final check with the bridge that the wind was within limits and reported to the captain, via the transmitter and hand flags, that all was ready. The captain ordered 'stand by to launch', after which the 'haul-back' cables were removed and the cordite charge inserted into the catapult breech. Flag 'F' was hoisted 'close up' to warn other ships that launch was imminent, and the captain ordered the directing officer to 'launch when ready'. The latter raised a green flag and circled it above his head, and the pilot opened the throttle to give full power and raised his hand over his head to signal readiness. Seeing this, the directing officer lowered his green flag to the deck and the catapult controller pulled a lever which fired the charge. A second later the crew felt the pressure of 2.75g forcing them back

into their seats and the aircraft was airborne. Flag 'F' was hauled down immediately.[4]

When the time came to return to 'mother', ships usually chose to hoist the aircraft on the starboard side. Preparations included manning the crash-boat, rigging the starboard boat boom with a towing pennant and testing the 'Thomas Grab' against an eyebolt on the deck. The crane was turned outboard with the quick-release coupling[5] on the Thomas Grab lowered to a height at which the aircraft's 'hooker-on' could easily reach it. The Thomas Grab was a clever arrangement in which the lower part of the unmated grab, to which was attached the quick-release coupling, was suspended by tricing lines, thin ropes that were kept taut by the crane driver using a small winch with a slipping clutch. This allowed the coupling to be kept steady without having to make constant movements with the main crane cable. Above the coupling, the tricing lines ran through the upper grab unit, which was attached to the main crane cable. The crane operator was a skilled sailor upon whom a lot depended in a rough weather recovery. He controlled the amount of cable paid out on the main winch with a lever in his right hand, and the height of the coupling, using the tricing winch with his left. Two steadying lines were passed out attached to a link on the 'Thomas Grab' and tended by sailors on deck.[6] A handling party stood ready with padded bearing-out spars and extra steadying lines.

The Walrus could set down safely on a sea with waves six feet high but, if necessary, there were procedures for the recovery vessel to provide a relatively calm patch on which the aircraft could alight. Once the aircraft arrived overhead, 'mother' started the recovery process by putting the wind 60 degrees on the starboard bow and hoisting Flag 'F' superior with Flag 'B' inferior at the dip on starboard yard-arm. When the captain ordered the recovery to begin, flags 'FB' were hauled 'close-up' to the yard-arm and the ship began a turn to starboard. As the bow passed through the wind the flags were hauled down smartly, the executive signal for action and an indication of wind direction to the pilot. The ship steadied with the wind 30 degrees on the port bow, making a 'lee' to protect the aircraft when it taxied up to the ship's side. The aircraft then

flew a left-hand circuit, aiming to land on the 'slick' of calmer water. Final approach was directly toward the ship, into the wind, at low speed using power to hold off just above the waves. As soon as the throttle was closed the Walrus landed in a flurry of spray and taxied towards the ship.[7]

Things happened quickly as the aircraft closed with the ship. The pilot had to make sure that he kept between the ship's bow and stern waves, avoiding the suction effect between them that would tend to pull the aircraft in towards the hull. One of the crew, usually the TAG, climbed out of the hatch, up pegs on the interplane struts fitted for the purpose, on to the top of the upper mainplane, where he attached a safety line to hold himself securely in place while the aircraft bucked in the swell. The 'hooker-on' position on top of the upper wing was the principal reason for having the propeller at the rear of the nacelle. Had it been situated at the front he would have had to climb aloft within inches of it. Also, being aft of the engine nacelle gave the propellers some protection from damage by spray. Due to the camber of the upper wing the rear-mounted propeller was lower than a front-mounted one would have been, making the height of the 'quick-release' coupling less critical. The observer stood up on the right-hand side of the cockpit with a boat-hook ready to grab the 'grass'[8] towing rope streamed aft from the boom. It was made fast well forward on the recovering ship so that the ensuing bight of rope took out any tendency to jerk the aircraft harshly once it was attached,[9] a technique widely used for launching and recovering sea boats. As soon as the towing rope was clipped to a link on the Walrus's nose, the aircraft's engine was shut down and it was pulled forward so that the quick-release coupling came within grabbing distance of the 'hooker-on'. Once it was caught, he could pull down on the coupling against the tension in the slipping clutch on the tricing winch to connect it to the aircraft sling fitted to the upper mainplane. When the coupling was secured the action of the tricing winch kept the cable from jerking as the aircraft rode the waves. At this point the 'hooker-on' removed a safety pin from the quick-release coupling so that, if things went wrong, he could release the aircraft back

on to the water. Once the Thomas Grab was safely mated and the aircraft was being hoisted he reinserted the pin. When ordered by the directing officer, the crane operator lowered the upper part of the grab and pulled hard up on the tricing winch control, pulling the top of the unmated lower portion upwards to lock into the upper portion, attaching the crane cable to the coupling. Once this happened the crane operator hoisted the aircraft on the main cable using the main winch control, and the pilot pulled a small lever in the cockpit to release the towing rope. The 'hooker-on' unclipped the steadying lines and passed them to the other crew members, who helped keep the aircraft nose-to-crane as it was hoisted over the deck. As the aircraft was moved over the deck, tackles could be attached to it to help it move securely back on to its trolley in rough weather, but these could be dispensed with by an experienced crew in calm conditions. The 'hooker-on' had not completed his task until the aircraft was back on its trolley and he had unclipped the coupling. The aircraft could then be prepared for another flight or folded and struck down into the hangar as necessary.

The French, German, Japanese and Italian navies also developed catapults for installation in cruisers and battleships. Like the US and Royal Navies these included both compressed-air and cordite-powered variants. In both France and Germany catapults were installed in transatlantic liners to shorten mail delivery times, and the Germans even designed commercial catapult ships designed to refuel Dornier Do 18 flying boats in mid-ocean and launch them on their way again. Although catapult installations appeared superficially similar, the different navies used them in different ways. In the RN catapult aircraft were seen as adding to the overall air capability of the fleet. Given the low aircraft numbers embarked in carriers at first this was reasonable, but by the mid 1930s the need to design every aircraft for catapult launch from a trolley severely limited their performance. The primary role of catapult aircraft was action information, giving the force commander an 'eye in the sky' that helped him to form a 'picture' of what the enemy was doing beyond the visible horizon. A Seafox from HMS *Ajax* was launched

The 'RAE 1921 Target' on its upward-sloping launching ramp on the destroyer HMS *Stronghold*.
(AUTHOR'S COLLECTION)

during the battle of the River Plate on 13 December 1939; a Swordfish floatplane played a prominent part in the Second Battle of Narvik in 1940; Walruses were launched by HM Ships *Renown* and *Manchester* in the action off Cape Spartivento and another by HMS *Gloucester* during the Battle of Matapan on 28 March 1941. The reconnaissance and shadowing roles were largely subsumed by the rapid expansion in the number of carrier-borne aircraft to the extent that, after 1943, the RN withdrew catapult flights from service and converted the hangars into mess decks, offices and cinemas. The gunnery-spotting role was rendered obsolete by the rapid adoption of gun-ranging and fire-control radar systems that could detect the impact point of shells to within a few yards. The USN used its catapult aircraft in a similar manner, but Japanese cruisers and battleships were equipped from the early 1930s to carry large numbers of aircraft, and these were relied on to perform the reconnaissance task, freeing the carrier aircraft to concentrate on the strike and fighter missions.

A number of unusual catapult installations illustrate an innovative British approach to the use of catapult aircraft at sea. They include the installation in the submarine M2, which had a small hangar, catapult and crane fitted forward of its conning tower. A special floatplane, the Parnall Peto, was designed for it and two prototypes were built. The crew of two were paid specialist allowances for both flying and service in submarines. The idea was that the submarine could operate in advance of the fleet as a scout, diving with or without the aircraft to avoid a concentration of hostile forces. The operation of the aircraft replicated, on a small scale, the operation of larger aircraft described earlier, except that the hangar door had to be sealed watertight after the aircraft was struck down before the submarine could dive. The M2 carried out a number of successful sea trials, but unfortunately was lost with her whole ship's company of 60 in West Bay, near Portland in Dorset, on 26 January 1932. Divers found her stern embedded in the sandy seabed with the bows high above the bottom. The hangar door and the hatch into the hull from the hangar were both found to be open. Experienced submariners believe that, because she was a large submarine, blowing all the tanks completely to surface took up to 15 minutes. The operational technique of getting the aircraft out of the hangar, spread and launched in the minimum time was to open the hangar door as soon as the superstructure emerged clear of the water, even though the stern ballast tanks were not yet pumped empty, holding the boat on the surface with forward speed acting on the hydroplanes. They must have failed, causing the stern to drop, dragging the open hangar under the surface. The rapid inrush of water would have caused M2 to dive stern-first into the bottom.[10] A witness, the master of a passing merchant vessel, reported seeing a submarine dive stern-first. The Royal Navy carried out no further experiments with submarine-launched aircraft. The IJN was the only navy to take the concept of operating aeroplanes from submarines further, and eventually developed the I-400 class, which could each carry up to three aircraft. During the Second World War the German Navy equipped U-boats, principally the ocean-going Type IX, with the Focke-Achgelis Fa 330 Bachstelze gyroplane kite, which was sent aloft under tow from a surfaced U-boat to extend the observer's range of vision when searching for Allied convoys.

Britain was the only nation to operate another type of catapult at sea, in the Catapult-Armed Merchant Ships, or CAM-Ships. These were an emergency measure to counter Focke-Wulf Fw 200 Condor long-range bombers from 1940 onwards. In many ways they were a throwback to the First World War, in that the fighters were 'one-shot' weapons that could not be recovered once they were launched. The aircraft were 'war-weary' Hurricanes, fifty of which were hastily fitted with catapult spools and designated Sea Hurricane Mark IA. The aircraft was fitted on to the catapult over the forecastle before the ship sailed, and stayed there, exposed to wind and weather, until it was launched in anger or craned off at the convoy's destination. The catapults themselves were crude trellis structures from which the aircraft were launched by rocket-propelled trolleys which did not prove very reliable. Great precision was necessary to regulate the rocket thrust,

and aircraft were sometimes launched close to their stalling speed or so fast that they sustained structural damage. In all there were 35 CAM-Ships, of which eleven were sunk by enemy action, including the first, SS *Michael E*, which was sunk in a convoy bound for Canada in May 1941. The first launch of a CAM-Ship fighter occurred on 4 June 1941, flown by Sub Lieutenant M.A. Birrell RN. In addition to these mercantile catapult ships the RN converted four ocean boarding vessels and the veteran seaplane carrier *Pegasus* (formerly *Ark Royal*) into naval manned fighter catapult ships. Lieutenant R.W.H. Everett RNVR, flying a Hurricane from one of these, HMS *Maplin*, achieved the first catapult fighter success when he shot down an Fw 200 on 3 August 1941.[11] By 1943 sufficient escort aircraft carriers were available, and the catapults were removed from the remaining CAM-Ships.

The most unusual British catapult application was a 'dead-weight' catapult fitted on the forecastle of the destroyer HMS *Stronghold* in 1924.[12] This consisted of a lattice structure on the bow, angled up at about 40 degrees from the horizontal and from which an unmanned 'flying bomb' was accelerated by a wire attached to a large bag full of water which was dropped into the sea. Improbable as it may sound, the system worked and twelve separate launches were carried out in 1924/25. The aircraft, an unmanned combat air vehicle or UCAV in today's parlance, was radio-controlled and intended to strike at shore targets from a safe distance at sea. It had a 200lb explosive warhead. The first version was known as the 'RAE 1921 Target' and, despite the limited radio technology of the time, it worked. An improved version, given the code-name 'Larynx', was produced in 1927, by which time an improved cordite-powered catapult was fitted to *Stronghold*. Larynx was intended to carry a 250lb warhead for a distance of 300 miles under radio control, and five launches achieved varying degrees of success in 1927. The weapon's major problem was terminal guidance, and shipborne trials ceased after the second series of trials but did continue ashore. It was eventually seen by the RAF as a rival to its manned bomber force and, in consequence, terminated.

CHAPTER 11

HMS *Implacable* described and compared

HMS *Implacable*, and her sister-ship *Indefatigable*, had the largest flight decks of the wartime British aircraft carrier force. Only those of the post-war *Eagle* and *Ark Royal* were bigger. She is seen entering Melbourne in 1946.

(AUTHOR'S COLLECTION)

By 1940 the three carrier navies had evolved a generation of capable and distinctive fleet carrier designs, and the demands of a global war led to further variants that could be mass-produced but which still needed credible capabilities including radar, homing beacons and action information systems for the command and control of air operations. In the space of five years they became not just the cornerstone of every fleet operation, but arguably the most important strategic weapons system in the British and US armed forces. They were certainly the only British force capable of taking the fight to the Japanese mainland in July and August 1945. HMS *Implacable*, one of the last two ships of the

HMS *Implacable* was one the first British aircraft carriers to be equipped with flight-deck tractors, one of which is visible in the foreground, but most aircraft moves were still carried out by men pushing the aircraft into position, a slow and labour-intensive operation.
(AUTHOR'S COLLECTION)

Illustrious group of armoured carriers, operated about eighty aircraft and had a ship's company of 2,300 in 1945. She is used as an example and compared with USN and IJN ships, light fleet and escort carriers.

Until 1944, when USN-style flight deck tractors were procured, all Royal Navy aircraft were man-handled by parties of seamen, detailed from the ship's company for work on the flight deck, assisted by squadron maintenance ratings.[1] By 1945 about thirty aircraft were kept permanently in a deck park,[2] and maintenance was compounded by the need to clean

aircraft that were coated with salt spray and soot from the funnel. The flight deck was designed to allow any type of naval aircraft to be flown off by day or night in any weather conditions in which the aircraft itself could be operated.[3] In the *Illustrious* group it was constructed from 3-inch armoured steel plates and was kept as small as possible, both to minimise the area of heavy plate required and to limit the horizontal area potentially exposed to enemy bombs and shells. Given the number of aircraft operated by 1945, the small deck was a design weakness and a bigger deck would have allowed the ship to achieve greater potential. There was a single hydraulic 'accelerator'[4] which moved a shuttle along a slot in the deck. A wire 'strop' was looped over this and hooked on to 'spools' on the aircraft. A 'hold-back' device was linked to the aircraft, and this had a weak link which broke when the aircraft was at full power and the accelerator was 'fired', giving maximum acceleration from the outset. In *Implacable* the unit was a Type H III capable of launching aircraft weighing up to a maximum of 20,000lb at end speeds of up to 66 knots.[5] Maximum acceleration was 2.75g. The accelerator was controlled from an adjacent position in the port catwalk.

Nine arrester wires were rigged on the after half of the flight deck, each capable of stopping aircraft up to a maximum of 20,000lb at an entry speed of up to 60 knots. The design allowed for three similar wires to be rigged at the forward end of the deck to allow aft-facing landings, but these were not fitted. The wires comprised 'centre-spans' or 'pennants' on deck which could be quickly replaced if worn, attached through couplings to wires reeved on to hydraulic rams under the deck between the 'deep-beams', girders that supported the flight deck, in the hangar roof. Two wires were attached to each retardation unit in the order 1 and 2, 3 and 4, 5 and 6, 7 and 8, numbered from aft, the aftermost wire being number 1. The ninth wire was a single unit known as a 'trickle' wire, since an aircraft engaging it would impact the after barrier but at a reduced momentum, minimising the amount of damage caused. The centre spans comprised 2½-inch special flexible steel wire rope, and each was supported by two 'bow-springs',

HMS *Implacable* gave the Royal Navy a deck which, while not perfect, was able to range a large strike and maintain a significant deck park. Fourteen Seafires and twelve Avengers are seen ranged here for a strike on the Japanese mainland in 1945. The Seafires are fitted with United States Army Air Force drop-tanks which doubled the type's radius of action.

(AUTHOR'S COLLECTION)

hydraulic supports either side of the centreline which held the wire 4 to 6 inches above the deck to help it engage arrester hooks. Maximum retardation was designed to be 1.5g, but the length of pull-out varied according to the position of the wire. The after wires had a maximum pull-out of 156 feet, central wires 144 feet and forward wires 120 feet. The trickle wire had a pull-out of only 40 feet. Control of the arrester gear was exercised from a position in the port catwalk.

There were three safety barriers, unofficially known as 'crash-barriers'. Each consisted of a wire net stretched across the deck between two stanchions which could be raised and lowered rapidly. The net itself was 3 feet high and its height between the stanchions could be raised and lowered between deck level and 6 feet. They were controlled from a position in the port catwalk, being lowered as soon as a landing aircraft was arrested and raised after it had taxied over them. Each had a pull-out of 40 feet. When in use, the after barrier limited the number of usable arrester wires to the after three, but it also had the flexibility to be used as a trickle wire for the forward barrier when laid flat on the deck, or to support landings over the bow if the forward arrester wires were rigged. Having three gave the flexibility to continue rapid recovery rates even after damage to one of the barriers. The flight deck was surrounded by 'catwalks' and safety nets. The former provided access points to the deck from below in addition to the control positions. Among the many items of

Although improvements had been made, landing a propeller-driven aircraft on the deck of a straight-deck carrier with a safety barrier was still dangerous. Seafire L.III PR240 of 880 NAS has engaged HMS *Implacable*'s barrier in July 1945. The two visible barrier stanchions are both in the down position and are more substantial pieces of kit than the USN equivalent. The wires of the nearer one have been disconnected to extricate the aircraft, which is being steadied by handlers.

(AUTHOR'S COLLECTION)

equipment stowed in them were fuel hoses, electrical power cables, tool boxes, aircraft chocks and outriggers ('U-shaped' metal bars that could be attached to the edge of the deck. When these were in position aircraft could be stowed with their tailwheels in the bar so that the only the main wheels were on the flight deck, minimising the aircraft's 'footprint'.) Fire-fighting equipment was stowed in catwalk lockers, and consisted of at least seven foam generators, three CO_2 extinguishers on trolleys with 40lb cylinders, and the fire main with its numerous access points and ready-use hoses. Wireless-telegraphy masts were fitted at intervals around the flight deck and were hinged so that they could be lowered to the horizontal during flying operations. A single mast on the starboard side, forward mounted the VHF direction-finding antennae, was kept in the raised position so that it was always available.

The DLCO had a working platform on the port side right aft from where he could see, and be seen by, aircraft on finals. Hinged panels were fitted at the

'Flyco' in British fleet carriers was still open to the elements in 1945, although this one in HMS *Indomitable* is at least rigged with an awning to shade 'Wings' from the tropical sun. Khaki uniforms were standard among officers in the BPF.

(AUTHOR'S COLLECTION)

forward part of the platform to protect him from windblast and to provide a contrasting background against which his bats could be seen, rather like the white screens on a cricket pitch behind the bowler. A padded escape chute was constructed by the platform, down which the DLCO could dive if an aircraft veered dangerously towards him as it crossed the round-down. In many ships a brightly painted 'dan-buoy' marker and its weighted 'sinker' were fitted near the DLCO so that, in the event of an aircraft going over the side, it could be dropped instantly to mark the position.

There were facilities for giving visual signals to aircraft on the state of the deck, although these were little used in 1945. They comprised panels on the deck and a horizontal signal mast for flags on the port side of the flight deck, opposite the island. Either flags or the panels could be used to indicate which types – fighter, spotter, torpedo etc – were to land on, and to give other instructions from the fleet signal book. These included flags to indicate 'normal landing', 'wind speed low', 'arrester gear not in use' and others which were issued to pilots on a printed card.[6] In earlier fleet carriers 'signal groups' of lights were fitted to convey the same messages at night. In extreme circumstances a number of ingenious schemes were evolved for communicating with aircraft that had suffered radio failure. These included painting 'bale out' in large letters on the flight deck in whitewash; it had the desired effect.

All British carriers were fitted with flight-deck lighting systems to allow aircraft to land-on at night or in reduced visibility. The Deck Landing Control System, centred on the 'batsman' using illuminated 'bats', remained the key to successful operation, but other lights gave cues which helped pilot orientation, depth perception and judgement of position relative to the ideal glide-slope and line-up with the flight deck. The system had undergone constant additions and was perhaps over-complicated in 1945, but was still expected to enable a darkened carrier to operate at night without giving away her position to surface vessels and with minimum risk of detection by enemy aircraft. It included the following lights:

Carrier identification groups, fitted in fleet carriers, comprised four white lights arranged in a square which flashed the deck recognition letter of the carrier in Morse code.

Port and starboard groups each consisting of three lights, red on the port side and green on the starboard, showed aircraft in the 'wait' on which side of the carrier they were flying.

Signal and homing light flashed the deck recognition letter or messages in Morse code. It was sited on the starboard side forward, with a second light to cover the blanked space aft of the island in fleet carriers.

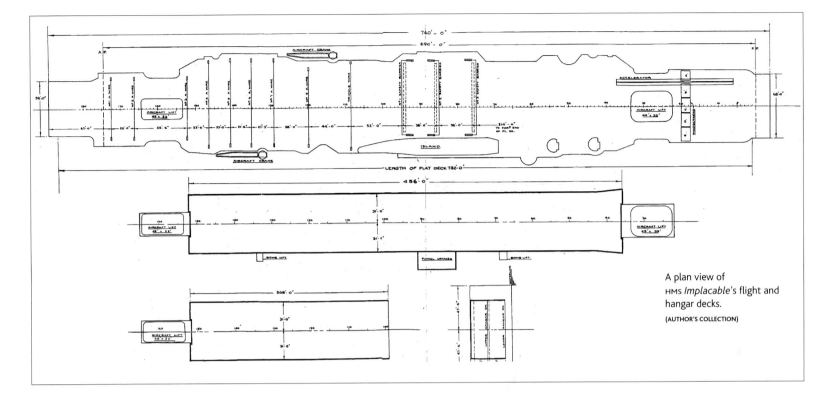

A plan view of HMS *Implacable*'s flight and hangar decks.
(AUTHOR'S COLLECTION)

Pillar lights were spaced at regular intervals, with three on each side of the flight deck, and were intended to be an extra indication of the deck's perspective for inexperienced pilots. They were 6 feet high and hinged to fall flat if touched by an aircraft's wingtip without causing damage, and were spaced 60 feet apart. When on the ideal approach path the pilot saw them as a single strip of light, the top of one pillar being aligned with the bottom of the next ahead.

Sector lights were fitted on either side of the deck, ideally 150 feet forward of the round-down. They each shone through a 30-degree horizontal sector aft and showed three colours in vertical sectors so that only one could be seen by the pilot, depending on his angle above the horizontal. From the horizontal to 5 degrees he saw red; between 5 degrees and 8 degrees, the ideal glide-slope, he saw green; and between 8 and 15 degrees he saw amber. By 1945 sector lights were stabilised in pitch and were considered a primary landing aid.

Round-down lights comprised up to 15 lights situated athwartships at the top of the curve of the after round-down to indicate the after end of the landing area. The centre three were red to help indicate the centreline; the outboard lights were green.

Outline lights were white and fitted along the outboard edges of the landing area to indicate its width, helping pilots turning finals to orientate themselves with the deck.

Direction lights comprised two lines of green lights either side of the centreline in the take-off area in the forward half of the flight deck. Most shone aft to enable pilots to keep straight during take-off. Those forward shone forward and were intended to indicate the forward end of the deck to pilots crossing the bows on entering the visual circuit. Direction lights were not fitted to escort carriers and in USN-supplied ships, but in their case the outline lights could be selected to shine forward.

Stanchion lights were another aid to take-off, and one was fitted on each side of the flight deck forward, showing the widest part of the take-off area.

Obstruction lights were red and fitted on or near structures or fittings above flight-deck level that might be a hazard to the operation of aircraft.

All flight-deck lighting was controlled from switches and dimmers located in the Flight Deck/Aircraft Control Room in the island.

Most British carriers were built with two lifts on the centreline at the fore and aft extremities of the hangar. In the early ships of the *Illustrious* group they were kept as small as possible to minimise the size of penetrations in the armoured deck, but this was found to be a crippling limitation on the size and type of aircraft that could be embarked. In *Implacable* and other ships of the later groups the forward lift was enlarged to be 45 feet long by 33 feet wide. This allowed a greater number of types to be struck down, but the forward lift served only the upper hangar. The after lift remained at the original 45 feet by 22 feet and served both upper and lower hangars. Both lifts could move aircraft weighing up to 20,000lb.

Implacable had two electrically-operated cranes, one on either side of the flight deck at hangar deck level aft of the island. Originally designed as seaplane cranes, they were fitted with power-operated tricing winches and wave-compensating gear, which helped in lifting boats and ditched aircraft, and in other uses including hoisting out fuel hoses to refuel escorts. They had a useful capacity to pick up an aircraft that had hit a barrier (a 'barrier prang') and hoist it outboard clear of the deck so that the next aircraft could land-on quickly. Like all electrical equipment on board, the cranes and crane drivers were the responsibility of the Torpedo Department. A mobile crane on the flight deck, capable of lifting 12,000lb, was intended primarily for the removal of crashed aircraft to clear the landing area, but had many other uses. Other flight-deck vehicles included four 'Clarkat' tractors for moving aircraft, and two fork-

A posed photograph of aircrew being briefed for one of the strikes on *Tirpitz* using a target model set up in the wardroom of a fleet carrier (note the patterned carpet under the model)
(AUTHOR'S COLLECTION)

lift trucks.

Control of activity on the flight deck was carried out in the Flight Deck Control Room in the island at flight-deck level. In the same office the functions of aircraft control were also carried out, and the term Aircraft Control Room, or ACR, gradually replaced the earlier name. The officer in charge was the Aircraft Control Room Officer (ACRO). He sat at a desk on which he had metal boards inscribed with accurate diagrams of the flight and hangar decks. On these he used magnetic shapes cut to the accurate dimensions of all aircraft embarked, both folded and unfolded, to indicate their positions. They were colour-coded green on top, indicating that the aircraft was serviceable, or red on the 'flip side', indicating that it was unserviceable. Each would have the number of the aircraft it represented written on it. The room contained voice-pipe[7] and intercom communication with Flyco, and a host of other equipment including a switchboard for night deck lighting and dimmer switches; hydraulic controls to raise and lower the W/T masts; hydraulic controls for the wind-breaks; control for the steam jet forward which indicated wind direction; and the arrester gear ready lamps. There was also an arrester gear control valve setting order device to transmit the required setting to the control position in the port catwalk, and a flying telegraph connected to a repeater in the engine control room. The last gave the 'state of the deck' to the officer in charge of the ship's main machinery and included 'ranging aircraft', 'crash on deck', 'take-off', 'first land-on', 'last land-on', 'crash in sea' and others. It had particular relevance as the engineer officer of the watch might need to accept machinery damage to keep a constant wind over the deck in action if aircraft were landing-on, and after a crash in the sea nearby he might expect rapid manoeuvring orders. All mechanical equipment on the flight deck was the responsibility of the ship's Marine Engineering Department, and sailors working on deck wore white surcoats with a black stripe, earning them the nickname 'badgers'.

Flyco was the control centre for all flying operations, and was situated on the port side of the island next to the compass platform from which the ship itself was controlled. In early carriers it had been open, but by 1945 it was partially closed in to make it habitable in foul weather. In *Implacable* a number of instruments were fitted to help 'Wings" control of flying operations. These included a wind speed and direction indicator, which could be selected between anemometers at the masthead and on the starboard bow. Indicators showed both lift positions and whether they were locked in place, arrester wire settings and readiness, and flight-deck lighting state. Controls were provided for the traffic lights, to enable Very lights to be fired to order an aircraft to 'wave-off' and to sound an alarm klaxon on deck. There was a gyro compass repeater showing the ship's course. Voice pipes were provided to the compass platform, ACR and operations room, and two-way intercoms to the DLCO platform, ACR, Aircraft Direction Room (ADR) and the Hangar Control Position (HCP). An exchange telephone and a broadcast system allowed 'Wings' to use loudspeakers on the flight deck, in the hangar, or the ship's main broadcast. On deck the loudspeakers were known as 'bull horns' and had to overcome the noise of a running range of aircraft engines. In consequence, at full volume in still air, they could be heard about three miles away.

The ship's Operations Room, or 'Ops Room', was situated in the island close to the Compass Platform and Flyco. It was originally known as the Air Operations Room, but as the flow of information needed to fight the carrier grew to encompass all forms of warfare, the name was changed. Originally it was used by aircrew [8] to get their orders before and after briefing, and was fitted with plots, chart tables, drawers, blackboards, a clock and even a bunk for the duty Air Staff Officer. The number of briefings and the material needed for them led to redesign and the use of other compartments as briefing and ready rooms. As the focal point of what had become the Action Information Organisation (AIO), the Ops Room was equipped with a General Operations Plot (GOP) on a large table and a Local Operations Plot (LOP) which displayed a moving, stabilised radar picture upwards on to a glass table. There was also a signal desk, an Army Liaison desk, 'state-boards' and a separated Air Staff Office. *Implacable* was the first carrier to be fitted with a small Bridge Mess with its own pantry and hot cupboards so that officers whose duties kept them in the island could have hot meals when required.

Fighter Direction techniques expanded rapidly after radar revolutionised aircraft operations. From 1940 all carriers had a room fitted out as a Fighter Direction Office, but it was gradually realised that radar enabled all aircraft missions to be controlled, including strikes and antisubmarine patrols, using techniques originally evolved for fighters. Thus, in *Implacable* and later carriers, the space was enlarged and renamed the Aircraft Direction Room (ADR). It was situated in the island, close to the Ops Room, and was part of the AIO. The ADR gave the facility for constant control of the carrier's own or other aircraft. Detections from the ship's radar sets were passed to the ADR, where they were plotted.[9] Reports from ships in company were passed on voice circuits, among them the Air Raid Reporting Net,[10] and plotted. Interceptor plots were placed in front of the main plot with information fed by 'filter plotters' to 'interceptor plotters' by intercom. In *Implacable* the individual direction officers each had radar Plan Position Indicators (PPI) which showed raw radar and Identification Friend or Foe (IFF) in addition to the intercept plotting board. They received target information by intercom or telephone and had R/T communication with their own aircraft. They each had a Radar Plot qualified rating as an assistant to help with communications. A senior direction officer sat behind the interceptor plots so that he could monitor overall activity. He had access to the flight deck and main broadcast systems as well as intercoms and telephones. Space was also provided for a Fleet Direction Officer if the ship was acting as a Flagship and a gunnery liaison officer to co-ordinate fighter defence with the ship's gunnery systems. The significant difference between a fleet carrier and an escort carrier was not in the design of the ADR, but in the number of stations at which direction officers and their assistants could work.

Hangars were the largest spaces and in *Implacable* the upper hangar was divided into three sections, A, B and C, by fire curtains. Their lengths, respectively, were 166, 124 and 166 feet; each was 62 feet wide but only 14 feet high. The lower hangar was divided into two sections, X and Y, by a fire curtain. These were, respectively 83 and 125 feet long, each 62 feet wide and 14 feet high. *Implacable* and her sister ship *Indefatigable* were the first British carriers that were not specified to operate floatplanes. Unfortunately this led to the hangar height being reduced from the 16 feet of the early *Illustrious* group to only 14 feet to reduce the amount of side armour, and thus top-weight, required. *Indomitable*, her half-sister, had an upper hangar 14 feet high and a lower hangar 16 feet high. The result of the low hangar height in the last group was that they could not operate USN-supplied fighters such as the Vought Corsair[11] and that they were severely constrained as to what aircraft they could operate, almost from the moment of their completion. This was a disastrous shortcoming in ships that had the biggest internal volume of any yet completed for the RN, and was to condemn them to very short operational lives because the cost of rebuilding the armoured hangars into a single structure with more height proved to be unafford-able. In addition to providing stowage for aircraft and the arrester gear mechanisms between the 'deep beams', hangars provided storage for large or bulky spare aircraft components. They were effectively 'closed, armoured boxes' that could only be entered on the lifts or through airlocks at the appropriate deck levels.

Hangars were controlled by a Hangar Control Officer (HCO) who operated in a Hangar Control Position (HCP) on the starboard side about 10 feet above deck level, giving a clear view of activity. There was an HCP in both upper and lower hangars. Both were fitted with extensive communications with direct lines to Flyco, the ACR, the ship's Damage Control HQ and secondary DCHQ, Avgas control compartments and the hangar access lobbies. Aircraft were packed tightly, three abreast, and it was difficult to manoeuvre the last two or three aircraft in when most of the space was filled. Hangars were brightly lit when aircraft maintenance was in progress, but switches were fitted to the lift platform that switched off the

A typical British fighter direction officer's position. This one is in an escort carrier; those in *Implacable* would have been similarly equipped but more numerous.

(AUTHOR'S COLLECTION)

The aircrew briefing room in a CVE. Fitted out to USN standards, it is rather better equipped than those in British-built fleet carriers.

(AUTHOR'S COLLECTION)

main hangar lighting when the 'keeps' were withdrawn, leaving only dim red safety lighting so that the ship's position would not be given away by the 'loom' of light when the lift platform descended below deck level. The main lighting comprised three rows of 500W lamps overhead, each one intended to be over the centreline of the three columns of aircraft in their stowed positions. The lights in the outer rows were spaced 41 feet apart, with the aim that each would be over the engine of a parked aircraft. The lights in the centre row were spaced 20 feet apart to give greater general lighting. Further 500W lights were fitted at intervals along the hangar bulkheads, and 136W low voltage hand lamps were provided with sockets on each side of the hangar at intervals of approximately 120 feet. Beside these sockets, there were connections for 220V portable hand lamps, floodlights and small portable tools. These could only be used under 'Fuel Safe' conditions in their particular hangar, and were enabled by a master switch in the HCP. An 'emergency off' master switch was fitted in each hangar access lobby.

Since the loss of *Ben-my-Chree* to a fuel vapour explosion British designers were concerned about the risk inherent in handling Avgas. The hangar fire-fighting arrangements in *Implacable* comprised a separate spray system in each of the five hangars, each supplied by three pumps. These worked at 90 psi and were cross-connected with the fire-main. Both used seawater. There were four connections to the fire-main in each hangar, with ready-use hoses and branch pipes (plain or jet/spray) nearby. Up to eight two-gallon hand-held extinguishers and numerous sand buckets were provided in each hangar, together with a single CO_2 extinguisher with a 40lb cylinder mounted on a trolley. Asbestos flame-resistant suits were stowed in lockers by the fire-points. Each hangar had access lobbies on both port and starboard sides, each of which contained spray-pump starter switches and alarm rattler controls; control buttons for power lowering the fire curtains, a clutch for changing from power to hand control if necessary and a handle for operating the fire curtains by hand. In the event of a serious hangar fire the HCO would order the fire curtains to be lowered, start the pumps, open the spray valves and close ventilation and exhaust. With the amount of water generated any fire was cut down quickly, but men in the hangar would be at considerable risk. The amount of water would rapidly become a problem, and if the upper hangar flooded to a depth of only two feet the ship's stability would be compromised. To clear the water away, eight-inch scuppers were fitted at intervals along the sides of the hangar. Hangar ventilation was achieved by drawing air in through inlets high in the hangar bulkheads and exhausting it directly by 17½-inch high-efficiency fans at deck level. Flaps could be closed in the exhaust trunking but the supply inlets were always open.

Aircraft on the flight deck and in the hangar were secured by lashing the aircraft to link plates, later known as ring-bolts, welded into the flight and hangar decks. In early carriers these were screwed into sockets in places where it was thought aircraft might need to be secured, three being provided per aircraft. This proved inadequate, and *Implacable* and *Indefatigable* were the first British carriers to be built with link plates welded into the flight and hangar decks in symmetrical lines. There were over a thousand on the flight deck alone. Each comprised a circular 'cup' welded into a circle cut in the deck; a bar at the top held a ring to which the aircraft lashing could be secured. It was designed so that the link was flush when the ring was down and it fell down facing forward. Thus an aircraft taking off would knock down an upright ring and pass over it. If a ring was mounted the wrong way round it might stand proud, and a passing tyre could not knock it flat and might burst. A good team of flight-deck handlers always kicked ring-bolts flat if they saw them standing proud for no good reason. The lashing itself consisted of a length of 45-hundredweight special flexible steel wire cable with a quick-release hook at one end and a shackle at the other. In the centre there was a turnbuckle which gave 15 to 18 inches of adjustment. In really heavy weather, handling parties were advised to back-up the wire lashings with 2½-inch hemp ropes, secured wherever possible.[12]

The aircraft fuelling system comprised pipes running round the hangars and flight deck, from which connections could be run to aircraft in almost

any position. It allowed six aircraft to be refuelled at the rate of 20 gallons per minute simultaneously, but with an air group of 80 aircraft in 1945 this was inadequate. The hose that connected the system to the aircraft used a Zwicky self-closing, trigger-operated delivery nozzle, exactly like the ones in use at filling-station forecourts today. Separate hoses and brass adaptors were provided to connect aircraft to fuel draining connections, the rate of defuelling depending on the number of pumps in operation. The fuel was piped back into the system and reused. *Implacable* had storage for only 94,650 gallons of Avgas.

The Royal Navy had a useful Photographic Reconnaissance (PR) capability by 1945, and most carriers were fitted with photographic arrangements to varying degrees of sophistication. Fleet carriers were capable of handling vertical photography, oblique photography, making mosaics for PR Interpreters and even making three-dimensional models of targets for strike briefings. Most fighter and strike aircraft were fitted with cameras to record details of weapons release and the analysis of

practices, and these, too, could be supported. All deck landings were filmed with movie cameras, but the film was only developed if there was an accident that needed to be investigated or debriefed.

Two large stores complexes aft of the after lift, on the upper gallery deck level, were racked for spare wings and other bulky items including engines and drop-tanks, and a further large compartment, situated right aft immediately below the flight deck, contained smaller stores items. The ship had extensive workshops capable of carrying out aircraft and component repair to a major level. These included specialist areas for parachute maintenance and fabric repair; engine stripping, cleaning and repairing; a metalworkers' shop; a spark-plug servicing bay; an electrical and instrument repair shop and workshops with test facilities for aircraft R/T, W/T and radar.

Implacable could stow over a thousand bombs of varying sizes and fifty-four torpedoes. The former were placed on British conversions of USN bomb trolleys known as Skid Number 1 Mod 1 in the bomb room, brought up on bomb lifts[13] and taken on the

USS *Bogue*, CVE 9, was similar to the large number of '*Attacker*' and '*Ruler*'-class ships operated by the Royal Navy under Lend-Lease arrangements. Like all American designs, the rectangular flight deck made no compromises and allowed the maximum number of aircraft to be ranged.

(AUTHOR'S COLLECTION)

same trolley, via the fusing point, to individual aircraft on deck. The speed of delivery depended very much on the drill of the bomb supply parties, which were made up with seamen from outside the Air Department, fusing personnel from the Air Gunner's party and loading personnel from the squadrons. Bombs of greater weight than 500lb had to be carried on modified torpedo trolleys. Aircraft designed for the USN, such as the Avenger, used special hoists which could lift bombs up to 1,600lb into place. The Royal Navy designed and used the similar Type 'C' hoist after 1945. Torpedoes were brought up special torpedo lifts from a torpedo assembly room amidships. Trolleys were designed to allow the weapon to be raised into its stowage under the aircraft. Fairey Barracudas of 828 and 841 NAS from *Implacable* carried out the last attack by Royal Navy aircraft using torpedoes on 28 October 1944 off the coast of Norway, sinking six merchant ships and driving a U-boat ashore.

The smaller *Tracker* and *Ruler*-class escort carriers (CVE) operated by the Royal Navy under Lend-Lease arrangements from the USN stand up well to comparison. They were capable of operating the same aircraft types as the fleet carriers up to a maximum air group size of about 30. HMS *Queen*, typical of the 23 ships of the *Ruler* class, was a versatile aircraft carrier, her major disadvantage being a top speed of only 18 knots, but endurance was more than double that of the fleet carriers, with 'spare' fuel to replenish escorts at sea if necessary. The most obvious difference, apart from sheer size, was the wooden flight deck,[14] the planks being laid on top of a mild-steel structure built over the basic hull. Lashing points were contained in cross-deck steel channels into which the anchor points could be slotted. Like the bigger carriers they had a single 'accelerator', nine wires and three barriers of similar capability. They were originally supplied with 1½ -inch diameter USN-pattern arrester wires, but these proved unsuitable for British-built aircraft hooks and were replaced by standard British 2½-inch centre-spans. The USN-designed barrier stanchions were power-operated but not designed to take any strain. The heavy barrier wire was held in place by a light wire and shearing

pin. When an aircraft hit the barrier the pin sheared and the wires pulled out. Unlike the British carriers, there were no forward-facing direction lights, but some of the forward outline lights could be selected to shine forward, achieving the same purpose. Another advantage of the CVEs was that the flight deck was rectangular with no round-down, allowing the whole deck to be used for aircraft ranges and deck parking. Using all the space available in the hangar and on deck, up to 90 aircraft could be ferried, and a number of CVEs, including *Queen* in 1944, were used exclusively as ferry carriers.

Another positive advantage was the hangar height. At 18 feet it placed no restrictions on the types of aircraft that could be struck down, and the two lifts were both similar in size to the larger, forward lift in *Implacable*. As supplied they had no fire curtains and no HCP, but these were fitted when the opportunity arose as the ships were brought up to operational standard. Some were also fitted with sophisticated AIO facilities including ADRs and AntiSubmarine Plots. The British suffered from a shortage of fleet carriers throughout the war and, in addition to convoy protection, CVEs were used as effective fleet carrier surrogates in strike operations off the Norwegian coast, in the Aegean and in the Indian Ocean.

In the last weeks of the war the first light fleet carriers entered service with the Royal Navy. Designed with half a cruiser's machinery and no complicated gunnery or fire control equipment, they achieved build times of just over two years for the first four ships and had a deck nearly the size of a fleet carrier for a fraction of the operating cost. They were among the most successful warship designs of their era, and a number were exported after 1945 when they became surplus to requirements. They, too, had high hangars, big lifts and 'level' flight decks without significant round-downs. The first sixteen had a low maximum speed of 24 knots which ultimately limited the launch envelopes of later generations of aircraft, but a second group, completed post-war, had double the machinery to give an extra 4 knots, making them very successful ships. One is still running in the Indian Navy, over sixty years after it was laid down.

The lighter USN pattern of barrier stanchion fitted in a British CVE. The lines of U-shaped holes are securing points for aircraft lashings, and the V-shaped boards at the top right are tailwheel guides to help aircraft line up on the single catapult.

(AUTHOR'S COLLECTION)

By comparison, the larger USN *Essex* class made no concessions to aerodynamic shape on the flight deck, both it and the single open-sided hangar deck being designed uncompromisingly to operate the largest number of aircraft. The hull was actually narrower than that of *Implacable*, but the flight deck was appreciably wider and its squared-off ends forward and aft allowed more aircraft to be ranged and parked. Air group size in 1945 was between 90 and 100 aircraft. The flight deck was wooden, supported by a steel superstructure over the armoured hangar deck, and had nine Mark 4 arrester wires aft and the capability to rig six forward for aft-facing landings. Each was capable of arresting aircraft up to 19,800lb at up to 55 knots. Later units of the class in 1945 had Mark 5 gear capable of arresting 30,000lb at up to 78 knots. Both marks had a shorter pull-out than British arresting gear. There were three barriers similar to those fitted in CVEs.

The first four units of the *Essex* class had two catapults on the flight deck forward and a third, double-ended unit athwartships in the hangar. Each was capable of launching aircraft up to 18,000lb at 78 knots; the latter was intended to launch aircraft out of the hangar. It was fitted in four ships but was seldom used, and was removed before 1945. A remarkable 240,000 gallons of Avgas were contained in hull tanks similar to those used for the ship's fuel oil. These could constitute a weakness, however, after action damage, making the ships vulnerable to fire. By using a completely standard main and auxiliary machinery installation in all ships and placing orders with only five shipyards, the build times for this class were incredibly short. One of the two civilian firms, Newport News Shipbuilding Co, built seven of the first eleven ships on four slipways between April 1941 and October 1944, with individual build times as low as 14 months, nearly a year less than a light fleet carrier in the UK.

The nearest IJN equivalents were the *Shokaku* and *Zuikaku*,[15] which were completed in 1941, just before the attack on Pearl Harbor. After the aberrations in *Akagi* and *Hiryu*, both the new ships had starboard-side islands with two typically Japanese downward-curving funnels. The flight deck was larger than that in most British carriers and had six arrester wires aft

A typical CVE hangar. HMS *Ravager* was a deck-landing training carrier, and the aircraft struck down include Fairey Fulmar nightfighters, Grumman Wildcats, Hellcats and Avengers and a Fairey Barracuda for the different pilot courses to use.

(AUTHOR'S COLLECTION)

and three forward. There were three barriers and three lifts, all on the centreline, the forward one being slightly larger than the other two. The normal aircraft complement was 72, with the ability to carry 12 more as dismantled reserves.

The hangar was a closed mild-steel box with no armour protection, as was the flight deck. In a British armoured carrier the blast from a 1,000lb armour-piercing bomb detonating in the hangar could be contained, although damage to aircraft and fittings would be devastating. Bomb blast in a USN carrier hangar would largely be vented through the open sides, but an explosion in a Japanese carrier was invariably spectacular.[16] The blast was contained initially by the closed hangar but, as the pressure built up, large areas of the structure were distorted, the flight deck being bulged upwards or blown out completely, similar damage occurring to the hangar walls. The 187,000 gallons of Avgas were carried in integral hull tanks surrounded by a thin screen of concrete, and these were liable to be cracked open by blast, causing explosion and intense fires. Inadequate ventilation design added to the problem, as did a disinclination to take damage control training as seriously as the subject deserved.

Both US and Japanese carriers had open forecastles which tended to throw spray back over the flight deck at high speed. They were vulnerable to damage in rough seas, unlike the 'hurricane bow' fitted to the British *Illustrious* and *Colossus* classes, a feature that also helped to smooth airflow past the hull when into wind for flying stations. A British-style streamlined bow was built into every USN carrier built or reconstructed after 1945.

Flying from a straight-deck carrier

A range of Grumman F6F Hellcats and TBF Avengers
on the second USS *Lexington*, CV 16.

Aircraft maintenance influenced aircraft carriers' ability to generate sorties and grew in importance with the technical complexity of the aircraft themselves, their engines, systems and weapons. It fell into two broad categories, planned and unplanned.[1] In 1945 the former comprised 'before flight' and 'after flight' inspections and 'Mainchecks' at set numbers of flying hours graded between 1 and 5. A Maincheck 5 was a major undertaking which entailed stripping the aircraft; removing the engine, weapons and sensors to look for hidden corrosion, cracks and damage. It was usually undertaken at an air yard ashore. Air Engineers attempted to even-out the major servicing events so that they did not all fall at once, make excessive demands on manpower and 'ground' the squadron until the work was complete. Most engines and components were 'lifed' by set numbers of flying hours and had to be replaced by new or refurbished items at appropriate Mainchecks. It was a judgement decision whether or not to replace items that were not yet life-expired in an airframe that was already stripped down for other work in order to save time and manpower later. This would assume that sufficient spares were available to cover the 'lost' hours caused by early replacement, and this was seldom the case in 1945, especially in the British Pacific Fleet.

Unplanned maintenance included the repair or replacement of failed or battle-damaged components and airframe structure. Before a period of sustained flying operations, air engineers would try to clear as much planned servicing work as possible to make the largest number of aircraft available and to have resources available for unplanned work. The type of flying programme had an impact on availability. The armoured carriers were designed, at first, to have an air group of only thirty-six aircraft, most of them TSR types, which were expected to be launched in small numbers throughout the day to find the enemy fleet, shadow it, slow it with torpedo attacks and spot the fall of shot of battleships' guns. Replacement aircraft in the maintenance carrier *Unicorn* were expected to be close at hand to replace combat losses. Reality in 1945 was different; air group size had grown to fifty-four in the early ships of the class and eighty

in the last two. About a third were kept in a permanent deck park and suffered from salt spray and soot from the funnel gases. Some of these even had to have major component changes on deck if room could not be found for them to be struck down. The requirement to launch frequent CAP and ASW patrols still existed, but the overriding requirement was the deck load strike. This was a 'pulse' of power intended to strike at the enemy at sea or on land with the maximum number of aircraft. Routine, hour-based maintenance was possible with the earlier method but difficult in the latter. A number of aircraft began to accumulate that could not be repaired or given the relevant Maincheck overnight to be ready for the dawn range. During the day squadron maintenance ratings worked flat out refuelling and rearming aircraft, with the result that the growing number of 'hours-expired' aircraft became a waste of space. In the worst cases they were stripped of useful components and literally pushed over the side. This may seem profligate in the twenty-first century, but the USN worked a very similar system and made even less attempt than the Royal Navy to return 'duds' to maintenance yards where they could be refurbished for further service. If the Pacific War had continued, the Royal Navy planned to use CVEs close to the fleet carriers in which deep maintenance work could have been undertaken to take some of the load off the operational squadron maintenance personnel. In addition to the need for maintenance, repair was a constant worry, as flying propeller-driven aircraft from straight-deck carriers was dangerous and losses were common, even without contact with the enemy. British and American carriers reckoned to lose up to 20 per cent of their aircraft in accidents on deck during protracted operations.

Flight-deck operations in British carriers reflected the cramped conditions caused by the increasing size of their wartime air groups, and the growing requirements for technical support and maintenance. The ship's company of *Illustrious* grew from about 1,400 in 1940 to 2,000 in 1945, with no real improvement in the quality and quantity of mess deck space. Every aircraft had to be manhandled from the hangar on to the lift and then aft into the range.

Tractors helped movement on deck from 1945, aircraft being steered by an 'arm' attached to the tailwheel, with chock-men walking by the main wheels in case ship motion caused the aircraft to slide. Marshallers had standardised orders to control the handling teams; 'tail amidships, come astern'; 'tail to starboard'; 'midships'. Once the aircraft was in position, the order 'stop – in chocks and lashings' was given and the handling team moved on to the next aircraft. It took training and skill to manoeuvre an aircraft into a narrow slot in the range, especially after hours on deck, and especially at night when there was no deck lighting and only minimal use of shaded torches was allowed. Aircraft supplied by the USN, such as the Corsair, had power folding wings, but British-built aircraft such as the Seafire did not, and every one of them had to be spread and folded by hand, another labour-intensive, physical and time-consuming activity. Aircraft only moved under their own power when taking off or taxiing forward of the barrier after landing. On all other occasions they were

pushed. Once ranged, every aircraft had to be started, warmed-up and tested, armed and, if necessary, refuelled in the range by squadron maintenance ratings.[2] Any that were found to be unserviceable had to be manhandled out of the range, others having to be moved to clear a path if necessary, and struck down. A replacement, if there was one, ranged in its place,[3] a procedure that might involve ranging half a dozen in order to extract the one required and then striking them down again. Space and time were critical factors.

Briefings for aircrew, the numbers of aircraft to be flown and launch and recovery times were included on the ship's flying programme, known as the 'Flypro', with other useful information such as the times of sunrise and sunset. Individual squadron programmes were produced by squadron Senior Pilots and showed the individual aircraft and aircrew to implement the Flypro. Commander 'Air', known as 'Wings', was responsible to the captain for making the flying programme happen as efficiently as

The North American B-25's wingtips overlap the deck edges in this photograph of the uss *Hornet*, CV 8, on passage for the 'Doolittle Strike'. Grumman F4F Wildcat fighters parked forward could have been launched by catapult if necessary, but could not have recovered to the ship. (AUTHOR'S COLLECTION)

possible. He had four principal assistants; the Operations Officer, whose team produced the Flypro; Lieutenant Commander 'Flying', known as 'Little f', who took charge of aircraft on deck and in the vicinity of the carrier; the Flight Deck Officer (FDO), who ran the deck; and the DLCO, who controlled deck landings. The ability of this group to work together as a team was of fundamental importance. The time between launches needed to be varied. On passage ASW patrols would be launched every three hours; if

A strike range of Supermarine Seafires and Fairey Fireflies on HMS *Triumph* during the Korean War in 1950.
(AUTHOR'S COLLECTION)

a continuous CAP had to be maintained with low-endurance aircraft such as the Seafire, a launch and recovery might be needed every 90 minutes. There was still room for individual initiative, however, and Commander C.L.G. Evans DSO RN, 'Wings' of *Implacable* in 1945, succeeded in exchanging several crates of whisky for a large number of USAAF 89-gallon drop tanks originally intended for Curtiss P-40 fighters. These raised the Seafire's endurance from a little over 90 minutes to over 4 hours, dramatically improving the potential of the whole air group and lengthening the period between launch and recovery operations.

With a manned, running range the carrier turned into wind minutes before the scheduled launch time and accelerated. Returning aircraft orbited the ship in the waiting pattern as, with seconds to go, she steadied into wind. After approval to launch by the captain, 'Wings' gave the 'affirmative' signal to the FDO, who waved away the chocks and raised his green flag. Flag 'Foxtrot', which would have been at the dip, was hauled close up. The pilot of the leading aircraft in the range opened up his engine to full power against the brakes, raising his right hand to show the FDO that he was ready to go. The latter lowered his flag and, as the aircraft began to skid forwards, the pilot released the brakes and accelerated forward. Before his wheels left the deck, marshallers were already bringing the next aircraft on to the centreline, and the FDO repeated the process until the range was airborne. Aircraft turned hard to port or starboard after leaving the deck so that their slipstream did not affect the next astern. Strikes were given a briefed 'form-up' area, usually some miles on either bow; fighter sections slipped into formation and headed straight for their briefed CAP station. Aircraft that went unserviceable in the seconds before launch taxied, or were pushed into the 'graveyard' forward of the island to let others get past them. The take-off interval between aircraft in a worked-up carrier was 20 to 30 seconds.

Recovering aircraft timed their circuit to start the turn on to finals as the last aircraft took off, the batsman having run from his position as FDO launching the range to his sponson, ready for the first aircraft. As each one crossed the round-down the batsman would give the 'cut' signal and the aircraft sank into the wires with a pronounced 'clang' as the hook struck the metal deck. In the hangar below, every landing sounded like a pile of scrap metal being dropped on the deck above, followed by the 'wheezing' of the wires running through their blocks. An actual crash sounded very different, with a prolonged scraping sound as the aircraft slid along the deck. As each aircraft came to rest, green-

surcoated 'hook-men' ran out from the adjacent catwalk to release it, and the pilot gave a burst of throttle to taxi forward as the barrier was dropped. As soon as he had passed it the 'talker' told the batsman that he was clear to bring on the next aircraft. The landing interval on most fleet carriers was less than 30 seconds. Once it was safely into Fly 1 each aircraft was marshalled more slowly into its shut-down spot, where it was chocked and lashed before the engine was switched off. Space was tight

The amount of deck available for take-off and landing could be increased by putting the tailwheels of alert fighters on outriggers so that only the part of the aircraft forward of the main wheels was over the deck, but it was ready to start in seconds. These are Wildcats of 853 Naval Air Squadron on HMS Queen in 1945.
(AUTHOR'S COLLECTION)

and the wheels could well be right at the deck-edge, leaving some pilots with no view of the deck at all, completely reliant on their marshaller. If the deck was not ready for whatever reason, the DLCO 'waved-off' the next aircraft and continued to do so until it was clear. A crash on deck, known as a 'prang', was rare but inevitable, given the stress and pace of carrier operations in wartime. USN-supplied aircraft, such as the Grumman Hellcat, proved far more robust deck-landing aircraft than the fragile Seafire, and their undercarriages often made the difference between an awkward but safe 'arrival' and a prang.

If there was a crash on deck, the flight-deck party reacted quickly to cut down any potential Avgas fire, rescue the pilot if possible and to clear the deck as quickly as possible in order to land-on any remaining aircraft. While 'Jumbo' the crane lurched out of its stowage aft of the island, fire hoses were run out with foam canisters and CO_2 cylinders ready for use. A team of red steel-helmeted 'firesuitmen' in protective asbestos overalls and gloves, equipped with fire-axes, were at constant readiness on deck whenever flying

was in progress, tasked with getting the aircrew quickly out of any wreck. The 'Fleet Standard' was to clear the crashed aircraft in 5 minutes or less. Often repairs were beyond the capacity of ship's staff and the wreck would have been pushed straight over the side. While crash removal took place, pilots left in the air orbited around the fleet, watching their petrol gauges and thinking their thoughts.[4]

Most launches from Royal Navy carriers before the jet age were free take-offs like the one described above. By 1945, however, it was common for the first few aircraft of a range to be 'accelerated' if a large range was to be launched. The first row of aircraft would thus only need space to be marshalled on to the accelerator. The advantages were that more aircraft could be ranged, or that aircraft could be launched at greater weight than the available wind over the deck would otherwise have allowed. The downside was that accelerated launches were slower, with delays of a minute or more between aircraft and consequent delays in forming-up the strike and taking departure towards the target. Another assisted take-

An athwartship catapult launch of a TBF Avenger from the hangar of the USS *Essex*, CV 9, in 1943.

(AUTHOR'S COLLECTION)

off technique involved fitting 'booster' rockets to cradles mounted on the wings, inboard. It was known as rocket-assisted take-off gear (RATOG). Up to four cylindrical rockets could be fitted on each side, the number depending on the aircraft's weight and the degree of assistance required to get airborne. Each rocket comprised a steel tube with a pressure plate screwed into the head, into which fitted the pressure igniter. A grid, locking ring and venturi formed the tail, and the charge consisted of a 'stick' of cordite. The method of operation was for the pilot to roll forward as normal and to press the RATOG firing button as the tail rose. The extra thrust continued until the cordite was expended, when the pilot jettisoned the gear, rockets, cradles and all into the sea.[5] For obvious reasons there needed to be a clear area behind the launching aircraft, and RATOG was unpopular with pilots for two very good reasons. Firstly, although the manual said 'the rockets fire simultaneously', there were occasions when they did not, and the resulting asymmetric thrust caused aircraft to spin uncontrollably into the sea. Secondly,

the same manual said that the cradles and rocket tubes would jettison from both sides of the aircraft together, but again there was a chance that only one side would go, and the resulting asymmetric drag, while not necessarily fatal. made the aircraft difficult to fly.

The key element of deck operations was the batsman. All were experienced pilots who had completed at least one front-line tour at sea; some were volunteers but the majority were not. They had to be on their platform for every recovery, day or night in any weather and, by the end of a prolonged period at sea, must have had exceptional arm muscles. They were trained ashore at RNAS Arbroath in Scotland, and at sea in the training carrier, which usually operated in the Firth of Clyde. A specialist training unit, 767 NAS, operated a variety of operational types as 'clockwork mice' with which DLCOs under training could practise. For many years the school was run by Commander R.N. Everett RN, a passionate believer in the importance of DLCOs. By 1945 the pressure of flying operations led to most

A 'pilot's-eye' view of the final approach to HMS *Illustrious* in 1953, when operating as a trials and training carrier. The batsman's position is on the platform just to left of the deck recognition letter 'Y'. The aerial on the pole mast to starboard of the funnel is the YE homing beacon.

(AUTHOR'S COLLECTION)

The raised barriers were always a concern to pilots landing on a straight-deck carrier. This Blackburn Firebrand is slightly high and has both barriers raised to stop it if it misses the wires. The square structure visible on the deck edge through the barriers is the batsman's wind-break.
(AUTHOR'S COLLECTION)

'Good approach, keep it coming'
signalled to a Swordfish from the
DLSO on a MAC-Ship.

fleet carriers having one or two assistant batsmen, who were also used to supervise the ranging of aircraft.

Deck landing required standardised instruction, practice and concentration, but was not the 'black art' that popular accounts portrayed it to be. For most piston-engined aircraft the ship and wind speed reduced the relative approach speed to about 50 knots, and the pilot's main concern was his attitude, maintained by an indicated air speed just above the stall. Line-up and vertical position relative to an ideal glide-slope on final approach were the responsibility of the DLCO. The RN and USN used similar signals that differed in meaning until 1945, when the BPF adopted USN signals. After the formation of NATO

The standardised system introduced in 1948 was based on the USN system, which had been used by the British Pacific Fleet in 1945. It was based on the concept of informing the pilot about his position relative to the ideal glide-slope; thus raised arms meant 'YOU ARE TOO HIGH', in effect 'GO DOWN', the very opposite of the former RN system. As can be imagined, the change produced confusion and a number of accidents among experienced pilots when it was introduced. (AD HOC PUBLICATIONS VIA ROGER CHESNEAU)

RN System 1937–1948

Lower flaps Steady Up nose Go down Go starboard Go up

Wave off Go port Drop hook Wheels down Lower nose Cut engine

Standardized System 1948 onwards

Too high Too low Too fast Too slow Starboard wing high Port wing high

Lower your hook Lower your undercarriage Wave off Roger Cut

in 1948 all navies adopted the USN system as standard, and this technique remained in use until the adoption of the mirror landing aid. There was no substitute for experience and speed of interpretation between batsman and pilot, but as long as the relative closing speed remained low, the time lag between error, appreciation, instruction and correction was acceptable. The piston engine's immediate response to throttle demands meant that, in the last resort, a late wave-off could be ordered and executed safely. The DLCO's aim was to bring aircraft safely over the pitching round-down to a point where he could safely give the 'cut' and the aircraft would 'drop' into the area covered by the arrester wires. That is why indicated airspeed was so important; too fast and the aircraft would 'float' over the wires in ground effect and crash into the barrier, too slow and the pilot risked stalling short of the round-down and spinning

into the sea. DLCOs soon developed an 'eye' for the speed of the aircraft they controlled, and it helped when they had experience on each particular type. The technique was never intended to give precise accuracy on to a particular wire,[6] and nor could it have been. The large number of arrester wires cancelled out errors in the exact point at which the aircraft touched down.

The technique of night deck landing resembled that used by day but made use of the extensive lighting arrangements on ship and flight deck. Aircraft would circle the carrier before joining the visual circuit. The DLCO used illuminated bats and the sector lights gave pilots confidence that they were in the right 'ball park' as they turned on to final approach. Night recovery needed practice, and few carriers had the luxury of time to allow for this in the middle war years. Night operations often took the

The first carrier landing by a twin-engine aircraft. Lieutenant Commander Eric Brown lands a Mosquito FB.VI on HMS *Indefatigable* on 25 March 1944. The port engine nacelle obscured the DLCO, who had to stand well inboard to be seen, and run for the catwalk after giving the 'cut'. This photograph was taken from a wartime cine-film and is not, unfortunately, of the best quality.

(AUTHOR'S COLLECTION)

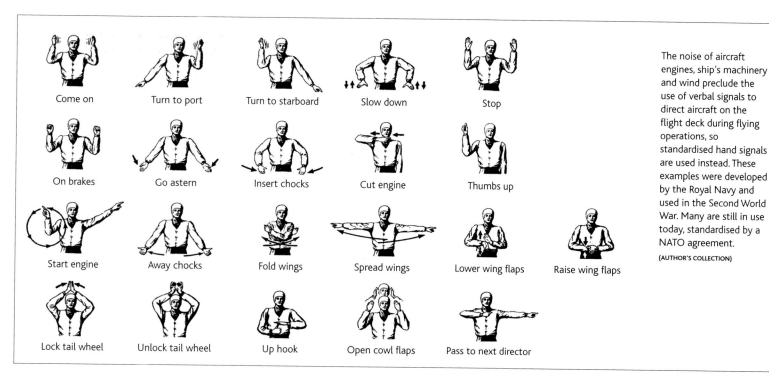

Come on · Turn to port · Turn to starboard · Slow down · Stop

On brakes · Go astern · Insert chocks · Cut engine · Thumbs up

Start engine · Away chocks · Fold wings · Spread wings · Lower wing flaps · Raise wing flaps

Lock tail wheel · Unlock tail wheel · Up hook · Open cowl flaps · Pass to next director

The noise of aircraft engines, ship's machinery and wind preclude the use of verbal signals to direct aircraft on the flight deck during flying operations, so standardised hand signals are used instead. These examples were developed by the Royal Navy and used in the Second World War. Many are still in use today, standardised by a NATO agreement.
(AUTHOR'S COLLECTION)

form of launches before sunrise and the recovery of fighters after sunset, when they had been in action. By 1945 the need for regular night operations was urgent, and HMS *Ocean* was completed as a specialised nightfighter carrier. Both *Implacable* and *Formidable* carried out night interdiction operations against Japanese targets ashore, but these were exceptions rather than normal operations in the BPF. Some nightfighters were operated from escort carriers operating on the Russian Convoy routes.

Two strike operations show the progress made by the Royal Navy in 'straight-deck' carrier operations between 1940 and 1945. The attack on Taranto was the first occasion on which carrier-borne aircraft attacked an enemy fleet in harbour. A small number of Swordfish used stealth to achieve surprise, launching from and recovering to HMS *Illustrious* at night about 170 miles from the target. The design of the ship and its operating technique limited the number of aircraft that could be used in the strike to a first range of twelve and a second of nine, one of which had to turn back when an overload fuel tank broke loose.[7] The last aircraft of this second range was 20 minutes late taking off because minor repairs had to be carried out following a collision with another aircraft as both moved out of the range to

Lieutenant Commander Brown makes the world's first turbojet-powered landing in Sea Vampire LZ551/G on 3 December 1945 on HMS *Ocean*.

(AUTHOR'S COLLECTION)

on the ship's ability to launch a deck-load strike.[8] Subsequent refits 'flattened' the deck aft and allowed larger ranges and a deck park to increase the ship's potential.

By July 1945 the strike operations carried out by the BPF required the most that could be achieved from the armoured carrier design. On 24 July 1945 the British carriers formed the fighting core of a highly mobile task force which ranged up and down the Japanese islands to achieve surprise and shock effect. Although the USN had the more effective *Essex* class carriers in some numbers, the disparity in air group sizes between British and American ships was

Lieutenant Commander G.R. Callingham carries out the world's first landing by a turboprop powered aircraft in Fairey Gannet prototype VR546 on HMS *Illustrious* on 19 June 1950.

(AUTHOR'S COLLECTION)

take off. Both ranges were limited in size by the excessive curvature of the round-down aft and the deck run needed ahead of the first aircraft for take-off. The accelerator was not used because it was thought that it would take too long to reload and the first aircraft off would waste fuel orbiting while waiting to form up with the last. It would also have delayed ranging, and therefore launching the second strike. The design of the flight deck thus had a major impact

not as great as has sometimes been stated, since the smaller *Independence*-class light carriers only carried about forty-five aircraft. Thus the USN Task Force 38 embarked 1,190 aircraft in ten fleet and six light carriers, an average of seventy aircraft. The British Task Force 37 embarked 255 aircraft in four fleet carriers, an average of sixty-four. On eight strike days off Japan in July and August 1945 British aircraft dropped a total of 460 tons of bombs on targets as

Landing-on in progress on the uss *Antietam*, CV 36, with an aircraft folding as it taxies forward over the barriers, photographed from the 'lead-ship' of a pair of Avengers waiting their turn to land.

(AUTHOR'S COLLECTION)

diverse as airfields, warships and other shipping, shipyards and harbour installations. Achievements compared favourably with those of the USN, although percentages are distorted by the smaller numbers deployed by the BPF. They included 447 enemy aircraft destroyed in the air and on the ground; an average of 0.28 per offensive sortie.[9] Despite USN attempts to keep IJN capital-ship targets to themselves, BPF pilots achieved good results. Lieutenant R.H. Grey DSC RCNVR won a posthumous VC for sinking a Japanese escort destroyer on 9 August 1945, losing his life in the process. British aircraft sank a total of 356,760 tons of enemy shipping; an average of 224 tons per offensive sortie.[10] British losses to deck-landing and other accidents remained higher than those of the USN, however, at 2 per cent of offensive sortie numbers compared with 0.55 per cent.[11]

British straight-deck carrier operating technique reached its zenith in the Korean War between 1950 and 1953. Throughout that period light fleet carriers of the Royal Navy and Royal Australian Navy (RAN) were maintained on task one at a time, supported by the maintenance carrier *Unicorn*. The Flag Officer Second-in-Command Far East Station noted the achievement of HMS *Theseus* in December 1950, a ship he described as a 'small but well-trained air group in a good light fleet carrier'.[12] He compared *Theseus*, which had an air group of thirty-three aircraft, with the BPF as it had been in May 1945, with an average air group of fifty-four aircraft. Despite having fewer aircraft *Theseus* flew 632 sorties in a period of 22 days' operations, compared with 562 sorties per carrier by the BPF in a period of 21 days, an outstanding achievement for which *Theseus*' air group was awarded the Boyd Trophy for 1950.[13]

Immediately after its resumption of full control over naval aviation, the Admiralty put pressure on the Ministry of Aircraft Production to manufacture high-performance aircraft for operation from flight decks. A series of trials demonstrated that the Air Ministry view that carrier-borne aircraft had, of necessity, to be of inferior performance was shown to be totally without foundation. Arguably the RAF's greatest contribution to naval aviation was the recovery of 46 Squadron's Hawker Hurricanes on to HMS *Glorious* in June 1940. If a handful of pilots with no previous deck-landing training could land 'high-performance' aircraft of a type that formed the bulk of Fighter Command's front line on a small carrier deck, the Admiralty saw at once that the way was open for similar aircraft to equip the navy's own fighter squadrons. Priority was given to the production of fighters for the RAF during the Battle of Britain, but Sea Hurricanes were adopted from January 1941, followed later in the year by Seafires[14] modified from RAF Spitfire Mark VCs. Such was the urgency to get them into service that deck-landing trials were carried out in HMS *Illustrious* in the Clyde during the Christmas week of 1941.[15] The trials were made using BL767, technically a 'hooked Spitfire' rather than a fully modified Seafire Mark I, flown by Lieutenant Commander H.P. Bramwell DSC RN.[16] The long nose

ahead of the cockpit obscured the pilot's view of both deck and batsman, so Bramwell tried two different landing techniques. First he tried a curving, steeply banked final approach off a tight circuit flown at 400 feet, keeping the batsman in sight and only levelling at the last moment to take the 'cut'. Then he tried a 'crabbing' approach, flying a longer straight approach on finals with the nose displaced to starboard by rudder and left bank applied to oppose the swing. The aircraft was kicked straight and levelled before closing the throttle at the cut. Bramwell preferred the first, as 'crabbing' only a knot or two above the stall risked flicking into a spin, especially when used by an inexperienced pilot. The trials were deemed to be 'sufficiently successful for production of the Seafire to be confirmed'.[17] The Seafire was never to be a good deck-landing aircraft, and was cursed with an undercarriage that was not up to the resilience required. It was so aerodynamically clean that if it was fast at the 'cut' it floated, without stalling, over the wires and into the barrier. In September 1942 another trial flown by Lieutenant E.M. 'Winkle' Brown RNVR cleared the Seafire for operation from escort carriers.

In April 1942 a force of sixteen North American B-25 Mitchell bombers led by Lieutenant Colonel 'Jimmy' Doolittle USAAF was launched from the USS *Hornet* to attack Tokyo, but there was never any question of landing them back on board. In the following year the Admiralty became disenchanted with the strike capability of the underpowered Barracuda, and tasked the RAE with evaluating the possibility of operating the de Havilland Mosquito VI fighter-bomber from the deck. The prospect was daunting, as the aircraft had a maximum weight of 21,600lb, 7,500lb more than the Barracuda II, and pilots' notes gave the landing speed as 110 knots. It had a wing span of 54 feet, making it a tight fit on the narrow deck of an *Illustrious*-class carrier. 'Winkle' Brown was chosen as the trial pilot and, together with his flying scientist Bill Stewart, they established how slowly on the approach the aircraft could be flown. It was clear that deck landing would require the aircraft to fly just above the stall with a lot of power, and two aircraft were especially modified with Rolls-

An Eastern Fleet Hellcat taxies into the deck park in Fly 1 after landing on HMS *Indomitable*. The lack of protective clothing worn by the handling party is surprising considering the ever-present risk of fire with aircraft fuelled by Avgas.

(AUTHOR'S COLLECTION)

Royce Merlin 25 engines giving +18lb of boost instead of the standard +12lb. To absorb that amount of power they were fitted with experimental, non-feathering, four-bladed propellers cropped to 12 feet 6 inches diameter so that they would not 'peck' the deck on pitching forward when the hook caught a wire.[18] There were concerns that the aircraft's wooden structure might not stand up to deck-landing stresses, and the RAE knew from the outset that failure of a single engine on take-off or on finals would be fatal. A reinforced 'Barracuda-type' arrester hook was fitted under the fuselage forward of the tailwheel.

The ADDLs were carried out at RNAS Arbroath, the deck-landing school, where there was a dummy deck complete with arrester wires. There Commander Everett acted as batsman throughout the trials ashore and afloat, and both he and Lieutenant Brown learnt from the outset that if the batsman stood in the normal position, relative to the wires, he would 'disappear' behind the port engine nacelle in the final stages of the approach. The first deck landing by a multi-engined aircraft took place on HMS

Indefatigable on the afternoon of 25 March 1944, off Ailsa Craig in the Clyde Estuary. Brown flew a fast, low slot and broke downwind. Abeam the island at 400 feet, he lowered the undercarriage, set flap to the intermediate position and selected the propeller pitch levers to fully fine. He continued further than usual downwind and turned on to final approach about a mile astern of the ship to fly a long straight approach at 75 knots IAS. His first impression was that he had the best view of the deck he had ever seen, with no engine in front of him; his second was to note that the batsman was in the centre of the deck so that he could be seen. The approach was steady, with only a small correction as the aircraft flew through the funnel gases at the stern. As it crossed the round-down the batsman gave the 'cut' and ran to the port catwalk; Brown eased the throttles back, knowing that the Mosquito had vicious stalling characteristics, and closed them about a foot above the deck to hit the deck in a three-point attitude, taking number 2 wire. When film was developed it was calculated that his speed into the wires was only

Dressed in his high-visibility suit, a USN batsman turns to look at a Corsair taking a wire on a CVL during the Korean War.

(AUTHOR'S COLLECTION)

66 knots. Subsequent take-offs and landings went well at gradually increased weights until the hook-bill broke on the third landing on 26 March. Fortunately Brown was able to open the throttles and take off to divert ashore.

The operation of heavy, twin-engined aircraft was proved viable, and Sea Mosquitoes saw service with the Fleet Air Arm, but not until after the war. The Royal Navy went on to achieve a number of deck-landing 'firsts' in the period immediately after the Second World War, most notably the first landing by a turbojet-powered aircraft, in December 1945. Again the pilot was 'Winkle' Brown, who by then had transferred from a temporary commission in the RNVR to a permanent commission as a lieutenant commander RN. The aircraft was LZ551/G,[19] a de Havilland Vampire prototype modified to interim Sea Vampire status by the installation of a tail hook, strengthened undercarriage and enlarged flaps. The ship, HMS *Ocean*, commanded by Captain Caspar John, later to become First Sea Lord, was at sea on 3 December 1945 and found conditions in the English Channel to be rough. A signal was sent to RNAS Ford, where the Vampire had spent the night, postponing the trial, but by the time it arrived Brown was already airborne. When Brown arrived over the ship, Caspar John took a judgement decision to let the trial proceed. He was conscious that 'beating the Americans to it' would be a considerable achievement for the Royal Navy.

Brown flew a standard circuit and, as he turned finals at 100 knots IAS, he was impressed by the view of the deck from the Vampire, this time with no engine nacelle to block out the batsman, but concerned by the amount of ship movement in both pitch and roll. He carried out a standard 'sinking approach' technique like that used by contemporary tailwheel aircraft (the Vampire had a nosewheel), easing back on the throttle and raising the nose before crossing the round-down. The batsman's 'cut' signal was of little value owing to the slow wind-down characteristic of the de Havilland Goblin engine, and the control inputs were intended to put the aircraft into the wires just above stalling speed. The hook took number 1 wire in a successful landing, although subsequent film analysis showed that the tail booms touched the deck. Free take-offs were followed by a further two uneventful landings, and then a fourth in which the aircraft touched down port wing low and damaged the trailing edge of the port flap. Repairs ashore included the removal of four square feet from the flaps to provide better wing-down clearance.

In his subsequent report[20] Brown spelt out the difficulty average pilots would have landing the Vampire on a carrier deck. The throttle response of the Goblin engine was poor, and once the throttle was closed on finals there would be no chance of opening it rapidly to overshoot. The slow wind-down meant that it would have to be closed progressively from about a quarter of a mile out, a difficult distance for the DLCO to judge with accuracy. The Admiralty wanted a second opinion, however, and tasked 'C' Squadron, the RN Test Unit at the Aeroplane and Armament Experimental Establishment (A&AEE) at Boscombe Down, to carry out a deck-landing assessment of LZ551/G on HMS *Triumph* in June 1946. The unit's commanding officer, Commander J.A. Ievers RN, strongly supported by his pilots, decided to make full use of the tricycle undercarriage and perfect deck-landing view. After a programme of ADDLs to ascertain the best technique they elected to fly a low, flat final approach with engine rpm kept high in the range where immediate response was available if required.[21] The aircraft was flown into the wires and the throttle was not closed until the hook had taken a wire and retardation was felt.[22] A series of sixteen faultless deck landings were carried out over two days on *Ocean* by Commander Ievers and two other pilots, Commander Randolph Pearson RN

and Commander 'Stan' Orr DSC AFC RN. Their collective opinion was that the Sea Vampire was simple and straightforward to deck-land provided the right technique was used.

The technique worked out by Ievers and his colleagues proved to be the basis of the jet-landing technique used by all carrier navies into the jet era, and is still used today. The USN caught up quickly and landed its first jet fighter, the twin-engined McDonnell FH-1 Phantom, on board the USS *Franklin D Roosevelt* on 19 July 1946. The Royal Navy's first twin-jet landing took place on 25 October 1948, when Gloster Meteor III EE387, fitted with a tailhook, landed on HMS *Illustrious*, which by then was operating as a trial and training carrier. The Royal Navy achieved two further 'firsts' before the end of the straight-deck era. On 19 June 1950 Lieutenant Commander G.R. Callingham landed a prototype Fairey Gannet, VR546, on HMS *Illustrious*; the first deck landing by a turboprop powered aircraft. On 8 November 1950 a Supermarine Type 510 swept-wing experimental jet aircraft piloted by Lieutenant 'Jock' Elliot RN landed on *Illustrious*, the first time that a swept-wing aircraft had landed on a carrier. The RAE believed that the operation of swept-wing aircraft would prove difficult, but twelve perfect landings were carried out on that day by Lieutenant Commander D.G. Parker DSO DSC AFC RN, Lieutenant Elliot and Mike Lithgow, a former naval pilot by then employed as a Supermarine test pilot. The approach speed was in the range 124 to 134 knots, depending on weight and, despite the unusual tailwheel undercarriage, the level powered technique was used, flying the aircraft into the wires. The DLCO proved to be of little value for anything but line-up. Take-offs in between landings were made using RATOG, with 15 knots of ship speed into a 25-knot wind giving 40 knots down the deck. On the next day the rockets failed to produce full thrust on one side and Lieutenant Commander Parker experienced an alarming swing to the left on take-off. His port wingtip hit the top of a gun turret but he retained control and flew safely ashore to land. Straight decks and their associated take-off and landing techniques had reached their limits.

Design innovation and the 'rubber deck'

The problem was not the arrested landing, but moving the aircraft after it had come to rest. This Sea Vampire is being dragged along the flexible deck on to a wooden trolley fitted with castors. Seawater from the fire main has been hosed on to the deck to lubricate it and help the aircraft slide.
(AUTHOR'S COLLECTION)

As the early deck landings by jet aircraft were analysed, scientists predicted that radical changes in both carrier technology and deck-landing technique would be required if new generations of aircraft, especially fighters, were to be operable. Wings designed for high speed at altitude were expected to lead to even higher launch and recovery speeds.[1] To make matters worse, 'high-speed' wings were expected to be too thin to accommodate the substantial undercarriages needed to absorb the ever-increasing impact velocities of deck landing. The search for a solution led Mr Boddington, head of the new Naval Aircraft Department at the RAE, to propose the use of aircraft without undercarriages, which would land on a flexible deck fitted over the conventional steel flight deck. In practical terms, he proposed transferring the pneumatic absorption of the deck-landing impact from the aircraft to the ship. The idea was based on the logic that other devices that enabled short take-offs and landings, the catapults and arrester-wires, were built into the ship rather than the aircraft, and the obvious fact that aircraft without undercarriages and their operating mechanisms would be lighter and enjoy better performance for given engine thrust than their conventional equivalents. The obvious drawbacks were the inability of aircraft without undercarriages to taxi after landing,[2] or to land on ships or airfields that did not have a flexible deck.

The Admiralty was sufficiently concerned about the need to land-on aircraft at speeds up to, and perhaps beyond, 135 knots that it funded trials into the concept despite the severe economic position in the immediate postwar years. The first flexible deck was built ashore at Farnborough and a second was built on the flight deck of the light fleet carrier HMS *Warrior*, recently returned from loan service with the Royal Canadian Navy. Both comprised rubber tubes made out of hosepipes, filled with compressed air and covered by a rubber membrane which formed the surface on which aircraft landed. A single USN Mark 4 arrester gear was fitted, with the actuating pistons situated fore-and-aft alongside the flexible-deck installation. This had a maximum pull-out of only 160 feet, which restricted the approach speed,

with the result that the deck could only be used under specified minimum wind conditions. Initial trials ashore were carried out by modified de Havilland Vampire TG286. Subsequent trial landings both afloat and ashore were carried out by Sea Vampire F.21s specifically strengthened to land with their undercarriages retracted.

Boddington's proposal involved aircraft flying a flat approach at a speed above the stall to pass low over the flexible deck with the hook down. The throttle was not closed, and each approach was treated as a potential 'miss' until the pilot felt the retardation when his hook took the single arrester wire. Trials ashore showed that the aircraft could actually fly away from contact with the deck if it did not catch the wire. The distance between the Sea Vampire's hook and the bottom of the aircraft was small, requiring the pass over the deck to be very low. The prototype flexible decks ashore and afloat were about 2 feet higher than their surroundings, making accurate height perception difficult. All the early landings were carried out by Lieutenant Commander Eric Brown RN, who was at pains to fly the required low passes accurately, but on one occasion he sank low on the approach to the deck at Farnborough and struck the ramp at the beginning of the flexible deck, causing a fair amount of damage to TG286. At sea it was noticed that, on several landings, he 'organised' the pick-up of the arrester wire by pushing the nose down and running the aircraft belly along the deck before reaching the wire in order to increase the chances of catching it.

The first flexible deck trials in HMS *Warrior* were carried out in November 1948, using the repaired TG286 and three Sea Vampire F.21s[3] operating from RNAS Lee-on-Solent. On 3 November Brown carried out a low pass over the deck in TG286 before landing successfully at a weight of 7,800lb and an indicated air speed of 96 knots, giving an entry speed into the wire of 61 knots. The wind over the deck was a steady 35 knots. After it had come to rest on the flexible deck, the aircraft was raised by crane so that its undercarriage could be lowered, and lifted on to the conventional flight deck forward of the rubber 'mat'. From there it carried out a free take-off to return to

Lee-on-Solent, using 300 feet of deck.[4] From 4 November landings were carried out using the F.21s at a weight of 8,600lb. Again an initial low pass was carried out, but on the first landing the port wing dropped and hit the arrester wire, although the landing was successful. In consequence the raised span of the arrester wire was reduced in width from 45 feet to 25 feet to give increased wingtip clearance in the event of a roll. A DLCO was positioned on the deck aft to monitor the aircraft's height on the approach and wave it off if it appeared to go low. He did not give a 'cut' signal since the aircraft was intended to 'fly through' the wire.

Problems were encountered on 9 November, when two attempts were made to land-on in VT805 at 14:45 and 14:50, but on each occasion the arrester wire struck the aircraft's booms, forcing it out of the hook. In both cases the aircraft made contact with, and ran along, the flexible deck before climbing away safely

without causing the pilot any concern. Cine records revealed that the shape of the hook needed to be modified to suit the conditions of pick-up associated with the lower entry speeds used in this stage of the trials. Modified hooks were made at Farnborough with a beak that was lengthened and with its angle closed by 18 degrees. Proof landings were carried out at Farnborough, and sea trials resumed on 23 November. These included off-centre landings and entry speeds up to 77 knots with retardations measured between 1.8 and 3.1g. The last landing was on 6 December in VT803, when an entry speed of 85 knots at 9,000lb was achieved with a wind over the deck of 22 knots and an indicated air speed of 107 knots. Unfortunately a high-pressure joint in the arrester gear failed, causing the retardation unit to bottom-out, subjecting the aircraft to a retardation of 5.4g. It had to be carefully examined before it could be flown ashore, and the arrester gear had to

The flexible deck installed over HMS *Warrior*'s conventional deck between the lifts, shortly after its installation. The ship is alongside in Portsmouth Dockyard.

(AUTHOR'S COLLECTION)

be repaired, so this phase of the trial programme was deemed to be complete after a total of twenty-one successful landings. On 25 November VT805 had been launched by *Warrior*'s BH 3 hydraulic catapult, the first time the RN had launched a jet-propelled aircraft with a nosewheel undercarriage from one of its aircraft carriers.

Further deck landings in *Warrior* were carried out in March 1949. For this phase two USN Mark 4 arresting gears were mounted in tandem, with the wire carried round the moving crossheads of both gears so that a total pull-out of 290 feet could be obtained, allowing for closing speeds up to 120 knots.[5] Five different pilots of varying levels of experience, in addition to Lieutenant Commander Brown, carried out the landings. Again these trials were successful insofar as they demonstrated the ability of aircraft without undercarriages to land safely on a flexible deck. They also demonstrated the fundamental flaw in the concept; once the aircraft slithered to a halt on the 'rubber deck' it was both difficult and slow to move away from the landing area.

Conventional landing rates by wheeled aircraft on to carriers with straight decks and barriers averaged about two per minute at the time. At closing speeds

of about 60 knots this meant that, as the first aircraft took a wire, the second should be turning finals 1,000 yards astern. Taking this distance as an acceptable minimum, Boddington argued that aircraft with a closing speed of 110 knots should be able to recover at the rate of one every 16 seconds, or about four per minute. Assuming that the wave-off signal for a deck that was not yet clear was left until the following aircraft was in to 200 yards, this allowed 12 seconds to clear the flexible deck after each landing. In reality, however, it took 5 minutes to clear aircraft off *Warrior*'s flexible deck, lifting them by crane and then either lowering them on to a trolley or holding them clear of the deck while their undercarriages were pumped down. With the large number of aircraft embarked in contemporary carriers, a landing interval of 5 minutes could never have been acceptable. NAD produced a number of ingenious ideas to overcome the problem, none of which was ever likely to be a practical success at sea. They included a ramp just forward of the landing area, down which the aircraft could be pulled, and side lifts on to which the aircraft could be dragged by wires and then struck down into the hangar. The least unlikely was the idea of dividing the deck with a nylon 'safety barrier'. As the aircraft

One theoretical advantage was the ability to rotate aircraft on their trolleys and pack them tightly, with overlapping wings, into low hangars. These aircraft are ashore at RNAS Ford in Sussex.

slithered to rest, a naval airman would have attached a wire cable to a ring on the aircraft's nose. A winch would then have pulled the aircraft rapidly forward over a lowered nylon barrier which would be raised once it had passed, very much in the style of conventional straight-deck operations. However, sorting out the jumbled mass of aircraft on their bellies in Fly 1 for the re-spot would have been a time-consuming and difficult evolution; the faster rate of recovery would have been achieved at the expense of a slower re-spot, leading, overall, to a lower total number of sorties in a given day's flying operations.

Separating launch and recovery operations led to proposals for separate launch and recovery decks, launching aircraft out of the hangar and landing on a flight deck above it, harking back to the slip decks in *Furious*, *Courageous* and *Glorious*. The best thing to emerge from this spate of design concepts was a proposal to offset the flexible deck radially to port of the ship's centreline, allowing aircraft to be pulled off it to starboard into Fly 2. Discussion about the merit of this proposal led directly to the brilliantly simple application of the angled deck that was to follow. This was a period of innovative thought like none that had gone before it, however, and bright ideas continued, with the result that work on the flexible deck was not finally abandoned until 1954. One ingenious 'spin-off' from the concept of the fighter without an undercarriage was to roll the aircraft a few degrees on their handling trolleys when they were struck down into the hangar so that the low wing of one could be parked under the higher wing of the next aircraft, increasing parking density. Lack of undercarriages would have made aircraft lower,

requiring less hangar height, but none of these so-called advantages was worth the difficulty of having to put aircraft on to trolleys to move them. The more scientists thought about the problems raised by the concept, the more far-fetched the proposed solutions became. Some of them never achieved any sort of contemporary solution; such as the need to have rubber 'mats' available at airfields throughout the world to which naval aircraft might be required to divert. Another that was never seriously addressed was the need for aircraft to carry pylons under their wings loaded with drop tanks and weapons, which might be ripped off or damaged as aircraft slithered along the flexible deck. The operation of helicopters and propeller-driven aircraft would always have required 'steel deck' space from which they could be launched and recovered.

The USN sent observers to witness the trials at Farnborough and at sea in *Warrior*. Representatives from the Military Requirements, Airborne Equipment, Research, Ship's Installations Divisions and the Naval Air Material Center evaluated the flexible deck and wrote, positively, about the potential advantages in aircraft performance. As late as November 1952 a classified report on the subject[6] spoke optimistically about the possibility of solving the deck-handling problems. It stated that:

In the canted-deck design, the landing area is slanted out to port from the fore-and-aft line of the ship at an angle of about 8 degrees. This means that the landing aircraft can be moved sideways a short distance to a parking area or elevator. One plan calls for the removal of the aircraft by means of a winch-powered tow line to drag the plane to a waiting trolley. On a conventional

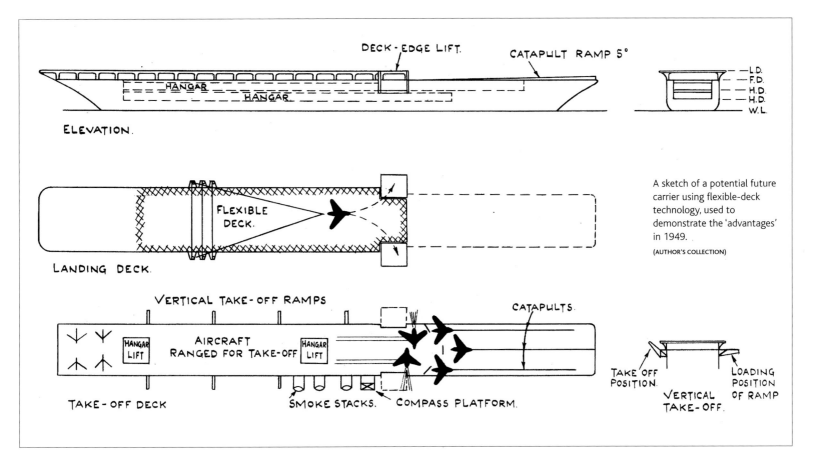

A sketch of a potential future carrier using flexible-deck technology, used to demonstrate the 'advantages' in 1949.

(AUTHOR'S COLLECTION)

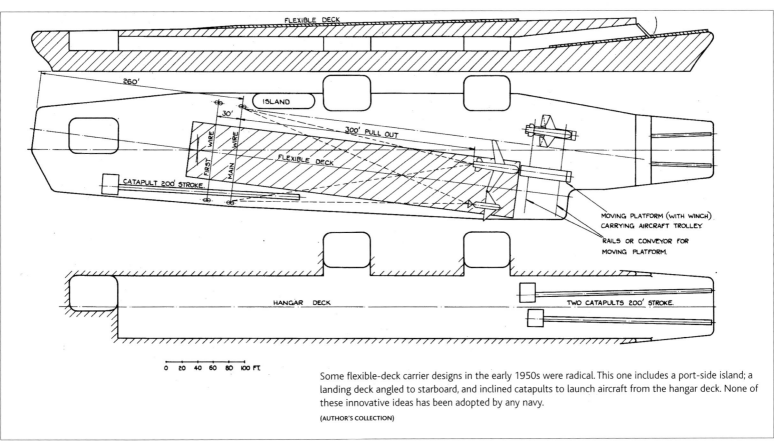

Some flexible-deck carrier designs in the early 1950s were radical. This one includes a port-side island; a landing deck angled to starboard, and inclined catapults to launch aircraft from the hangar deck. None of these innovative ideas has been adopted by any navy.

(AUTHOR'S COLLECTION)

A Sea Vampire on its trolley after being pulled off the 'rubber deck' at RAE Farnborough.
(AUTHOR'S COLLECTION)

HMS *Warrior* alongside Fountain Lake Jetty in Portsmouth Dockyard, showing the flexible deck being installed in 1948.
(AUTHOR'S COLLECTION)

carrier equipped with a flexible deck, dragging the plane 150 feet to the edge of the mat by winch would take about 15 seconds. Because of the shorter towing distance, this time would be considerably reduced in the canted-deck configuration.

The USN also noted the potential for parking aircraft closer together because their trolleys would have free-castoring wheels.

A final attempt to solve the handling problem was put to both navies by the RAE in 1952.[7] This entailed designing aircraft with 'taxiing wheels' which could be lowered after the landing to allow the aircraft to taxi or be moved without needing trolleys. By then the concept was all but dead, and the idea of increasing aircraft weight and complexity by adding an undercarriage upon which it could not land found no favour with the operators. In the event, better aircraft design and carriers with angled decks and steam catapults meant that the problem of landing-on high-performance aircraft was solved in a less complicated way, and the flexible deck experiment was terminated in 1954. Although it appears bizarre in hindsight, the concept did at least show the innovative lengths to which designers were prepared to go to take deck-landing capability into the supersonic era.

CHAPTER 14

Transformation

A Douglas AD-1 Skyraider about to be launched during
trials of the prototype steam catapult in HMS *Perseus* by
the US Navy. The wire strop is tensioned against the
shuttle and the hold-back is visible just aft of the tailwheel.
(AUTHOR'S COLLECTION)

By 1944 aircraft technology had advanced rapidly to the point where the operation of new aircraft types was constrained by the aircraft carriers already in service, and even by those still under construction. Turbojet powered fighters were in the forefront of the new technology, offering significantly improved performance in the air, but they were larger and heavier than the aircraft they would replace and used greater quantities of a fuel that was not, at the time, refined in Britain, and had to be imported from the USA. Their significantly higher launch and recovery speeds required more deck space to operate them at a time when the Royal Navy had invested heavily in 'straight-deck' carrier production, with seven fleet carriers [1] and twenty-four light fleet carriers [2] ordered or under construction. By then, British and American carriers were operating aircraft with take-off weights up to 15,000lb and landing weights in the region of 10,000lb. Take-off speeds were generally about 80 knots and landing speeds about 70 knots.

The beneficial effect of the ship's speed into the natural wind meant that the contemporary hydraulic catapults with end speeds in the region of 60 knots were seldom used at maximum pressure, and arrester wires, capable of stopping aircraft with a speed of 60 knots relative to the deck, were seldom required to operate to their full capacity except in an emergency. Thus initial acceleration and deceleration loads on the aircraft were kept within reasonable limits and the life of the ship's machinery was not shortened by excessive use at maximum capability. The need to conserve airframe life had been a minor consideration, and with the cost of a new Seafire at only £9,000 and a Corsair little more, many airframe lives were brief. Between 1940 and 1945 the maximum airborne speed of fleet fighters had increased from the 215 knots of the Gloster Sea Gladiator to the 358 knots of the Corsair. Each new generation had seen an increase in aircraft weight, with average increase of 100 per cent in the five years. Landing speeds over the same period had increased by roughly 20 knots, but the last generations of piston-engine fighters flew from carriers that had originally been designed to operate Swordfish, which had lifted off the deck at 11,000lb and 55 knots and landed-on at 7,000lb and

40 knots. Fortunately the ships and their machinery had been designed with an element of 'stretch', but by 1945 this had been largely used up.

Having evolved a viable landing technique for jet aircraft in 1946, the RN turned to the problem of arresting them safely. Existing wires could stop a 15,000lb aircraft at up to 60 knots, [3] but the safety barriers were totally unsuitable. Without the solid mass of the engine and its bearers to take the first impact, the load fell on the wing leading edges, and the pilot's exposed position just a few feet behind the streamlined nose was dangerous, the main hazard being the top, transverse, strand of the barrier. The USN recognised the problem and adopted a large nylon net, with the top strand held some twelve feet above the deck, and broad vertical tapes spreading the load of deceleration evenly along the leading edges of unswept wings. When the first operational squadrons of jet fighters, Supermarine Attackers, embarked in HMS *Eagle* in 1951 they formed part of a mixed jet/piston powered air group, and jet recoveries used USN-supplied nylon barriers.

The prospect of operating aircraft of steadily increasing weight from the existing British carriers drove the Royal Navy to pioneer a major advance in launching equipment. In 1945 the standard assisted-take-off apparatus, by then known as a catapult, was the hydro-pneumatic BH 3, designed originally to launch an 11,000lb aircraft at 66 knots from a trolley running along a track 60 feet long. By adopting the USN 'tail-down' technique, in which the aircraft was towed down the catapult track by a strop pulled by a shuttle, the load was increased to 14,000lb at about 70 knots. By 1950 the hydraulic catapult had been developed further into the BH 5, fitted into HM Ships *Eagle, Albion, Bulwark* and *Centaur*. This was capable of launching a 30,000lb aircraft at up to 85 knots end speed, but it represented the extreme limit of the technology using wires and pulleys. It imposed an acceleration of up to 5g on airframe and aircrew and, while this was within the tolerance of both when applied progressively, there was nothing progressive about the action of the BH 5, which achieved its maximum speed after only a third of its travel, 30 feet in the case of *Eagle*. This required aircraft to be especially structurally strengthened, adding weight that could be put to other use or, better still, eliminated.

Catapult development work by the Royal Navy in the Second World War involved a flywheel similar to that which had been used to drive catapults in the USS *Lexington* and *Saratoga* in the late 1920s, but work stopped in 1945 when a better alternative was adopted. Credit for this is due to Commander C.C. Mitchell RNVR, who had proposed the use of a 'slotted cylinder' catapult powered by steam to the Admiralty in the 1930s, but there had been no need for it at the time and it was not progressed. The catapult developed by the Germans to launch the V1 'flying bomb' used a similar concept, and Mitchell was able to acquire component parts through the British Intelligence Operational Survey Team to hasten trials in the UK. The result was a catapult in which rams were driven along parallel cylinders by steam pressure. A cradle linked the rams so that they ran together along the cylinders, and provided the structure on which the shuttle was fixed. This ran at flight-deck level, pulling the aircraft by means of a wire strop attached to hooks on the aircraft. Rubber seals ran along the top of the cylinders, and were forced open by devices on the leading edges of the cradle and resealed behind it to allow its passage without significant loss of steam pressure. The high-pressure steam was provided from the ship's boilers and 'stored' in huge accumulators at up to 4,000 psi. The steam pressure applied to the rams was regulated to give the desired end speed dictated by aircraft weight and the wind over the deck generated by ship speed and natural wind. Initial acceleration was gradual, full speed not being reached until the shuttle had travelled some two-thirds of the length of the cylinders. Known as the steam catapult, the new device was essentially simple and eliminated the miles of wire-rope reeving which gave the necessary mechanical advantage to the short piston-stroke of the hydraulic catapult, and which was the primary cause of its unserviceability. The energy potential of the new catapult was far greater, a welcome feature given the rapidly increasing weight of new naval aircraft designs.

The Admiralty immediately saw the potential of the design and gave a development contract to a Scottish engineering firm, Brown Brothers & Co, which Commander Mitchell joined when he was demobilised from the RNVR. After extensive trials ashore, the prototype steam catapult, BXS 1, was erected in a new structure on the deck of the maintenance and repair carrier HMS *Perseus* at Rosyth Dockyard early in 1951. The spring and summer were occupied with sea trials, at first with wheeled trolley dead loads and surplus aircraft with their wings cut off. Next the latter were used with their engines running at full power, and finally manned operational aircraft were launched. The whole series of launches was completely successful, and such was the enthusiasm of the USN observers that a repeat of the trial programme was run in the USA between December 1951 and March 1952, during which period *Perseus* launched 140 dead loads and aircraft. The aircraft could not land-on, and had to be lifted on to the deck by crane before the days' trials, flying ashore to land after launch. The USN acquired the manufacturing rights for its own steam catapult production as part of the Mutual Defence Aid Programme's benefits, and work began in the USA in April 1952. The first trial catapult was commissioned at NAS Patuxent River in December 1953, and the first live launch from an operational carrier took place six months later, on 1 June 1954, when the USS *Hancock* launched a Grumman S2F-1 Tracker. The first British carrier with steam catapults, HMS *Ark Royal*, began contractor's sea trials four days later but did not commission for operational service until February 1955. Her BS 4 catapults could launch a 15,000lb aircraft at 100 knots in a distance of 100 feet, the end speed dictated by considerations of ram deceleration rather than energy limitations. Steam catapults with longer tracks could launch aircraft at greater weights and higher end speeds, and by 1962 the USS *Enterprise* was fitted with C 13 versions, 250 feet long, which could launch 85,000lb aircraft at up to 140 knots. Extensions of catapult tracks were possible while carriers were in refit. *Ark Royal*, for example, had two such improvements; the first extending the bow catapults to 160 feet and the second replacing the starboard one with a waist

HMS *Perseus* carrying out steam catapult trials in July 1951. The BXS 1 prototype is under the long structure built on to the upper deck of this former maintenance carrier. A de Havilland Sea Hornet is attached to the catapult ready for launch, and other aircraft aft include another Sea Hornet, a Fairey Firefly, a Grumman Avenger and a Short Sturgeon.

(SYD GOODMAN COLLECTION VIA MARITIME BOOKS)

catapult 200 feet long. The USN eventually improved on the speed at which aircraft could be loaded on to the catapult by replacing the wire strop with a T-shaped bar on the nose oleo of carrier-borne aircraft. This was lowered on to the shuttle, and retracted with the undercarriage after launch.

While catapult trials were carried out in *Perseus* in 1951, the NAD at the RAE undertook a high-speed closing trial to evaluate the problems likely to be encountered by future generations of naval aircraft in deck landing, from the perspective of both pilots and batsmen. A Sea Vampire made a series of downwind approaches to HMS *Illustrious*, giving closing speeds of up to 140 knots. The standard shallow approach was used, with the 'cut' ordered by the batsman, but such was the size of the circuit that had to be flown that the batsman could only be seen distinctly just before he gave the cut, with the aircraft only 100 to 150 yards from the round-down. Thereafter he was unable to appreciate errors in height or line quickly enough to be able to signal them in time for the pilot to be able to make any corrections. Subsequent trials ashore demonstrated

A 'pilot's-eye-view' of the angled deck painted on HMS *Triumph* in 1952. The image was taken from a cine film of the approach and is unfortunately of poor quality. It shows the markings and the fact that, because the angled deck centreline was displaced to starboard of the axial deck centreline, the DLCO had to move on to the deck, to starboard of his normal position, to be within the pilot's field of view.

(AUTHOR'S COLLECTION)

that constant-power approaches and power-on landings at a steeper angle of descent of about 3 degrees did not result in the heavier landings expected of them. Since by then the only value of the batsman in jet landings had been his assessment of the 'cut' position, he no longer had anything to offer, although there was no immediate replacement. The steeper approach with power on became the standard landing technique, with the additional benefit that it allowed the touchdown point to be nearer the round-down in calm sea conditions and gave greater clearance between the hook and round-down when the ship was pitching in rough weather. Even then, however, the 12,000lb jets in service, landing at 100 knots, needed two-thirds of the deck clear for their

arrested landings, and the amount of deck space forward of the safety barrier for a park was restricted, limiting the size of a strike that could be recovered in a single operation. Any further encroachment by faster and heavier aircraft would make the deck park unusable, with the forward lift included in the landing area. If carriers were not to be forced to return to the 'clear deck' method of the 1920s, a new technique was required. With the only new carriers in prospect based on pre-1945 designs, the RN did not have the luxury of specifying new, larger ships and was forced to find a new technique if its carrier force was to remain viable. With its larger flight decks the USN did not see the problem with quite the same immediacy, but was concerned nonetheless.

Considerable thought went into the problem, and a new technique was evolved by another serving naval officer, Captain D.R.F. Campbell RN, who was the Deputy Chief Naval Representative at the Ministry of Supply (MoS). Longitudinal separation of the landing and parking areas, with the latter forward of the former with a safety barrier between, was becoming difficult. Lateral separation, with the two areas alongside each other, was seemingly impractical if the ship's beam was not to be extended to unacceptable dimensions. Inspired by some of the concept designs put forward during the rubber-deck trials, in which the flexible landing mat had been offset from the ship's centreline to allow aircraft to be pulled clear of the deck for further aircraft to land, Campbell put forward the idea of radial separation. By rotating the axis of the landing deck so that it was at an angle to the centreline of the ship, several attractive and positive benefits were achieved. Even a slight angle brought the forward end of the landing deck to the edge of the flight deck at a point well aft of the bows, effectively lengthening the space available for aircraft to be arrested. The area to starboard could be used as an expanded parking area, and the sum of the length of the two areas was greater than the length of the original axial flight deck. Even better, the angled deck gave approaching pilots a clear deck with no need for a barrier to separate them from parked aircraft, and if they missed all the wires (an event subsequently known as a 'bolter') they could simply

HMS *Centaur*, the only ship of her class to be completed to the original 'straight-deck' design, is seen carrying out her acceptance trials in 1953.

(AUTHOR'S COLLECTION)

Immediately after her acceptance trials HMS *Centaur* was modified with the 'interim' angled deck seen here. It involved the fitting of a modest extension to port, the realignment of a reduced number of arrester wires and a landing area painted $5\frac{1}{2}$ degrees to port of the ship's centreline.

(AUTHOR'S COLLECTION)

The first ship to be fitted with a full 8-degree angled deck was the USS *Antietam*, seen here during USN angled-deck trials off the Virginia Capes in January 1953.

(US NAVAL HISTORICAL CENTER)

Royal Navy pilots were also given the chance to evaluate USS *Antietam*'s angled deck in 1953. A Sea Vampire leaves the angled deck after a 'roller' touchdown with the hook raised, off Portsmouth.

(AUTHOR'S COLLECTION)

open the throttle and fly away for another circuit to land. The new jet technique of landing with power on exactly suited landing on the new type of deck, known at first as a 'skew-deck' in the Royal Navy and 'canted-deck' in the USN, but soon renamed by both and referred to ever since as the angled deck.

The deck had to be angled to port on all existing carriers, because the repositioning of the island with its funnel uptakes would have presented too daunting a task. However, the RN did study the option of angling the deck to starboard in the early 1950s, so that the finals turn from a left-hand circuit would be through 170 rather than 190 degrees, but the sketch design work came to nothing. The ship used to validate the concept of the angled deck was the light fleet carrier HMS *Triumph*, and her preparation was simple. The arrester wire pennants were removed

as they were aligned with the axial deck and could not, easily, be repositioned. An angled deck was painted into place, with its centreline extending from the starboard quarter to a point on the port deck edge abreast the island. In February 1952 all RN aircraft currently in service and under development carried out flying trials involving low approaches to the angled deck, controlled by a batsman. No actual 'touch-and-go' roller landings were made as there were doubts about the length of the painted deck. The USN was kept informed at every stage of the experiment, quickly appreciated the value of the new deck layout, and adopted it immediately. Trials similar to those on *Triumph* were carried out on to a deck painted on an *Essex*-class carrier in the spring of 1952, and in the summer the attack carrier USS *Antietam*, another ship of the same class, was taken in hand for

The Deck Landing Mirror Sight fitted in HMS *Albion*. The mirror was attached to its framework through a series of gears which enabled it to be moved up and down to compensate for different hook/eye distances.
(AUTHOR'S COLLECTION)

modification. The port-side deck-edge lift was extended outboard and the triangular area between the lift and the port after deck edge filled in by mild-steel plating covered by wood, consistent with the remainder of the flight deck. The beam across the angle was extended from 136 feet to 154 feet. The centreline of the angled deck began only slightly to

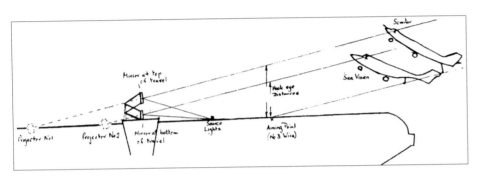

The path the hook needed to follow to catch the target wire was constant but the distance from the hook to the pilot's eye-line differed with different aircraft types. To compensate for this, the mirror had to be adjusted up and down and the angle of the source lights had to be adjusted.

(AUTHOR'S COLLECTION)

starboard of the ship's centreline, but such was the size of the extension that a 10-degree angle was possible with a full-width landing area extending over its full length. The arrester wires had to be repositioned to line up across the new landing area. *Antietam*'s reconstruction was completed at the end of 1952, and on 12 January 1953 her commanding officer, Captain S.G. Mitchell USN, flying a North American SNJ Harvard training aircraft, carried out the first-ever arrested landing on an angled deck. Trials on *Antietam* continued for much of 1953 with complete success. They included a visit to Portsmouth in the autumn, where a range of Royal Navy operational aircraft landed-on. Batsmen were used to give height corrections for all aircraft on finals, and to give the 'cut' for piston-engine aircraft.

Higher landing speeds exposed the problem that, by the time a batsman had appreciated an error, signalled a correction to the pilot and the latter had interpreted it, it was often too late for the correction to be of practical use. With even higher landing speeds in prospect, the problem was serious. Since the late 1930s RN carriers had been fitted with 'Sector Lights', [4] glide-path indicators in which the beam depth in each sector was three degrees, within which a pilot could not see that he was building up an increasing rate of descent or climb. [5] Again the answer came from a serving naval officer, Commander H.C.N.

Goodhart RN, Captain Campbell's assistant at the MoS. He had an engineering background and had flown Hellcat fighters during the Second World War. His solution consisted of a large mirror, facing aft, and a source light placed 150 feet aft of it from which light was projected into the mirror. By tilting the mirror back slightly, an ideal predetermined but adjustable glide-slope indication was shown to pilots on final approach with the reflected 'blob' of light, soon to be known universally as the 'meatball' or simply 'the ball', in between datum bars on either side of the mirror. If the 'ball' appeared exactly between the datum bars, the pilot's eye was exactly on the glide-slope. If it appeared high he was high and if it appeared low he was low. Reaction time lags were reduced to the pilot's alone, potential misinterpretations of hand signals were eliminated and, by selecting the optimum colours and brilliance for the source lights, the visual pick-up range of the landing signals was considerably increased. In practice more than one source light was provided, each with a different power supply, so that the equipment could not be 'taken out' by a single electrical circuit failure. The equipment was known as the Deck Landing Mirror Sight (DLMS), [6] and the Admiralty tasked RAE Farnborough with producing suitable hardware for trials on the airfield and at sea.

The first prototype mirror was installed in HMS *Illustrious* in October 1952. The reflecting surface was convex, intended to spread and diffuse the reflected light over a wide horizontal angle so that it could be seen and interpreted throughout the turn on to final approach. It consisted of a sheet of polished steel secured to a curved backboard, and the datum bars on either side of the mirror were also mirrors made out of sheet steel and angled at 45 degrees to provide a contrast by reflecting the sky. It was a crude device, but showed sufficient promise to warrant the construction of a more sophisticated mirror with better optical properties. This had an aluminium-faced mirror and aft-facing green lights as datum bars on either side, together with a gyroscopic stabilisation system designed by Mr D. Lean of the RAE, who was responsible for the practical development of the sight. The stabilised sight was able to cancel out the effect of ship pitch which, if uncorrected, would result in pilots seeing the 'meat ball' constantly moving up and down relative to the datum bars, making it difficult to maintain an accurate glide-slope.

In June 1953 this improved mirror was installed on the starboard side of HMS *Indomitable*'s flight deck, about 200 feet ahead of the round-down. A series of trial landings by operational aircraft followed which were witnessed by Canadian, USN and US Marine Corps (USMC) observers, aircraft being flown by American as well as British pilots. The mirror sight demonstrated all that had been hoped for it; approaches were accurate, simple to execute and possible in all 'flyable' conditions of light and weather. The exact point at which the hook hit the deck could be selected with considerable accuracy by adjusting the tilt of the mirror. This solved the problem of giving the pilots of aircraft with high approach speeds adequate glide-slope information which could be interpreted in a timely manner, and led immediately to further benefits that had not, at first, been considered. First, the number of arrester wires could be reduced from an average of twelve in 1950 to just four, a significant saving in flight-deck machinery requirements. The reduction in the number of wires meant that those fitted could be sited well forward of the round-down and as near as possible to the centre of pitch, allowing greater clearance between the tailhook and the round-down during rough-sea landings. The new mirror sight and the angled deck together allowed recoveries that were not only more accurate but safer than before. The rate of sink at touchdown was measured during this trial and it was demonstrated that the new 3½-degree, no-cut, no-flare technique, in effect 'flying the aircraft into the deck', resulted in a sink-rate that was less than that experienced in the shallow approach and 'pole forward to the deck' technique that was standard at the time.

Several improvements were made in the light of the June 1953 trials. The sight was made adjustable vertically to take into account the different 'hook-eye' distances of different naval aircraft, and the reflecting surface was reversed, a concave parabolic reflecting surface being adopted which focused the beams from the source lights and gave good horizontal beam width. The number of source lights was increased from two to four. Thus modified, the mirror sight was installed on the port deck edge of HMS *Illustrious*, again about 200 feet forward of the round-down, from where it could be seen throughout the last 90 degrees of the turn on to final approach. Pilots for this third series of trials were drawn from 703 Squadron, the

RN Service Trials Unit; the RAE; the A&AEE at Boscombe Down in Wiltshire and the US Navy. Between them they flew Sea Vampires, a Gannet and a hooked Meteor. Westland Wyverns were flown by 813 Squadron pilots. Each pilot carried out between thirty-five and forty night Mirror Assisted Dummy Deck Landings (MADDLs), as well as a full

The Projector Sight was a considerable improvement on the mirror and removed the need for source lights. This example fitted in HMS *Ark Royal* IV shows the four jacks on which it was raised and lowered and the Projector Sight Officer at his control position.
(AUTHOR'S COLLECTION)

programme of day landings at RAE Farnborough before embarking in *Illustrious* in November 1953. The trials were an unqualified success, and the sight was accepted for immediate use by angled-deck carriers of the Royal Navy and US Navy. Both continued to use batsmen to control piston-engine aircraft landings for some while afterwards, the mirror being less easily seen over their long engine cowlings than the bats right aft on the port quarter.

The first carrier to be completed with both the angled deck, albeit an interim one of only 5 degrees, and a mirror sight was HMS *Albion* which left the builder's yard on 26 May 1954. She was followed quickly by the USS *Hancock*, which completed a modernisation with steam catapults and the angled deck. The first ship to commission with all three new developments incorporated during modernisation was the USS *Shangri-La* in early February 1955. Three weeks later, on 25 February 1955, she was followed by HMS *Ark Royal*, the first carrier to be completed with the three developments installed during construction. Before the end of 1955 other new carriers including the USS *Forrestal* and HMAS *Melbourne* were completed with the new technology. Within the space of a year a revolution in carrier operating technique had been completed that was of as great significance as the appearance of HMS *Dreadnought* had been half a century before. In both cases the appearance of the new design had rendered all predecessors obsolete, but in the case of the aircraft carriers, older ships could be successfully modernised to the new standard.

Several other British developments of the 1950s deserve mention, but were not adopted by the USN. These included the Catapult Aircraft Line-up Equipment (CALE) gear. This consisted of two sets of rollers recessed into the flight deck at the after end of the catapult, one on either side of, and at right angles to, the centreline of the catapult track. The forward section of each set of rollers could be raised to act as chocks to stop the aircraft in the right place relative to the catapult, and the rollers could either be rotated, turning inwards towards the track, or declutched to turn freely. The inboard rollers on each set were declutched to correspond to the distance between the main wheels of the aircraft to be

launched, so that if it arrived off-centre the rotating rollers moved it sideways until it was resting on the free rollers, aligned with the catapult and able to be attached to the hold-back and catapult shuttle. CALE gear first appeared in HMS *Eagle* in 1951, and its adoption resulted in improved launching efficiency. By the 1960s, however, the new generation of jets such as the McDonnell Douglas Phantom and Blackburn Buccaneer were fitted with nosewheel steering. This allowed accurate taxiing, and in the last refit of the Royal Navy's last conventional carrier, HMS *Ark Royal*, the CALE gear was no longer considered necessary and removed. It was replaced by white lines painted on to the deck to which the aircraft could be accurately and quickly steered. It may be that the USN's early adoption of nosewheel steering was responsible for the lack of interest in CALE gear.

Both the RN and USN saw a need for jet-blast deflectors (JBDs). The thrust from a running range of propeller-driven aircraft had always made the flight deck a dangerous place for the unwary, but the introduction of jets made it more so. The effect of a twin-engine jet fighter at full power of over 20,000lb static thrust on the catapult could be felt down the entire length of the deck, and protection had to be provided for the aircraft handlers directing the stream of aircraft up the deck, and even for the aircraft waiting their turn to launch within 50 feet of the heat, noise and blast, especially behind aircraft using afterburner (reheat in USN terms) for launch. Let into the deck at an angle behind the catapult track, JBDs were jacked up hydraulically as soon as the aircraft had taxied on to the launching position and were not lowered until the catapult had been fired. They were first used by the USN aboard the wooden-decked *Essex*-class carriers, which also had to have steel plates let into the deck behind the catapults to prevent damage to the flight deck. The first British JBDs were installed in *Victorious* during her reconstruction, and JBDs were subsequently fitted to all operational British carriers. Later generations of aircraft needed developed, watercooled JBDs and, in order to operate the F-4K version of the Phantom with its two Rolls-Royce Spey engines, each giving 20,500lb of static thrust, the RAE developed four-plate

watercooled JBDs. [7] These were to have been fitted in all British carriers but, with the political decision to run down the carrier force in 1966, they were only fitted in *Ark Royal*.

Subsequent development of aids to carrier flying took the form of improvements rather than radical innovations. From 1961 the mirror was replaced by the Deck Landing Projector Sight (DLPS), in which the mirror was replaced by a vertical stack of twelve 'spotlights'. Stabilisation in pitch was provided by a slide moving up and down in front of the lights, which showed all of one light and half of the lights above and below it, making the 'ball' appear to move seamlessly. The bottom two were coloured red to indicate to pilots that they were dangerously low. The DLPS had several advantages over its predecessor. It was visible at a greater range, since pilots were looking at projected rather than reflected light, and the source lights of the mirror sight had tended to light up the side of the carrier, making it less secure when darkened at night. Two DLPSs were fitted in every RN carrier, the master to port and a standby to starboard. The latter had the green lights of its datum arms replaced by a 'Hi-Lo' which served as a vertical localiser, a bit like the old Sector Light, for pilots about a mile out, too far to see the 'ball' clearly, and then as a datum bar for the final approach.

Catapults were lengthened to launch heavier and faster aircraft, and continue in use in several of the world's navies including those of the USA, France and Brazil. The angled deck has not yet been improved upon, although the cancelled British CVA01 design of 1966 featured a reduced angle offset to port of the ship's centreline to create what were,

A Gannet AS 4 on the CALE gear abaft one of HMS *Eagle*'s catapults in 1956. The flight deck engineer in the lighter overalls is fitting the hold-back, attached to the rear of the nose oleo, to the retaining block on deck. His colleague in the darker overalls is holding the port loop of the launching strop ready to attach it to the hook visible above the hinge of the bomb-bay door. He will then hold it in place until it is correctly tensioned by moving the shuttle forward before being ordered clear. The chocks forward of the CALE gear will be lowered hydraulically when the aircraft is tensioned and ready for launch. (AUTHOR'S COLLECTION)

in effect, parallel landing and launching/parking decks. British arresting gear was greatly improved in the late 1960s with the adoption of the Direct Acting Gear. Its basic feature was a perforated cylinder containing fluid which was expressed by a piston drawn along its length by the engaged arrester wire. The rate of deceleration was controlled by the steadily reducing diameter of the holes along the top of the cylinder. Compared with earlier systems it was simpler, smoother, less demanding in terms of weight, space and steel wire, and gave a constant pull-out regardless of the weight of the aircraft arrested. It was fitted in *Ark Royal* during her 'Phantom Refit'.

A number of aircraft innovations in the 1950s added significantly to their ability to operate off carrier decks. There is insufficient space to describe them all, but several are illustrative. The Admiralty recognised that carrier-borne aircraft represented the ideal antidote to the large number of cruisers being produced for the Soviet Navy in the early 1950s. Specification NA.39 was issued in 1953 for a long-range strike aircraft capable of attacking at very low level, below the radar cover of ships and shore targets. The project team in the Admiralty also had the courage to 'freeze' the specification in 1955 when the Blackburn B-103, later to be named the Buccaneer, was selected for production. It would have been only too easy to continue adding to complexity and cost.

The Blackburn team, under the leadership of Barry Laight, realised that NA.39 required a lot of performance from a relatively small aircraft if it was to operate from existing carriers. It had to be very clever indeed, because high speed at low level required the smallest possible wing to minimise gust response, whereas operating from a carrier required a big wing that allowed reasonable launch and landing speeds compatible with contemporary catapults and arrester gear. Achievement of the specified range required fuel efficiency that was as yet unheard of, using turbojets with the minimum thrust to achieve the flying performance. What made the B-103 stand out was the adoption of boundary layer control (BLC), achieved by blowing hot, high-pressure bleed air from the engines out of thin slits in front of the flaps. This technique had been pioneered in the USA by John Attinello of the National Advisory Committee for Aeronautics (NACA, later the National Aeronautics and Space Administration [NASA]). A basic version was used by aircraft such as the USAF's Lockheed F-104 Starfighter and the RN's Supermarine Scimitar, and reduced their landing speeds by about 10 knots. Blackburn took the idea much further, however, with assistance from Dr John Williams of the NPL and Lewis Boddington of the Naval Air Department of the RAE. Together they investigated blowing air right across the wing from tip to tip in conjunction with steeply angled flaps and 'drooped' ailerons. Model tests showed dramatic results, nearly doubling the lift of a conventional wing and reducing the landing speed by as much as 25 knots. The Buccaneer design stemmed from this work and featured relatively small 'blown' wings. 'Blowing' the underside of the tailplane allowed this surface, too, to be dramatically reduced in size but still powerful enough to counter the significant nose-down pitch change that occurred when flap was selected. The Buccaneer benefited from another piece of NACA research in that it was an early, if rather crude example of the principle of 'area-ruling' pioneered by Richard Whitcomb. This reduced drag by forming the cross-sectional area of an aircraft into a smooth, streamlined curve from nose to tail, achieved by reducing the area of the fuselage in line with the wing which would otherwise have formed a 'peak'.

The Buccaneer achieved a low-level radius of action of 500 miles on internal fuel by using two scaled-down de Havilland Gyron engines known as Gyron Juniors. Together these gave 14,000lb of static thrust and very low specific fuel consumption with the boundary layer bleed system in operation, just enough to achieve the specified attack speed of Mach 0.85. For the first time in the Royal Navy the specification did not call for the aircraft to be able to carry out a free take-off from the deck, and satisfactory performance relied on catapult launch and arrested recovery. When disembarked ashore the early Buccaneers required a very long runway, and it was accepted that performance with these engines in the circuit would be marginal, especially if one engine was shut down for some

reason. At sea without a diversion, early Buccaneers were landed into the nylon barrier if attempting single-engine recoveries. Later Buccaneers, the S.2 version, had Rolls-Royce Spey engines which combined even better specific fuel consumption statistics with a total of 22,000lb of static thrust, giving the aircraft a far better performance in the circuit and on a single engine. Buccaneers had distinctive 'clamshell' airbrakes at the after end of the fuselage. Unusually these were opened for landing, allowing the throttles to be set at nearly full power to provide 'bleed' air without causing high speed. Overshoots were performed rather more by closing the air brake than by opening the throttles. The brakes were kept open on deck and in the hangar as this significantly reduced the aircraft's length.

Another aircraft development was the Audio Air Speed Indicator (Audio ASI), developed in Britain

in the late 1950s. Trials with a Meteor T.7, in which the eyes of pilots on final approach were filmed, showed that they spent 56 per cent of the time looking ahead at the runway and the remainder looking at instruments, especially the ASI. A prototype Audio ASI was flown in a Hawker Sea Hawk in 1954 and tested during a series of landings on HMS *Albion*. These were successful but the equipment was not fitted as standard until some time later. It was fairly basic, and comprised a detector unit fed from the pitot-head, a two-tone sound box and an on/off/volume control. It became operative when the undercarriage was selected down. Above the optimum landing speed the pilot heard high-pitched 'pips', the interval decreasing until a steady note was heard. If speed decreased below the optimum a series of deeper-toned 'beeps' were heard that got deeper and slower as speed decreased. The problem with the

Early British JBDs were flat steel plates raised hydraulically to an angle behind each catapult to deflect the jet blast clear of the deck. The most sophisticated were the four-plate, water-cooled JBDs installed in HMS *Ark Royal* to cope with the launch of Phantoms in re-heat. Note the remarkable 40 inch nose extension on the British F-4K version of the Phantom; double the extension on the contemporary USN F-4J variant. The DLPS is raised to the highest position to allow aircraft to taxi past close to it with their wings spread.

(AUTHOR'S COLLECTION)

two parallel rows of slots to indicate angle of attack on an instrument in the cockpit. This showed a circle when on the correct angle of attack, or nose-up/nose-down chevrons either side of it when adjustment needed to be made. The RN evaluated the device in a Sea Venom in HMS *Eagle* in 1958 and adopted it generally in 1960. In some aircraft it was successfully linked with the Audio ASI system.

The USN was less constrained by warship dimensions in the years after 1945 than the Royal Navy, and was able to derive greater benefit from the transformational technology pioneered by the British in the large hulls of the *Forrestal, Kitty Hawk, John F. Kennedy, Enterprise* and *Nimitz* class carriers. In Britain the mistaken view persisted that hull size was closely related to total cost, with the result that designs were constricted, placing limitations on flying operations. Too much emphasis was placed on stowing aircraft in the hangar rather than flying them from the deck, whereas in the USN the 'battle flexi-deck' was evolved to allow launches, recoveries, refuelling and rearming to take place concurrently on the flight deck. As aircraft designs improved, the USN was able to reduce the number of aircraft types embarked from about eight in the 1970s [8] to just three [9] when the EA-18G Growler replaces the long-serving EA-6B Intruder in 2010. This is a major achievement, and allows greater standardisation of aircraft support and maintenance infrastructure within a task force. Taken with significant improvements in the designed serviceability of the new aircraft and their avionics, this has allowed the size of air groups to be reduced from about 100 to about 85 while still producing the same effect. In turn, this has made the 'flexi-deck' even more efficient. All helicopters embarked in USN task forces form part of the carrier air group and can be rotated to other ships from the parent ship. It would have been fascinating to see how the designed parallel deck of the projected British CVA01 design would have compared with the greater angles used on all US carrier decks, but the scheme has never been revived. The new British carriers *Queen Elizabeth* and *Prince of Wales* have thankfully been designed to embrace the importance of size, and have the potential to operate a mixed air group of about fifty aircraft.

A Buccaneer S1 of 800 Naval Air Squadron with wheels, flaps and hook down on finals to HMS *Eagle*. It has drooped ailerons and the air-brake is in the normal, open position for deck landing and has flown a wider circuit than usual to allow the 'chase-plane' to stay behind and below to take the photograph. The aircraft is to starboard of the wake, lining up with the angled deck and the wind is down the angle, blowing the funnel smoke to starboard, clear of the aircraft's approach path.

(AUTHOR'S COLLECTION)

Audio ASI was that the actual speed on finals varied with fuel remaining, and therefore aircraft weight. The ASI could not be reset in flight by the pilot to the required speed, so it tended to be disregarded. The USN came up with a rather more useful item when it appreciated that the aircraft's angle of attack on finals was a constant, whereas speed was not. To help pilots fly the correct angle the USN produced the Airflow Direction Detector (ADD). This was a probe that stuck out at right angles from the fuselage and rotated as the result of the airflow impinging on

CHAPTER 15

Flying from an angled-deck carrier

The FDO of HMS *Victorious* shows the Royal Navy's launching technique in 1966. The green flag is raised, the red hidden behind his back as a Buccaneer S.2 of 801 Naval Air Squadron sits in the flying attitude with its nosewheel lifted off the deck by the launching strop tensioned against the bridle.

(AUTHOR'S COLLECTION)

HMS *Victorious* commissioned in 1958 as the first British carrier with a full 8-degree angled deck, two parallel-track steam catapults in Fly 1, mirror landing aids and the first JBDs in an RN carrier. The huge aerial of her Type 984 'three-dimensional' radar topped her small island, and her Aircraft Direction Room (ADR) was equipped with the Comprehensive Display System (CDS), the most advanced system of operational display and control to emerge in the pre-computer era. Although the ship was small compared with the new USN *Forrestal* class, there was some justice in contemporary Royal Navy claims that she was one of the world's most advanced carriers. A similar but slightly smaller carrier, *Hermes*, completed in 1959.

The 'third-generation' jets in service by 1958 were too big and heavy to manhandle, and all movements were made by tractors attached to the aircraft nosewheels by towing arms which were equally able to pull or push. Each was manned by a team of four, comprising a leading airman director with a yellow surcoat, a tractor driver and two 'chock-men', all with blue surcoats. A supply of chocks and lashings were carried on the tractor. Each squadron supplied sailors to sit in cockpits to work the aircraft's brakes during moves. These were usually known as 'brake-numbers' in the RN, or sometimes as the USN equivalent, 'brake-riders'. As soon as each aircraft was positioned in the range the main wheels were chocked and either four or eight lashings fitted, depending on ship motion or the predicted sea state. Care had always to be taken to ensure that these led in differing directions.[1] To enable the tractor teams to range aircraft accurately, making full use of the deck space available, the deck was considered to have a number of spots. On *Hermes* the numerals 1 to 10 were painted on the deck and intended for helicopter operations, 11 to 30 were not marked on the deck, but were intended to indicate exactly where the tractor teams were to position fixed-wing aircraft. As with all other RN ship numbering systems, odd numbers were to starboard and even to port. The small British decks placed considerable constraints on how aircraft could be ranged, and the ACRO's instructions were explicit:[2] 'Use 14, 16, 18 and 20 spots for spread

Buccaneers; 21 and 23 spots are for folded Buccaneers. Use 22, 26, 30, 29, 27 and 25 spots in that order for [de Havilland] Sea Vixens. Sea Vixen tankers must be spread to refuel and must, therefore, use 22 or 29 spots.' Before the first launch of the day, if there had been no aircraft arrests for 72 hours, space had to be left for tractors to carry out slow pull-outs on the arrester wires as part of their maintenance schedule. The time limit was reduced to 24 hours when tractors were used to pull out the wires. Aircraft wheels and lashings had to be positioned clear of the catapult tracks because the 'badgers' needed to carry out light shots as part of their maintenance procedures. Liquid oxygen for use in Sea Vixens, Buccaneers and Phantoms could not be produced until a minimum of two hours had passed since leaving harbour, so fixed-wing flying could not, realistically, be programmed until some hours after that. As soon as the deck was declared serviceable the aircraft were moved into the standard range as quickly as possible. Fixed-wing squadron maintenance personnel were responsible for getting 'weight chits', showing the exact weight of each aircraft, to Flyco in good time for 'f' to calculate the catapult settings for the next launch. Movement on deck was controlled by the ACRO while aircraft were being spotted, but once aircraft started the deck became the responsibility of the FDO. Overall responsibility for implementing the flying programme rested with 'f'.

By the 1960s aircraft used Palouste high-pressure air starters rather than the cartridge starters of previous generations. 'Firesuitmen' stood by in case of emergency and directors were positioned along the deck to control the start process and bring aircraft out of the range and on to the catapults. Most were leading airmen, but the key position was the 'Y' Director who marshalled aircraft between the two bow catapults. He was usually an experienced petty officer airman, and his job was made more exciting by the fact that the wind over the deck was usually considerable as he directed aircraft on to the catapults. 'Little f' supervised the process of start-up and taxiing aircraft from his control position in Flyco. This was by now a fully enclosed and extensively glazed compartment projecting some distance to port of the island on the 02 deck level. The extension had proved necessary to enable 'f' to have a clear view of aircraft on finals to the angled deck both by day and by night. Deck movement was ordered by 'traffic lights' positioned in banks so that they could be seen from any part of the deck. Instructions for fixed-wing aircraft used 'steady' lights, which shone constantly, and those for helicopters used flashing lights. When no taxiing was allowed the lights remained red. After start-up a fixed amber traffic light allowed fixed-wing lashings to be removed and the aircraft to taxi forward. A flashing amber allowed helicopter lashings to be removed but, since they seldom taxied, the chocks were left in place. Taxiing placed a constraint on ship movement and, while the ship would usually minimise the amount of time spent into wind by turning while the range taxied forward, the angle of heel applied to the deck had to be kept to a minimum

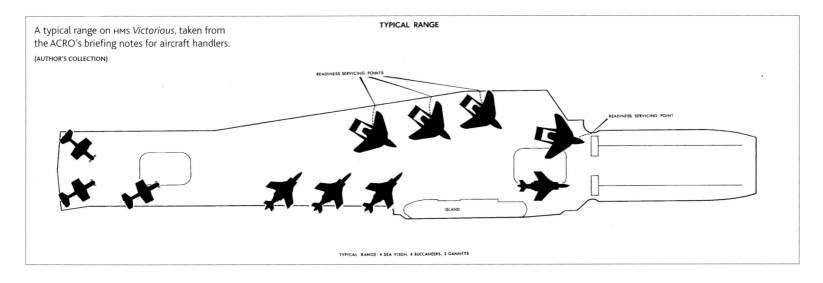

A typical range on HMS *Victorious*, taken from the ACRO's briefing notes for aircraft handlers.

(AUTHOR'S COLLECTION)

TYPICAL RANGE

READINESS SERVICING POINTS

READINESS SERVICING POINT

ISLAND

TYPICAL RANGE: 4 SEA VIXEN, 4 BUCCANEERS, 3 GANNETS

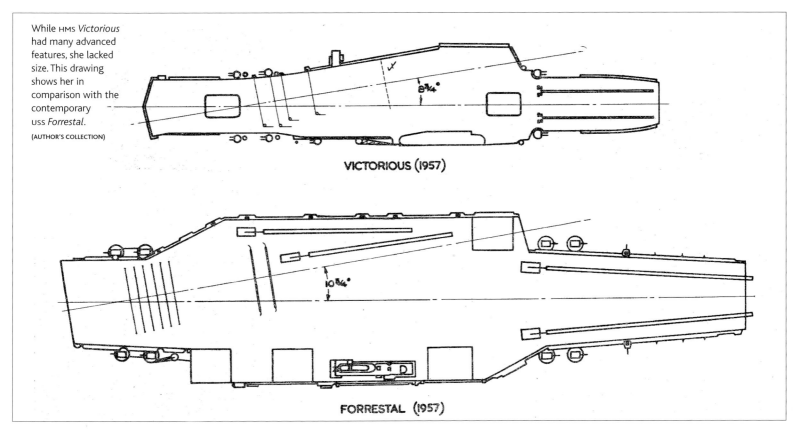

While HMS *Victorious* had many advanced features, she lacked size. This drawing shows her in comparison with the contemporary USS *Forrestal*.

(AUTHOR'S COLLECTION)

VICTORIOUS (1957)

FORRESTAL (1957)

Tractors were used regularly to pull out arrester wires for maintainers to work on them when no flying was taking place. Two tractors coupled together are seen here on HMS *Albion*, pulling out arrester wire number three, which was capable of stopping a 30,000lb aircraft at up to 75 knots. Note the deck-landing mirror sight on a sponson on the port side amidships, and the SAR helicopter parked at the after end of the angled deck.
(AUTHOR'S COLLECTION)

Opposite: The parking spaces created by angling the landing deck to port are shown with particular clarity in this photograph of the new HMCS *Bonaventure* as tugs tow her out of the Harland and Wolff shipyard, Belfast, in 1957. Unlike other Commonwealth aircraft carriers she had a hull number, 22, painted on the flight deck, rather than a deck-recognition letter. Note how the starboard after part of the flight deck has been extended to starboard.
(AUTHOR'S COLLECTION)

by a relatively gentle turn. Catapult launching potentially required more manpower than free-stream take-offs had done, and several steps were taken to 'automate' the loading process. The CALE gear was the first of these, complemented by a new technique in which both the strop and the hold-back were fitted to aircraft in the range but held clear of the deck by lanyards while it taxied forward. This allowed the hold-back to be dropped into its slot as the aircraft taxied over it, and the strop to be dropped on to the shuttle when the aircraft was ideally placed. Tensioning was achieved by moving the shuttle forward until the strop was taut and the hold-back took the strain. The steady forward movement in this process reduced the number of men required, as the aircraft no longer needed to be 'shunted' into position. 'Badgers' were responsible for ensuring that everything was in place, and Badger 1 gave a 'thumbs-up' to the FDO when it was.

Although *Victorious* could, in theory, launch an aircraft from the starboard catapult while landing another on the angle, it was more usual to operate cyclically, with a recovery following immediately on completion of a launch, and a gap to re-spot or 'elephant tango' the aircraft from the previous recovery into a new launch range. Large 'pulses' of strike aircraft could be interspersed when required with the more standard launches of aircraft for CAP and AEW barrier patrols. At 34,000lb fully loaded, the Supermarine Scimitar was considerably heavier than the 15,200lb Sea Hawk it replaced, and it was tensioned on the catapult in a new way. The aircraft was put into a flying attitude before launch by the strop pulling against the hooks, which were positioned so that when tensioned, the nosewheel was raised up off the deck. The tail rested on a 'skid' aft which lowered with the undercarriage. The same technique was used by the Buccaneer, which replaced the Scimitar in service, but the Phantom, designed to meet USN specifications, used a different method. Its nose oleo was extended by 20 inches when the aircraft was positioned on the catapult, to achieve a flying attitude. When the type was procured for the Royal Navy there were concerns that even this would not be enough to launch the aircraft safely from the

short steam catapults of British carriers, and the nose oleo was modified to give a 40-inch extension. After launch, the oleo compressed to its normal height before retracting, a process that lengthened the time taken to retract the gear fully. In practice, USN F-4 J Phantoms were able to launch successfully during cross-deck operations.

The process of launching comprised aircraft being directed forward and on to the catapult. Once the aircraft was in position, 'badgers' ensured that the hold-back was in place and the strop hooked over the shuttle. 'Badger 1' gave the catapult operator in the 'howdah' the signal to move the shuttle forward to tension the aircraft into the launch position. When happy that all was well, he ordered his men clear, gave a thumbs-up to the FDO and scrambled clear himself. British carriers had four FDOs who operated in teams of two with each of the two watches of aircraft handlers. Usually 1 and 3 worked with one watch and 2 and 4 with the other. The senior FDO was usually a lieutenant commander and the others lieutenants. Some of them were aircrew, the remainder former naval airmen who had earned commissions. All catapult launches were controlled by an FDO, using flag signals. When the 'badgers' ran clear he would raise a green flag and rotate it slowly to instruct the pilot to move his throttles forward to full power. A naval airman held a board up where the pilot could see it, a 'last reminder' that brakes were off and cockpit checks complete. At full power the pilot would raise his right hand to 'salute' the FDO and confirm that he was ready to launch. Then the FDO would glance up to confirm a steady green traffic light giving command approval to launch, and look over his shoulder to see that the area ahead of the carrier was clear of other ships. If anything went wrong in the aircraft, the pilot shook his head instead of saluting and the FDO raised a red flag, slowly lowering (and hiding) the green so that the catapult operator could not mistake his moves for the order to launch. A tractor pushed the aircraft back and moved it to the 'graveyard'. This takes a while to read, but in practice it took less than a second, at the end of which the FDO lowered the green flag and the catapult operator pressed the button to 'fire' the

HMS *Albion*'s Fly 1 packed with Sea Hawks and Sea Venoms after a recovery during the 1956 Suez Intervention, *Operation Musketeer*.
(AUTHOR'S COLLECTION)

catapult.

As soon as the launch was completed, with the last aircraft climbing away, the ship adjusted course by a few degrees to put the wind down the angled deck. Wires were raised and the pieces of catapult equipment that stood proud of the deck, such as the hold-back block, were removed and stowed. The sight would be manned, tested and set on the appropriate hook/eye distance for the first aircraft due to recover. As aircraft returned to the carrier they joined the waiting orbits; jets in high and low waits on the port quarter at 2,000 and 1,000 feet, and turboprops in a single wait on the starboard quarter at 1,500 feet. They usually remained and kept an eye on launch activity to spot any delays. Assuming there were none, the first aircraft would have its wheels on deck within a minute of completion of the launch. The time at which wheels were briefed to be on the deck was known as 'Charlie time', and being adrift (late) was

a 'cardinal sin'. Delay could disrupt the Flypro, besides keeping the ship needlessly into wind.

The circuit technique was to leave the wait and fly down the starboard side of the ship at 400 feet or less with groups of aircraft in echelon starboard, the position abreast the island being known as 'the slot'. The ship's course for both launch and recovery was known as the Designated Flying Course (DFC),[3] and all circuits were flown relative to it, even if the ship was still turning when aircraft were at the slot. When using normal R/T procedures the leader called 'slot' with his section's call-sign as he passed the island, after which he continued ahead of the ship on the DFC for about a mile[4] before carrying out a hard level break to port through 180 degrees to the downwind leg. Other aircraft turned to port after him at 15-second intervals. Speed was washed off by selecting airbrake at the start of the turn so that the undercarriage and partial flap could be selected down

A range of Sea Hawks fire their cartridge starters in unison on HMS *Eagle*. The mirror sight is visible just under the tail of the fourth aircraft from forward. At the time *Eagle* only had an interim angled deck with a small extension to port, allowing much of the original close-range armament to remain in place. Six-barrelled Bofors mountings and their directors are visible. (AUTHOR'S COLLECTION)

A Gannet is directed on to HMS *Eagle*'s starboard catapult. The dotted white line visible under the tailhook shows the ideal path for the nosewheel to follow to arrive on the CALE gear in the right place. The director has his feet astride the catapult so that the shuttle can pass between them when it is retracted. (AUTHOR'S COLLECTION)

and pre-landing checks completed while on the 'downwind' leg. The circuit distance was judged so that the wingtip appeared to pass down the centre of the axial deck, and a radio call 'downwind' with the fuel state was made by individual aircraft. When level with the island the aircraft turned port on to finals, selected full flap and maintained attitude and power to intercept a 3-degree glide-slope just aft of the ship. Because of the angle, the full turn would be through more than 180 degrees, but line-up was easy and straightforward. The mirror sight was visible from halfway through the turn, allowing early power adjustments to get 'into the groove'. When the aircraft were established in the final turn and the sight was visible, individual pilots transmitted 'finals – 4 greens[5] - sight'.

From the late 1950s most aircraft were fitted with audio airspeed indicators and ADD instruments that showed the correct angle of attack, leaving the pilot's eyes free to concentrate on the sight, with occasional glimpses at the brightly painted angled deck

centreline. For peacetime flying training, voice transmissions were made to indicate aircraft positions in the visual circuit, both for 'f' and to help other aircraft slot into the pattern without confliction. Once an air group was worked up to full efficiency, however, voice transmissions were dispensed with and aircraft were operated under silent conditions known as 'zip-lip'.

In the late 1950s the mirror sight was operated by a Mirror Control Officer (MCO), whose job it was to ensure that the sight was set for the appropriate 'hook-eye' distance of the aircraft on final approach, and was stabilising correctly. Like the DLCO before him, the MCO was assisted by a naval airman who acted as a 'talker', checking that each aircraft had its wheels, flaps and hook down. The projector sight, introduced in 1960, featured an improvement in that the operator, now known as the Projector Sight Officer (PSO), could view the approaching aircraft through a glass panel, rather like an aircraft gunsight. This was calibrated with a cross to show the ideal glide-slope,

The USN launch technique differs in that the 'shooters' use their hands rather than flags, and the F/A-18C is linked to the shuttle by a 'nose-tow' bar attached to the nose oleo. The hold-back is attached to the rear of the same oleo. Note the two sailors in green surcoats sitting on the open catapult control position.
(US NAVY)

and was stabilised by the same system as the sight itself. Looking through it from a seated position at aircraft on finals, the PSO could see firstly that the sight was stabilising correctly relative to the horizon and, just as importantly, could see whether aircraft were high or low, left or right of the ideal glide-slope. A control panel was situated below the glass panel, from which the sight was controlled, and daily checks were carried out before flying started. The accurate information provided by this display led the RN to make a further improvement in flight safety, replacing the PSO, who often doubled as a flight-deck officer, by an experienced pilot known as the Landing Safety Officer (LSO). He was able to grade pilots' deck-landing skills and give brief instructions to help them on finals if required. Like his predecessors he had a 'talker' and, in addition, a 'writer'; a second naval airman with a note-pad who jotted down his terse calls to aircraft for subsequent debriefs, and noted which wire the aircraft caught. The 'talker' was responsible for telling the LSO that the deck was clear after each landing, before the next aircraft could land. If it was not clear, or if the approach was unsafe, the LSO could 'wave-off' the aircraft for another circuit by flashing red lights over the sight's datum bars. The LSO's call took the form 'Roger' if the aircraft was on glide-slope and lined-up correctly. Corrective calls started with 'slightly low/high'; lined up a 'little left/right' graduating to a more imperative 'come left/right' or 'you are low' if the aircraft diverged from the ideal. Often aircraft sank a little as they passed through the turbulence astern of the ship and the LSO called for a 'little power', but if the aircraft appeared to be sinking, especially near the round-down, the call would be an emphatic 'power'. The USN continues to train LSOs for each type of aircraft embarked, and they man a sponson on the port side aft, where the batsmen had formerly stood. A camera mounted under armoured glass in the flight deck films every approach, and they can be watched on screens in briefing areas, ready

The Phantom was expected to be a tight fit in the existing generation of Royal Navy aircraft carriers. This study of XT865 of 'C' Squadron, A & AEE Boscombe Down, on the forward lift of HMS *Eagle* during trials shows just how close the tolerances were.

(AUTHOR'S COLLECTION)

rooms, the Primary Flying Control Position (Prifly) and the bridge. Regrettably this excellent system had no equivalent in the Royal Navy.

Each deck landing was graded by the LSO, and squadrons kept records on their briefing room bulkheads showing every pilot's deck-landing performance, the 'grades' being a matter of individual pride. Blue indicated a perfect final approach and landing that took the target wire; green a good safe approach; amber an adequate approach and landing with some cause for comment; and red an unsafe recovery. For an approach that started slightly high and left, corrected to the roger, went low in close, needed a little power and took number two wire, thus gaining a 'green' grade, the 'writer's' pad

would read 'SH – LUL – R – R – LIC – LP #2 G. Most pilots would select full power on hitting the deck in case they had a 'bolter'.

As soon as the aircraft stopped, having taken a wire, two 'hook-men' (naval airmen wearing green surcoats) ran out from the catwalk to ensure that the wire dropped from the hook. Usually tension in the wire pulled the aircraft back slightly after it had stopped and the wire fell away, but occasionally it needed to be pulled clear. When clear, the wire was reset by the operator, and snaked away aft to its ready position. The next aircraft could not land until it had done so. The aircraft on deck was directed to raise flaps, fold and taxi away fast to clear the wingtip safety line so that the next aircraft was clear to land. The

A Buccaneer S.2 of 801 Naval Air Squadron halfway down HMS *Victorious*' port catapult in 1966. The Buccaneer on the starboard catapult has its wheels against the CALE gear chocks, but has yet to have its hold-back slotted into the retaining block on deck. The 'Y' Director is already giving the 'brakes off' signal to bring the next aircraft on to the port catapult. 'Flyco', at the top right of the picture, is a more sophisticated, enclosed structure than the earlier open platforms. The square structure between the catapults is the 'howdah' or catapult control position, which, unlike its USN equivalent, was enclosed. It was lowered flush with the deck when not in use.
(AUTHOR'S COLLECTION)

Left: A good recovery; the leading Gannet rolls its wings level as it crosses the round-down lined up with the angled-deck centreline. The second aircraft is backing it up a minute astern, and the curved wake shows that the carrier has just steadied on to the DFC. She would still have been turning when the aircraft 'slotted' into the circuit.

(AUTHOR'S COLLECTION)

A Gannet AEW.3 of 849C Flight seconds before taking a wire on HMS *Victorious*.

(AUTHOR'S COLLECTION)

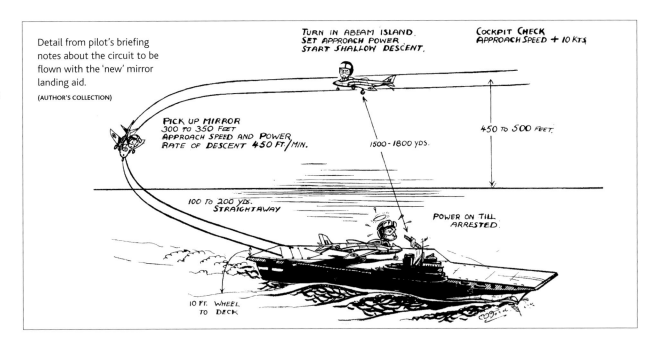

Detail from pilot's briefing notes about the circuit to be flown with the 'new' mirror landing aid.

(AUTHOR'S COLLECTION)

A 'pilot's-eye-view' of HMS *Ark Royal*'s deck seconds before landing. Line-up is good but the 'meatball' is slightly below the datum bars, showing that the aircraft is slightly below the ideal glide-path. The dustbin-shaped object at the rear of the island, just to the right of 'Flyco', is the radome for the Type 963 CCA Radar. Note the good view of the final approach area enjoyed by 'Flyco'.
(AUTHOR'S COLLECTION)

interval between aircraft was about a minute, giving time for the wire to reset and the aircraft ahead to move clear. Third-generation jets like the Buccaneer could fold their wings while the flaps were still housing, but the Gannet's Fairey Youngman flaps had a complicated operating mechanism which would have been damaged had the wings started folding before the flaps were fully housed. Crews tackled the problem of clearing the landing area as a team effort. The pilot selected flap up as soon as the aircraft came to rest, and began to taxi, following the director's signals when the hook was clear; the observers called 'flap up' as soon as they saw it housed, allowing the pilot to select wing fold. Gannets usually recovered last so that their relatively slow movements did not cause a fast jet behind them to overshoot.

Aircraft handlers were taught that their signals should be given in the manner in which they were meant to be obeyed. Thus signals telling the pilot to clear the landing area were given with urgency requiring fast action,[6] but when the aircraft was handed off to the parking directors in Fly 1 the signals were slow and deliberate, requiring careful taxiing close to the deck edge. Once the aircraft were in position, handlers placed chocks and squadron maintainers lashed the aircraft and attached ladders for the crew to climb out. Often squadrons used little wooden 'hand carts' to carry all the kit they needed out to the aircraft. Engines were only shut down when the aircraft was securely lashed. Aircrew needed to be particularly careful moving across the deck into the island to sign-in their aircraft, as they had to pick their way past aircraft that could still be running or even taxiing, lashings that criss-crossed past each other, and a gale-force wind that blew down the deck if the recovery was not yet complete. The 'cardinal sin' was to drop maps and briefing notes, which would blow, uncontrollably, down the deck.

The re-spot after the recovery was preplanned by the ACRO, who marked up a board with the deck spots to be occupied by individual aircraft. For ease of reference this was hung in the ACR window in some carriers. Aircraft that had declared themselves unserviceable in flight needed to be struck down and serviceable aircraft had to be ranged from the hangar,

A drawing showing what the pilot sees on finals at night (no pilot I know of has been persuaded to take a photograph at this point). The new lighting system introduced with HMS *Victorious* was effective, and night deck landing gave a wonderful sense of achievement once you caught a wire.

(AUTHOR'S COLLECTION)

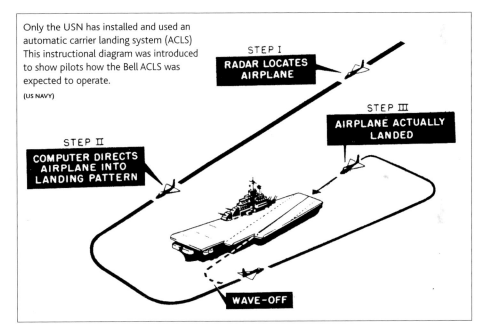

Only the USN has installed and used an automatic carrier landing system (ACLS) This instructional diagram was introduced to show pilots how the Bell ACLS was expected to operate.

(US NAVY)

STEP I
RADAR LOCATES AIRPLANE

STEP III
AIRPLANE ACTUALLY LANDED

STEP II
COMPUTER DIRECTS AIRPLANE INTO LANDING PATTERN

WAVE-OFF

so in ships that had an arrester wire over the after lift this needed to be dragged clear to get the lift into use as quickly as possible. All tractor teams moved to Fly 1 after the recovery, and, as soon as armed aircraft were declared safe by the squadrons and re-spot positions for each aircraft were known, moves began. It was considered better to re-spot before refuelling and rearming to allow sufficient time to prepare the aircraft for its next sortie. Splitting the squadron manpower and equipment between two deck spots with a move between them, which might be delayed by a number of factors, seldom achieved the desired

Aircraft that could not land normally were arrested by a nylon barrier which took five minutes to rig, sited forward of the wires. This Gannet AEW.3 of 849C Flight has lost its nosewheels and is landing into the barrier as a precaution.
(AUTHOR'S COLLECTION)

Unable to lower its hook, this Sea Hawk of 806 Naval Air Squadron in HMS Eagle has landed into the barrier, which has stretched out as intended to absorb the aircraft's momentum. Some damage was possible if the nylon cut into the wing leading edges.
(AUTHOR'S COLLECTION)

The ACRO's desk in HMS *Hermes* in 1968, showing aircraft positions after a recovery, before the re-spot. The upper panel shows the largely empty hangar.
(AUTHOR'S COLLECTION)

results. Although an 'elephant tango', in which aircraft taxied under their own power back down their deck to points near their 'pit-stop' spots, seemed attractive, it seldom worked, because aircraft tended to be packed too tightly into Fly 1 after the recovery and could not reverse into their new spots. Movement by tractor invariably proved quicker and more effective. In any carrier, no matter what the size, the recovery of an aircraft with 'hung-up' live weapons could disrupt the flying programme. The aircraft needed to be parked on a safe heading in the 'graveyard' area while armourers worked out how to remove the weapon safely.

Operations at night or in poor visibility followed similar lines, but required specialised techniques and training. Pilots would normally qualify in day operations and build up their levels of skill and confidence for at least six months before operating at night. The transition involved a substantial number of hours night flying in the weeks before embarkation and three sessions of 'duskers', landings in twilight conditions, to get used to the different visual cues given by the flight-deck lighting. After that, a concentrated series of night launches and recoveries were made to achieve full qualification.

For night deck moves, marshallers would use

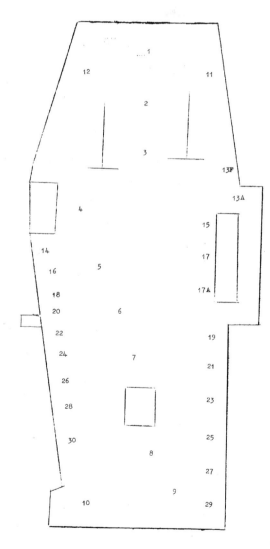

Detail from the ACRO's briefing notes, showing flight-deck parking spots in HMS *Hermes*.
(AUTHOR'S COLLECTION)

uss *George Washington*, CVN 73, an example of the *Nimitz* class which is, without doubt, the most effective aircraft carrier design of naval aviation's first century.

(US NAVY)

illuminated wands to direct aircraft. These comprised plastic tubes attached to torches and were colour coded. Marshallers used yellow, FDOs green and red, and 'badgers' blue. Signals from the pilot in the cockpit could not be seen, so aircraft used their navigation lights to indicate their status. 'On steady dim' indicated manned, ready to start-up; 'on flashing dim' indicated engines started ready to taxi. Irregular flashes of the taxi-light indicated that the aircraft had a problem. Signals such as 'on brakes' or acknowledgement of the check-board on the catapult could be given by turning the navigation lights off for a pause and then back on again. Once the aircraft was on the catapult the navigation lights were selected to 'steady dim' to indicate 'ready to launch'. If the pilot had a problem at this late stage he switched the navigation lights off and could use radio to call Flyco unless the 'zip-lip' state prevented it. Once launched, navigation lights were switched to 'steady bright' or 'off', depending on the operational need.

Straight-deck carriers had used a 'wash' of light to show the landing area. This failed to give good enough depth perception, and by the 1960s the scheme was replaced by white floodlights mounted on the island and its masts, which were rather like theatre stage lights. They threw across the deck carefully shaped beams which could be varied from bright, for aircraft maintenance on deck in peacetime, to a dim loom of light which was used for aircraft recovery. The light was projected through a tube fitted with 'cut-outs' which prevented the source light from being visible beyond the deck edge. Since the lights were angled downwards they could only be seen from the deck, and the loom of light was not visible beyond half a mile. The result gave an effective three-dimensional impression, improving pilots' depth perception inside half a mile as they approached the deck. The number of lights let into the deck was simplified to show the pilot the round-down at the after end of the deck and the angled deck centreline. This arrangement gave a clear indication of line-up without the plethora of confusing lights that had been used before. A 'turning light' was retained on the island in case pilots short of fuel had to fly an emergency visual circuit and needed

Although the technology of modern aircraft carrier operations has been largely inspired by the Royal Navy, US Navy carrier designs have consistently made the best use of it. This is the uss *Enterprise*, CVN 65, the first nuclear-powered aircraft carrier and, at the time of her completion in 1961, the largest mobile object ever built by man. Her 10-degree angle is obvious, but the aircraft parked in Fly 1 obscure two of her four steam catapults. At over 1,100 feet long she can not only operate a large air group (over ninety aircraft are visible on deck, more than many smaller nations possess), but also large aircraft within the group, such as the A-5 Vigilantes parked aft, which contrast strikingly with the diminutive Douglas A-4 Skyhawks nearby. Like the Royal Navy, the USN favoured a 'flop-spot' for the SAR helicopter, in this case an SH-2 Seasprite, on the angled deck abeam the island.

(A.D. BAKER III)

Taken just as the aircraft is about to cross the round-down of HMS *Centaur*, this photograph shows us to be lined up on the angled-deck centreline but slightly high. The 'meatball' on the mirror landing aid is above the datum lights in the top left corner of the mirror. The 'dustbin'-shaped object on the rear of the island is the weatherproof cover for the Type 963 CCA radar. A Gannet AEW.3 is tucked as tightly as possible into Fly 3 with its tail over the side, and Sea Vixens are lined up against the wingtip safety line.

(AUTHOR'S COLLECTION)

assistance to judge the point at which they should turn finals. It showed red from 30 degrees to 90 degrees on the port beam, and amber from 90 to 145 degrees. It was screened so that it could not be seen on the final approach.

The principal difference between day operations and those at night or in low visibility was the method of recovery. Night visual circuits were no longer considered safe, and by 1956 Carrier Controlled Approach (CCA) radar Type 963 was introduced. This was capable of detecting an aircraft the size of a Sea Hawk out to 15 miles, and of tracking aircraft out of pre-briefed marshalling points to which they were

directed by the 'homer' in the ADR using conventional radar such as Type 982. The marshalling points were at a bearing and range from the carrier, with each aircraft holding heights stepped up at 1,000-foot intervals to give separation. Turboprop aircraft such as the Gannet had the lowest stack height at 2,000 feet; the fast jets were usually much higher to conserve fuel. When the recovery started, jets were ordered to descend at 330 knots and 7,000 feet per minute through an 'Alpha Arc' to maintain 5,000 feet and 220 knots.[7] They were then fed through a 'Bravo Gateway' inside the range of CCA radar, where they changed radio frequency and were taken under control by an Air Traffic Control Officer (ATCO) who arranged the aircraft into a stream at one-minute intervals. Gaps were usually left in the line so that 'bolters' could be fed back into the stream without using the fuel needed to go 'to the back of the queue'. Gannets were usually taken out of the stack last as they were slower and generally, but not always, had greater endurance.

Once through the 'gate' the aircraft were directed to turn on to the DFC, descend to 2,000 feet and change to the final control frequency. Two ATCOs on different frequencies handled alternate talk-downs. Before starting they each checked with Flyco that the deck was ready to receive the aircraft, and with the LSO that he was ready. 'Little f' in Flyco monitored both frequencies to know what was coming next. At 8½ miles pilots were told to carry out cockpit checks and reduce speed to 150 knots. At 5 miles they were told to 'commence a slow descent, as for a 3-degree glide-path', at which point they selected full flap. Type 963 gave accurate bearing information but was not accurate in height, so the finals controller gave advisory heights such as 'now at 4 miles, you should be passing 1,600 feet; now at 3 miles, you should be passing 1,200 feet'. Pilots adjusted their rates of descent to match this ideal glide-slope. The minima for this type of approach were a 300-foot cloudbase and/or three-quarters-of-a-mile visibility, and the aircraft were flown down to that point on instruments until the controller called: 'At three-quarters of a mile look up for sight'. The landing then continued by using visual cues in much the same way as a day landing. It sometimes happened that the LSO could see the aircraft navigation lights before decision height and would tell the pilot to 'keep it coming', even if he had not 'called the ball'. If no visual contact was made, the pilot overshot to be fed back into the recovery stream for another attempt.

For convenience, the types of recovery were designated Case 1, 2 and 3 in the 1960s. Case 1 indicated visual recoveries to visual circuits, and was the most often used by day. Case 3 indicated a radar feed-in to a CCA, and was invariably used at night. Case 2 was an amalgamation of the two, used when there was low cloud base but good visibility in daylight; it was not used often, but indicated a radar feed-in to the visual circuit. HMS *Ark Royal* had her Type 963 radar replaced by the more capable USN SPN 35 CCA radar during her 'Phantomisation' refit. This was a much more capable set that gave greater ranges, allowing the CCA supervisor to control aircraft in the stack positions. It gave accurate height as well as bearing data, allowing a more accurate approach which lowered the minima to 200 feet and half a mile. Night deck landing, when everything worked properly, was an exhilarating experience, and I look back on my own landings as among the most satisfying achievements of my flying career.

Position information relative to the carrier was even more important, given the low fuel states with which the jets recovered. In 1958 the Royal Navy began to replace the YE homing beacon with the Tactical Air Navigation System (TACAN). Beacons were fitted to *Ark Royal*, *Eagle*, *Victorious*, *Hermes* and *Centaur* which gave, when selected, accurate bearing and range information out to the limit of UHF range. At high altitude this could be as much as 100 miles. The display in the cockpit was a simple analogue dial which showed the bearing of the selected beacon with a pointer against a compass card and numbers indicating the range in nautical miles. TACAN beacons were mounted ashore as well as on ships.

Helgicopters

CHAPTER

A Westland Wasp HAS.1 at Alert 5 on the tiny flight deck of the 'Tribal'-class frigate HMS *Nubian*. The pilot is not in the photograph, but would be close by and could man, start and launch the helicopter within the alert time. The flight deck was actually a lift that lowered the aircraft into the hangar below for maintenance, covers being placed over the top to form a roof. The wheels are set at 45 degrees so that when the lashings are removed the helicopter would tend to rotate rather than slide.

(AUTHOR'S COLLECTION)

Helicopters, the first true vertical take-off and landing (VTOL) aircraft, were immediately recognised as being useful for embarked operations from ships other than aircraft carriers. The first practical type was the Sikorsky R-4, which flew in prototype form in 1943 and carried out landing trials on a tanker modified with a rectangular wooden flight deck, the SS *Bunker Hill*. This was the first landing by a helicopter on a ship at sea.[1] A joint board was established to carry forward the development of the new type and evaluate its potential uses; members included representatives of the USN, Royal Navy and US Coastguard. A number of R-4s, named Hoverfly in British service, were procured for the Royal Navy, and one of them embarked on a merchant ship, the

SS *Daghestan*, off the north-eastern US coast for a practical trial of its usefulness in convoy defence. It operated off a flight deck made of wooden slats that was 90 feet long by 40 feet wide and, as a practical precaution, the Hoverfly was fitted with pontoon floats in case it came down in the sea. There was no hangar and the aircraft remained exposed to the elements throughout its time on board. The Hoverfly was 47 feet 11 inches long and had a rotor diameter of 38 feet, so it fitted comfortably on to the deck and could, with caution, land across it. It weighed up to 2,600lb and was distinctly underpowered by its single 245 hp Franklin engine, which limited it to visual search for surfaced U-boats in the immediate vicinity of a convoy, but the trial did at least show that

A Sikorsky R-4, the first practical helicopter design, carrying out deck landing trials on the SS *Bunker Hill*, a tanker modified with a rectangular wooden flight deck, in 1943.

helicopters could operate from ships at sea fitted with flight decks. Two R-4s were subsequently embarked in the ship on an operational convoy across the Atlantic, but extremely rough weather limited the amount of flying achieved.

In 1946 the 'River'-class frigate HMS *Helmsdale* was fitted with a small flight deck aft and carried out a series of experiments to evaluate a helicopter as part of a small warship's weapons system. The pilot was Lieutenant Alan Bristow RN, the Service's first helicopter pilot and the first to land on a small warship deck.[2] The trial showed that, while the Hoverfly could only realistically carry a pilot and an observer with a pair of binoculars on sorties of reasonable length, the potential for a more powerful helicopter able to carry both sensors and weapons was enormous.

There were immediate roles at sea for the early helicopters, the most obvious of these being combat search and rescue (SAR). Both Royal Navy carriers and naval air stations used the obsolescent Supermarine Sea Otter biplane amphibian in the role, but the new Sikorsky S-51 Dragonfly, manufactured under licence in the UK by Westland Aircraft, had obvious advantages, as it could be fitted with an hydraulically powered winch capable of lowering a net to 'catch'

survivors in the water, or a hook and underarm strop to lift them. In the Korean War it also proved that it could fly behind enemy lines, land to pick up 'downed' aircrew and take off again to fly them to safety. With a reasonable fuel load, pilot and winchman the Dragonfly HR.3 could pick up two survivors. The first carrier flight went to sea in HMS *Indomitable* in January 1951.[3] The first 'live' helicopter rescue was carried out during Korean operations by HMS *Glory*'s Dragonfly on 14 May 1951, when Stoker McPherson was recovered after falling overboard.[4] Dragonflies replaced destroyers in the daytime 'plane-guard' role during flying operations, and hovered close to the deck during all launches and recoveries. They were able to react instantly when an aircraft was lost over the side or ditched close to the fleet after crossing the coast with battle damage. As an example, Lieutenant Fraser's Hawker Sea Fury suffered an engine failure while he 'slotted' to starboard of *Glory*'s island on 1 March 1952, and ditched. The 'plane-guard' Dragonfly had him out of the water and on deck in only ninety seconds, probably quicker than he would have been on deck in his own aircraft! The ship's helicopters rescued a total of four ditched pilots and four from behind enemy lines during *Glory*'s tours of duty off the Korean coast. The ship's flights were

A USN S-51 Dragonfly helicopter on loan to HMAS *Sydney* III as a 'plane-guard' hovers to port of the flight deck as the carrier turns to starboard into wind. Its nose is canted into the natural wind to make hovering easier as the ship turns. A Fairey Firefly is running on the catapult, ready to launch.

(ROYAL AUSTRALIAN NAVY)

also valuable for transferring passengers, mail and urgent spare parts between ships of the battle group, and eventually Dragonflies equipped nine carrier flights.[5] Westland could not produce Dragonflies fast enough, and several carriers, including *Theseus* and HMAS *Sydney*, operated 'borrowed' USN S-51 flights.

Despite helicopters' obvious advantages, difficulties were encountered integrating even a two-helicopter SAR flight into fixed-wing carrier operations. Rotor blades had to be folded and spread manually, and the spread blades covered a large area.[6] The blades themselves were vulnerable to gusts and propeller blast.[7] The early Dragonflies had composite wood-and-fabric blades and were not operated at sea by the Royal Navy. Until fully engaged the rotors were sensitive to wind direction, and restrictions known as Ship Helicopter Operating Limits (SHOLs), were placed on start-up procedures, launch and recovery. These had to be taken into account by 'f' when positioning the plane-guard before a fixed-wing launch. Most ships learnt to keep a 'flop spot' clear to land-on helicopters for refuelling without getting in the way of other flight deck activity. Unlike fixed-wing aircraft, helicopters could not check full engine power by running up against the brakes before they took off. To cater for this, 'tie-down' points had to be fitted that would allow the aircraft to remain firmly chained to the deck while full power was selected as

The survey ship HMS *Vidal* was the first unit of the Royal Navy to be built with a flight deck and helicopter hangar aft. The hangar is visible here by the aftermost sea-boat, with its deck aft of it, above the quarterdeck. The embarked helicopter, usually a Westland Dragonfly, was used to carry survey parties ashore to remote locations and for aerial photography. The hangar is little different in design from the 'box-like' structure built on to the French ship *Foudre* in 1912.
(AUTHOR'S COLLECTION)

HMS *Undaunted* was the first Royal Navy frigate to be fitted with a flight deck aft capable of operating a small antisubmarine helicopter. Trials of the Saunders-Roe P.531, which eventually entered service as the Westland Wasp, were carried out from 1959, and the deck was left in place after their successful conclusion although, with no hangar, the ship had no permanent embarked flight. This unique view of the deck was taken seconds before she sank in the Atlantic as a target after being hit by a torpedo from the nuclear submarine HMS *Swiftsure* in November 1978. Note that, unlike British aircraft carriers, which have a single deck-recognition letter, destroyers and frigates have two; in this case UD for *Undaunted*.
(AUTHOR'S COLLECTION)

one of many maintenance procedures. Access to these points and a clear area around them had to be left when other aircraft were ranged or parked, especially at night, when a lot of deep maintenance took place. Another difference was that helicopter ground runs had to be carried out by pilots because of the inherent dangers when engaging or disengaging rotors.

Most carriers operated the 'plane-guard' from an area of deck roughly amidships. This gave space to angle the helicopter into the felt wind to engage the rotors, and allowed easy access to the 'graveyard' if it went unserviceable on start-up. There was also space for the second helicopter to be ranged quickly to replace it if necessary. The area in Fly 1 was not considered as good, since any delay in launching would block the deck for a fixed-wing launch from a straight-deck carrier, and the area aft was likely to get in the way of an aircraft range before the next launch. As with so many aircraft, helicopters responded better to constant flying operations, and long periods at sea improved the operators' skills.

The early small-deck experiments had shown other useful capabilities, and a growing number of minor

A Wasp launches from the *Leander*-class frigate HMS *Galatea*. The technique is to lift using full power, move out to port and, once clear of the superstructure, lower the nose to accelerate away forward. The 'shapes' at the port yard-arm indicate that the ship's ability to manoeuvre is constrained, in this case by operating the helicopter. (AUTHOR'S COLLECTION)

Left: A Sea King on final approach to the cruiser HMS *Tiger*. The recovery technique is to slow into a hover to port of the deck about 40 feet above the water and then move across the deck over the eye-line and land on the circle. Although two circles and eye-lines are marked on the deck, only one could be used at any one time. The hangar was big enough for four Sea Kings. (AUTHOR'S COLLECTION)

The FDO signals landing instructions to HMS *Falmouth's* Wasp. The 'board-like' objects either side of the cockpit are flotation bag covers, and the object above the right-hand cockpit window is part of the aimer's sight for AS.12 air-to-surface missiles.

(AUTHOR'S COLLECTION)

war vessels and auxiliaries were fitted with hangars and a flight deck aft. The first was the survey ship HMS *Vidal*, followed in 1955 by the Antarctic patrol ship HMS *Protector*, one of the first ships to operate the new licence-built Sikorsky S-55, known in British service as the Whirlwind. Helicopters proved particularly useful in the survey role because of their ability to move parties of men and equipment between sites and, if necessary, to take them well inland and support them. These ships pioneered the Royal Navy's helicopter operating techniques, which continue in use virtually unchanged in the twenty-first century. Flight decks were usually only capable of operating a single helicopter, even if more could be stowed in the hangar. Before flight the aircraft was pushed aft

by hand into the centre of the deck, facing fore and aft, the blades were spread, and 'before-flight' checks carried out. Deck operations were supervised by one of the ship's officers or warrant officers who had undergone specialist FDO training for the task. He wore a headset connected to an intercom and sought permission from the captain for each stage of helicopter launch and recovery. After engine start, the rotors were held stationary by a rotor brake acting on the transmission between the main and tail-rotor gearboxes. Once the deck was within SHOLs and permission had been gained, the FDO signalled the pilot to release the brake and engage rotors, using bats exactly like those once used by batsmen on carriers. For take-off, the FDO requested the appropriate SHOL over the deck and ordered the flight maintainers to remove the lashings. There were no aircraft handlers in small ships' helicopter detachments. When removed, the lashings were shown to the pilot to 'prove' that they were clear,[8] but the chocks were left in place. The FDO used his bats to signal the take-off and the pilot carried out a 'towering climb', moving to port of the superstructure. When there were two pilots the non-flying pilot would kept his eyes 'inside' the cockpit to check power settings and a positive rate of climb, a function that was particularly important at night. There was no difference between day and night techniques but the deck and superstructure were dimly illuminated for the latter.

The recovery was straightforward with the ideal wind on the port bow between 10 and 20 knots. By day there was no circuit. The helicopter turned on to the ship's heading, aiming to come to a hover to port of the flight deck and about 15 to 20 feet above it. Royal Navy deck markings evolved to show a white circle at the ideal landing point. A white line was painted athwartships beneath where the pilot sat in the ideal hover, known officially as the 'eye line' and to most pilots as the 'bum line'. A second white line was painted fore-and-aft between the eye line and the hangar door, continuing up the hangar door when it was shut. These helped compensate the pilot for the fact that, when he hovered over the landing spot, he could not see the flight deck immediately underneath him and relied on the FDO and visual cues to help him land in the ideal place. Again, day and night techniques were the same, but a line of lights on the rear of the hangar gave a horizon and the deck was floodlit like a miniature version of a carrier. As the pilot decelerated to the hover the FDO signalled 'come forward' with his bats until the ideal spot was reached. When it was, he signalled 'steady' with his arms outstretched and then, when the deck was steady and in limits, he signalled the pilot to move over the deck until he was over the ideal spot, when he would again signal 'steady'. With experience, pilots learnt to use visual cues on the superstructure and the deck edge to position themselves accurately, and relied less on the FDO. Helicopter FDO signals were

advisory except that, as in fixed-wing flying, a wave-off was mandatory. Once the helicopter was well placed over the deck the FDO signalled 'come down' and the pilot descended to land firmly, lowering the collective-pitch control lever fully as the wheels touched. The helicopter was chocked and lashed when the pilot signalled the FDO that he was ready. Once lashed, the helicopter was shut down and stowed in the hangar. All navies have slightly different techniques, and the USN has white lines painted across the deck at 45 degrees to port and starboard so that helicopters effectively carry out 'angled-deck' landings into a wind put down the relevant line. This has the advantage of giving less turbulence than the Royal Navy's 'fore-and-aft' system. As more-sophisticated helicopters entered service, improved landing systems were devised to recover them in rough weather. The Royal Canadian Navy took Westland Sea Kings to sea in its frigates in the 1960s and designed the 'Bear-Trap' system, in which a wire, attached to a trolley running along rails built into the flight deck, was winched up to the helicopter hovering over the deck, and attached to it. The pilot then increased power slightly and an operator in the hangar hauled the aircraft down and 'locked' it to the trolley, which could then tow it into the hangar after shut-down and fold. Similar systems have been adopted by the USN for the SH-60 LAMPS helicopter and by the Royal Navy for the Merlin. The widely exported Agusta-Westland Lynx had a harpoon which locked into a circular grid built into the deck. The main wheels were canted and the nosewheel could be turned to allow the helicopter to rotate about the harpoon into the relative wind. The collective-pitch lever could be lowered to give negative rotor pitch, effectively forcing the helicopter on to the deck.

Day approaches were uncomplicated, and early helicopters seldom operated far enough away from their parent ship to need navigational aids, but night recoveries needed a little more sophistication. Ships built or modified to operate helicopters had their navigational radars sited to port of the foremast, from where they had no obstructions over the ship's port quarter. Helicopters were directed to the port quarter at a height of 200 feet, 3 miles out, for an approach

Even on an aircraft carrier, helicopters did not have much space in which to land. Here a Sea King of 824 Naval Air Squadron lands on the 'flop-spot' in Fly 3 aft of the island in HMS *Ark Royal*. The director and a fire-suitman are to the left, the squadron duty officer is to the right, and a number of air engineers wait to do a 'turn-round' inspection.

(AUTHOR'S COLLECTION)

10 degrees starboard of the ship's heading. This gave the pilot a better aspect to see visual cues than a stern approach. At half a mile the radar controller advised the pilot to set up a descent, passing advisory heights while the pilot reduced speed to achieve visual contact before hovering to port of the flight deck at 50 feet. A glide-slope indicator exactly like the sector light was mounted on the hangar roof on a gimbal that compensated for ship movement in pitch. It showed a green sector approximating to the ideal glide-slope, red for low and amber for high. In conditions of really low visibility the helicopter was told to descend to 50 feet early and controlled to fly along the wake at low speed. Flares were thrown into the ship's wake and look-outs were posted to watch

for it. Air traffic control officers only serve in carriers, and the control of helicopters in small ships is carried out by operations branch officers and ratings.

The introduction of turbojet-powered helicopters in the late 1950s brought types into service that were capable of operating from relatively small warships but had the ability to lift a viable quantity of weapons and sensors. The Saunders-Roe P.531 carried out trials from a small flight deck fitted right aft on the Type 15 frigate HMS *Undaunted* in the autumn of 1958, using the operating techniques that had by then become standard. With fuel for a one-hour flight and a single pilot it was capable of carrying a Mark 44 homing torpedo to ranges considerably beyond the ship's antisubmarine mortars, taking advantage of the practical ranges achieved with the Royal Navy's new Type 177 medium-range sonar. Launched from deck-alert with less fuel, the helicopter could carry two torpedoes to enable it to carry out a second attack if the first failed. When Saunders-Roe joined the Westland Group the P.531 was developed as the Westland Wasp, and was built in sufficient numbers to embark in every destroyer and frigate built from the early 1960s, beginning with the 'Tribal' and *Leander* classes. The technique of using a radar-guided Wasp armed with torpedoes to prosecute a sonar contact was refined into what the RN called the MATCH[9] System, and it proved extremely successful. Other navies adopted different methods. The USN used unmanned torpedo-carrying drone helicopters,[10] but technology was not up to controlling them accurately and many simply disappeared over the horizon. The RAN developed the Ikara torpedo-carrying missile, essentially an unmanned aircraft fired from a frigate and controlled to drop a Mark 44 torpedo over a sonar contact. This was probably a better ASW weapon than the Wasp, but lacked its flexibility. Wasps extended the visual search range of their parent vessel, could act as utility helicopters and carry missiles to engage small warships such as fast patrol boats. The MATCH System proved so successful that variations have been adopted by all the world's navies, including the USN, which evolved LAMPS[11] in stages from the late 1970s.

British helicopter decks tended to be platforms aft of box-like hangars, except in the 'Tribal' and 'County' classes. In both of these, helicopters were a late substitution in the design for a battery of antisubmarine mortars, and the helicopter facilities

A Lynx HAS.2 hovers over the flight deck of HMS *Arrow* to pick up a load during the South Atlantic Conflict in 1982. The grid in the centre of the landing circle mated with a 'harpoon' device on the underside of the helicopter to hold it in place after landing. The weatherbeaten flight deck recognition letters 'AR' are just visible aft.
(AUTHOR'S COLLECTION)

Helicopters can refuel in flight by hovering to winch up a hose from a warship with a flight deck too small for them to land on, a process known as helicopter in-flight refuelling (HIFR). This Wessex HAS.3 of 820 Naval Air Squadron is practising HIFR from a corner of the cruiser HMS *Blake*'s deck.

(AUTHOR'S COLLECTION)

had to be fitted in around immovable aspects of the design. In the 'Tribals' the hangar was a box-like structure just forward of the after gun mounting, and the helicopter landed on top of it. The flight deck was, in fact, a small lift, and the helicopter was struck down by turning it through 90 degrees, lashing it securely and literally lowering it into the hangar. Portable panels were then fixed in place to form a weatherproof roof. This ingenious arrangement worked well with the Wasp but could not have taken anything bigger. Fortunately it never had to, even in the ships that were sold to Indonesia, as that country retained Wasps in service. In the 'Counties' the flight deck was placed between the Seaslug missile launcher on the quarterdeck and its Type 901 radar, which had to be an exact distance from the launcher. Consequently the hangar was situated forward of the radar aerial and the Westland Wessex helicopters had to be pushed, by hand, around the port side of the 901 structure into the hangar from its port side. The available space was so confined that the bulkhead had to be angled inboard to allow the starboard wheel to run along a 'slot'. The helicopter's outer wheel was only 6 inches from the deck edge, and the turn to starboard into the hangar had to be made by putting the inner wheel on to a small turntable. There was no room for a mechanical handler, and the 13,600lb helicopter had to be pushed in and out of the hangar by hand.

The Whirlwind offered sufficient capacity to carry several marines into action, and the Royal Navy's first front-line helicopter squadron was formed to operate from jungle bases during the Malayan Emergency in the 1950s. Several ferry carriers were used for experiments as helicopter carriers during the same period and proved extremely successful. During the Suez Crisis in 1956 the light fleet carriers *Ocean* and *Theseus* were brought out of the Training Squadron and quickly adapted for use as amphibious assault ships. The conversion was straightforward because much of the hangar space had been converted into accommodation and the original Avgas fuel system was still operable. The flight deck provided a large 'heliport' and the lifts could be used to bring 'sticks' of marines up from the preparation areas to man the

aircraft. After an intense work-up period a total of twenty-two helicopters of 845 NAS and the Joint Helicopter Development Unit (JHDU) was used to fly 45 Royal Marine Commando ashore under fire on 6 November 1956 in the first operational helicopter-borne amphibious assault in history. The order to land was received in the carriers at 07:40, and by 10:21 helicopters had landed 415 marines, three anti-tank guns and 15 tons of equipment.[12] The Landing Zone headquarters was established near the de Lesseps statue. Twelve helicopters of the JHDU, with their RAF and Army pilots and maintainers all new to carrier flying, landed on *Ocean* to refuel and emplane more marines during the assault and launched again together in only nine minutes. After the assault the two helicopter carriers acted as primary casualty receiving ships, and one marine was back in *Ocean*'s sick bay only 20 minutes after his original take-off in an assault stick.

Two larger light fleet carriers, *Bulwark* and *Albion*, were subsequently converted into dedicated 'commando carriers'. This entailed the removal of all fixed-wing flying facilities, the conversion of the mess-decks formerly used by the embarked air group's sailors into troop accommodation, and the use of the former air weapons magazines as stores for small-arms ammunition and everything else the Commandos would need ashore for fourteen days of intense fighting or longer periods of low-intensity operations, from barbed wire and sandbags to rations, clothing and toilet paper. Water and fresh bread were particularly important. A specialist team of Royal Marines assault logistics experts was embarked to ensure that supplies reached the landing ground in an organised and efficient manner to keep the marines in action. This was the key to the commando carrier's success. Helicopters in Malaya had represented an efficient means of transporting patrols across jungle that was difficult to penetrate, but an airborne assault on a hostile shore needed greater sophistication. At first Whirlwind helicopters were used, which proved their worth in the Kuwait Crisis in 1961. They were replaced from 1962 by the more effective turbine-powered Wessex, which was capable of carrying up to sixteen fully equipped marines over

short distances and smaller numbers further. Helicopters had the advantage that they could pass over the shoreline to assault specific objectives inland. Tactical bases, known as 'eagle bases', could be set up ashore to give raiding parties mobility, and vehicles up to and including Land-Rovers could be carried as underslung loads to act as prime movers for light artillery, anti-tank guns and trailers loaded with ammunition. The size of the assault wave to be put on the ground would dictate the number of helicopters

and their fuel state. Marines were grouped into 'sticks' which followed trained guides from the mess-decks, up to the hangar, and thence by lift to the flight deck. They were taken to specific helicopters and, once they were clear of the deck, the guide marked a paper 'chit' with the number of the stick, the identity letter of the helicopter and the time of take-off, and 'posted' it in a box at the base of the island. From there the chits were taken to the Amphibious Operations Room, the former ADR, so that every stick or stores load could

This Wessex HU.5 is too big to land on HMS *Tartar*'s flight deck, but HIFR would be possible. In fact it is hovering over the deck to winch down passengers.
(AUTHOR'S COLLECTION)

An Agusta-Westland Merlin HM.1 firmly lashed to HMS *Iron Duke*'s flight deck in rough weather.
(AUTHOR'S COLLECTION)

be tracked.

Different techniques were used for the initial assault wave in the two British commando carriers. Both had nine helicopter spots painted on the former angled deck and Fly 1 areas, and a 'dumping and access' area to starboard, but the after part of the deck was often filled with vehicles, reducing the number of spots available.[13] Both ships operated squadrons of twenty-two Wessex by the late 1960s and early 1970s. *Bulwark* moved vehicles into the hangar and to the starboard side of the deck to clear the maximum number of spots, bringing eight into use. Helicopters were ranged on these and launched with more fuel than the minimum necessary for the assault. They orbited the ship at low level while eight more, fuelled for the assault and parked folded in Fly 1, were spread and towed on to spots, loaded with their sticks and launched, the process taking ten to fifteen minutes. The first eight then landed-on, picked up their sticks and launched to join the assault. Sixteen aircraft was a good number to put a rifle company ashore, the aircraft flying at very low level in tactical elements of four. *Albion* also packed vehicles tightly away from the landing spots, but the helicopters were ranged as tightly as possible, with the minimum clearance, over the available deck area without using the painted spots. The result was a range of up to fourteen helicopters, which were launched from aft to forward to avoid problems with rotor downwash. Getting the sticks into helicopters and removing lashings was slower, but the overall effect was a 'faster' first wave, albeit with a smaller military force in the initial assault. The risks in this technique were greater; damage was caused and at least one Wessex lost when the rotor disc of one helicopter hit the tail rotor of the next ahead on take-off in 1972, causing it to go over the side, fortunately without fatal casualties. In both cases it was a command decision whether to break down into a shuttle or to continue to fly in tactical formations after the first assault. The former method got things ashore more quickly.

The first two commando carriers were valuable ships, even though they had not been designed for the role. The later *Ocean* was designed for the role and featured several improvements, including separate hangar and vehicle stowage decks, the latter having access to the deck via a ramp. Wide assault passageways and ladders were designed to make it easier for fully-equipped marines to move through the ship to their embarkation points. The USN has led the world in pioneering the design of amphibious carriers, and continues to operate them in large numbers.

The appearance of lightweight sonar sets capable of lowering a transducer into the water from helicopters hovering 40 to 50 feet above the sea caused considerable interest in both the USN and RN from the early 1950s. The first piston-engine helicopters, such as the Sikorsky S-55, were incapable of lifting weapons in addition to the sonar, aircrew and a meaningful fuel load, so had to be operated in hunter/killer pairs on sorties of short duration, adding to the numbers that needed to be embarked. The first practical ASW helicopter was the Bell Model 61, a tandem-rotor design powered by a single 2,400hp Pratt & Whitney R-2800-50 engine that enabled it to lift off at a maximum weight of 26,500lb. Designated HSL by the USN, it showed considerable promise, albeit without a flight control system that would have enabled it to operate at night or in bad weather. The Admiralty ordered eighteen in 1953, but these were cancelled during the financial cutback a year later that followed the ending of hostilities in Korea. For a while interest centred on the Bristol Type 191, a tandem-rotor British design with potential similar to the HSL, but the naval version was cancelled in 1957.[14]

Both tandem-rotor designs were big, the Type 191 with both rotors turning was 87 feet long, over 30 feet longer than a Sea King,[15] and each rotor had a diameter of 48 feet 7 inches. Trials were carried out with a Type 191 in HMS *Eagle*, which showed it to be cumbersome and difficult to operate alongside fixed-wing aircraft, leading Rear Admiral A.R. Pedder, Flag Officer Aircraft Carriers (FOAC) to state that helicopters could not operate from fleet carriers without seriously degrading the vessels' ability to operate in their primary role as fixed-wing carriers. Following trials with Sikorsky Whirlwind HAS.21

helicopters provided by the USN under the MDAP, however, the Admiralty Board decided at its meeting on 13 October 1955[16] that helicopters represented better ASW platforms than fixed-wing aircraft. After the cancellation of the two tandem-rotor types, a single-rotor Westland helicopter based on the Sikorsky S-58 but fitted with a British turbine engine, sonar and flight control system was accepted as the future ASW platform. Since it was not expected in service until 1960 at the earliest, a version of the Whirlwind fitted with a British engine and designated HAS.7 was adopted as an interim type. Unlike the USN, the Royal Navy could not afford to operate separate ASW and strike carriers; nor could it dilute strike potential by embarking both fixed- and rotary-wing ASW aircraft in strike carriers. Helicopters were vital for the close-in defence of task forces, and therefore the integration of helicopters into air groups had to be made to work. The Admiralty did not accept FOAC's view, and ordered further trials to recommend solutions. Consequently, 845 NAS, the Royal Navy's first operational helicopter ASW unit, was embarked in the light fleet carrier *Bulwark* in 1958, together with squadrons of day and nightfighters and a flight of AEW aircraft. These trials were entirely successful and revealed that, far from limiting the carrier's usefulness, the presence of a helicopter squadron within the air group increased the ship's capability. After an incident in which two tankers collided and caught fire off the Persian Gulf, and the helicopters of 845 NAS were used to ferry fire-fighting, salvage and rescue teams across to one of the stricken ships, the squadron was awarded the Boyd Trophy for 1958.[17] From 1958 helicopters began to replace Gannet ASW in carriers, and from 1961 the Wessex replaced the Whirlwind.

Helicopter operations from fixed-wing carriers proved to be quite straightforward, with few of the early worries borne out by experience. As a 'rule of thumb' the Director of Air Operations and Training (DAOT) believed that the space required to stow ten Wessex in a hangar equated roughly to that required for three Buccaneers.[18] Two helicopters were kept in the SAR role with no sonar, one of them usually operating from the angled deck overhan g near Flyco. It was manned, started-up and launched about ten minutes before the start of a fixed-wing launch, and remained airborne until the subsequent recovery was complete. In the interval between serials it performed useful functions such as delivering mail and passengers to other ships in the task force. In the Far East a frequent task for the SAR helicopter was to drop smoke floats ahead of the carrier to see if there was any natural wind to assist marginal fixed-wing launches. Firm rules were laid down regarding the operation of ASW helicopters. They were usually launched in pairs in between fixed-wing cycles, with clear space into which they could be dragged clear of the angled deck if they went unserviceable on start-up. They were commonly briefed to maintain a 'ripple two', in which two helicopters were kept airborne in the task force antisubmarine screen. Wherever possible, helicopters were landed on other ships to refuel, but they returned to 'mother' to change crews from time to time. Refuelling was carried out with the rotors turning, one of the two pilots remaining in the cockpit during the crew change in case the aircraft started to resonate or suffer an unserviceability that needed rapid action. Helicopters returning to the ship during fixed-wing operations hovered outboard of the 'plane-guard', gradually forming a line as more came back to meet their 'C' time. The turn-round was timed not to conflict with the re-spot after a recovery, preferably using a part of the deck that allowed tractor teams to tow other aircraft past them. The period between fixed-wing operations was a good time to shut down a helicopter that required maintenance and start up another to launch and replace it.

As the number of war-built carriers declined, the USN also adopted mixed carrier air groups with both fixed- and rotary-wing types, although the Lockheed S-3 Viking, the last fixed-wing ASW aircraft, is being phased out of service without a direct replacement in 2008. Contemporary carrier air groups embark two helicopter squadrons, one each of MH-60R 'sea-control' and MH-60S 'utility' Seahawks. Some of each are detached from the carrier to other ships in the battle-group, including both warships and auxiliaries.

Short Take-Off, Vertical Landing

The iconic image of a transonic strike aircraft in the
hover is as fascinating in the twenty-first century as it
was four decades ago, when this photograph was taken.
(AUTHOR'S COLLECTION)

Royal Navy interest in fighters with a vertical-take-off capability dates back to 1945, when a specification was drawn up for a quick-reaction interceptor to counter Japanese kamikaze aircraft that had broken through the fleet's outer defences. In the early 1950s VTOL was believed to be a logical 'next step' to solve the problem of increasing conventional landing speeds. However, Admiralty interest in the Hawker P.1127 VTOL technology demonstrator was limited at first because it did not even match the performance of the obsolescent Sea Hawk, let alone the Scimitar and Buccaneer that had been procured to replace it. One of the prototypes, XP831, landed on HMS *Ark Royal* on 7 February 1963,[1] flown by Hawker test pilot Bill Bedford, who had no previous deck-landing experience. The large flight deck presented few problems for the pilot, and the island gave good visual cues for the hover and landing. The P.1127 did cause the ship some problems, however, and her captain at the time, Captain M.P. Pollock MVO DSC RN, recalled that the aircraft had insufficient fuel to fly from Hawker's airfield at Dunsfold in Surrey to the operating area in Lyme Bay, off Dorset.[2] It deployed to Exeter Airport to be nearer, but *Ark Royal* still had to close the coast to within the 10-fathom line[3] to give the aircraft fuel enough to return to Exeter if it could not land on the deck.

In the postwar era after 1945 the Admiralty issued a number of statements of requirement for new aircraft carriers which consistently took a robust line on the need for CCA radar, visual landing aids and extensive facilities for the effective command and control of air operations. After the trauma of CVA01's cancellation in February 1966, the stated requirements for the projected 'Maritime V/STOL Aircraft' became markedly more timid and it was hoped, at first, that helicopter glide-slope indicators and navigational radars would suffice for night and adverse-weather recoveries. The RAE at Bedford was tasked with evaluating the need for specialist equipment in ships to support V/STOL fighter operations but, following the closure of the former Naval Aircraft Department,[4] it already lacked the expertise to view the new technology in a realistic perspective. This resulted in several 'blind-alley' developments which subsequent experience proved to be unnecessary. This was particularly disappointing because practical experience had been gained in 1966 when a P.1127 took part in a trial from the commando carrier HMS *Bulwark* alongside the ship's Wessex helicopters, at the instigation of her commanding officer, Captain D.B. Law RN, a strong advocate of short take-off/vertical landing (STOVL) fighters. In his report[5] he noted the relative ease with which the P.1127 had operated from the deck, and the lack of any difficulty interfacing its operations with those of helicopters. He strongly advocated procuring the type to operate from commando carriers in support of amphibious operations, and to give a limited air-defence capability for the fleet by day. His ideas had considerable merit but, coming only days after the cancellation of the new carrier project, they were rejected by the new First Sea Lord, Sir Varyl Begg, a man who seldom allowed reality to cloud his judgement that Britain could no longer afford aircraft carriers, as being an attempt to cling on to carrier aviation by another means.

The design of the support carriers (CVS) that became the *Invincible* class was strongly influenced from the outset by the potential requirement to operate STOVL fighters, and their need for a runway determined the eventual tonnage, since a long, unobstructed flat deck with an island structure displaced to starboard was clearly a more efficient means of operating helicopters as well. The Directorate of Naval Operational Requirements (DNOR) began to evaluate the design's potential for the operation of fighters in 1971,[6] two years before the first of class was laid down, and one year before full-scale development of the Sea Harrier was authorised. Sea Harrier support arrangements were finalised and incorporated into the first ship well before the requirements for the improved mark of Sea King helicopter, the last of which were not accepted until 1979, only months before completion.

Night and adverse-weather recovery requirements caused concern, since the RAF had no intention at the time of operating its own Harriers at night from anything but a major airfield with ground controlled approach (GCA) radar and a long, well-lit runway. In fact, despite a decade of trials in the UK, there was

A prototype Hawker P.1127 carries out a rolling take-off along a white line painted on the former angled deck centreline during trials of the type in HMS *Bulwark* in June 1966. As soon as it is clear, the Wessex HU.5 helicopters in Fly 1 will be ranged quickly on to spots for take-off. They already have their port engines running, and tractors are attached to their tailwheels to pull them aft. The trials showed that Harriers and helicopters could work together with remarkable ease.

(AUTHOR'S COLLECTION)

little knowledge of STOVL operations in anything but benign weather conditions by day. Carrying out the decelerating transition to the hover alongside a ship in the open ocean with little fuel remaining was expected to be difficult without good visual cues, because the test pilots tasked with evaluating it had no knowledge of conventional deck landing and were unable to make realistic comparisons. Among the 'blind-alley' developments sponsored by the RAE was a system of visual landing aids known as the Horizontal Approach Path Indicator/Close Approach Indicator (HAPI/CAI). These used three separate stabilised platforms that emitted red and white lights that were hard to interpret and contravened NATO Standardisation Agreements. They were intended to give a broad approach band like the discarded sector light, but a pilot could not see a rate of descent develop until it was potentially rapid, needing a major control input to correct. The system had no green lights because the RAE scientists believed that they 'would be difficult to discern at half a mile range', though the existing DLPS had green datums visible beyond that range, and both ships and aircraft are required by law to have green starboard lights visible at five nautical miles. HAPI/CAI also had the disadvantage that the 'on glide slope' indication was a red light, at variance with every other RN, USN and NATO system, in which red indicated danger through being too low. The projector sight had given a precise glide-slope indication from which the slightest deviation could be corrected by a small control input, and the solution was to fit a modified version of it on the island, just aft of Flyco, from where pilots used its accurate glide-slope information from the selection of the hover stop at half a mile right down to a hover position off the port beam, 50 feet above flight-deck level.[7] In this application I named it the Deck Approach Projector Sight (DAPS).

The need to home fast jets into visual contact with the ship was given attention and, surprisingly, the Directorate of Naval Air Warfare (DNAW) discounted the use of TACAN despite its recent extensive use in conventional carriers because it was an active emitter that would 'not be used in wartime operations'. Eventually a device known as Microwave Aircraft Digital Guidance Equipment (MADGE), which had recently won a NATO competition for a rough-area landing aid ashore, was selected for this application. It used 'line of sight' frequencies and was deemed to be more secure in use than TACAN. The USMC evaluated a similar device known as Marine Corps Remote Area Landing System (MRALS) in the USS *Tarawa*, an LPH, but did not adopt it at sea. A MADGE processor in the aircraft gave glide-slope

information derived from a transmitter on the stern of a CVS, but the system suffered a number of drawbacks. It only had a range of 10 miles, and so could not be used to home aircraft from their operating areas. Worse, it only operated in a 90-degree sector aft of the ship, so aircraft could not use it to set up a recovery until they were close to the stern and the ship was virtually steady into wind. In the absence of CCA radar such as SPN 35, Sea Harriers had to rely on the ship's navigational radar being used to give a 'bearing only' approach, in which height information was advisory. If the Emission Control (EMCON) policy allowed, Sea Harriers could carry out an approach with their own radar locked on to the ship, a technique that, with practice, was more accurate than the navigational radar method.

Invincible was designed to launch STOVL fighters from a runway 450 feet long which was angled 1 degree to port to clear the Sea Dart missile launcher and its protective 'zareba' just aft of the open forecastle. By the time they reached the forward end of the runway, aircraft would have accelerated to an IAS of about 90 knots. With a typical wind over the deck of 20 knots this gave an end speed of 110 knots as the aircraft left

The first deck landing by a VTOL fast-jet was carried out by the P.1127 prototype XP831 on HMS *Ark Royal* (IV) on 7 February 1963. The pilot for this historic landing was Hawker's Bill Bedford, who had no previous deck landing experience.

(AUTHOR'S COLLECTION)

A Sea Harrier FRS.1 launches from HMS *Ark Royal*'s 12-degree ski-jump. The shimmer of exhaust gases shows that the nozzles have been rotated to about 40 degrees below the aircraft's centreline as it follows a curved trajectory after launch.

(AUTHOR'S COLLECTION)

the deck, well below the stalling speed of the small wing. To compensate, the pilot selected the nozzles about 50 degrees down from the horizontal and raised the nose slightly to give optimal wing incidence. Much of the aircraft weight was, thus, borne by engine thrust, but a proportion was still directed aft and accelerated the aircraft in straight and slightly climbing flight. Seconds later, when speed had increased to the point where the wing provided sufficient lift for normal flight, the nozzles were rotated aft and the aircraft was flown conventionally. This short-take-off technique allowed aircraft to launch up to 30 per cent heavier than a vertical take-off would have allowed. It was possible to do even better, however, and another 'bright idea' from a serving Royal Navy officer produced a major improvement in STOVL launch technique. Lieutenant Commander D.R. Taylor RN was carrying out a period of aeronautical engineering study at Southampton University when he put forward the idea of the 'ski-jump' for launching aircraft with swivelling nozzles that greatly enhanced their ability to operate from small carriers. It was subsequently adopted by a number of navies including those of India, Spain, Italy and Thailand but not, surprisingly, the USN.

The P.1127/Kestrel/Harrier/Sea Harrier series of aircraft were particularly well suited to this form of short take-off since, being designed to hover, they were equipped with a system of duplicate flying controls that operated when the wing was not giving lift and the normal flying control surfaces had no airflow on which to act. In wing-borne flight the aircraft was controlled by conventional elevators, ailerons and rudder. When the nozzles were rotated below 10 degrees these surfaces continued to move but, in addition, a series of 'puffer' jets, fed via an array of pipes that delivered air bled from the engine, provided forces that moved the aircraft in pitch, roll and yaw. The pilot's control input to the 'puffer' jets was made by deflecting his controls in the 'normal' manner to actuate both systems. When the nozzles were raised to the horizontal, only the conventional control surfaces remained active. The US Marines elected to retain the 'flat launch' since it allowed more space for the operation of helicopters from

their ships, which had the advantage of a deck run nearly twice as long as that in *Invincible*. A flat-deck launch, however, left the aircraft low and slow over the sea in the 15 seconds after take-off. At night or in bad weather this increased the 'fear factor' and the pilot had little time to eject if anything went wrong. Another British limitation was that Sea Harriers were not always able to take off at their maximum weight from the short deck run in the *Invincible* class.

A Sea Harrier lands on HMS *Illustrious*. Tractors are already linked to two others, ready to push them aft into the range. Less than 10 feet separate the landing aircraft from the Sea King parked in the shadow alongside the island.
(AUTHOR'S COLLECTION)

In his paper,[8] Lieutenant Commander Taylor examined several ways of launching STOVL aircraft more effectively, including the use of catapults, tubes that were elongated rapidly by compressed air pressure, and even a platform at the after extremity of a large lever which would have hurled the aircraft into the air like a boulder from a medieval ballista. In practice such a system would have rendered the aircraft uncontrollable. The most elegant proposal, however, was the curved ramp or 'ski-jump' at the forward end of the flight deck, which causes the aircraft to leave the deck after nozzle rotation at the apex of a curve at a speed which was very much less than that required for a flat deck take-off. This effect translated into a shorter deck run, higher launch weight, or both. A 20-degree ski-jump offered a launch speed reduction of 30 knots, at a given aircraft weight, compared with a flat deck. At the highest aircraft weights used in strike missions this represented a 30 per cent reduction in the end-speed

A Sea Harrier FRS.2 of 800 Naval Air Squadron lands on a CVS aft of four RAF Harrier GR.7s during a combined embarkation by several squadrons from Joint Force Harrier. A second Sea Harrier is coming to the hover off the port quarter, the puffs of smoke indicating a high power setting with water selected. Note the Sea King parked tight in against the island in Fly 3, and the tractors ready to move the Sea Harriers once they are on deck.

(AUTHOR'S COLLECTION)

required, which, because distance depends on speed squared, reduced the deck run required by about 50 per cent. At the lower weights used on fighter missions the decreased end speed requirement represented a 40 per cent reduction in velocity, requiring a deck run of only about a third of that needed for a flat-deck launch. Alternatively, from a longer deck run the end speed remained comparable with that achieved on a flat launch, only about 4 knots being lost 'climbing the hill'. The aircraft was thus effectively launched with 30 knots 'excess' end speed, and could carry 30 knots multiplied by 66lb per knot, equalling roughly 2,000lb more payload than on a flat-deck take-off.

A ski-jump was erected from Fairey medium girder bridge components at RAE Bedford, and trials were conducted which showed that a 15-degree ramp imposed a vertical loading of 2.5g on a Sea Harrier during the launch. No structural changes were deemed necessary to the airframe, but it was decided to alter the compression ratio of the undercarriage to give more flexibility and better performance. Theoretically, launch performance continued to increase with ski-jump angle, but in practical terms there was an optimum end speed corresponding to maximum launch weight, and this was achieved by a minimum angle, the size of which was derived from the radius which avoided the undercarriage being a limiting factor at that weight. This effectively sized

the ski-jump, since excess load factor was proportional to end speed squared divided by the radius of the curve. In practice, the ideal radius for the Harrier/Sea Harrier family lay in the range 600 to 800 feet. The application of Euclid's theory then determined how long and how high the actual ski-jump structure needed to be for a given exit angle. The size of the structure grew markedly after 12 degrees, and this was a disincentive to considering bigger angles. *Hermes* and *Ark Royal* were fitted with 12-degree ski-jumps from the outset. After an initial, timid 7-degree structure, *Illustrious* and *Invincible* were upgraded to 12 degrees in the 1980s.

The greatest single weakness of the *Invincible* design was the narrow flight deck, much of it made even narrower by the long, low island structure. The original plan for the flight-deck markings showed a centreline on the STOVL runway, and two large circular helicopter landing spots aft of the island and a single one forward. The adoption of the ski-jump eliminated the forward spot, and an ill-considered attempt was made to add landing spots along the port side of the runway by painting circles to port of the island. These actually touched the deck edge[9] and were never used. Opportunity was taken during early sea trials to work out a better system of markings.[10] Both helicopter and Sea Harrier pilots lost sight of the deck immediately underneath them as they moved across the deck in a high hover, but accurate

An overhead view of HMS *Ark Royal*'s flight-deck markings, showing the black centreline, eye-lines and numbered landing spots designed by the author. The photograph was taken on 1 July 1985, when the ship entered her base port, Portsmouth, for the first time, still wearing the red ensign. The aircraft aft is a Fairey Swordfish, its presence organised by the author to illustrate the historic importance of the ship's name. The aircraft forward is a Sea Harrier of 899 Naval Air Squadron. The amount of space wasted to starboard of the island and on the open forecastle is clearly evident.

(AUTHOR'S COLLECTION)

After her reconstruction, the STOVL runway in HMS *Hermes* was angled one degree to starboard, an arrangement unique to this ship. This photograph was taken by the author while flying in a Wessex HU.5 helicopter during the ship's Sea Harrier clearance trials, which took place in 1981. It shows the deck layout, with the 12-degree ski-jump forward. The object on the forward edge of the former angled deck, to port of the runway, is a projector sight that I placed there for the trial to prove the concept of the Deck Approach Projector Sight (DAPS) under realistic conditions. The production DAPS was later mounted on the island. In 2009 the ship continues in service in the Indian Navy as INS *Viraat* in much the same configuration and operating Sea Harriers.

(AUTHOR'S COLLECTION)

line-up fore and aft was helped by new centreline 'tramlines' consisting of white lines five feet apart with black paint between them. These stood out well against the light grey painted deck, and night lighting was fitted along the white lines to give similar cues at night. White 'eye lines', like those on the helicopter decks in destroyers, were painted athwartships but without circles. The lines were numbered so that pilots could be given a numbered spot on which to land, the ideal being for pilots to land with their backside exactly over the starboard 'tramline' at its intersection with the designated, numbered, eye line. Sea Harriers always landed on the starboard 'tramline' to allow tractor drivers room to manoeuvre the aircraft once the nose tow-bar was connected. Helicopters landed with the right-hand pilot over the port 'tramline' for a rotors-running turnaround to give more space on the cramped deck. Full-stop landings were carried out like Sea Harriers, with the right-hand pilot over the starboard 'tramline', again to give tractor crews room to manoeuvre.

It is difficult to understand why the flight-deck design was so bad when it is compared with exploratory STOVL designs of the 1950s, in which the merit of a wide deck on a ship of roughly the same length as *Invincible* was well understood. The narrow deck and long, inboard island combined to make cross-deck landings extremely difficult and, therefore, reduced the tactical flexibility that a well-designed ship would have enjoyed. In consequence the *Invincibles*, like their conventional predecessors, were forced to turn into wind for virtually every launch and recovery, and aircraft had to land fore-and-aft if tractor teams were not to spend a long time trying to move them clear. The narrow deck was further blighted by two centreline lifts which obtruded into the runway. If the forward lift stuck below flight-deck level, a not uncommon occurrence in the early years of the class, it effectively prevented all but a vertical take-off by Sea Harriers because the 'hole' left insufficient deck run for even a lightweight rolling take-off. Ironically the lifts were among the few pieces of equipment designed for CVA 01 to be used in a subsequent design. The scissors supports obviated the need for balance weights and, in theory, the lift

could be loaded from the side as well as along the centreline. The *Invincible* hangar, however, was so narrow and awkwardly shaped that, realistically, aircraft could only be loaded on to the lifts fore and aft. The hangar was designed to support Sea Harriers in the forward half and Sea Kings aft. The facilities built into those areas for them could not easily or affordably be transposed. Unfortunately this was out of synchronisation with the way the aircraft were ranged on deck; Sea Harriers were ranged aft and the Sea Kings amidships and forward. While not of critical importance, the arrangement led to the need for a lot of tractor moves on deck that frequently caused 'traffic jams' as aircraft were ranged aft to be towed forward, and vice versa.

Aircraft moves in the last generation of conventional carriers were carried out by tractor teams of aircraft handlers. To reduce numbers the *Invincible* Scheme of Complement (SOC) reduced the tractor team to two, the director and a driver, and the squadrons were required to provide three chock/lashing numbers in addition to the brake number. Superficially this 'lean' approach reduced manpower requirements, but the drawback was that squadrons needed constantly to provide hands for aircraft moves and found themselves short of junior rates. Expensively trained air mechanics effectively took the place of less expensively trained naval airmen. The CVS were among the RN's first 'lean-manned' warships, and savings were made in a number of areas.[11] To compensate, hands were taken from every department to carry out 'whole-ship activities' such as replenishment at sea (RAS). The 'knock-on' effect was that the flying task was difficult to maintain when hands were detailed off for other tasks. The flight-deck party was divided into two watches, one headed by the FDO and the other by a CPO 'Captain of the Flight Deck'. Under each was a PO Aircraft Handler and four directors, not enough to maintain Sea Kings ripple-flying with Sea Harriers at deck alert if hands were taken away for 'whole-ship' tasks. Of course the 'off-watch' watch could be used, but there is a limit to how long men can work effectively and safely without a break.[12]

From completion of the first ship in 1980, a

A typical range of Sea Harriers on HMS *Ark Royal*. The ship has undergone several changes. The Type 909 radar dome has gone from the after part of the island, and the missile launcher and its zareba have been removed forward, allowing the flight deck to be enlarged and extended and the missile magazine to be used for air weapons.

(AUTHOR'S COLLECTION)

number of aviation shortcomings in the CVS had to be put right, and this absorbed my time in DGA (N) for over two years. The low island made it difficult to mount flight-deck floodlights without their sources being visible at a distance from the deck. Ideally, the light units would best be mounted angled down at 45 degrees, with each covering a small area of deck. In *Invincible* they were only 10 degrees below the horizontal and had to achieve a big 'throw' of light across the deck. On the after bulkhead of the island they shone directly into the eyes of pilots hovering before landing, and illuminated the aircraft so that it could be seen a considerable distance from the ship. Flyco, on the other hand, was four decks above the flight deck and, in the ship as originally designed, 'f' when seated at his control console could not see any part of the deck. The compartment had to be redesigned and rebuilt as a matter of urgency before

any of the ships were declared operational.[13] Workshop space was always minimal, and when a Sea King AEW squadron was embarked in 1986 a portable workshop had to be embarked in the hangar to support it. A mezzanine deck was added over the forward part of the forward hangar to hold bulky aircraft spares such as main rotor gearboxes, for which there was no designed stowage. Extra stowage and shelves were constantly added throughout the hangar to provide space for the growing amount of equipment that needed to be embarked as aircraft requirements grew in service.

Sea Harriers were moved in the hangar by mechanical handlers, brought up the forward lift and moved aft along the flight deck by tractor teams to be ranged around the after part of the flight deck. In calm conditions four lashings were attached, in rougher weather eight. The nose oleo was chocked.[14]

HMS *Ark Royal* (V)'s hangar shortly after completion, looking from aft to forward past the 'scissors structure' of the after lift. The central section visible is narrow, constrained by four other lifts for removing the ship's Rolls-Royce Olympus gas turbines. The well of the forward lift is visible forward beyond the Wessex and Sea Harrier.
(AUTHOR'S COLLECTION)

uss *Boxer*, LHD 4, with AV-8B Harriers ranged aft and helicopters forward. Designed for amphibious assault operations, these ships can carry a large number of Harriers in an alternative sea-control mission. Many warship types have 'through-decks' to operate all sorts of aircraft more effectively. (US NAVY)

The need for support systems had been kept to a minimum and so, unlike the Buccaneer twenty years earlier, there was no capacity to run navigational and system alignment information to the aircraft by cable, so latitude/longitude and ship's head information had to be written on a chalk board and held up by a naval airman for the pilot to read once he had started his engine.[15] Pilots manned their aircraft twenty minutes before the planned launch time and started their engines ten minutes later on Flyco's command. The Sea Harrier had an auxiliary power unit (APU) that was used to start the Bristol Pegasus and provide power before the main alternator came on line. It was a simple and reliable method of starting the main engine. The Sea Harrier's navigation, heading and attitude reference system (NAVHARS)[16] could be aligned using power from the ship before start-up, but usually 'dumped' information on engine start. It was much better aligned when the engine-driven alternator was running. Alignment required the ship to remain steady for at least one minute, as any swing introduced errors into the system. Once the Sea Harriers were started and aligned, command approval was sought for them to taxi and traffic lights were selected to amber as the ship turned into wind gently to avoid too much deck motion. Yellow-coated directors marshalled the aircraft forward and on to the runway centreline. The exact take-off distance

required by the first aircraft off was calculated by the Squadron Duty Officer and the details were passed to Flyco; 500 feet[17] was typical for aircraft loaded with weapons. Pilots calculated the nozzle setting required at take-off and pre-set the hover stop on the nozzle selector quadrant as part of their pre-take-off checks. Keeping accurately aligned and in the centre of the runway was easy with the white tramlines stretching ahead to the top of the 'ski-jump', and in addition to the director's signals, pilots could see the 'distance-to-go' marks on the deck.

Sea Harriers usually launched in sections of two or divisions of four or more. Before launch up to six aircraft were lined up tightly along the centreline, each close up behind the aircraft in front. As little as 20 feet was common; blast was not a problem and, since the aircraft did not have reheat, exhaust temperatures were not excessive. Once the aircraft were on the centreline, each pilot in turn selected nozzles down and advanced the throttle to check engine acceleration. Ship's heading was entered into the NAVHARS as soon as the ship was steady on the DFC, and the aircraft was held on the brakes with the engine at 55 per cent power. Flyco obtained command approval to launch and, when it was given, selected the traffic lights to green. The FDO controlling the launch raised a green flag, circled it and lowered it to the deck while the pilot slammed the throttle forward to select 100 per cent power, releasing the brakes as the aircraft began to slide forward with the Pegasus rapidly spooling up, and accelerated rapidly along the deck. If there was any pitch motion the FDO lowered his flag as the bow pitched down so that it would be rising as the aircraft left the ski-jump. Subsequent aircraft were launched at intervals of ten seconds or less; the FDO raising his green flag quickly for the next as the first moved forward, and it was perfectly possible to launch six aircraft in a minute. Launch rates as fast as this had never been achieved with catapults, and the capability was one of the bonuses of STOVL operation. For a second the ski-jump would seem like a wall ahead of the aircraft, obscuring the sea, then it had gone behind and beneath the aircraft. As the wheels left the deck the nozzle lever was pulled to the selected position, usually between 35 and 50 degrees, and the aircraft flew away. It was as simple as that.[18]

Recovery by day followed the established Royal Navy pattern, with aircraft homing in section to a wait position on the ship's port beam. When pilots were satisfied that there would be no delay in the recovery they dumped fuel down to the minimum needed for a circuit to land. If delay was at all likely it was imperative that Flyco passed this information out sooner, rather than too late. As the ship turned into wind to start the recovery, Sea Harriers slotted fast at 600 feet or less and the break into the circuit was a hard 4g turn with airbrake out and the throttle closed to wash the speed back to 300 knots. Downwind checks were carried out with the nozzles selected 15 degrees down, and the throttle was gradually advanced as the undercarriage was lowered. The finals turn was begun as the ship's stern appeared to pass the port wingtip, with speed reduced to about 150 knots, the nozzles progressively lowered and the throttle advanced so that the engine began to take weight from the wings. It was important that the pilot maintained a steady 8 degrees of 'alpha'[19] in the decelerating transition to the hover, as any heavy-handed control inputs might lead to a high nose attitude, low airspeed and a consequent departure from controlled flight, usually with fatal consequences. The 'danger zone' was from about 120 down to 40 knots. The pilot's aim was to put the aircraft into a position about 150 feet above the water, lined up with the DFC behind and slightly to the left of the ship, with the aircraft's weight transferred to the four columns of thrust from the engine and low forward airspeed. There was no fuel for an overshoot, and the pilot selected the nozzle lever to the braking stop, angling the nozzles as far forward as they would go, 10 degrees forward of the vertical. He used the speed trimmer on top of the throttle which made fine nozzle adjustments up to 10 degrees either side of vertical, known as 'nudging', checking engine temperature as the aircraft came to the hover alongside the landing point designated by a director. The Sea Harrier carried 50 gallons of demineralised water that was pumped into the engine to give peak hover

An AV-8B of the USMC seconds after a rolling take-off from the 'flat' flight deck of the uss *Wasp*, LHD 1. Another AV-8 is parked on the side lift.
(US NAVY)

performance, without overheating the engine, for 90 seconds. Landings using this system were known as 'wet committed', and as soon as the water started pumping there was no stopping it.

Having 'nudged' the aircraft into a high hover alongside the landing point, the pilot used gentle control inputs to move over the deck, usually on to 4 or 5 spot amidships, where pitch motion had least effect but where the long island seemed alarmingly close. Looking out of the Flyco windows, 'f' was able to look pilots in the eye only a few feet away as they landed. Any 'green' wind from the starboard bow gave a degree of turbulence which had to be corrected as the aircraft sat in the hover. To land, the pilot closed the throttle by half an inch and, as the aircraft began to settle, opened it again to compensate for the hot exhaust gasses which were reingested into the intakes as the aircraft moved lower over the deck. The aim was to achieve a solid landing on all four wheels. Any attempt to be gentle was not recommended, as it took too long and continued hot gas reingestion could cause the Pegasus to 'pop-surge'. If that happened the aircraft would drop 'like a manhole cover' for the last twenty feet. Endurance at 'wheels on' was typically less than a minute.

Vertical recoveries offered a number of options. A group of aircraft could be given one landing spot each, but this tied up a number of directors and needed a large area of the small deck to be clear. A better option was to bring aircraft alongside at one-minute intervals to land on a single spot, and then taxi them clear quickly. It was prudent to have a second 'flop-spot' available in case of unforeseen snags. As soon as each aircraft was safely on deck, the director gave the pilot the 'off-brakes' signal and marshalled it clear of the landing area.[20] Another advantage of STOVL operations was that, with their high thrust-to-weight ratio, Sea Harriers were easy to taxi, and if the nozzles were rotated forward of the vertical they could even taxi backwards. This feature could be used to 'walk' or 'elephant tango' aircraft back into the range after a recovery, but in practical terms it was often quicker to shut them down and tractor them aft.

Night operations were similar but more

The adoption of STOVL aircraft operating from medium-sized aircraft carriers has allowed a number of navies to become members of the aircraft carrier 'club', and to operate as effective allies alongside the US Navy. This photograph shows a formation of allied aircraft flying over INS *Viraat* (the former HMS *Hermes*) during *Exercise RIMPAC 2007*. The formation includes two F/A-18 Hornets of VF 102, the 'Diamondbacks' from the USS *Kitty Hawk*. The two aircraft on the near side are Indian Navy Sea Harriers, and the two on the far side are Indian Air Force Jaguars.
(US NAVY)

frightening. Lights along the tramlines allowed a similar launch technique to that used by day to be employed. The major difference was the recovery, in which the aircraft were homed to a wait position and then taken into a carrier controlled approach. The pilot was passed ranges at which he selected the nozzles down to carry out the decelerating transition to the hover. At 200 feet he was instructed to 'look up for the sight' and continue the approach using visual cues. All night approaches were monitored by a squadron pilot in Flyco using a specially calibrated sight like a head-up display, known as the LSO Sight, through which any deviation from the ideal approach could be detected and the pilot warned. Night transitions to the hover were far from easy and required skill and concentration.

The USN showed considerable interest in the ski-jump at first, and one was assembled at the USN test centre at NAS Patuxent River for evaluation. Hundreds of launches were carried out with AV-8 STOVL aircraft, and even by conventional aircraft such as the F-14, F/A-18, T-2 Buckeye and E-2. The latter group used smaller angles and benefited from the ballistic trajectory followed after launch, but were unable to derive the full benefit without the ability to use engine thrust to bear some of the aircraft weight. Russia has developed another variation in which conventional fighters with a very high thrust-to-weight ratio are launched off a short deck using a ski-jump, but land-on using a tailhook and conventional arrester wires. This technique, known as short take-off but arrested recovery (STOBAR), has been exported to India, which intends to use MiG-29K fighters from a new generation of STOBAR carriers. The technique has the advantage that aircraft can be launched quickly in large numbers, and that the conventional arrested recoveries are less stressful and more easily controlled than vertical landings. China has acquired the former Russian STOBAR carrier *Varyag*, and is believed to have plans to refit it for operations in the next decade.

The British-designed Harrier and its American AV-8 derivatives remain the world's most successful operational STOVL aircraft, and are the key enabler that has allowed several medium-sized navies to retain or incorporate fixed-wing aviation in their order of battle. India, Spain, Italy and Thailand have built or procured carriers that are capable of operating a mix of helicopters and Harriers, the latter in the fighter, strike and reconnaissance roles. India was the first, and procured a version of the British Sea Harrier which was operated from light fleet carriers purchased from Britain and fitted with ski jumps.[21] Spain followed with a version of the AV-8A which it sold secondhand to Thailand when it procured AV-8Bs to replace them, and Italy procured AV-8Bs from the outset. Although these small air groups fall short of the USN capability, they offer a marked improvement over the two-dimensional fleets they augmented and give a significant national capability. Both Spanish and Italian Harriers have struck at targets in Afghanistan from carriers in the Indian Ocean. India intends to replace its Sea Harriers with Mig-29K STOBAR fighters, which will operate from a new generation of carriers; one is being built in India and another is being converted in Russia to meet Indian requirements. Spain and Italy, like Britain, have stated their intention to procure the F-35B Lightning II STOVL version of the Joint Strike Fighter to replace the Harrier from the end of the next decade.

What might have been

An artist's impression of the cancelled HMS
Queen Elizabeth, CVA 01. The original hangs
on my study wall, and I have spent hours
studying it and wondering what if …?
(AUTHOR'S COLLECTION)

The methods of deck landing and take-off, the ships and their equipment described in the preceding chapters were real and their impact on naval aviation tangible. In the same period, however, the Royal Navy pursued a number of designs and concepts that showed considerable ingenuity but which, for various reasons, were never built. Had they been, carrier flying might have followed a different path, and their loss has made a significant impact on British capability.

An 'airfield' made of ice

In 1943 Project 'Habbakuk' investigated the construction of an 'unsinkable aircraft carrier' made of ice. The originator was Mr Geoffrey Pyke, a scientist acting as Director of Programmes at Combined Operations Headquarters. Winston Churchill seized on the proposal and stated that he attached 'the greatest importance to the examination of the idea. The advantages of a floating island, or islands, if used only as refuelling depots for aircraft, are so dazzling that they do not, at the moment, need to be discussed. There would be no difficulty in finding a place to put such a stepping-stone in any of the plans of war now under consideration.'[1] An investigative committee set up in September 1942 found that ice alone was insufficiently strong as a building material for the hull in contemplation. Pyke believed he had solved the problem by incorporating a binding substance, wood pulp or sawdust, which produced a material created by freezing but with a compressive resistance similar to concrete at about 3,000lb per square inch. Imaginatively named 'Pykrete', it was created in laboratory quantities in the UK,[2] but the vast amounts needed could only be made in Arctic Northern Canada, and in April 1943 a team was sent to work with the Canadian National Research Council and the British Admiralty Technical Mission, both based in Ottawa.

Their Directive[3] required study into a number of specialised applications, including a 3,000-foot-long base for long-range aircraft; an aircraft carrier 2,000 feet long; an advanced fighter base 1,250 to 1,500 feet long; a cargo ship; an oil tanker, or a combination of these. The study group dismissed all but one. The long-range base was beyond the existing knowledge of materials and facilities. The fighter base could not be built as small as the directive dimensions because of the need for wall thickness and extensive refrigeration machinery. The cargo and tanker versions were found to have too small a deadweight capacity in relation to the size and cost of the vessel, only about 5 per cent of the displacement, making them completely uneconomical in comparison with normal merchant vessels. Attention therefore focused on the aircraft carrier, and a design emerged that would have been 2,000 feet long, 300 feet wide, with a draught of 150 feet and a freeboard of 50 feet. It would have displaced 2,000,000 tons. A speed of about 6 knots was to be provided by steam-powered turbo-electric machinery driving propellers in twenty-six pods mounted along the hull sides. The 'hot' machinery would have been insulated from the Pykrete hull which, in turn, needed wooden cladding on the outside to keep its form. Vast refrigeration plants were needed to keep the Pykrete at its ideal temperature, and the ship would have been far from unsinkable if it suffered any damage to the hull or the refrigerating plant. A model 'Habbakuk' was tested at the NPL in Teddington in the UK, and an experimental Pykrete ship, sixty feet long by thirty feet wide, was built in Canada. The study group eventually recommended cancellation, however, because the construction effort needed in a remote Arctic site would have been enormous and the cost of a single 'Habbakuk' was computed to be considerably more than double that of a conventional fleet carrier. Despite, or perhaps because of, the small-scale experiments there was no real confidence that the ship could actually be built and operated.

Operationally, the Pykrete carrier was never fully developed, but the NPL model showed that the ship could ride waves up to a thousand feet long and fifty feet high without significant deck motion, and the hangars were big enough to take aircraft as big as the de Havilland Mosquito without folding wings. In the Atlantic there was usually sufficient natural wind for free take-offs from a deck that size, but turning into wind at only 6 knots would have presented problems. Machinery would have been difficult to maintain because, with its enormous draught, 'Habbakuk' could not have entered any Royal Dockyard or dry dock for refit and nor, with its enormous mass, could it realistically have been moored in deep water. Even the need to clean marine growth off the vast underwater area of the hull would have been an enormous problem. 'Habbakuk' was a wartime 'bright idea' that was taken further than it deserved, but it can be said to have raised Royal Navy awareness of the value of size in more conventional aircraft carriers.

The definitive British wartime carrier design

During the Second World War the Admiralty saw very quickly some of the advantages of USN design practice, and acted to incorporate them in a new fleet carrier design, known by the name allocated to the lead ship, *Malta*. By 1942 the size of an air group was measured by the number of aircraft that could be operated from the deck, rather than the number of aircraft that could be struck down into the hangar. The design process began in 1943 as an 'improved *Implacable*', but, following a strong input by the Fifth Sea Lord, Admiral Boyd, the weight of operational opinion caused the design to be changed to a larger carrier with an open-

sided hangar so that aircraft engines could be run up before they were ranged on deck, and the flight deck was more nearly rectangular than previous British designs in order to range the maximum number of aircraft before launching a strike, and to recover the maximum number into Fly 1 after a strike. A total of four lifts was specified; two centreline and two side-lifts on the port side. The latter were spaced fore and aft of the barriers so that the after one could be used to range running aircraft after the deck range had launched, and the forward one could be used to start striking-down aircraft while a recovery was still in progress. It was planned that up to eighty aircraft could be launched from the deck, supplemented by another twenty running in the hangar to follow them. The island, which contained aircraft direction rooms and radar offices as well as the compass platform and flag bridge, was so large that it was split into two, with a central gap level with the after barrier.

The flight deck was not armoured, and some thought was given to surfacing it in wood to give an easily-repairable skid-resistant surface like USN ships,

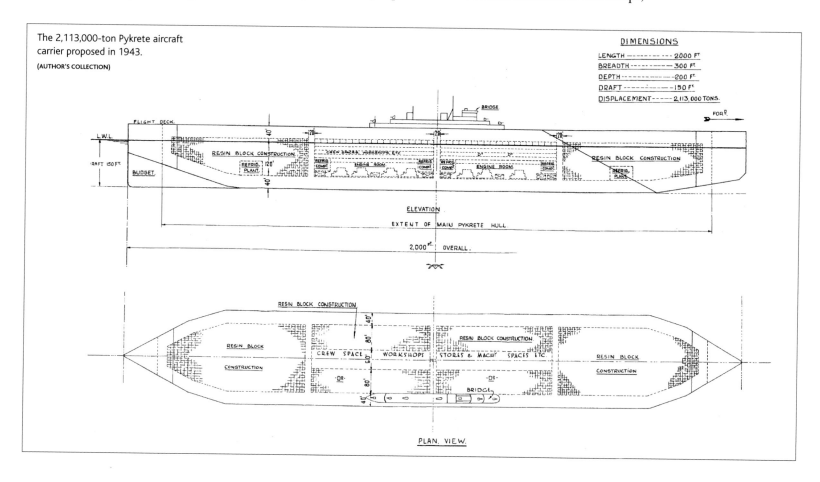

The 2,113,000-ton Pykrete aircraft carrier proposed in 1943.

(AUTHOR'S COLLECTION)

but the final design specified mild steel with a number of expansion joints at intervals. Four ships of this class were ordered[4] in 1943, but none was laid down and the orders were cancelled after the war's end. While there were obvious economic reasons for this, the loss of these ships hurt the Royal Navy badly. As a later and better design than the two fleet carriers left under construction, in my opinion they offered a much better long-term prospect. The big deck would have made the operation of large, multi-engined aircraft straightforward and, although it could not be known at the time of their cancellation, the un-armoured structure of the deck would have been far more adaptable than the armoured 'boxes' in the *Illustrious* group, making the incorporation of a fully-angled flight deck, like that in the USS *Antietam*, a less expensive process than that required for *Victorious*, *Eagle* and *Ark Royal*. Like the US vessel, the forward side lift could have been used as the forward part of the sponson to support the angled deck, with a triangular section built in astern of it. Another big

advantage of the *Malta* design was internal volume, space in which new aircraft, systems and the men to man them could be accommodated. All the carriers that were completed or converted for RN service after 1945 were relatively small, cramped, and imposed severe restrictions on the aircraft they operated. If two *Malta*-class ships had been laid down in 1946[5] they could have absorbed all the transformational features built into the new *Ark Royal* and the converted *Victorious* at less cost and in a shorter timescale. The result would have been ships at least as capable as the USN *Midways*, able to operate second-generation turbojets in large numbers without restriction. Their loss poses one of the most significant 'what-ifs' in post-1945 RN history.

Large and small carrier concepts in 1954

By 1953 DNAW was alarmed both at the cost and complexity of *Victorious*' modernisation, and plans to modernise *Implacable*, *Indefatigable* and several light fleet carriers in turn were cancelled. A series of

An impression of the 'Habbakuk' aircraft carrier drawn by G.H. Davies and published in the *Illustrated London News* of 2 March 1946.

(ILLUSTRATED LONDON NEWS)

meetings chaired by the Directorate of Tactics and Staff Duties (DTSD) were held, which led to consensus of opinion in the Admiralty that a light fleet carrier 700 feet long and of 20,000 tons displacement should be capable of operating VTOL aircraft when they entered service in the long term, and a significant number of N.113[6] turbojet fighters and helicopters in the short term. A rough sketch was produced to illustrate the staff thinking, and DNC was tasked to produce a design. It was accepted that arrester wires and catapults would be so close together that concurrent landing and take-off would not be possible. The resulting design had dimensions similar to the 1942 light fleet carriers and reflected DNC's view that, since the ships would be required to operate conventional aircraft first, the flight-deck design should be governed by this consideration,[7] but that features considered suitable for VTOL operation should be included where possible.

The sketch design allowed a landing area angled 6½ degrees off the centreline and similar in size to that projected for the new *Hermes*, plus a single steam catapult with a stroke of 180 feet. Two small hangars were connected to the flight deck by a single central lift, and there was deck parking space for about six fighters and several helicopters. An advantage of the central lift was its accessibility from most parts of the flight deck; the big disadvantage of the single lift and catapult was that a mechanical failure of either would put the ship out of action. The potential as a VTOL carrier was interesting, and compared favourably with *Invincible*, designed more than a decade later. The key feature was a landing circle of the largest practical diameter in the region of the ship's centre of pitch and roll, to enable landings to be made into any relative wind. This put a premium on flight-deck width rather than length, and the sketch showed a width across the sponsons that was fully 20 per cent of the ship's length, allowing full advantage to be taken of the flexibility of aircraft that could land vertically on to a small area in clear, daylight conditions. Aircraft could have landed into almost

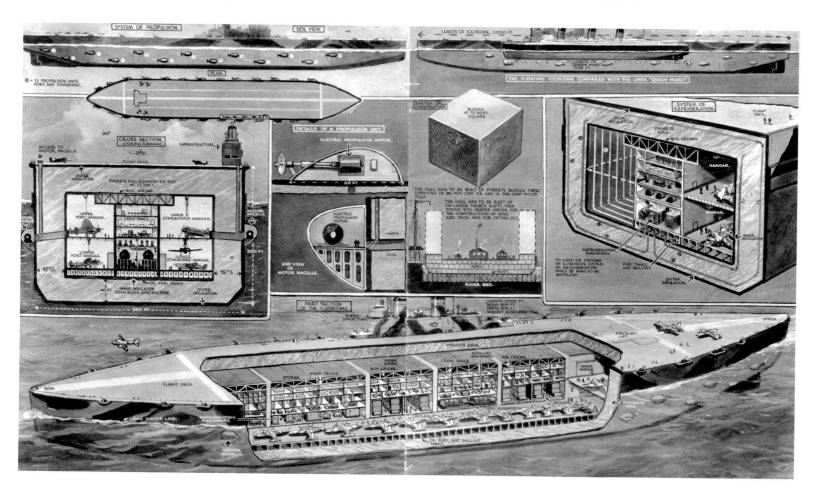

The deck plan of HMS *Malta* as designed in 1945. The dotted lines show the dimensions of the single hangar deck.

(AUTHOR'S COLLECTION)

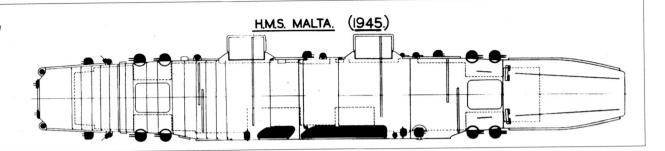

H.M.S. MALTA. (1945.)

The author's sketch of how HMS *Malta*'s flight deck might have appeared had she been completed to a revised design, on the lines of HMS *Victorious*'s conversion, in 1957.

(AUTHOR'S COLLECTION)

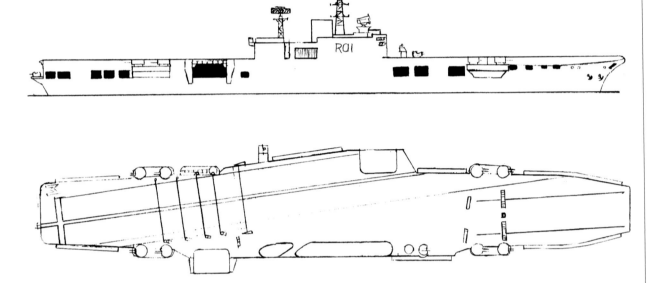

A sketch design prepared in 1954 for an 'affordable' aircraft carrier capable of operating STOVL aircraft.

(AUTHOR'S COLLECTION)

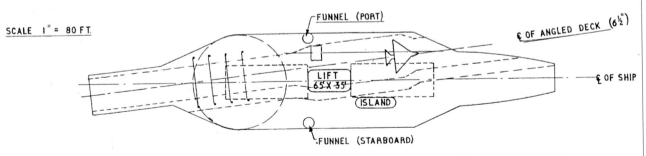

20,000 TON CARRIER (TO OPERATE N.113 ETC.) SUITABLE FOR CONVERSION TO V.T.O. AIRCRAFT

SCALE 1" = 80 FT.

FUNNEL (PORT)

℄ OF ANGLED DECK (6½°)

LIFT 65' X 35'

℄ OF SHIP

ISLAND

FUNNEL (STARBOARD)

DIMENSIONS.
LENGTH 695' (AS 'COLOSSUS')
WIDTH 144' (21% LENGTH)
2 HANGARS 125' X 50' (APPROX.)

CHARACTERISTICS FOR V.T.O A/C.
LANDING CIRCLE 72 FT RADIUS.
ALTERNATIVE SMOKE DISCHARGE
THROUGH PORT OR STARBOARD FUNNEL.

CHARACTERISTICS FOR CONVENTIONAL A/C.

DECK PARK	20
HANGAR	8
TOTAL	28

SINGLE CATAPULT 180 FT STROKE.
MK.13 ARRESTER GEAR - 4 WIRES.
LANDING AREA AS 'HERMES'.
SINGLE LIFT (CAN NOT BE USED WHEN LANDING ON.)
ANGLE 6½° APPROX.

NOTES UNDERLINED IN RED AND GREEN
REFER TO SIMILARLY COLOURED DETAILS ON SKETCH

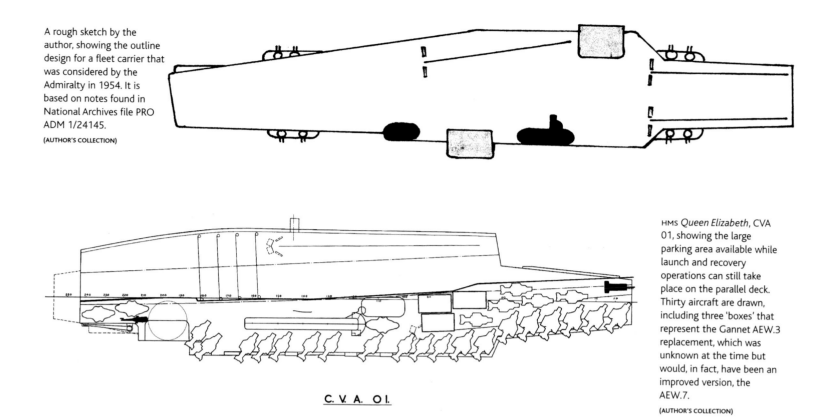

A rough sketch by the author, showing the outline design for a fleet carrier that was considered by the Admiralty in 1954. It is based on notes found in National Archives file PRO ADM 1/24145.

(AUTHOR'S COLLECTION)

C. V. A. O I.

HMS *Queen Elizabeth*, CVA 01, showing the large parking area available while launch and recovery operations can still take place on the parallel deck. Thirty aircraft are drawn, including three 'boxes' that represent the Gannet AEW.3 replacement, which was unknown at the time but would, in fact, have been an improved version, the AEW.7.

(AUTHOR'S COLLECTION)

any relative wind up to 50 knots in strength and taxied into a parking area to allow the next astern to recover after an interval of seconds. The small island might have caused turbulence when landing with a strong wind on the starboard bow, but its modest size would have minimised the problem. By night or in poor visibility some form of radar assisted recovery along the ship's centreline from astern would have been required, but was not included in the sketch. With hindsight the design is interesting and represents an early attempt to design a CVS that was not burdened by the armament of a destroyer and the boats of a battleship, and the ridiculous requirement to 'look like a cruiser'. Unfortunately it was forgotten by the designers of *Invincible*.

Another interesting feature was the small hangar complex. The intention was to keep serviceable aircraft on deck, using the hangar only for deep maintenance. Again this contrasts favourably with the mediocre design of *Invincible*, in which the cramped, narrow deck made parking difficult, while a considerable amount of space was wasted under the boats stowed to starboard of the island. In the 1954

carrier, aircraft could taxi to starboard of the island, making maximum use of a very flexible deck. Two funnels were proposed, one to port and one to starboard, which would, in theory, have allowed smoke to have been discharged from either side so that aircraft making cross-deck landings could land into clear air, a complicated idea that might well have proved unnecessary, given practical experience with STOVL aircraft. Considering it was sketched six years before the first flight of the Hawker P.1127 prototype, the 1954 carrier showed a remarkably well considered appreciation of what would be required. It is a pity that the design was not carried forward.

In another of the minutes on the subject[8] Captain Bolt[9] made several interesting comments. He felt that a new generation of light fleet carriers needed only a modest design effort by contemporary standards, cost much less than larger carriers and offered a quick solution to the fleet's shortage of flight decks. They would be suitable for sale to Commonwealth and foreign navies and, if built in significant numbers, could be concentrated in formations of two or more to give the same effect, but more flexibly, than a single large carrier. Not the least of his arguments was the observation that such ships would counter the argument that new generations of aircraft could only be operated from very large and extremely expensive ships. It is difficult to fault his logic.

At the same time DNC put considerable effort into the design of a new fleet carrier, similar in size to the *Malta* class. Design 'C' included an 8-degree angled deck and side lifts, but the most unusual feature was the decision to incorporate two separate starboard side islands a considerable distance apart. These reflected the need to provide funnels serving two machinery groups that were widely separated to provide resistance to battle damage. The idea had some merit, as each island presented a smaller obstruction to aircraft movement than a single large structure, but the fact that they interfered with two separate parking areas was, in my opinion, a demerit. Design work on large carriers continued throughout the 1950s, but the Admiralty failed to win approval to order any.

Queen Elizabeth – the CVA 01 Project

The most developed RN large carrier project after 1945 was known by its NATO designation as Strike Carrier Number 1, or CVA 01 for short. The name *Queen Elizabeth* was allocated to it in 1964,[10] but not publicly announced at the time. Between 1961 and 1965 much effort went into the design of the flight deck and aviation arrangements. This had input from a Fleet Work-Study team who examined theoretical 'best practice', moderated by a 'future planning group' comprising officers from DNAW and DGA (N), a cross-section of operational aviators, test pilots and air engineering officers. Among these were Captain Eric 'Winkle' Brown RN and Captain P.C.S. 'Pat' Chilton RN, both test pilots with experience of USN equipment, capability and practice. They had the advantage of some years of operation with the new carrier technology including the angled deck, but believed it possible to do even better on a design that started with a 'clean sheet of paper'.

They held the view that the ideal carrier would have three separate 'lanes' for launching, recovery and parking, all with access to and from the hangar. The angled deck had the positive effect of creating two lanes with a reasonable amount of parking space, but had two negative effects. Firstly, the landing area split the parking areas Fly 3 and Fly 4, isolating the latter during recoveries. If the landing area could be moved to port, Fly 3 and 4 could be amalgamated to give a more flexible parking area which was fully accessible during recoveries. Secondly, a large number of pilots, when questioned, felt that at night or in conditions of poor visibility the first view of the angled deck centreline occurred very late, giving little time for significant correction if it was necessary. Most confirmed that the first thing they saw was the wake, especially when the carrier was at high speed, but this was of little practical use for lining up on the angled deck. If the landing 'lane' could be made parallel to the ship's centreline, night and adverse weather recoveries would be assisted. Fears that funnel smoke would interfere with aircraft on finals over the wake led to the design of 'cyclone generators' on the outboard sides of the two 'macks' (combined masts and stacks). These were intended to draw smoke away from the approach path, and models worked well in windtunnel experiments. The outward-jutting structures were conspicuous in artist's impressions of the design.

The design team at Bath took in this advice and evaluated runways that were completely offset to port. Providing two completely parallel lanes within the 184 feet total width allowed for the design proved impossible, however, but models showed that an offset runway angled 2¾ degrees to port virtually achieved the same effect, giving a large expanse of deck to starboard for launching, parking and moving aircraft.[11] The theory was that, during constant launch and recovery operations, known in the USN as the 'battle flexi-deck', aircraft would turn right after an arrested landing and taxi quickly clear of the wingtip safety line into an arming and refuelling area, effectively a 'pit-stop' lane, on the starboard side aft. Unserviceable aircraft would be struck down into the hangar on the side lift. Replacement aircraft could be ranged into the same area. After their pit stop aircraft would taxi, or be tractored, to the catapult on the starboard side of Fly 1. In effect this would create an anticlockwise flow around the deck, but with the difficulty of how best to define the taxi paths that would allow aircraft moving in different directions to pass each other safely. The elegant solution was to create a taxi path 34 feet wide outboard of the island, known as an 'Alaskan Highway', along which the aircraft moving forward could pass, allowing a constant flow of aircraft to and from the pit-stop area. A useful amount of space for parking remained in Fly 2 and Fly 3 as this flow continued. A rectangular area at the after end of Fly 3 was intended as a 'flop-spot' for helicopters to operate from, clear of fixed-wing operations.

Conservatively, the designers felt that a deck-edge lift sited forward would be vulnerable to wave damage, so a lift near the ship's centreline was substituted. This was positioned to one side of the hangar and operated by a scissors mechanism so that it could be loaded from three sides to make the most use of the available space. This was almost the only feature of the design to be carried forward into the *Invincible* class and, unfortunately, it proved unreliable for a decade before major alterations were made to the design. The flight deck was optimised for continuous, concurrent operations, but large deck-load strikes could be undertaken with a more conventional range aft, feeding the two catapults, one in Fly 1 and the other at the forward end of the angled deck. At 250 feet long, both were to be the largest steam catapults ever built into a British carrier, and they would have been fed with steam from their own dedicated boiler room. During the recovery of a deck-load strike the whole space to starboard of the runway would have been used, both lifts striking down aircraft as the recovery continued. Another innovative feature for a British design was the provision of a roller shutter at the port after end of the hangar which, when opened, allowed aircraft to carry out ground runs over the quarterdeck without having to be ranged on to the flight deck. The idea stemmed from a similar arrangement seen by British officers on the after end ('fantail') of the USS *Enterprise*, CVAN-65, when she commissioned in 1961. To clear space for the Sea Dart missile system and its engagement arcs, the round-down at the after end of the flight deck was some feet forward of the quarterdeck, but this posed no problem as the arrester wires themselves were considerably further forward than those in early carriers, near the ship's centre of pitch. The area aft of Fly 3 was left open for a crane and a number of boats. It is probable that, had *Queen Elizabeth* gone into service, the boats would have been landed and the flight deck extended to enlarge the pit stop and helicopter operating areas. Most RN warships had their old-fashioned boats removed in the 1990s, replaced by Rigid Hulled Inflatable Boats (RHIBs) that were more easily launched and operated.

The intention was to operate the ship with a dedicated air group of thirty-six fast jets, four AEW aircraft and eight helicopters.[12] Considerable thought had been given to the operation of joint formations of P.1154 STOVL fighters, but the attempt to combine light strike and all-weather fighter capability into a single innovative design proved difficult and it was cancelled. The operation of RAF squadrons equipped with naval aircraft, or of Harrier STOVL aircraft in the reinforcement role, was always considered to be important by the Admiralty, and the normal air group did not take up all the available space. The design allowed two-thirds of the embarked aircraft to be struck down into the hangar and two-thirds to be parked on deck. Thus a 'spare third' was available for a reinforcement squadron. In the 1960s the RN practised the concept of flying replacement Buccaneers over considerable distances with in-flight refuelling to enlarge the air groups of carriers or replace losses.[13]

The design was complete and ready to be put out to tender in 1966, when the Labour Government of the day cancelled the project to reduce defence expenditure. Her loss was the traumatic beginning to a long period of decline which has sapped the morale, as well as the fighting capability, of the Royal Navy. In my opinion her design marked the high point of British carrier design and, at the time of writing, USN interest in the design has been stimulated by the studies into potential improvements that can be incorporated in CVN-21, the design that will follow the last of the *Nimitz* class into production. I was able to arrange for a windtunnel model of CVA 01 to be sent to the USA for study by the F-35 ship-compatibility team at Fort Worth.

Cross-deck operations

An AD-1 Skyraider of VA 52 from the USS *Ticonderoga* lands on HMS
Victorious during *Exercise Crosstie* in the South China Sea during 1961.
The exercise was designed to test the capability of the RN and USN to
cross-operate aircraft, and Skyraider, Skyhawk, Skyray and Demon
aircraft operated from *Victorious* while Scimitars, Sea Vixens, Gannets
and Whirlwinds operated from *Ticonderoga*.

(US NAVY)

In the 'network-enabled' twenty-first century it is taken for granted that warships of different navies can communicate with each other, exchange tactical data and replenish with standardised solids and liquids, including fuel from each other's auxiliaries, while deployed. The operation of aircraft from other navies and even most nations' own air forces has yet to achieve the same level of interoperability despite the emphasis placed by governments on joint and coalition operations.

American entry into the Second World War in December 1941 led to closer co-operation between the Royal Navy and the US Navy, and when fleets operated together it was inevitable that aircraft of one navy would land on the other's aircraft carriers. The first foreign aircraft to land on a USN carrier was Sea Gladiator N2274, flown by Captain H.L. St J. Fancourt RN, the commanding officer of RNAS Hatston in the Orkney Islands. This occurred in April 1942, when the USS *Wasp* deployed to join the Home Fleet at Scapa Flow. In the weeks that followed, part of *Wasp*'s air group disembarked to Hatston to work-up in European conditions while their ship ferried forty-seven RAF Spitfires to Malta. [1] That same year saw Colonel J.H. Doolittle's B-25 bombers embarked in the USS *Hornet* for their strike on Tokyo. Unlike the Spitfires, which could, in an emergency, attempt to land back on the carrier, the B-25s stood no chance of recovering to the ship.

Allied co-operation went a step further in 1943, when HMS *Victorious* was lent to the US Pacific Fleet for six months. Initial differences in equipment and

The first foreign aircraft to land on a USN aircraft carrier. Captain H.L. St J. Fancourt RN, commanding officer of RNAS Hatston, near Kirkwall in the Orkney Islands, lands on the USS *Wasp* on 20 April 1942 while the ship was temporarily attached to the Home Fleet at Scapa Flow. (US NAVY)

technique were overcome, and the ship worked closely with the USS *Saratoga*, at one point the only operational US carrier in the Western Pacific. Once confidence was gained the two carriers capitalised on each other's strength, and with her better fighter control capability *Victorious* embarked all the task-force fighters, both RN and USN. [2] The strike squadrons, all equipped with Avengers, operated from *Saratoga*. In 1944 the loan was repaid when *Saratoga* was lent to the British Eastern Fleet for operations in the Indian Ocean. Her experienced air group was able to teach the recently formed Royal Navy squadrons a great deal about the long-range strike missions, which were not yet common in the European Theatre and which they would have to undertake in the Pacific a year later. Both navies

A Corsair from HMS *Victorious* serving with the British Pacific Fleet in 1945 lands on the USS *Shangri-La*, CV 38. *Victorious*'s deck recognition letter, 'P', has been painted on over HMS *Illustrious*'s 'Q', showing that the aircraft is a replacement that has been refurbished by the Fleet Air Maintenance Group.

(AUTHOR'S COLLECTION)

A Royal Australian Navy Skyhawk of 805 Naval Air Squadron carries out deck-landing practice on HMS *Hermes* in 1968. At the time HMAS *Melbourne* was being modernised, and the presence of the British carrier in Australian waters allowed RAN pilots to become deck qualified on their new aircraft, which had recently replaced Sea Venoms.

(AUTHOR'S COLLECTION)

benefited from the exchange of ideas, not least the USN, which was impressed by the Royal Navy's ability to operate F4U Corsairs from the relatively small decks of the *Illustrious*-class carriers. The Americans had previously rejected the type as being too difficult to deck-land because of its long nose ahead of the cockpit, which deprived the pilot of a good view of the deck. By 1945 most aircraft operated by the British Pacific Fleet were USN types supplied under Lend-Lease arrangements. They were so heavily modified that they were not compatible with airframes that came direct from US stocks. Different engineering practice in the USA and the British Empire meant that even the screw threads in British and US aircraft differed, and maintenance ratings working on each variant had to be issued with different toolkits. The need for specialist tools, weapon attachment points,

fuel and oils can make a significant impact on the ability of aircraft carriers to operate another nation's aircraft. Eventually NATO partly solved the problem with specialist publications and tool packs.

After the war the RN and USN continued to operate closely, and regular cross-decking exercises helped them remain abreast of each other's operating practice. In 1948 standardised deck-landing techniques were introduced which, theoretically, led to all NATO navies operating in the same way, although some local differences remained common. In the weeks before the outbreak of the Korean War HMS *Triumph* and USS *Valley Forge* operated together in the waters off Japan, greatly enhancing their ability to act together when North Korea unexpectedly attacked the South. During the next thirty years British and American aircraft frequently practised cross-deck

A Phantom FG.1 of 892 Naval Air Squadron on the USS *Saratoga*'s starboard bow catapult during a deployment in the Mediterranean in 1969. The 'shooter' has his arm outstretched as the order to 'fire' the catapult, and the aircraft will launch in seconds. The cables leading back from the catapult strop are part of the 'Van Zelme' gear that returned the strop after each shot for further launches, rather than having it fall into the sea. The squadron embarked in *Saratoga* to gain sea experience with its new aircraft before *Ark Royal* completed her special 'Phantom' refit. There were problems with the non-watercooled JBDs, which were melted by the FG.1's reheat at first. Later launches had to be made without reheat at lighter weight.
(US NAVY)

Sea Harriers of 801 Naval Air Squadron attract an interested crowd of 'goofers' (RN slang for spectators) as they land on the USS *Ranger*, CV 61.
(US NAVY)

Opposite: United States Navy F-4 Phantoms and A-6 Intruders parked in Fly 1 on HMS *Ark Royal* (IV) in 1976. The author had just landed the Gannet AEW.3 seen at the forward end of the park, between the RN Phantoms and Buccaneers.
(AUTHOR'S COLLECTION)

US Marine Corps AV-8B Harriers and an MV-22 Osprey operating from HMS *Illustrious* during an exercise off the US east coast in 2007. The lack of a dedicated Royal Navy air group for these ships has made the embarkation of foreign aircraft from the USA, Spain and Italy a common occurrence since the Sea Harrier was withdrawn prematurely from service.
(US NAVY)

operations and acted as 'spare decks' for each other in NATO Strike Fleet and Pacific manoeuvres. When HMS *Ark Royal* (IV), the Royal Navy's last 'conventional' aircraft carrier, paid off in 1978, however, the smaller STOVL carriers were unable to land USN 'tailhook' jets and the practice largely ceased for fixed-wing aircraft. Sea Harriers could, of course, land on virtually any deck, including those designed for helicopters. Renewed British interest in large-deck carriers will hopefully lead to a return to inter-operability, especially if the ships are equipped with catapults and arrester wires.

An F-4J Phantom II of VF-102 flown by the USS *Independence* Air Group Commander being towed into Fly 1 on HMS *Ark Royal* during cross-deck operations in which the author took part in April 1975. Note the tow-bar attached to the aircraft's nose wheel and the chock-man walking alongside the port main wheel ready to secure the aircraft as soon as it stops moving. Both ships were operating in the Atlantic off the Eastern coast of the United States.

(AUTHOR'S COLLECTION).

In January 1964 HMS *Centaur* went a step further than basic cross-decking when she formed the core element of the British forces used to quell the East African Army mutinies at the short-notice request of their newly independent governments. She embarked two RAF Belvedere helicopters to help her own Wessex helicopters with troop movements. Her own Sea Vixen and Gannet squadrons were retained, and she embarked 45 Royal Marines Commando with some of its vehicles and equipment, and the 16/5 Lancers with their light armoured cars, both from the garrison at Aden. A plan, known appropriately as *Operation Squeeze*, was worked out to clear the port catapult and landing area to enable Sea Vixen and Gannet sorties to be flown if necessary. It involved launching the two

Belvederes and most of the Wessex to clear space in the hangar to strike down the bulk of the military equipment. Fortunately it was not needed. The armoured cars were landed by the ship's cranes on to lighters chartered for the purpose close inshore.

Combined operations have been repeated many times since 1964, the most recent being the use of HMS *Ark Royal* (V) as a helicopter landing platform (LPH) operating RAF Chinooks during the assault on Iraq in 2003. Like the Belvederes in *Centaur*, they were too big to be struck down into the hangar. Aircraft carriers are big ships with many flexible uses other than the obvious ones, and the twenty-first century will demonstrate increasing flexibility in their employment.

An artist's impression of HMS *Queen Elizabeth*, showing an F-35B Lightning II in the hover off the port quarter before landing. Flyco is visible on the port side of the after island; the compass platform is at the forward edge of the forward island. The plume of hot air below the F-35B shows that the nozzles are in the hover position. Interestingly the UK is considering 'rolling vertical landings' in 2008. In these the aircraft lands on the runway with low forward airspeed, about 60 knots, with nozzles down, giving some wing lift to augment engine thrust in order to land at greater weight. The drawbacks are that an overshoot after a baulked approach is not possible, and stopping without restraint after landing places a great strain on the braking system.
(BAE SYSTEMS)

Taking-off from and landing on warships at sea has reached a point where technology is demonstrating the capability to take over from the inputs of human pilots. At the time of writing, only the US Navy has installed and made use of an automated carrier landing system (ACLS), although the UK has carried out practical demonstrations of a system capable of controlling the decelerating transition to the hover and subsequent carrier landing of a modified Harrier. The ensuing system may have a part to play in the control logic that is fitted to the STOVL variant of the Joint Strike Fighter.

Once it is in widespread use, automatic landing technology will bring significant changes in the way aircraft carriers are operated. Until now pilot-controlled landings have required considerable practice, although lately not as much as in the days of propeller-driven aircraft, batsmen and barriers. Computers mean that much of the practice can be carried out synthetically, but their power and reliability mean that taking pilots out of carrier-borne aircraft has become a practical possibility. The USN plans to carry out deck-landing trials with the Northrop Grumman X-47 unmanned combat air vehicle (UCAV) in 2011,[1] 100 years after Eugene Ely landed on USS *Pennsylvania*. The Service also announced in 2008 that it expects the eventual replacement for the F/A-18 E/F Super Hornet to be

an unmanned aircraft entering service from about 2025.

The advantages that UCAVs have over manned aircraft include simplicity, as they do not need ejection seats, oxygen systems and structures sized to take seated aircrew. Once the human limitations are removed they can fly long-duration, dull, dirty and dangerous missions which would otherwise be limited by crew fatigue, and can pull far greater 'g' loads than a human pilot could tolerate. Not the least of their advantages is the reduction in training, since their automatic systems do not need to fly a set number of hours per month to maintain flying currency. The remote pilots who control their airborne mission time can be trained using simulated sorties generated by computers, reserving the airframes themselves exclusively for operational flying missions. The X-47 may well be manoeuvred on the flight deck by marshallers using hand-held controllers, and loading on to the catapults will follow an automatic sequence.

The French Navy identified aircraft carriers as a key element of its revival after 1945, and has gradually built up a viable force, culminating with *Charles de Gaulle*, to date the only nuclear-powered strike carrier built outside the USA. It operates an air group of indigenous Dassault Rafale strike fighters and Super Frelon helicopters, together with Grumman E-2C

The French nuclear-powered aircraft carrier *Charles de Gaulle* anchored in the Solent during the ceremonies to mark the 200th anniversary of the Battle of Trafalgar in 2005. The only nuclear-powered carrier to be built outside the USA, she has an island mounted unusually far forward, shown clearly in this photograph. Her two deck-edge lifts are both on the starboard side of the deck, visible aft of the island, posing some limitations on the extraction of aircraft from the forward part of the hangar.
(AUTHOR'S COLLECTION)

Hawkeyes purchased from the USA. In the early postwar years the French Navy purchased the light fleet carrier HMS *Colossus*, renamed *Arromanches*, from Britain, and relied heavily on British operating techniques and aircraft such as the Seafire and Aquilon, a licence-built version of the Sea Venom. United States Navy influence grew with the addition of two light carriers, the *Bois Belleau*, formerly the USS *Belleau Wood*, and *La Fayette*, formerly the USS *Langley*, together with the procurement of US aircraft such as the F4 Corsair and F8 Crusader. The USN gave the French Navy assistance with the design of *Clemenceau* and *Foch*, the first carriers to be built in France since the conversion of *Bearn* in the 1920s. Both ships operated aircraft of French design, such as the Super Etendard, in addition to US-supplied types, and developed a distinctive French style of operation, although USN influence remains discernable. Unlike the Royal Navy, the French Navy has never lost its focus on conventional fixed-wing operations using catapults and arrester wires to launch and recover aircraft, and continues to see advantages in the technology. The Service plans to build a new carrier that will be larger than *Charles de Gaulle* but conventionally powered and based on the British *Queen Elizabeth* design. It will be built from the outset with catapults, wires and an angled deck. Although France has contributed to the British design costs, a firm order has yet to be placed at the time of writing. Two large helicopter carriers, *Mistral* and *Tonnerre*, have recently been completed to add to the French Navy's impressive expeditionary capability.

Flight-deck technology is likely to undergo continual changes intended to reduce the need for large numbers of men to operate aircraft. The next-generation USN carrier design is CVN 21, due to follow the last *Nimitz*-class ship, *George H.W. Bush* (CVN 77), in construction, completion of the first ship, to be named the USS *Gerald R. Ford* (CVN 78), being set for 2015. The second will follow in 2019. The hull will be similar in size to that of a *Nimitz*, but with redesigned internal arrangements to improve weapons supply and allow systems that require 30 per cent less manpower. The CVN 21 design will incorporate a new, more efficient nuclear powerplant,

Unmanned Combat Air Vehicles (UCAVs) are growing rapidly in importance as the twenty-first century progresses. This artist's impression shows an X-47 seconds before landing on a US Navy aircraft carrier, a view that will be commonplace two decades from now.
(US NAVY)

the Electro-Magnetic Aircraft Launch System (EMALS), Advanced Arrester Gear (AAG) and an electricity-generation capacity nearly three times greater than that of *Nimitz*. The expanded flight deck will allow increased sortie generation rates, and the small island, sited further aft than in previous designs, will allow more space for 'pit-stop'-style aircraft turn-around work between sorties. The design is impressive, and shows that the USN has every intention of maintaining its lead in carrier operations well into the twenty-first century.

There is growing international interest in aircraft carriers of every size and operational capability. In addition to the projected new French carrier and the two large STOBAR carriers under construction for the Indian Navy, significant helicopter carriers capable, if required, of operating STOVL fixed-wing

An artist's port-bow impression of HMS *Queen Elizabeth*, showing the design at the time a contract was signed for her and her sister-ship *Prince of Wales* in July 2008. In early designs the ski-jump covered the full width of the deck forward, but by 2008 it covered only half the width, allowing a substantial deck park in Fly 1 to starboard of it. Five F-35B Lightnings IIs are parked in Fly 1, a further six in Fly 3, and one is lined up on the runway aft. A Merlin helicopter is parked right aft. Note the two islands giving separate intakes and exhausts for the two widely separated machinery spaces below, and the two lowered side-lifts on the starboard side amidships and aft. No lift serves the forward half of the hangar.
(BAE SYSTEMS)

An impression of the USS *Gerald R. Ford*, as the first CVN 21-class aircraft carrier for the US Navy is to be named. The design features an enhanced flight deck capable of greater sortie rates than a *Nimitz*-class carrier, and improved weapons movement capacity that will more than double the rate at which smart munitions can be delivered. Northrop Grumman and the US Navy have, in my opinion, produced the outstanding design against which all aircraft carriers in the next fifty years will have to be compared.

(NORTHROP GRUMMAN)

aircraft, are being designed and built in Spain, Italy, Australia, South Korea, Japan and, potentially, China, to play their part in the future development of carrier aviation.

The British Strategic Defence Review (SDR) of 1998 identified two new aircraft carriers as 'the key component in the continuing shift towards expeditionary forces'.[2] Design studies for these two ships, to be named *Queen Elizabeth* and *Prince of Wales*, considered every type of ship from small STOVL carriers to large ships with catapults and arrester wires. The final design is flexible, allowing the ships to be completed or converted to support STOVL or conventional operations and, at 65,000 tons they are to be the largest ships ever ordered for the Royal Navy. At last British politicians comprehended the importance of size[3] when approval was given for these ships to proceed. A contract for both ships' construction was signed on 3 July 2008 between BVT Surface Fleet, a consortium formed by BAE Systems and VT Shipbuilding. *Queen Elizabeth* is optimistically scheduled by the MoD for completion in 2014, and her sister ship two years after that. No firm order has

been placed by the MoD for the F-35B Lightning II, the aircraft for which it has stated a preference as a Harrier replacement. The 'B' model flew for the first time in 2008, and once it has completed its development the first British squadron will have to form and work-up in the USA, because the sophisticated facilities needed to train the crew and support it will not exist in the UK until after that date. The first British unit is, in the manufacturer's judgement, unlikely to be declared operational before 2018. In consequence *Queen Elizabeth* can be expected to be completed with a ski-jump and to have an initial air group of Harrier GR.9, Sea King ASaC.7 and Merlin HM.1 aircraft, all of them decades old and only remaining available in small numbers. The projected 'out of service' date for the Harrier is 2018, so the timescale is already critical. Whatever their air group over their projected life-span of 50 years, these ships have considerably more potential than their small, cramped and much-modified British predecessors, and will give the Royal Navy the opportunity to play a major part in advancing carrier aviation in its second century.

Notes

CHAPTER 1

[1] J.D. Brown. Unpublished notes on the early history of naval aviation.

[2] Zeppelin LZ4 gained a world endurance record by staying aloft for 12 hours in August 1908. *Documents Relating to the Naval Air Service 1908-1918*, edited by Captain S.W. Roskill DSC RN, published by the Navy Records Society in 1969.

[3] A.E. Cowton, *With the First in the Field*, privately published by Mrs Cowton, Norwich, 1963.

[4] J.D. Brown. Unpublished notes on the early history of naval aviation.

[5] Norman Polmar, *Aircraft Carriers*, Macdonald & Co, London, 1969.

[6] Hugh Popham, *Into Wind – A History of British Naval Flying*, Hamish Hamilton, London, 1969.

[7] Duralumin, presumably taken from the material delivered for the airship, which was the first aircraft in the world to make use of it.

[8] Lieutenant Commander Jack Waterman RD RNR, *The Fleet Air Arm Story*, Old Bond Street Publishing Company, London, 1974.

[9] Lieutenant Commander P.K. Kemp RN, *Fleet Air Arm*, Herbert Jenkins, London, 1954.

[10] J.D. Brown notes.

[11] R. Sturtivant & G. Page, *Royal Navy Aircraft Serials and Units 1911-1919*, Air-Britain (Historians), Tonbridge, Kent, 1991.

[12] C.F. Snowden Gamble, *The Story of a North Sea Air Station*, Oxford University Press, London, 1928.

[13] *Ibid*.

[14] R.D. Layman, *Before the Aircraft Carrier*, Conway Maritime Press, London, 1989.

CHAPTER 2

[1] D.K. Brown, *The Grand Fleet – Warship design and development 1906-1922*, Chatham Publishing, London, 1999.

[2] J D Brown. Notes on early naval aviation in the possession of the author.

[3] *Ibid*.

[4] Lieutenant Commander Michael Apps RN, *The Four Ark Royals*, William Kimber, London, 1976.

[5] Admiral Lord Jellicoe, *The Grand Fleet*, Cassell, London, 1919.

[6] H.A. Jones, *The War in the Air*, The Clarendon Press, Oxford, 1928.

[7] *Ibid*.

[8] C.F. Snowden Gamble, *The Story of a North Sea Air Station*, Oxford University Press, London, 1928.

[9] D. Young, *Rutland of Jutland*, Cassell, London, 1963.

[10] Air 1/668 in the National Archive, Kew.

[11] C.R. Samson, *Fights and Flights*, Ernest Benn, London, 1930.

CHAPTER 3

[1] Letter from the C-in-C Grand Fleet to the Admiralty, written in July 1915. In the author's collection.

[2] ADM 1/8430, quoted in Captain S.W. Roskill, *Documents Relating to the Naval Air Service 1908-18*, Navy Records Society, 1969. Hereafter referred to as RNAS Documents.

[3] Air 1/636, quoted in *RNAS Documents*.

[4] Flight Commander C.H.K. Edmonds RNAS. Report of Flight on 14 August 1915, quoted in *RNAS Documents*.

[5] Captain Donald Macintyre, *Wings of Neptune*, Peter Davies, Kingswood, Surrey, 1963.

[6] *RNAS Documents*.

[7] H.A. Jones in *War in the Air* gives the pilot's name as Towler, but in his Report of Proceedings the Commanding Officer of HMS *Vindex* refers to him as Fowler. Since the captain knew him personally I have used the name quoted in the report.

CHAPTER 4

[1] Air 9/2. 'Air Staff Report on Seaplane Operations', dated 13 February 1924, in the National Archive.

[2] J.D. Brown. 'Documents relating to Early Naval Aviation' by the Head of the Naval Historical Branch, now in the author's archive. Hereafter referred to as J.D.B. Documents.

[3] B.A. Smart. Papers in the archive of the Fleet Air Arm Museum at RNAS Yeovilton, and R. Cronin, *Royal Navy Shipboard Aircraft Developments*, Air Britain (Historians), Tonbridge, 1990.

[4] If no valve were fitted to the bag, the air within it would expand when the aircraft climbed to altitude, eventually causing the bag to burst. Remembering to insert the bung was of primary importance before ditching!

[5] R. Cronin, *Shipboard Aircraft Developments*, Air Britain (Historians), Tonbridge, 1990.

[6] Flight Commander D.G. Donald RNAS. Flying log book in the archive of the Fleet Air Arm Museum at RNAS Yeovilton.

[7] A.C. Sharwood papers and copy of flying log book in the archive of the Fleet Air Arm Museum.

[8] A.W. Jose, *The Royal Australian Navy: The Official History of Australia in the War of 1914-18*, Volume IX, University of Queensland in association with the Australian War memorial, 1928.

[9] R.D. Layman, 'The Shipboard Catapult', *Warship International* Number 3, US Naval Records Club. 30 September 1970.

[10] J.D.B. Documents.

[11] After the formation of the Royal Air Force on 1 April 1918, Culley became a Lieutenant RAF. See next Chapter for notes on the impact of the RAF on naval air operations.

[12] R. Cronin. *Shipboard Aircraft Developments*.

CHAPTER 5

[1] *Furious* was referred to as a 'large light cruiser', 'light battle-cruiser' and in other, less complimentary, terms before her conversion. The straightforward term battle-cruiser seems, to me, to define its original role adequately, and I have used it in this work.

[2] Vice-Admiral Sir Richard Bell Davies VC CB DSO AFC, *Sailor in the Air*, Peter Davies, 1967; reprinted in paperback by Seaforth Publishing, Barnsley, 2008.

[3] There has been some confusion about the actual Sopwith Pup flown by Dunning on 2 August 1917. In Ray Sturtivant's *Royal Navy Aircraft Serials and Units 1911-1919* the first landing is said to have been carried out by N6452. The same author, with J.M. Bruce and Gordon Page in *The Sopwith Pup*, makes the same statement in the individual aircraft histories, but in Chapter 18 demonstrates conclusively that N6453 was the first to land. Chapter 18 quotes from the diary of Petty Officer Walter O. Porter, who was present during all of Dunning's flights and who worked on both aircraft. In it he states clearly that N6453 was the first to land. An analysis of the photographs of the three landings and subsequent experiments by Squadron Commander Busteed show that the first two landings were by an aircraft with a white repair patch on the lower starboard aileron. This was still evident on N6453 weeks after 7 August. The aircraft in which Dunning died was beyond doubt N6452, which was subsequently written off charge. It had

no white patch on the lower starboard aileron and could not, therefore, have been the aircraft used on 2 August 1917. I confirm that N6453 was the first aircraft to land on HMS *Furious*. The same aircraft was used in subsequent trials with take-off platforms in HMS *Repulse*.

[4] As a comparison, the Blackburn Buccaneer was designed 35 years later as a turbojet powered, low-level-strike aircraft capable of flying from a carrier deck. Its wings were designed to give minimum gust response at low level over the sea and it had a wing loading of about 100lb per square foot.

[5] L.F.E. Coombs, 'Engine Management', *Air Enthusiast*, Volume 2 Number 2, February 1972.

[6] While in the 'off' state the propeller continued to turn in the airflow, turning the engine as it did so. The engine would have remained hot for a short while, so the response to an 'on' demand should be instantaneous. Once the engine had cooled, it might not be. With such a low wing loading the Pup would have been a very good glider if the engine would not re-start and the pilot had space to manoeuvre.

[7] When wind hits the slab-sided hull of a ship it is blown upwards, tending to lift aircraft as they move through it. This is known as cliff-edge effect.

[8] J.M. Bruce, G. Page and R. Sturtivant, *The Sopwith Pup*, Air-Britain (Historians), Tunbridge Wells, 2002.

[9] At pilot's eye level the wheels would have been lower, nearer the deck.

[10] D.G. Moore, *Early Bird*, Putnam, London, 1963.

[11] Desmond Young, *Rutland of Jutland*, Cassell, London, 1963.

[12] *Early Bird*.

[13] Norman Friedman, *British Carrier Aviation*, Conway Maritime Press, London, 1988.

[14] The official Admiralty designation for the Sopwith Pup was the Sopwith Type 9901, from the airframe number of the first aircraft. Pups modified with skid undercarriages were designated Type 9901a.

[15] *Early Bird*.

[16] *Rutland of Jutland*.

[17] *British Carrier Aviation*.

[18] Contained in ADM 137/1956, *Report of the Advisory Committee on Naval Aeronautics*.

CHAPTER 6

[1] Some years after the end of the First World War, Williamson was awarded £500 from the Royal Commission on Awards to Inventors. The hearings that took place before the committee make it clear that the award was made in respect of his 1915 design for an aircraft carrier. The award is quoted in an unreferenced Admiralty letter dated 6 November 1925.

[2] D.K. Brown, *The Grand Fleet – Warship Design and Development 1906-1922*, Chatham Publishing, London, 1999.

[3] Details of the early flying trials have all been extracted from a letter from Lieutenant Colonel R. Bell Davies to the Admiral Commanding Aircraft, Grand Fleet, contained in the National Archive as part of Air 1/667.

[4] It is significant that the report refers to the 'fore-and-aft' wires as 'retaining gear' intended to hold the aircraft on deck, and not as 'arrester gear' intended to arrest their forward motion. The distinction has not previously been fully appreciated by many writers.

[5] Again, details are taken from Air 1/667.

[6] A left deflection can be compared to hitting the ball fore-handed at tennis in terms of muscle movement; a right deflection can be compared to hitting back-hand. Few tennis players have a stronger back-hand than fore-hand stroke, and pilots find a left turn instinctively easier for the same reason.

[7] The same wires that had been fitted in *Furious*, removed after her unsuccessful landing trials.

[8] Torpedo aircraft with fixed undercarriages were designed with separate units unconnected by an axle so that the torpedo could fit between them under the fuselage and be dropped without risk of snagging any part of the chassis.

[9] The empty weight of the Strutter was 1,259lb; the T.1 was 2,199lb.

[10] Captain S.W. Roskill DSC RN, *Documents Relating to the Naval Air Service, Volume 1 1908-1918*, Navy Records Society, 1969.

[11] N. Friedman, *British Carrier Aviation*, Conway Maritime Press, London, 1988.

[12] *Ibid*.

[13] T.C. Hone, N. Friedman & M.D. Mandeles, *American and British Carrier Development 1919-1941*, Naval Institute Press, Annapolis, Maryland, 1999.

[14] D.K. Brown, *The Grand Fleet*.

[15] This is one of the areas where the RAF's utopian view that naval aircrew needed no specialist training and could be drawn from a pool of aircrew trained to fly over the land was shown to have no foundation in fact. Navigation over the sea was recognised as needing specialist training very soon after the RNAS had been absorbed into the RAF, and the function of navigation has been carried out by naval officers trained as observers since 1921.

[16] While aircraft were provided by the RAF, the term Senior Aviation Officer was used at first, followed from 1924 by Wing Commander 'Flying'. Once the Royal Navy resumed full control of its embarked aviation, the officer in charge of a carrier's air department was known as Commander 'Air' and, for the sake of continuity, this term has been used throughout this work.

[17] 'The First Pearl Harbor – The attack by British torpedo planes on the German High Seas Fleet planned for 1918', by the author, *Warship 2007*, Conway, London, 2007.

[18] Comprising four flights of torpedo aircraft, a strike co-coordinator's aircraft without a torpedo and two fighters.

[19] All miles quoted in this work are nautical miles, a nautical mile being 2,025 yards.

[20] This was another area where RAF hopes of manning carriers with men on temporary attachment from the metropolitan air force proved unworkable.

[21] Further evidence, if it were needed of the Royal Navy's enthusiasm to use aircraft for a growing number of tasks.

[22] N. Friedman. Report of Proceeding quoted in *British Carrier Aviation*.

[23] *Ibid*.

[24] Hone, Friedman & Mandeles, *American and British Carrier Development*.

CHAPTER 7

[1] Later Sir Stanley Goodall KCB RCNC, Director of Naval Construction (DNC).

[2] N. Friedman, *US Aircraft Carriers, an Illustrated Design History*, United States Naval Institute, Annapolis, Maryland, 1983.

[3] *Ibid*.

[4] H.T. Lenton, *American Battleships, Carriers and Cruisers*, Macdonald, London, 1968.

[5] I am unsure about the part played by pigeons in US Naval Aviation, but in the RNAS they were often carried in flying boats and other aircraft patrolling the North Sea. In the event of a ditching they were released to carry news of the aircrews' survival to the parent air station. Some pigeon lofts were fitted in seaplane carriers.

[6] Norman Friedman, *US Aircraft Carriers*.

[7] Cdr David Hobbs MBE RN, 'The Aircraft Carrier – the experience of its conception, procurement and operation', contained in *The Face of Naval Battle*, Allen & Unwin, Crow's Nest, New South Wales, Australia, in co-operation with the Royal Australian Navy Sea Power Centre, 2003.

[8] Thomas Wildenberg, *Destined for Glory – Dive-bombing, Midway and the Evolution of Carrier Air Power*, Naval Institute Press, Annapolis, Maryland, 1998.

[9] Adolphus Andrews Jr., *Admiral with Wings – the career of Joseph M Reeves*, Bachelor's thesis published by Princeton University in 1943.

[10] *Ibid.*

[11] The date of the establishment of an independent Royal Air Force. The first day of April is known in England as April Fools' or All Fools' Day. The name derives originally from a church festival known as Holy Fools' Day, which has evolved into the present names. Traditionally, jokes are played on the unsuspecting until noon, after which time the person playing the prank is designated the fool.

[12] T. Wildenberg, *Destined for Glory*.

[13] N. Friedman, *US Aircraft Carriers*. The exact composition of the air group is believed to have been 12 fighters, 12 spotters, 4 torpedo bombers, plus 6 seaplanes held dismantled in the holds for potential operation when the ship was at anchor.

[14] Clark G. Reynolds, *Admiral John H. Towers – the struggle for air supremacy*, Naval Institute Press, Annapolis, Maryland, 1991.

[15] *BuAer Newsletter*, 11 September 1926.

[16] T.C. Hone, N. Friedman & M.D. Mandeles, *American & British Aircraft Carrier Development*, Naval Institute Press, Annapolis, Maryland, 1999.

[17] *Ibid.*

[18] *Ibid.*

CHAPTER 8

[1] N. Friedman, *British Carrier Aviation – The evolution of the ships and their aircraft*, Conway Maritime Press, London, 1988. Hereafter referred to as *British Carrier Aviation*.

[2] Later, as First Sea Lord, to achieve the regaining of full control of naval aviation for the Royal Navy in 1937.

[3] A larger ship than *Argus* and, therefore, more representative of the generation of carriers in prospect.

[4] CB 3307(1) *Naval Staff History – Second World War. The Development of British Naval Aviation Volume 1.*

[5] *Ibid.*

[6] *Ibid.*

[7] *Ibid.*

[8] *Argus* (1918), *Hermes* (1924), *Eagle* (1924) and *Furious* (1925).

[9] The first aircraft to land-on was a Sopwith 2F.1 Camel. Others that took part included Parnall Panthers, Bristol Fighters, Sopwith T.1 Cuckoos and de Havilland D.H.9As.

[10] The two were brothers-in-law and it was believed, therefore, that they must be able to communicate with each other. The resulting agreement accepted the Admiralty's term 'Fleet Air Arm' for the air units that operated at sea and stipulated that up to 70 per cent of pilots and all observers and telegraphist air gunners would be naval personnel trained for flying duties by the RAF.

[11] Small floodlights on a pole shaped to throw a carefully shaped fan of light on to the deck.

[12] Commander C.A. Jenkins OBE RN, *Warship Profile No.24 – HMS Furious, Part II: 1925-1948*, Profile Publications, Windsor, 1972.

[13] R. Sturtivant and D. Cronin, *Fleet Air Arm Aircraft, Units and Ships 1920 to 1939*, Air Britain (Historians) Ltd, Tunbridge Wells, 1998.

[14] J.L. Bartlett, 'Brief History of the Development of Aircraft Carriers and Arresting Gear', paper written when he was Deputy Director of Naval Construction (Design), dated 11 September 1953 in the author's archive.

[15] NID 3683/29.

[16] NAD 3683/29.

[17] Outline DNC ideas on the arresting gear were described in Paper DO 191/30, supported by Drawing DNC 26/100.

[18] Initiated in DNC Docket D 0543/30.

[19] Application Number 1876/31.

[20] The captain, a non-aviator, would have taken advice from his senior aviation specialist, an RAF wing commander seconded to the Fleet Air Arm who would have been well aware of the Air Ministry desire to reduce, rather than increase and streamline, the size of embarked air groups.

[21] Work on the Mark II gear was abandoned when the potential success of the Mark III hydraulic gear was recognised. It would have been an improved friction gear with a watercooled brake.

[22] The order, CP 72673/40, was placed with MacTaggart Scotts on 28 August 1940.

[23] Ordered under CP 22079/42.

[24] N. Friedman, *Historical Innovation – Carrier Aviation Case Study*, distributed by the Office of the Secretary of Defense, Washington, 24 June 1994. In the author's archive.

[25] Figures taken from 'Development of British Naval Aviation' Volume 1.

[26] M 0775/31 in Case 2385 quoted in 'Development of British Naval Aviation' Volume 1.

[27] *Ibid.*

[28] Introduced by CW 4954/32.

[29] Sir Thomas Inskip, Minister for Defence Co-ordination, awarded full control of embarked naval aviation, including the airfields and air yards needed ashore to support it, to the Admiralty in July 1937. Two years were allowed for the change-over, which in fact was completed in May 1939. He decided to leave aircraft that could not embark under RAF control ashore in the newly formed Coastal Command.

CHAPTER 9

[1] HMS *Exeter*'s Supermarine Walrus was set on fire during the Battle of the River Plate in December 1939 and jettisoned along with the ship's ready-use Avgas supplies.

[2] Catapult aircraft were expected to have wheeled undercarriages substituted for floats in wartime to improve their performance. Those that were still fitted with floats could still land on a carrier deck, however, as the Admiralty specified floats that were strong enough to sustain deck landings.

[3] M 0560/27 quoted in *Development of British Naval Aviation*, Volume 1.

[4] A 0229/39 dated 3 June 1939.

5 British Prime Minister Stanley Baldwin made a speech in November 1932 in which he said, on Air Ministry advice, that 'I think it well for the man in the street to realise that there is no power on earth that can protect him from being bombed. Whatever people may tell him, the bomber will always get through.' Given the acceptance of this dogma by the British Cabinet throughout the 1930s, Admiralty acceptance that fighter defence of the fleet was not possible, with all the consequences of that mistaken assumption, was inevitable.

6 In the RNAS during the First World War and the US Navy in the Second World War, fighter pilots who shot down five or more enemy aircraft were deemed to be 'aces'. Unfortunately the Admiralty took the view that official recognition of the top-scoring pilots would be 'divisive' and refused to use the term 'ace'. Pilots who fought successful actions in the air were awarded the Distinguished Service Cross or, in exceptional circumstances, the Distinguished Service Order. In all, 32 RN pilots shot down five or more aircraft in operations between 1939 and 1945.

7 'Fundamentals of the Airflow over Aircraft Carriers', Admiralty File dated 10 November 1943, in the author's collection.

8 Paper by the author included in *The Face of Naval Battle*, edited by John Reeve and David Stevens, Allen & Unwin, Crows Nest, NSW, Australia, 2003.

9 H. Van Willigenberg, 'Graf Zeppelin afloat: Germany's aircraft carrier – What might have been', *Air Enthusiast*, Issue 92, 2001.

10 Led by Commander The Master of Sempill and including Squadron Commander Rutland in the group.

11 Mark R. Peattie, *Sunburst, the Rise of Japanese Naval Air Power 1909-1941*, Chatham Publishing, Rochester, Kent, 2001.

12 *Ibid.*

13 J. David Brown, *Aircraft Carriers*, one of a series of World War 2 Fact Files, Macdonald and Jane's, London, 1977.

CHAPTER 10

1 R.D. Layman, 'The Shipboard catapult – its history and evolution', *Warship International* No.3, 30 September 1970, Naval Records Club of Toledo, Ohio.

2 The trial officer was Lieutenant Commander (later Admiral of the Fleet Sir) Caspar John, who became First Sea Lord in 1961.

3 Lieutenant Commander T.C. Horsley RNVR, *Find, Fix and Strike – The Story of the Fleet Air Arm*, Eyre and Spottiswoode, London, 1943.

4 *Find, Fix and Strike.*

5 Similar to the Robinson disengaging gear used to slip sea boats.

6 *Catapult Ships*, an Instructional film produced by the Admiralty in 1940.

7 *Ibid.*

8 'Grass' rope was chosen because it floated.

9 A wooden toggle was fitted into the tow-rope some feet from the end to stop the weight of the bight pulling the end back through the block.

10 T.C. Treadwell, *Submarines with Wings – The past, present and future of aircraft-carrying submarines*, Conway Maritime Press, London, 1985.

11 K Poolman, *The Catafighters*, William Kimber, London, 1970.

12 R.D. Layman. 'The Shipboard catapult'.

CHAPTER 11

1 As the importance of handling grew, it became common for sailors with flight-deck experience to work permanently on deck, and these became the core of a specialised 'Aircraft Handler' Branch in 1945.

2 Including all of 828 NAS's Grumman Avengers, which were too tall to be struck down into the hangars.

3 The details quoted here are drawn from CB 04335 *Aircraft Carrier Handbook – 1943*, published by the Airfields and Carrier Requirements Section of the Admiralty in December 1943. A copy of the book is contained in ADM 239/361 at the National Archive at Kew.

4 Until 1945 the Royal Navy referred to assisted take-off mechanisms in carriers as accelerators to differentiate them from the 'catapults' fitted in battleships and cruisers. With the demise of catapult flights the term 'catapult' became universal in the late 1940s.

5 For weights over 14, 000lb a lower end speed had to be accepted.

6 S 416 – *Carrier Flying Signals* (frequently revised). A copy of the January 1942 edition is in the author's archive.

7 Voice-pipes continue to be fitted in key areas in RN warships because virtually nothing can go wrong with them.

8 Usually limited to commissioned pilots and observers. Surprisingly, even as late as 1945, there was a reluctance to allow rating aircrew to be given the full intelligence briefing, some of which would have been classified.

9 A vertical Perspex board sited to face the Direction Officers. Radar Plot ratings stood behind the plot and marked information on it with chinagraph pencils, writing backwards so that the information could be read by the officers.

10 The contemporary exchange of information in what is known as 'Network Centric Warfare' is no different in theory but uses more advanced methods.

11 The Corsair was 15 feet 1 inch high folded.

12 BR 830 – *Securing Gear for Naval Aircraft.*

13 The British conversion was to make the trolley slightly smaller so that it would fit into British bomb lifts.

14 Oregon pine was used extensively, being readily available on the west coast of the USA where the ships were built.

15 The names translate as 'Heaven-Bound Crane' and 'Lucky Crane'.

16 J.D. Brown, *Aircraft Carriers World War 2 Fact Files*, MacDonald and Jane's, London, 1977.

CHAPTER 12

1 Commander David Hobbs MBE RN, *Moving Bases – Royal Navy Maintenance Carriers and MONABS*, Maritime Books, Liskeard, Cornwall, 2007.

2 Hugh Popham, *Into Wind – A History of British Naval Flying*, Hamish Hamilton, London, 1969.

3 Squadron serviceability states, known as 'Mayflies' were produced daily by the unit AEOs. During a range squadrons would try to keep the serviceable aircraft that remained in the hangar close to the lift, but this might not always be possible.

4 *Into Wind.*

5 AP(N) 144, *Naval Aircraft Handbook*, 1958 edition, published by the Admiralty.

6 Although Commander Everett might not agree with this statement.

7 Some of the Swordfish came from HMS *Eagle*, which did not take part in the battle because of damage caused by near-miss bombs in an earlier operation.

[8] Before 1939 British policymakers gave RAF Bomber Command the responsibility for attacking enemy fleets in harbour. The experience of war, including the appalling losses suffered by Bomber Command off the German coast in the autumn of 1939, led to carrier-borne aircraft assuming the task. There were, in any case, too few bombers in the Mediterranean Theatre.

[9] The equivalent USN statistics for the period were 2, 408 aircraft, averaging 0.22 per sortie.

[10] USN equivalent figures were 924, 000 tons and 90 tons per offensive sortie.

[11] *Naval Staff History – Development of Naval Aviation*. Notes for the unpublished third volume in the author's collection.

[12] FO2FE/2960/11 dated 19 January 1951, quoted in BR 1736 (54), *Naval Staff History – British Commonwealth Naval Operations, Korea 1950-1953*, 1967.

[13] Awarded annually by Admiral Dennis Boyd, who had been captain of *Illustrious* at Taranto, for the most outstanding feat of naval aviation in the year.

[14] Known at first as Sea Spitfires, but shortened to Seafire before the type entered service.

[15] *Illustrious* had been damaged by a collision with *Formidable* in heavy seas on 16 December 1941. There had been no time to repair the deck on the port side forward, and the trial team accepted the consequent reduced flight deck width.

[16] J.D. Brown, *Seafire – The Spitfire that went to Sea*, Ian Allan, Shepperton, 1973.

[17] *Ibid*.

[18] Captain E.M. Brown, *Wings on My Sleeve*, Weidenfeld & Nicolson, London, 2006.

[19] A '/G' suffix on an aircraft's serial number indicated a prototype or experimental aircraft that was considered so secret that it had to be kept under guard when not flying.

[20] Included in early jet deck-landing papers in the archive of the Fleet Air Arm Museum at RNAS Yeovilton.

[21] *Ibid*.

[22] Flying a tailwheel aircraft 'into the deck' would have caused it to land on the main oleos and, most probably, to bounce over the barrier. That is probably why Brown elected to use the old technique, but, as Ievers discovered, it was not a problem that applied to aircraft with tricycle undercarriages.

CHAPTER 13

[1] The amount of lift from a given wing varies with the square of its velocity through the air – the 'V-squared Law'; thus the amount of lift generated by a 'high-speed' wing will be reduced by the reduction in velocity squared.

[2] L. Boddington, 'Effects on Layout and Design of Future Carrier operating Undercarriage-Less Aircraft', RAE Naval Aircraft Technical Department Technical Memorandum NAD 14, January 1949, in the author's collection.

[3] VT795, VT803 and VT805.

[4] Lieutenant Commander E.M. Brown RN, RAE Naval Aircraft Department Technical Memorandum NAD 11, dated December 1948, covering deck landing trials in HMS *Warrior*, in the author's collection.

[5] L. Boddington, 'Progress Report on Stage 5 Flexible Deck Programme', RAE Naval Aircraft Department Technical Memorandum NA43, undated, in the author's collection.

[6] 'Rubber Carrier Decks may be on the Way', Confidential Report by the US Naval Air Material Center, November 1952 (subsequently declassified), a copy of which is in the author's collection.

[7] *Ibid*.

CHAPTER 14

[1] *Audacious* (later *Eagle*), *Irresistible* (later *Ark Royal*), *Eagle*, *Malta*, *Gibraltar*, *New Zealand*, *Africa*. The last five were cancelled in 1945.

[2] *Colossus*, *Vengeance*, *Venerable*, *Glory*, *Ocean*, *Theseus*, *Triumph*, *Warrior*, *Perseus*, *Pioneer*, *Majestic*, *Magnificent*, *Leviathan*, *Powerful*, *Hercules*, *Terrible*, *Albion*, *Bulwark*, *Centaur*, *Elephant* (later *Hermes*), *Hermes*, *Arrogant*, *Monmouth* and *Polyphemus*. *Leviathan* was never completed, and the last four were cancelled in 1945.

[3] Maximum all-up weight of the Sea Vampire was 12, 660lb.

[4] Described in Chapter 11.

[5] For example, if the pilot saw the green sector light at the start of his approach he might be at the top of the three-degree sector and descending rapidly through it; by the time the light changed to red, his rate of descent could be too high to correct, with the risk of hitting the after round-down. The converse would also be true, with a climb from the bottom of the green into the amber sector leading to a 'high-in-close' situation in which the aircraft hook might miss all the arrester wires.

[6] Legend has it that initial evaluation of the system was carried out in Captain Campbell's office with a small mirror provided by his secretary. The datum was represented by a dab of lipstick on the mirror, and the source light by the reflected top of the lipstick container. The merit in the concept and its simplicity were immediately obvious.

[7] 892 Squadron embarked its Spey-engined Phantoms in the USS *Saratoga* in 1969 and the jet blast melted the carrier's mild steel JBDs, with the result that, subsequently, the aircraft had to be launched at lower all-up weight without reheat.

[8] Typically North American RA-5C Vigilante, Douglas KA-3D Skywarrior, Grumman A-6E Intruder and EA-6B Intruder, Vought A-7E Corsair II, Grumman F-14A Tomcat and E-2C Hawkeye, and Sikorsky SH-3D Sea King.

[9] F/A-18 E/F Hornet and the closely similar EA-18G Growler, E-2D Hawkeye and MH-60 Seahawk in 2010.

CHAPTER 15

[1] If they all led aft, for instance, nothing would stop the aircraft rolling aft, allowing the lashings to go slack and then break when the they took the 'jerk' of the aircraft weight. A Buccaneer was lost overboard from HMS *Ark Royal* in 1973 in just this way. Usually at least two lashings, leading in different directions, would be attached to the nose oleo.

[2] HMS *Hermes* ACRO Instructions dated 1968, in the author's collection.

[3] DFC is the term used in the RN. The USN term is Base Recovery Course (BRC).

[4] 10 seconds at 360 knots.

[5] Three undercarriage legs and a tailhook indicated down by green lights on in the cockpit.

6 CB 04484 *Aircraft Carrier Handbook*, 1966 edition.

7 *Ibid.*

CHAPTER 16

1 Autogyros had operated from ships, including HMS *Furious*, in the 1930s, but these were short take-off and landing (STOL) rather than VTOL machines which proved not to have any great naval application.

2 He subsequently left the RN to form his own helicopter operation, known internationally as Bristow Helicopters.

3 Commander David Hobbs, *Aircraft Carriers of the Royal and Commonwealth Navies*, Greenhill Books, London, 1996.

4 *Ibid.*

5 In addition, fifteen naval air stations, starting with RNAS Lossiemouth in 1953, had Dragonfly SAR flights.

6 The rotor diameter of a spread Dragonfly was 49 feet.

7 The early Dragonflies had composite metal, wood and fabric blades. Only the HR.3 version with metal blades operated at sea.

8 An accident occurred in the destroyer HMS *Devonshire* when a non-standard chain lashing was left on the helicopter at night, causing it to break up and ditch when it took off. This emphasised the importance of showing the pilot that all lashings were clear. The problem was a new one, as fixed-wing aircraft invariably taxied, with lashings removed, from start-up to a take-off position before launch, effectively proving that lashings were clear.

9 Medium Antisubmarine Torpedo Carrying Helicopter.

10 The DASH System; Drone Antisubmarine Helicopter.

11 Light Airborne Multi-Purpose System.

12 'HMS *Ocean* and HMS *Theseus* in *Operation Musketeer*', *Flight Deck*, winter 1956, published by the Admiralty's Naval Air Warfare Division.

13 Both commando carriers were fitted with four small landing craft known as Landing Craft Vehicles and Personnel (LCVP), capable of taking up to thirty-six marines or a Land-Rover to the beach. A large pontoon was carried on the flight deck to ferry trucks ashore.

14 A similar version, the Bristol Type 192, was eventually developed for the RAF and operated in the 1960s as the Westland Belvedere.

15 A Sea King is 54 feet 9 inches long and has a rotor diameter of 62 feet.

16 Fifth Sea Lord Minute 2058 dated 21 October 1955, contained in ADM 1/25901.

17 Awarded annually to the squadron that performs the most outstanding feat of naval aviation.

18 AOD/D 95/60, dated 10 October 1960; contained in ADM 1/27685.

CHAPTER 17

1 H.C.H. Merewether, *Prelude to the Harrier – P.1127 Prototype Flight Testing*, HPM Publications, Beirut, Lebanon, 1998.

2 R. Johnstone-Bryden, HMS *Ark Royal IV*, Sutton Publishing, Stroud, 1999.

3 Ten fathoms equals 60 feet. At the time, *Ark Royal*'s draught was 36 feet, leaving little margin for error. There can be little doubt that, although this was a significant 'first', the P.1127's mediocre performance detracted from the Royal Navy's enthusiasm for STOVL fighters.

4 Quickly run down and closed after the cancellation of CVA 01 in 1966 on the misplaced assumption by the Ministry of Defence that 'there was no further use for it'.

5 HMS *Bulwark* 01/15, 29 March 1966, in the author's collection.

6 DNOR 22400/4, 15 December 1971, contained in papers held by the Naval Historical Branch in Portsmouth.

7 I was the carrier desk officer in DGA (N) at the time, and played a prominent part in getting the projector sight put into production and fitted to the three *Invincible*-class ships and HMS *Hermes*. The sight was exported to India for use on the Indian Navy's Sea Harrier carriers.

8 Lieutenant Commander D.R. Taylor RN, 'The Operation of Fixed-Wing V/STOL aircraft from Confined Spaces', the author's M Phil thesis, written in 1973 and published by the University of Southampton in 1974.

9 Thus about one third of the 'landing scatter area' that surrounded the circle was actually off the flight deck. Even test pilots refused to land on them in early flying trials.

10 I achieved this by sitting down with squadron pilots and talking through the minimum markings they needed to achieve a safe landing, before having the result drawn up by DGA (N) draftsmen. The result was simple, efficient and continues in use today.

11 The original Scheme of Complement for the CVS, contained in NSR 7097 of 1979, was 926. By 1997 the authorized Scheme with an embarked staff was 1,250; a 26 per cent increase. In the same period the original starboard part of the junior rates' dining hall was converted into a staff planning room, reducing the amount of space available in which the increased number of junior rates could eat by 30 per cent.

12 Using men from the off-watch watch would solve the problem in the short term, but in a long period at sea the effect would be debilitating and could not be sustained.

13 I achieved this by using wooden consoles mocked up in the as-yet-unfinished Flyco of *Ark Royal* at Swan Hunter's yard in Newcastle. By moving them around I was able to finalise a layout in which 'f' was moved close to the windows from which he could look down on the deck, and the controls could be positioned in such a way that he could easily select them.

14 Chocks are the only items of equipment that have survived unchanged from the earliest days of naval aviation.

15 The information was passed to the airman by 'f' in Flyco, broadcasting it on the flight-deck loop, often with many calls for repetition. When I was 'f' in *Ark Royal* the best airman, by far, for this task was a sailor from Newcastle who was a genius at discerning numbers from the crackling loop transmissions.

16 The Sea Harrier was the first British military aircraft to display primary flight information on a head-up display, the Head-up Display and Weapon Aiming Computer system (HUDWAC). In the alignment process the aircraft's actual heading had to be dialled in to align the system with reality.

17 The deck run available was increased to 550 feet when the 12-degree ski-jump was installed.

18 Details of Sea Harrier launches and recoveries do not refer to any single event or sortie, and are based on my own experience with 801 Naval Air Squadron in HMS *Ark Royal* during 1985-87.

19 'Alpha' is the relationship between angle of attack and airspeed, and is displayed to the pilot on an instrument next to the head-up display.

[20] Sea Harriers land with their brakes off ashore and with them on when deck landing. 801 NAS had a routine whereby any pilot could call 'bananas, bananas' on sorties, reminding the others to check that their brakes were as they should be for the landing in prospect.

[21] INS *Vikrant*, formerly HMS *Hercules*, and INS *Viraat*, formerly HMS *Hermes*.

CHAPTER 18

[1] 'Habbakuk' Directive issued to K.C. Barnaby Esq and Lieutenant R. Thorneycroft RNVR on 9 April 1943. A copy is in the author's collection.

[2] The ideal mix was 86 per cent ice with 14 per cent wood pulp, and the material was to be frozen in cubes with 20-foot sides. The keel was to be laid down as a timber 'raft' which would be towed into sheltered deep water for the construction blocks to be built on to it.

[3] *Ibid.*

[4] *Malta*, *Gibraltar*, *Africa* and *New Zealand*. *Africa* had originally been intended as one of two further sister ships intended to follow *Irresistible* and *Audacious* that became *Ark Royal* and *Eagle*. Some sources claim that *Malta* was actually laid down and the keel subsequently scrapped on the slipway, but I have found no evidence to confirm this.

[5] Of course, the Admiralty could not have known, beforehand, of the difficulties that would be encountered in modernising *Victorious* to operate jets, but it was understood that there were many 'unknowns' to complicate the work. A larger hull to a later design would surely have been a better starting point.

[6] The type that entered service as the Scimitar in 1958.

[7] Director of Naval Construction Minute dated 9 November 1954, in File TSD 123/53, opened on 26 May 1953, a copy of which is in the author's collection.

[8] DNAW DD(M)/24/53, dated 26 May 1953; contained in TSD 123/53.

[9] A most effective director of the Naval Air Warfare Department who was largely responsible for the NA.39 Project that led to the successful Blackburn Buccaneer.

[10] CVA 02 and CVA 03, had they been built, were to have been named *Duke of Edinburgh* and *Prince of Wales*.

[11] My understanding of the process that led to the CVA 01 flight-deck design is based on notes I made after conversations with Captain E.M. Brown RN, Captain P.C.S. Chilton RN and Lieutenant Commander 'Lofty' Wreford RN, all members of the future planning group. Captain Brown gives an account of the design in the third edition of his autobiography *Wings on my Sleeve* (Weidenfield & Nicolson, London, 2006).

[12] Comprising two squadrons, each with twelve Buccaneers; one squadron of twelve Phantoms; one squadron of four Gannet AEW aircraft; one squadron of six Sea King ASW helicopters and a ship's flight of two utility/SAR helicopters.

[13] Two Buccaneers of 803 NAS used air-to-air refuelling to fly from RNAS Lossiemouth in Scotland to HMS *Hermes* off Gan, in the Indian Ocean, a distance of roughly 6,000 miles, while I served in her in 1968. Admiral Le Fanu, the First Sea Lord, flew as the observer in one of these aircraft.

CHAPTER 19

[1] They flew ashore on 20 April 1942. Two days later only seventeen were left operable after German air attacks on the island.

[2] Both carriers operated versions of the Grumman F4F Wildcat, known in the RN as the Martlet.

CHAPTER 20

[1] The aircraft is larger than a Sea Vixen but about the same weight, and is intended to operate in a mixed air group with conventional manned aircraft. It is expected to fly for the first time in 2009.

[2] The same statement appeared in the 1998 Strategic Defence Review, the 2003 Defence White Paper 'Delivering Security in a Changing World', and the 2004 'Future Capabilities' White Paper.

[3] An industry spokesman once briefed me that 'air is free and steel is cheap'. He meant that the increased cost of a volumetrically larger ship is not commensurate with the increased volume. The systems cost far more than the basic steel structure.

Bibliography

Admiralty, *Aircraft Carriers* Part 1, 1918.

——, *Aircraft Carriers* Part IV, *Aeroplanes Carried in Fighting Ships*, 1918.

——, *Fleet Air Arm*, HMSO, London, 1943.

——, Naval Staff History *The Development of British Naval Aviation 1919-1945*, Volume 1

——, Naval Staff History *The Development of British Naval Aviation' 1919-1945*, Volume 2

——, Naval Staff History *The Development of British Naval Aviation, 1919-1945.* Unpublished Volume 3 in the Archive of the Naval Historical Branch in Portsmouth.

——, AP (N) 71 *Manual of Naval Airmanship*, 1949 edition.

——, *Progress in Naval Aviation*, editions from 1940 to 1956.

——, CB 04335 *Aircraft Carrier Handbook*, 1943 edition.

——, CB 04484 *Aircraft Carrier and Commando Ship Handbook*, 1972 edition.

——, *DAOT Quarterly Newsletter on Naval Aviation.* Issues from 1949 to 1958.

——, AP (N) 144 *Naval Aircraft Handbook*, 1958 edition.

——, *Flight Deck* magazine, August 1944 to 1980 issues.

Air Enthusiast magazine, Key Publishing, various issues.

Air International magazine, Key Publishing, various issues.

Allward, M., *Buccaneer*, Ian Allen, Shepperton, 1981.

Apps, M., *Send Her Victorious*, William Kimber, London, 1971.

Australian Naval Aviation Museum Foundation, *Flying Stations, the Story of Australian Naval Aviation*, Allen & Unwin, St Leonards, NSW, Australia, 1998.

Bell Davies, R., *Sailor in the Air*, Peter Davies, London, 1967.

Biggs, M.J., *Vampire LZ551/G*, Fleet Air Arm Museum, Yeovilton, 1993.

Braybrook R., *V/STOL – The Key to Survival*, Osprey, London, 1989.

Brown, D.K., *The Grand Fleet*, Chatham, London, 1999.

——, *Nelson to Vanguard*, Chatham, London, 2000.

——, & Moore, G., *Rebuilding the Royal Navy*, Chatham, London, 2003.

Brown, E.M., *Wings of the Navy*, Jane's, London, 1980.

——, *Wings on My Sleeve*, Weidenfeld & Nicolson, London, 2006.

Brown, J.D., *Carrier Operations in World War II*, Volume 1, Ian Allan, Shepperton, 1968.

——, *Carrier Air Groups – HMS Eagle*, Hylton Lacy, Windsor, 1972.

——, *Carrier Operations in World War II*, Volume 2, Ian Allan, Shepperton, 1974.

——, *Carrier Fighters*, Macdonald, London, 1975.

——, *Aircraft Carriers*, Macdonald & Jane's, London, 1977.

——, 'Carrier Technique', manuscript notes, undated.

Bruce, J.M., Page, G., & Sturtivant, R., *The Sopwith Pup*, Air-Britain, Tunbridge Wells, 2002.

Cronin, D., *Royal Navy Shipboard Aircraft Developments 1912-1931*, Air Britain, Tunbridge Wells, 1990.

Crosley, M., *They Gave me a Seafire*, Airlife, Shrewsbury, 1986.

——, *Up in Harm's Way*, Airlife, Shrewsbury, 1995.

Davies, B., *Fly No More*, Airlife, Shrewsbury, 2001.

Doust, M.J., *Phantom Leader*, Ad Hoc Publications, Ringshall, 2005.

——, *Buccaneer S1 from the Cockpit*, Ad Hoc Publications, Ringshall, 2007.

Ferguson, H.M., 'Deck Landing Projector Sight', Undated manuscript.

Flypast magazine, Key Publishing, various issues.

Frame, T.R., Goldrick, J.V.P., & Jones, P.D., *Reflections on the Royal Australian Navy*, Kangaroo Press, Kenthurst, NSW, Australia, 1991.

Francillon, R.J., *Japanese Aircraft of the Pacific War*, Putnam, London, 1979.

Friedman, N., *Carrier Air Power*, Conway, London, 1981.

——, *The Postwar Naval Revolution*, Conway, London, 1988.

——, *British Carrier Aviation, the Evolution of the Ships and their Aircraft*, Conway, London, 1988.

——, *US Aircraft Carriers*, Naval Institute Press, Annapolis, 1983.

Grimes, A., 'Angled Deck Trials', RAE Technical Note 242, 1952.

Grove, E., *Vanguard to Trident*, The Bodley Head, London 1987.

Hanson, N., *Carrier Pilot*, Patrick Stephens, Cambridge, 1979.

Harding, R., (Ed) *The Royal Navy 1930-2000, Innovation and Defence*, Frank Cass, London, 2005.

Hobbs, D.A., *Aircraft of the Royal Navy since 1945*, Maritime Books, Liskeard, 1982.

——, *Aircraft Carriers of the Royal and Commonwealth Navies*, Greenhill, London, 1996.

——, *Royal Navy Escort Carriers*, Maritime Books, Liskeard, 2003.

——, *Moving Bases, Royal Navy Maintenance carriers and MONABs*, Maritime Books, Liskeard, 2007.

Hone, C.T., Friedman, N., & Mandeles, M.D., *American and British Aircraft Carrier Development 1919-1941*, Naval Institute Press, Annapolis, 1999.

Horsley, T., *Find, Fix and Strike*, Eyre and Spottiswoode, London, 1943.

Jenkins, C.A., *HMS Furious 1917-1948*, Parts 1 and 2, Warship Profile Numbers 23 and 24, Profile Publications, Windsor, 1972.

Johnstone-Bryden, R., *HMS Ark Royal IV*, Sutton, Stroud, 1999.

Jones, C., *Wings and the Navy 1947-1953*, Kangaroo Press, Kenthurst, NSW, Australia, 1997.

Kealy, J.D.F., and Russell, E.C., *A History of Canadian Naval Aviation*, Queen's printer, Ottawa, 1967.

Laming, T., *Buccaneer – The Last All-British Strike Aircraft*, Patrick Stephens, Sparkford, 1998.

Layman, R.D., 'The Shipboard Catapult', *Warship International* magazine, 1970.

——, *The Cuxhaven Raid*, Conway, London, 1985.

——, *Before the Aircraft Carrier*, Conway, London, 1989.

——, *Naval Aviation in the First World War*, Chatham, London, 1996.

——, & McLaughlin, S., *The Hybrid Warship*, Conway, London, 1991.

Leahy, A.J., *Sea Hornet from the Cockpit*, Ad Hoc Publications, Ringshall, 2007.

Longmore, A., *From Sea to Sky*, Geoffrey Bles, London, 1946.

Lowry, T.P., & Wellham, J.W.G., *The Attack on Taranto*, Stackpole Books, Mechanicsburg, 1995.

Lyon, D.J., *HMS Illustrious 1939-1956 Technical History*, Warship Profile Number 10, Profile Publications, Windsor, 1971.

Macintyre, D., *The Wings of Neptune, the Story of Naval Aviation*, Peter Davies, London, 1963.

——, *Aircraft Carrier, the Majestic Weapon*, Macdonald and Co, London, 1968.

Masters, A.O., *Memoirs of a Reluctant Batsman*, Janus, London, 1996.

Moore, W.G., *Early Bird*, Putnam, London, 1963.

Morgan, D.H.S., *Hostile Skies*, Weidenfeld & Nicolson, London, 2006.

Nicholl, G.W.R., *The Supermarine Walrus*, Foulis, London, 1966.

Nordeen, L.O., *Harrier II – Validating V/STOL*, Naval Institute Press, Annapolis, 2006.

Norman, J.G.S., *Firefly from the Cockpit*, Ad Hoc Publications, Ringshall, 2007.

Peattie, M.R., *Sunburst, the Rise of Japanese Naval Air Power 1909-1941*, Chatham, London, 2002.

Popham, H., *Sea Flight*, William Kimber, London, 1954.

——, *Into Wind, A History of British Naval Flying*, Hamish Hamilton, London, 1969.

Reynolds,. C.G., *The Fast Carriers, the Forging of an Air Navy*, Naval Institute Press, Annapolis, 1992.

Roskill, S.W., *The Naval Air Service, Volume 1 1908-1918*, Navy Records Society, 1969.

Rotherham, G.A., *It's Really Quite Safe*, Hangar Books, Belleville, Ontario, Canada, 1979.

Royal Aircraft Establishment, 'Skew Deck Layout for Carrier Flight Decks', Technical Paper NA 45, 1951.

Schofield, B.B., *The Attack on Taranto*, Ian Allan, Shepperton, 1973.

Snowden-Gamble, C.F., *The Story of a North Sea Air Station*, Oxford University Press, London, 1928.

Snowie, J.A., *The Bonnie – HMCS Bonaventure*, Boston Mills Press, Ontario, Canada, 1987.

Soward, S.E., *Hands to Flying Stations, Canadian Naval Aviation 1945-1954*, Volume 1, Neptune Developments, Victoria, 1993.

Stevens, D., *The Royal Australian Navy*, Oxford University Press, Melbourne, 2001.

——, & Reeve, J., *The Face of Naval Battle*, Allen & Unwin, Crows Nest, NSW, Australia, 2003

——, & Reeve, J., *Sea Power Ashore and in the Air*, Halstead Press, Ultimo NSW, Australia, 2007

Sturtivant, R., & Page, G., *Royal Navy Aircraft Serials and Units 1911-1919*, Air-Britain, Tunbridge Wells, 1998.

——, & Cronin, D., *Fleet Air Arm Aircraft, Units and Ships 1920-1939*, Air-Britain, Tunbridge Wells, 1998.

——, & Burrow, M., *Fleet Air Arm Aircraft 1939-1945*, Air-Britain, Tunbridge Wells, 1995.

——, Burrow, M., & Howard, L., *Fleet Air Arm Fixed-Wing Aircraft since 1946*, Air-Britain, Tunbridge Wells, 2004.

Sueter, M.F., *Airmen or Noahs*, Sir Isaac Pitman & Sons, London, 1928.

Swanborough, G., & Bowers, P.M., *United States Naval Aircraft since 1911*, Putnam, London, 1990.

Thetford, O., *British Naval Aircraft since 1912*, Putnam, London, 1962.

Till, G., *Air Power and the Royal Navy 1914-1945*, Jane's, London, 1979.

Treadwell, T.C., *Submarines with Wings*, Conway, London, 1985.

US Department of Defense, *Historical Innovation – Carrier Case Study*, Washington, 1994.

Ward, N.D., *Sea Harrier Over the Falklands*, Leo Cooper, Barnsley, 1992.

Warship World magazine, Maritime Books, various issues.

Watton, R., *The Aircraft Carrier Victorious*, Conway, London, 1991.

Weaver, D.G., *The History of HMS Queen*, David Weaver, Hong Kong, 2004.

Wildenberg, T., *Destined for Glory: Dive-Bombing, Midway and the Evolution of Carrier Air Power*, Naval Institute Press, Annapolis, 1995.

Young, D., *Rutland of Jutland*, Cassell, London, 1963.

Index